Biographical Dictionary of Transcendentalism

BIOGRAPHICAL DICTIONARY OF TRANSCENDENTALISM

Edited by
Wesley T. Mott

Greenwood Press
Westport, Connecticut • London

Library of Congress Cataloging-in-Publication Data

Biographical dictionary of transcendentalism / edited by Wesley T. Mott.
p. cm.
Includes bibliographical references and index.
ISBN 0–313–28836–4 (alk. paper)
1. Transcendentalists (New England)—Biography—Dictionaries.
2. Authors, American—19th century—Biography—Dictionaries.
3. Authors, American—New England—Biography—Dictionaries.
I. Mott, Wesley T.
B905.B56 1996
810.9'384—dc20 95–45187
[B]

British Library Cataloguing in Publication Data is available.

Library of Congress Catalog Card Number: 95–45187
ISBN: 0–313–28836–4

First published in 1996

Greenwood Press, 88 Post Road West, Westport, CT 06881
An imprint of Greenwood Publishing Group, Inc.

Printed in the United States of America

The paper used in this book complies with the Permanent Paper Standard issued by the National Information Standards Organization (Z39.48–1984).

10 9 8 7 6 5 4 3 2 1

Copyright Acknowledgments

For
Merton M. Sealts, Jr.

Contents

Preface

The *Biographical Dictionary of Transcendentalism* is a comprehensive guide to the major persons associated with Transcendentalism in the United States. Focus is on those who shaped this movement of theological innovation and literary experiment in New England from the 1830s to the Civil War.

The 204 alphabetically arranged entries cover figures most prominent in 19th-century and modern accounts of Transcendentalism and in the public and private writings of the leading Transcendentalists themselves—writers, theologians, philosophers, educators, scholars, politicians, scientists, artists, reformers. Included are significant American and international antecedents, mentors, friends, relatives, and disciples who lived until at least 1830, as well as those who carried on, transformed, or memorialized the spirit of Transcendentalism after 1865, and important contemporaneous authors whose stances toward the movement may have been aloof, critical, or antagonistic but whose writings in various ways engaged with Transcendentalism.

The definitions, assumptions, and scope of the movement are explained in the entry ''Transcendentalism'' in the *Encyclopedia of Transcendentalism* (Greenwood, 1996), a volume that includes entries on philosophical and literary antecedents and sources who died before 1830 and on philosophical concepts, genres, periodicals, events, and places associated with Transcendentalism. Cross-references to the *Encyclopedia* in this *Dictionary* are indicated by a double asterisk(**).

The *Dictionary* is intended to complement such excellent biographical and bibliographical resources as the *Dictionary of American Biography* (in the process of being superseded by the *American National Biography*); Joel Myerson's *Dictionary of Literary Biography* volume *The American Renaissance in New England* (Gale, 1978); Myerson's *The Transcendentalists: A Review of Research and Criticism* (MLA, 1984); and excellent biographical and critical studies of several of the leading Transcendentalists. Entries, then, are not comprehensive biographies but emphasize the subjects' *significance to American Transcendentalism.* Following birth and death years, entries explain the person's place in, contribution to, influence on, or other relation to American Transcendentalism.

Cross-references to other entries in the *Dictionary* are indicated by an asterisk (*). Each entry concludes with selected references to significant modern, and historically important, scholarship. Reference items are chosen that stress, where possible, the person's link to Transcendentalism. For many figures, little modern scholarship is available, and older studies or sources may still be indispensable. The index will help locate topics not covered by separate entries and cross-referencing, such as individual writings by Transcendentalists.

Ninety scholars from a wide range of fields and backgrounds have contributed to this volume. Within common purpose and scope, freedom of interpretation and expression have been encouraged as in keeping with the rich diversity of Transcendentalism. I am grateful to the authors not only for their own research but also for responding to countless queries. I especially thank Joel Myerson for reviewing the project at its early stages; Ronald A. Bosco, Robert E. Burkholder, James Duban, Benjamin F. Fisher, Philip F. Gura, and Kent P. Ljungquist for recommending several contributors; Sterling F. Delano, Lee Fontanella, and David M. Robinson for reviewing specific items; and the Concord Free Public Library (Marcia Moss, curator), the American Antiquarian Society, and the libraries of Boston University and Worcester Polytechnic Institute for their indispensable help with research. Thanks also to my daughter, Sarah T. Mott, for her help with the manuscript; to production editor Desirée Bermani and copy-editor Susan E. Badger for their professionalism; and to Dr. George F. Butler of Greenwood Press for his guidance.

"The office of the scholar," said Emerson, "is to cheer, to raise, and to guide men by showing them facts amidst appearances." This volume is dedicated to Merton M. Sealts, Jr., of the University of Wisconsin at Madison, who has fulfilled his office by his scholarly example and his friendship.

Wesley T. Mott

Guide to Abbreviations and References

An asterisk (*) denotes cross-reference to an entry in this volume. A double asterisk (**) denotes cross-reference to an entry in *Encyclopedia of Transcendentalism* (Greenwood, 1996). Terms may be cross-referenced to a different form of the term or different part of speech (e.g., ''Swedenborgianism'' may be cross-referenced to ''Swedenborg, Emanuel,'' or the adjective ''Unitarian'' to the noun ''Unitarianism''). And a word highly charged in the Transcendentalist setting may be cross-referenced to an entry with a slightly different turn of phrase (e.g., ''miracles'' to ''Miracles Controversy'').

A person's full name is given at the beginning of each entry. Thereafter in the entry, the person's surname is given by initial only, without period (e.g., Sarah Margaret Fuller is ''F''). Where more than one person with the same surname appears in a given entry, the first initial of the person's given name may be used, without period (e.g., Lidian Jackson Emerson is ''L,'' and John Thoreau, Jr., is ''J''). Women who were better known by married name may be referred to interchangeably by initial of given name *and* by initial of married surname, as appropriate to the context (e.g., Caroline Sturgis Tappan is ''C,'' ''CS,'' and ''T'' in her own entry).

STANDARD REFERENCE SOURCES

B&M	Robert E. Burkholder and Joel Myerson. *Emerson: An Annotated Secondary Bibliography* [1816–1979]. Pittsburgh: Univ. of Pittsburgh Press, 1985.
B&M2	Robert E. Burkholder and Joel Myerson. *Ralph Waldo Emerson: An Annotated Bibliography of Criticism, 1980–1991*. Westport, Conn.: Greenwood Press, 1994.

Buell	Lawrence Buell. *Literary Transcendentalism: Style and Vision in the American Renaissance*. Ithaca: Cornell Univ. Press, 1973.
Cooke	George Willis Cooke. *An Historical and Biographical Introduction to Accompany* The Dial. 2 vols. Cleveland: Rowfant Club, 1902.
Corr	*The Correspondence of Henry David Thoreau*. Edited by Walter Harding and Carl Bode. New York: New York Univ. Press, 1958.
CW	*The Collected Works of Ralph Waldo Emerson*. Edited by Alfred R. Ferguson et al. 5 vols. to date. Cambridge: Harvard Univ. Press, 1971–.
DAB	*Dictionary of American Biography*. Edited by Dumas Malone. 20 vols. New York: Scribners, 1928–37.
Dahlstrand	Frederick C. Dahlstrand. *Amos Bronson Alcott: An Intellectual Biography*. Rutherford, N.J.: Fairleigh Dickinson Univ. Press, 1982.
DLB	*Dictionary of Literary Biography*. Detroit: Gale.
DNB	*Dictionary of National Biography*. Edited by Leslie Stephen and Sidney Lee. 22 vols. London: Oxford Univ. Press, 1950.
EBib	Joel Myerson. *Ralph Waldo Emerson: A Descriptive Bibliography*. Pittsburgh: Univ. of Pittsburgh Press, 1982.
EL	*The Early Lectures of Ralph Waldo Emerson*. Edited by Stephen E. Whicher, Robert E. Spiller, and Wallace E. Williams. 3 vols. Cambridge: Harvard Univ. Press, 1959–72.
EP	*The Encyclopedia of Philosophy*. 8 vols. Paul Edwards, editor in chief. New York and London: Macmillan, 1967.
Frothingham	Octavius Brooks Frothingham. *Transcendentalism in New England: A History*. New York: G. P. Putnam's Sons, 1876; rpt. Univ. of Pennsylvania Press, 1972.
Gohdes	Clarence L. F. Gohdes. *The Periodicals of American Transcendentalism*. Durham: Duke Univ. Press, 1931.
Gougeon	Len Gougeon. *Virtue's Hero: Emerson, Antislavery, and Reform*. Athens: Univ. of Georgia Press, 1990.
Harding	Walter Harding. *The Days of Henry Thoreau*. New York: Knopf, 1965; enl. ed., New York: Dover, 1982.
Heralds	*Heralds of a Liberal Faith*. Edited by Samuel A. Eliot. 3 vols. Boston: American Unitarian Assn., 1910.

Howe	Daniel Walker Howe. *The Unitarian Conscience: Harvard Moral Philosophy, 1805–1861*. Cambridge: Harvard Univ. Press, 1970.
Hutchison	William R. Hutchison. *The Transcendentalist Ministers: Church Reform in the New England Renaissance*. New Haven: Yale Univ. Press, 1959.
JMN	*The Journals and Miscellaneous Notebooks of Ralph Waldo Emerson*. Edited by William H. Gilman et al. 16 vols. Cambridge: Harvard Univ. Press, 1960–82.
L	*The Letters of Ralph Waldo Emerson*. Vols. 1–6 edited by Ralph L. Rusk; vols. 7–10 edited by Eleanor M. Tilton. New York: Columbia Univ. Press, 1939, 1990–95.
Matthiessen	F. O. Matthiessen. *American Renaissance: Art and Expression in the Age of Emerson and Whitman*. New York: Oxford Univ. Press, 1941.
Miller	Perry Miller. *The Transcendentalists: An Anthology*. Cambridge: Harvard Univ. Press, 1950.
Myerson	*The Transcendentalists: A Review of Research and Criticism*. Edited by Joel Myerson. New York: Modern Language Association of America, 1984.
*NET*Dial	Joel Myerson. *The New England Transcendentalists and the* Dial *: A History of the Magazine and Its Contributors*. Rutherford, N.J.: Fairleigh Dickinson Univ. Press, 1980.
PJ	Henry D. Thoreau. *Journal*. Gen. ed. Robert Sattelmeyer. In THE WRITINGS OF HENRY D. THOREAU. 5 vols. to date. Princeton, N.J.: Princeton Univ. Press, 1981–.
Pochmann	Henry A. Pochmann. *German Culture in America: Philosophical and Literary Influences, 1600–1900*. Madison: Univ. of Wisconsin Press, 1957.
PN	*The Poetry Notebooks of Ralph Waldo Emerson*. Edited by Ralph H. Orth et al. Columbia: Univ. of Missouri Press, 1986.
Richardson	Robert D. Richardson, Jr. *Myth and Literature in the American Renaissance*. Bloomington: Indiana Univ. Press, 1978.
Robinson	David M. Robinson. *The Unitarians and the Universalists*. Westport, Conn.: Greenwood Press, 1985.
RP	Henry D. Thoreau. *Reform Papers*. Edited by Wendell Glick. Princeton: Princeton Univ. Press, 1973.

Rusk	Ralph L. Rusk. *The Life of Ralph Waldo Emerson.* New York: Scribners, 1949.
Sermons	*The Complete Sermons of Ralph Waldo Emerson.* Edited by Albert J. von Frank et al. 4 vols. Columbia: Univ. of Missouri Press, 1989–92.
TN	*The Topical Notebooks of Ralph Waldo Emerson.* 3 vols. Edited by Susan Sutton Smith, Ronald A. Bosco, and Glen M. Johnson. Columbia: Univ. of Missouri Press, 1990–94.
W	*The Complete Works of Ralph Waldo Emerson.* Edited by Edward Waldo Emerson. 12 vols. Centenary Edition. Boston: Houghton Mifflin, 1903–04.
Wr	*The Writings of Henry David Thoreau.* Walden Edition. 20 vols. Boston: Houghton Mifflin, 1906.

JOURNALS AND PERIODICALS

AL	*American Literature*
AQ	*American Quarterly*
ARLR	*American Renaissance Literary Report: An Annual*
Atl	*Atlantic Monthly*
ATQ	*American Transcendental Quarterly*
BB	*Bulletin of Bibliography*
BoQR	*Boston Quarterly Review*
BPLQ	*Boston Public Library Quarterly*
BRPR	*Biblical Repertory and Princeton Review*
BuR	*Bucknell Review*
CE	*College English*
ChEx	*Christian Examiner*
CHR	*Catholic Historical Review*
ChReg	*Christian Register*
CM	*Century Magazine*
CS	*Concord Saunterer* (Thoreau Society)
EIHC	*Essex Institute Historical Collections*
ESP	*Emerson Society Papers*
ESQ	*Emerson Society Quarterly* (1955–71); *ESQ: A Journal of the American Renaissance* (1972–)
FR	*French Review*
GaR	*Georgia Review*

GrMag	*Graham's Magazine*
HLB	*Harvard Library Bulletin*
HMo	*Harvard Monthly*
HTR	*Harvard Theological Review*
IntR	*International Review*
JAAC	*Journal of Aesthetics and Art Criticism*
JHI	*Journal of the History of Ideas*
JR	*Journal of Religion*
MLN	*Modern Language Notes*
MP	*Modern Philology*
MQ	*Midwest Quarterly*
NAR	*North American Review*
NCL	*Nineteenth-Century Literature*
NEMag	*New England Magazine*
NEQ	*New England Quarterly*
NHR	*Nathaniel Hawthorne Review*
NJM	*New Jerusalem Magazine*
NLH	*New Literary History*
NR	*Nassau Review*
NYH	*New York History*
PAAAS	*Proceedings of the American Academy of Arts and Sciences*
PAAS	*Proceedings of the American Antiquarian Society*
PAH	*Perspectives in American History*
PAPS	*Proceedings of the American Philosophical Society*
PBSA	*Papers of the Bibliographical Society of America*
PhR	*Philosophical Review*
PMHS	*Proceedings of the Massachusetts Historical Society*
PMLA	*PMLA: Publications of the Modern Language Association of America*
PUUHS	*Proceedings of the Unitarian Universalist Historical Society*
RALS	*Resources for American Literary Study*
SAQ	*South Atlantic Quarterly*
SAR	*Studies in the American Renaissance: An Annual*
SB	*Studies in Bibliography*
SIR	*Studies in Romanticism*
SP	*Studies in Philology*

SPAS	*Studies in Puritan American Spirituality*
StN	*Studies in the Novel*
TJQ	*Thoreau Journal Quarterly*
TSB	*Thoreau Society Bulletin*
UCPMP	*University of California Publications in Modern Philology*
UQ	*Universalist Quarterly*
WM	*Western Messenger*
WWR	*Walt Whitman Review*

A

AGASSIZ, JEAN LOUIS (1807–1873), a natural scientist and acquaintance of Transcendentalists, helped create an awareness in America of the importance of the study of natural history.** He founded the Museum of Comparative Zoology at Harvard University and was a pioneer in making scientific studies an integral part of the curriculum of American schools. Born in Switzerland, the son of a Protestant clergyman, A entered medical school at Zurich and after two years enrolled in Heidelberg, where he developed a special interest in natural history. The following year, he transferred to the University of Munich, where he came under the influence of Ignaz von Dollinger, an embryologist whom he credited as the source of his scientific training. He enrolled in Erlanger, where he received his doctorate in philosophy, and later returned to Munich to complete his degree in medicine. He never examined a patient but pursued his studies in glacial geology, paleontology, and ichthyology. His first published works were in ichthyology. His first wife, Cecile Braun, was a natural history artist and drew the pictures of fossils and live fish that appeared in many of his books. A accepted a post at Neuchatel as a naturalist and soon turned it into one of the major research centers in Europe. While there, he published over 200 works on his research, including his famed *Principles of Zoology* (1848).

The last 25 years of A's life were spent in America. He accepted an appointment to teach natural history at the new Lawrence Scientific School at Harvard and was appointed to the board of regents of the Smithsonian Institution in Washington, D.C., whose natural history division he helped plan. In America, A's interests were as varied as they had been in Europe. He and his second wife, Elizabeth Cary, opened a school for young women in Cambridge, Massachusetts, which became the precursor of Radcliffe. A often worked in the laboratory of Cambridge High School, which he then found better equipped than the one at Harvard. In time, however, he built Harvard's laboratory into one of the nation's finest.

A found a kindred soul in H. D. Thoreau* and often visited Walden Pond.** Thoreau sometimes sent A varieties of reptiles and fish for his laboratory, and A paid him well. On one occasion, Thoreau and A offended R. W. Emerson's* sensibilities while dining by talking about turtles mating. A was a member of the Saturday Club,** which was conceived as a forum for ideas and included poets, historians, scientists, lawyers, and ministers, many of whom were of the new breed of mid-19th-century Transcendentalists. They met at the Parker House for dinner and discussed current topics of intellectual interest, the most recent of which was evolution. Darwin's* *The Origin of Species* was published in 1859, and almost immediately, A took issue with it. A held to the idea that separate creation was essential in his philosophy of nature,** and for the rest of his life, he openly denied the theory of evolution. As a lifelong student of fossils, he concluded that the changes that living entities undergo during their embryonic growth coincide with the order of succession of the fossils of the same type in past geological ages. He carried his belief to racism by arguing that blacks were created separately and were a different species from whites. Most of his students had abandoned his creationist theory by the time of his death.

References: See *Correspondence Between Spencer Fullerton Baird and LA* (1964), ed. Elmer C. Herber; Jules Marcou, *Life, Letters, and Works of LA*, 2 vols. (1896), with annotated list of publications and papers; Edward Lurie, *LA: A Life of Science* (1960); Louise Hall Tharp, *Adventurous Alliance: The Story of the A Family of Boston* (1960); and Lane Cooper, *LA as a Teacher* (1917), an excellent account of A, who wanted most to be remembered simply as a teacher, including anecdotes as told by his students.

Raymond L. Muncy

ALCOTT, AMOS BRONSON (1799–1888), educator, philosopher, conversationalist,** essayist, and poet, was a central figure among the Transcendentalists. He played an active role in the various reform efforts associated with Transcendentalism; and because of the typically extreme positions he struck, he was frequently singled out as representing the excesses of the movement. Always committed to, and himself an exemplar of, the Transcendentalists' belief in self-culture, A was born on a farm near Wolcott, Connecticut. His scant formal education ended when he was 13; poverty prevented him from going to Yale as he had hoped, and for the rest of his life, he read and learned on his own. Years later, A captured these boyhood experiences in *New Connecticut: An Autobiographical Poem* (1881).

The most formative events in his early life occurred during a series of peddling trips to Virginia and the Carolinas (1817–23). On these trips, he witnessed the evils of slavery, an experience that later led him to join the antislavery movement and embrace other humanitarian causes. Also, while staying at a Quaker** community, he became deeply impressed with the idea of man's "inner light"; though never becoming a Quaker, A was convinced of the spirituality of all humans. Feeling energized and hopeful that he could help reform society,

A returned to New England and for the next decade and a half pursued what he clearly believed to be his calling in life, teaching. In part to record his experiences, A began keeping a journal** in 1826; soon these yearly journals grew to several hundred pages each and included trenchant comments on his contemporaries as well as the various events and issues of the day. As H. Thoreau* thought of his Journal, A eventually came to regard the volumes as his life's work.

Following a frustrating stint teaching in rural Connecticut, where his progressive ideas about education met with resistance, A moved to Boston in 1828 and taught with success in an infant school. There he met Abigail May, whom he married in 1830. Shortly after his marriage, he and Abba moved to the Philadelphia area, where he taught for four years. This period marked an important turning point in A's intellectual development, for he became immersed in the literature and philosophy of Idealism.** Once enamored of Aristotle, Bacon, Locke,** and other philosophers in the tradition of empiricism and sensationalism,** he now devoured the works of Plato,** Proclus,** Plotinus,** other Neoplatonists,** Goethe,* and French eclectic philosopher V. Cousin,* who was popularizing Kant,** Fichte,** and Schelling.* Of English writers, he favored Wordsworth,* Coleridge,* and Carlyle.* Most revelatory was Coleridge's *Aids to Reflection*, which he read in an edition prepared by J. Marsh.*

By early 1834, having concluded that he could not thrive as a teacher in Philadelphia, A yearned for a wider and more receptive field of action. In the summer of 1834 with the help of his onetime mentor the Rev. W. E. Channing* and E. Peabody,* Channing's former amanuensis and a progressive teacher herself, a school was gathered for him. Steeped in the theories of the celebrated Swiss educator Pestalozzi** and holding up as his teaching models Socrates, Pythagoras, and Jesus, A opened his "School for Human Culture" in the Masonic Temple in September 1834 with Peabody as his assistant.

Characterized by its open spaces, its comfortable atmosphere and A's inductive methodology, avoidance of corporal punishment, and belief in the divinity of children, the Temple School** was a model of education reform,** attracting the young sons and daughters of Boston's elite. Peabody's *Record of a School* (1835; rev. ed. 1836) and A's *Conversations with Children on the Gospels* (2 vols., 1836–37) were designed to spread his ideas and increase enrollment, but many parents and patrons objected to the radical nature of some of A's methods, especially as revealed in the latter book. In his frank, wide-ranging discussions on the New Testament, A's students conversed on such subjects as the pain of Christ's circumcision and the meaning of birth. A was excoriated in the press, and parents withdrew their children from the school. Deep in debt and in despair, he closed the Temple School in 1838. Another attempt at running a similar school, in 1838–39 at his own home, also failed, this time as a result of refusing to dismiss an African-American student. Never again would he teach. Ironically, even as he was being assailed in Boston, A had gained disciples elsewhere—in Providence, Rhode Island, and in England, France, and Prussia.

If the decade of the 1830s proved disappointing in terms of his career, A's private life was one of relative happiness. His three daughters—Anna (b. 1831), Louisa May,* and Elizabeth (b. 1835)—provided much joy. A's observations of his girls' spiritual, moral, and psychological growth, though never published, are remarkable for their insight into childhood development, especially the one entitled ''Psyche,'' the record of Elizabeth's early years.

During this period, A met R. W. Emerson,* and they soon became the best of friends. Emerson regarded A as ''a god-made priest'' and invited him to join the Transcendental Club.** At the meetings of this group and in other settings, A enjoyed testing his ideas against those of the leading Transcendentalists, including C. Francis,* F. H. Hedge,* G. Ripley,* T. Parker,* W. H. Furness,* S. M. Fuller,* J. F. Clarke,* O. Brownson,* J. S. Dwight,* J. Very,* and Thoreau.

In 1840 a fourth daughter was born, Abby May, and A realized his dream of moving to Concord** to be near Emerson. In the same year, he contributed 50 ''Orphic Sayings'' to *The Dial*,** the magazine's title having in fact been suggested by him. Unsympathetic reviewers ridiculed them for being oracular, mystical, and vapid. By far the two most significant events of this period were his trip to England in 1842 and his subsequent attempt to found a utopian community at Fruitlands.** During his trip to England, funded primarily by Emerson, A visited Carlyle and a number of prominent British reformers, including C. Lane* and others who ran Alcott House, an experimental school founded near London by J. P. Greaves* and modeled directly on the Temple School.

A, with Lane and his son, returned to America in the fall of 1842. In January 1843, while forming plans for a New Eden and lecturing on the ills of the age, A was arrested for refusing to pay his poll tax, a characteristic act of conscience that a few years later was repeated for similar reasons by Thoreau, who in *Walden* praised his friend highly.

By late spring a suitable location was found for the proposed ''consociate family,'' a 90-acre farm near Harvard, Massachusetts, which was purchased with Lane's money. The Alcotts, the Lanes, and a few others moved there on 1 June. Like the Temple School, Fruitlands reflected A's belief that reform of society could not take place until individuals were regenerated. Rigorously enforced vegetarianism and early morning cold water baths characterized the physical discipline. From the beginning, however, there were problems. Lane and A refused on principle to use animal labor to work the fields, did not get the crops in early enough, and went off on lecturing tours during harvest season. Few people ever stayed there; many who did found little spiritual compensation and felt A dictatorial and inflexible in matters of diet and regimen. The experiment collapsed when Lane nearly converted A to celibacy, forcing Abba to make her husband choose between the conjugal family and the consociate family. In early January 1844 the Lanes and Alcotts parted company. Putting a humorous spin on the failure that nearly destroyed her father, Louisa May 40 years later gently satirized Fruitlands in ''Transcendental Wild Oats'' (1873).

Although he remained idealistic in his aspirations for reform, he never again took such a personal risk. Over much of the next decade, the family moved from place to place in New England before returning permanently in 1857 to Concord, where they finally settled at ''Orchard House.'' Always regarding money as an evil, A was never a good provider for his family. Even his position as superintendent of Concord's public schools (1859–65) did not pay enough to sustain the family. Until the poverty of what Louisa May called her ''pathetic family'' ended in 1868 with the publication of the autobiographical *Little Women* and subsequent successful writings, the family survived on gifts from friends and family and the meager earnings of what Abba and the girls made sewing or doing domestic work.

From 1855 until a stroke incapacitated him in 1882, A made a series of conversational tours of the West. While only modestly rewarding in monetary terms, A basked in the limelight of being lionized as the ''Sage of Concord.'' In 1868 he published *Tablets*, a collection of edited manuscripts he had worked on for 20 years covering such subjects as friendship, children, the family, conversation, politics, religion, and human culture. It also contains A's speculations about what he called genesis and lapse. *Concord Days* (1872) includes characterizations of famous Concordians, accounts of past conversations, comments on A's favorite authors, and thoughts about the ideal church. In 1877 he published *Table Talk*, a selection of scripturelike apothegms, or ''philosophemes'' as he termed the sayings, on such topics as reading, gardening, education, temperance,** and village life. Perhaps his most accomplished literary achievement is *Sonnets and Canzonets* (1882), which paid eloquent tribute to family members and friends, notably Channing and his poet-nephew Ellery,* Emerson, Thoreau, Furness, Fuller, Parker, N. Hawthorne,* W. Phillips,* and W. L. Garrison,* nearly all of whom A had outlived.

In 1879, two years after the death of Abba, in what proved to be the last chapter of his intellectual life, A began the Concord School of Philosophy.** The school, which was quite successful, met every summer until his death and drew people from all over America. Lecturers included, among others, A (until his stroke), Hedge, W. T. Harris,* D. Wasson,* F. B. Sanborn,* E. Cheney,* T. W. Higginson,* and W. H. Channing.* A had at last, it seemed, found the success that had so long eluded him; his stroke, however, made him unable to write and barely able to talk for the last six years of his life. The ''world-builder with olympian dreams,'' as Emerson once described A, died on 4 March 1888 in Boston at the home of Louisa May, who died two days later. He was buried in Concord in Sleepy Hollow Cemetery** with his family; nearby are the graves of Emerson, Thoreau, Hawthorne, Peabody, and others whom he numbered among his friends.

References: Many of A's manuscripts remain unpublished. Almost all of this material is in the Alcott-Pratt collection at Harvard. Odell Shepard's *The Journals of BA* (1938) prints but a small fraction of these voluminous records. Complete individual volumes have been published in their entirety: Joel Myerson's edition of the 1836 journal in *SAR* 1978: 17–104; Larry Carlson's two-part edition of the 1837 journal in *SAR* 1981: 27–

132 and *SAR* 1982: 53–167. A's 1838 journal has also been published in a two-part format by Carlson: *SAR* 1993: 161–244 and *SAR* 1994: 123–93. Also important is Richard L. Herrnstadt, ed., *The Letters of BA* (1969). Letters missed by Herrnstadt can be found in Frederick Wagner's two-part ''Eighty-six Letters (1814–1882) of A. BA,'' *SAR* 1979: 239–308 and *SAR* 1980: 183–228.

Of the many private and public 19th-century accounts of A, several need singling out. Significant personal commentary appears in *JMN* and *L.* Of special note, too, is Emerson's ''ABA'' in *The New American Cyclopaedia*, ed. G. Ripley and C. A. Dana* (1858). The centrality of A to the Transcendental movement is perhaps best appreciated in O. B. Frothingham* (1876). The first extended biography of A was published by F. B. Sanborn and W. T. Harris, *A. BA: His Life and Philosophy*, 2 vols. (1893).

Discussions of A's Fruitlands venture can be found in Sanborn, *BA at Alcott House, England, and Fruitlands, New England (1842–1844)* (1908), and Clara Endicott Sears, *BA's Fruitlands* (1915). A's career as a teacher and his theories about childhood are the subject of George E. Haefner, *A Critical Estimate of the Educational Theories and Practices of A. BA* (1937); Dorothy McCuskey, *BA, Teacher* (1940); Sherman Paul, ''A's Search for the Child,'' *BPLQ* 4 (April 1952): 88–96; and Charles Strickland, ''A Transcendentalist Father: The Child-Rearing Practices of BA,'' *PAH* 3 (1969): 5–73.

See Hubert H. Hoeltje, *Sheltering Tree: A Story of the Friendship of Ralph Waldo Emerson and ABA* (1943). An insightful discussion of A's theory of conversation is in Buell (1973). The best full-scale modern biographies of A are Odell Shepard, *Pedlar's Progress: The Life of BA* (1937), and Dahlstrand (1982).

Larry A. Carlson

ALCOTT, LOUISA MAY (1832–1888), most noted for her classic children's books, especially *Little Women* (1868–69), was born in Germantown, Pennsylvania, the second of four daughters born to A. B.* and Abigail May Alcott. LMA grew up in Boston and Concord,** Massachusetts, where she was a contemporary of the Emerson* and Hawthorne* children. Although she would never declare herself a Transcendentalist, having been too young to be an active participant, she could not help but be affected by its philosophy and actions. As a neighbor and friend to many of the major Transcendentalists, including Emerson and H. Thoreau,* A was greatly influenced by their ideas, especially in her attitudes toward self-reliance and reform. However, she also saw the impractical results of their ''castles in the air.''

Her first hard lesson as a Transcendentalist philosopher's daughter came when B. Alcott and C. Lane* established Fruitlands** in 1843. Ten years old at the beginning of her family's stay at Fruitlands, A knew well the value of practicality. Despite her early age, she absorbed the pleasant events and difficult times at the consociate community, and she later remembered that it was a practical woman—her mother—who made it work for as long as it did. The existing scraps of her 1843 diary and her subsequent publication of ''Transcendental Wild Oats'' in 1873 perhaps provide a unique view of the real life that was the foundation for the philosophical one. One cannot read A's fictionalized account without feeling that the experience at Fruitlands, although lasting less than a year, deeply affected her entire family. The satiric ''Transcendental Wild Oats'' pokes fun at an ill-planned venture. Yet A also recognized the nobility of the utopian experiment: ''Transcendental wild oats were sown broadcast that year, and the fame thereof has not yet ceased in the land; for futile as this crop seemed to outsiders, it bore an invisible harvest, worth much to those who planted in earnest. . . . Fruitlands was the most ideal of all these castles in Spain.'' However, her first experience in Transcendental living would not be the end of difficult times.

The 1850s also proved trying for ''the Pathetic Family,'' as LMA often called the Alcotts. With Bronson trying to secure some type of successful work, usually lecturing, the family moved often, and the two older girls held odd jobs, from keeping school to going out to service. In 1858, when the family eventually settled into their new Concord home, Orchard House—or Apple Slump as A irreverently called it—she confessed in her journal:** ''All seem to be glad that the wandering family is anchored at last. . . . The old people need an abiding place; and now that death and love have taken two of us away, I can, I hope, soon manage to care for the remaining four.'' That same winter, she wrote again of Bronson's inability to earn money: ''Dear man! How happy he will be if people will only listen to and *pay* for his wisdom.'' Despite Bronson's failure to support the family, A was proud of his intellectual abilities. She once wrote a friend and asked, ''Did I ever tell you what Mr. Emerson once said . . . to me! 'Louisa, your father could have talked with Plato.**' Was not that praise worth having?''

A relished Emerson's words, and her relationship with him helped develop her strongest ties to Transcendentalism. When Emerson died in 1882, A confided in her journal that he was ''the man who has helped me most by his life, his books, his society. I can never tell all he has been to me from the time I [was] . . . a little girl, . . . up through my hard years when his essays on Self Reliance, Character, Compensation,** Love & Friendship helped me to understand myself & life & God & Nature.**'' As a teenager, A was greatly influenced by *Goethe's* Correspondence with a Child*. The book, which documents the strong pupil-master relationship between the 13-year-old Baroness Bettina von Arnim and the 58-year-old German author, inspired A ''to be a second Bettine, making my father's friend my Goethe.'' Like the young Bettine, A wrote many letters to Emerson; however, she never sent them, choosing instead to leave ''wild flowers on the doorsteps of my 'Master' '' and to sing ''Mignon's song in very bad German under his window.''

Her reading, too, was greatly influenced by Emerson. Often she would ''venture into Mr. Emerson's library and ask what I should read, never conscious of the audacity of my demand, so genial was my welcome.'' Emerson would lead her around his library until she chose the proper work. When she selected a book beyond her comprehension, her neighbor would smile and reply: '' 'Wait a little for that.' '' A noted that ''[f]or many of these wise books I am waiting still . . . because in his own I have found the truest delight, the best inspiration of my life.'' Later, she would encourage her own young admirers to do the same. In 1884, she wrote to a young girl: ''Have you read Emerson? He is called a Pantheist** or believer in Nature instead of God. He was truly *Christian* & saw God *in* Nature, finding strength & comfort in the sane, sweet influences of the great Mother as well as the Father of all.'' She claimed that Emerson ''did much to help me to see that one can shape life best by trying to build up a strong & noble character through good books, wise people's society, an interest in all reforms that help the world, & a cheerful acceptance of whatever is inevitable.'' A once said that having known Emerson was ''the greatest honor and happiness of my life.''

Despite her admiration for the Transcendentalists, A could not help but find humor in these great sages, as well as the town of Concord and the literary pilgrims who journeyed there, hoping to glimpse one of its noted authors. In a letter to the *Springfield Republican* in 1869, A declared that since so many tourists now flocked to this ''modern Mecca,'' a new hotel called ''The Sphinx's Head'' was to be established. Here, the curious sightseers could partake of ''Walden** water, aesthetic tea, and 'wine that never grew in the belly of the grape.' '' The hotel itself, she claimed, would be furnished with ''Alcott's rustic furniture, the beds made of Thoreau's pine boughs, and the sacred fires fed from the Emersonian wood-pile.'' And for those hoping to glimpse a famous Transcendentalist, telescopes would be ''provided for the gifted eyes which desire to watch the soarings of the Oversoul, when visible, and lassoes [*sic*] with which the expert may catch untamed hermits, or poets on the wing.'' Despite her ability to view Transcendentalism with a wary eye, A's own writing was flavored with its ideas and with reminders of her close association with its leaders.

Even her characters recall her famous Transcendental neighbors. Thoreau forms the basis for at least two characters. David Sterling, who ''devotes himself to his flowers and leads a very quiet life'' in *Work: A Story of Experience* (1873), is A's idealized portrayal of the poet-naturalist. In fact, the book's heroine, Christie Devon (obviously based on A herself), marries young Sterling. In A's first novel, *Moods* (1864), she creates another picture of Thoreau in the character of Adam Warwick (the book's title comes from Emerson). Many of her works, including *Little Women* (1868–69), *Little Men* (1871), and *Rose in Bloom* (1876), are filled with the idea of self-reform. What else could one expect from a woman who grew up in the literary hotbed of Transcendentalism and once signed her letters, ''Yours, for reforms of all kinds''?

References: A's own discussion of Transcendentalism can be found in her ''Transcendental Wild Oats'' and ''Recollections of My Childhood,'' both reprinted in Daniel Shealy, Joel Myerson, and Madeleine B. Stern, *LMA: Selected Fiction* (1990). See ''Reminiscences of Ralph Waldo Emerson'' in *Some Noted Princes, Authors, and Statesmen of Our Time*, ed. James Parton (1885), for her memories of Emerson. The most informative biography is Madeleine B. Stern, *LMA* (1950; rev. 1971). Useful esp. for A's early life is Madelon Bedell, *The Alcotts: Biography of a Family* (1980). A's private writings are in Joel Myerson, Daniel Shealy, and Madeleine B. Stern, eds., *The Selected Letters of LMA* (1987), and *The Journals of LMA* (1989). Critical discussions include Sarah

Elbert, *A Hunger for Home: LMA's Place in American Culture* (1987), and Joy A. Marsella, *The Promise of Destiny: Children and Women in the Short Stories of LMA* (1983). Bibliographical sources are Madeleine B. Stern, *L's Wonder Book* (1975), which has an excellent primary bibliography, and Alma J. Payne, *LMA: A Reference Guide* (1980). Madeleine B. Stern, *Critical Essays on LMA* (1984), gives contemporary reviews plus new and reprinted essays.

Daniel Shealy

ALEXANDER, JOHN WHITE (1856–1915), was an American painter born near Pittsburgh, tangentially connected to the Transcendentalists via his portrait of W. Whitman.* Although A's artistic merit rests primarily on his portraits, he was also a prominent painter of murals. His concentration on the figure rather than on landscape** and his European training, which emphasized painting from a model rather than from nature,** reflect a definite breaking away from the Hudson River School of the previous generation.

Completed in 1889, A's portrait of Whitman was donated to New York's Metropolitan Museum of Art in 1891. That year the painter wrote to the poet, "I am delighted to have been the means of giving to future generations a portrait of you that is certainly one of my best works." Whitman's friend J. Burroughs,* however, was not impressed, calling the portrait "an emasculated Whitman—failing to show his power and ruggedness." Other literary figures who sat for portraits by A include O. W. Holmes,* Mark Twain, and William Dean Howells.

REFERENCES: For a discussion of A's life, an in-depth look at his style, a partial list of notable sitters, and examples of his painting plus a selected bibliography, see *JWA/1856–1915/Fin-de-Siecle American* (1980).

Heidi M. Schultz

ALLSTON, WASHINGTON (1779–1843), the leading American painter of his generation, was for the Transcendentalists the ideal type of the Romantic artist. A South Carolinian, A graduated from Harvard College in 1800, married W. E. Channing's* sister Ann in 1809, and lived in Cambridge during his last years (1818–43). In Cambridge, A wrote and spoke often to intimate groups on aesthetic theory at his Cambridgeport home. R. W. Emerson* was strongly influenced by his ideas, although A mistrusted the Transcendentalists as radicals. The statement in Emerson's "Art" (*Essays: First Series*) that "the painter should give the suggestion of a fairer creation than we know" is central to A's aesthetics. Almost more important than A's work was his example of the imaginative artist's self-sufficiency, even in workaday Boston. Commenting on A in *The Dial*,** M. Fuller* found his career a demonstration that "the poetical mind . . . may unfold to its due perfection in an unpoetical society."

A's canvases, with their haunting mood and glowing colors, make him a founder of Romantic landscape** painting. His friendship with Coleridge* in England made him an early messenger between the European Romantic movement, with its insistence on the primacy of thought and feeling, and New England. Yet A could not break free from academic rules of biblical and history painting, and modern critics like Nathalia Wright have seen both A and his work as ''escapist,'' retreating from any task that faced him with threats to his inner balance.

To Emerson's generation, the inner block that kept A from finishing his most ambitious work, *Belshazzar's Feast*, could be glamorized: He had put the life of the mind before mere worldly accomplishment. However, Emerson's verdict, in an 1839 journal entry, was that ''A's pictures are Elysian: fair, serene, but unreal. I extend the remark to all the American geniuses . . . they lack nerve and dagger.'' The Transcendentalists profited from A's Idealist** aesthetic but came to demand more vital and contemporary expressions of it.

References: The most recent in-depth study of A's art, without much attention to his life, is the exhibition catalog by William N. Gerdts and Theodore Stebbins, *''A Man of Genius'': The Art of WA (1779–1843)* (1979). The editorial apparatus in Nathalia Wright, ed., *The Correspondence of WA* (1993), makes it superior to Jared Flagg's *Life and Letters of WA* (1892). E. P. Richardson, *WA: A Study of the Romantic Artist in America* (1948), puts A in his context and details his relationship with the Boston intellectual world. Of more recent considerations, David Bjelejac, *Millennial Desire and the Apocalyptic Vision of WA* (1988), stresses A's conservatism and clarifies the differences between A's and Emerson's thought.

M. David Samson

ANDREWS, STEPHEN PEARL (1812–1886), was an eccentric reformer and philosopher infused with the Transcendental spirit that saw analogies in science and religion, mind and matter. Influenced by the great movements of his time, Protestantism, democracy, socialism, and Transcendentalism, all of which asserted the supremacy of the individual in society, he attacked any infringements upon individual freedom, from slavery to the oppression of labor, from press censorship to religious orthodoxy. In the effort to assert individual sovereignty, his career intersected almost every social movement in America.

During the 1840s, A championed abolition** and tried to free the slaves of Texas. Shortly after, he introduced Isaac Pitman's shorthand into the United States in the hope of enabling slaves to read. In 1851, with J. Warren,* he helped found a community of sovereign individuals, ''Modern Times,'' on Long Island, New York, and wrote *The Science of Society*. During the 1860s, he developed the Pantarchy, a ''Grand Composite Order of Government'' for a new universal society. In the 1870s, he wrote on Universology and Integralism for *Woodhull & Claflin's Weekly*, published his *Basic Outline of Universology*, and campaigned for Victoria Woodhull as first woman president of the United States. At this period, he also devised a universal language, Alwato, for the United States of the World that he envisioned.

Failing in most of his attempts, A fought a succession of windmills, and at his death, it was said that ''[t]he world at large is unable to determine whether he was a crank or the founder of a great system of philosophy.'' Certainly he was a touch of both. His mind was a Transcendental mind, searching for the oneness of all things, and his attempted reforms were based upon the Transcendental belief in the freedom and sovereignty of the individual.

REFERENCES: The only full-length biography of A is Madeleine B. Stern, *The Pantarch: A Biography of SPA* (1968). A collection of A papers is housed in the State Historical Society of Wisconsin at Madison.

Madeleine B. Stern

B

BACON, DELIA SALTER (1811–1859), historical lecturer and Shakespearean** critic, though not herself a Transcendentalist, intrigued some members of the group with her theory that W. Shakespeare of Stratford did not write the plays attributed to him. B, of a Calvinist (see Puritanism**) Connecticut family, arrived on the Boston scene in 1850 at the urging of C. H. Dall* in order to pursue her career as historical lecturer. Both Dall and E. P. Peabody* acted as her sponsors in the Boston area and introduced her into a wider circle.

When in 1852 B became increasingly consumed with her theory of non-Shakespearean authorship, Peabody, B's chief confidante on this point, introduced her to R. W. Emerson.* He found her a persuasive but not fully convincing advocate of her thesis. He admired the acuteness with which she could read the plays to the tune of her own theory and endorsed her work in a letter to the publisher George P. Putnam, declaring, with typical enthusiasm for one of his newly discovered geniuses, "I have seen nothing in America in the way of literary criticism, which I thought so good." For the next few years, Emerson devoted considerable time and effort to putting B in touch with his acquaintances in England (including T. Carlyle*) and to finding her a publisher in America. But acting as her agent proved difficult, and finally exasperated, Emerson ended his efforts. B, now armed with a letter of introduction from Peabody, appealed to N. Hawthorne,* then in Liverpool. Hawthorne, though he had no confidence in her theory, nevertheless wrote the introduction to *The Philosophy of the Plays of Shakspere Unfolded* (1857) and even personally paid for its publication. The work was immediately panned by critics in both England and America. Shortly afterward, B suffered a mental collapse from which she never recovered and died in an institution for the insane. Emerson never fulfilled his intention to write about this talented but unbalanced woman.

References: The standard biography is Vivian Constance Hopkins, *Prodigal Puritan: A Life of DB* (1959). Dall included a brief chapter on B in her book *What We Really*

Know About Shakespeare (1885), and Hawthorne's account of his dealings with her, ''Recollections of a Gifted Woman,'' appears in *Our Old Home* (Centenary Edition, 1970). Recent treatments of B's interactions with the Transcendentalists include Helen R. Deese, ''Two Unpublished Emerson Letters: To George P. Putnam on DB and to George B. Loring,'' *EIHC* 122 (April 1986): 101–23; and Deese, ''A New England Women's Network: Elizabeth Palmer Peabody, Caroline Healey Dall, and D S. B,'' *Legacy: A Journal of American Women Writers* 8 (fall 1991): 77–91.

Helen R. Deese

BANCROFT, GEORGE (1800–1891), historian and diplomat, was the son of a liberal Congregational minister and was from an early age encouraged to take up the pulpit. In 1811, he attended Phillips Academy, and two years later, he entered Harvard. After graduating in 1817, he spent two years at Germany's University of Göttingen studying, among other subjects, German and French literature. He began translating Goethe,* Schiller,** and other European poets and in a letter from A. Norton* was warned against developing such ''German affectations.'' After he received his Ph.D. from Göttingen in 1820, Bancroft traveled to Berlin to study Oriental languages and Higher Criticism.** Here he became acquainted with Schleiermacher* and Goethe. In 1822, he returned to America and took a position at Harvard, tutoring Greek.

B also occupied several pulpits but was not satisfied with this or the tutorship. With his friend J. G. Cogswell, he attempted to import educational concepts he had encountered in Europe into a new venture, the Round Hill school, which after eight years failed. With a growing penchant for Democratic politics and his diplomatic abilities, B served as secretary of the navy (1845–46), minister to England (1846–49), and minister to Berlin (1867–74).

But B is best known for his ten-volume *History of the United States*, which appeared at intervals from 1834 to 1875. The first volumes struck sympathetic chords within Transcendentalist ranks. O. Brownson* and G. Ripley* lauded B's analysis of Quakerism** (2: 326–404). Ripley wrote B in 1837 to discuss the comparison between the Quakers' ''inner light'' and the Transcendentalists' intuition. ''The chapter on the Quakers must of course excite great attention—& if it be comprehended—great opposition, from those who deem the salvation of the world dependent on an outward light, and every appeal to the inborn law a folly & an offence.''

B also contributed significant translations and reviews of German literature, a major influence on Transcendentalism. For the *North American Review*,** he provided articles on Schiller (October 1823), Goethe (October 1824), and Herder** (January 1825), including translations of representative works. In 1827, he initiated a series of six articles on ''German Literature'' for the *American Quarterly Review*, examining recent publications and literary culture. He also contributed several translations to the third volume of Ripley's *Specimens of Foreign Standard Literature*,** edited by J. S. Dwight.* B's early and direct exposure to German literature, philosophy, and culture preceded by many years the flowering of American Transcendentalism.

References: See M. A. DeWolfe Howe, *Life and Letters of GB*, 2 vols. (1908); Russel B. Nye, *GB: Brahmin Rebel* (1944), and his *GB* (1964); and Robert H. Canary, *GB* (1974). On B's social and political background, see also Arthur M. Schlesinger, Jr., *The Age of Jackson* (1950). On his contribution to the dissemination of German literature, see Pochmann (1957). See also Nye's "The Religion of GB," *JR* 19 (July 1939): 216–33. For Ripley's letter, see Mathew David Fisher, "A Selected Annotated Edition of the Letters of George Ripley, 1828–1841" (Diss., Ball State Univ., 1992). Most of B's letters are in the Massachusetts Historical Society.

Mathew David Fisher

BARTOL, CYRUS AUGUSTUS (1813–1900), Unitarian** clergyman and author, was a prominent figure in Boston religious and intellectual life between 1836 and 1889, his years as pastor of the historic West Church. He was a close observer of, and often participant in, the major controversies in the Unitarian Church over Transcendentalism, denominationalism, and scientific radicalism in the 19th century. B was an independent thinker who often dissented from the common beliefs of groups with which he was associated: the Transcendentalists, American Unitarian Association, Free Religious Association,** and sometimes even the majority of the West Church.

B came from a Calvinistic background in his native Freeport, Maine. He graduated from Bowdoin College in 1832 and the Harvard Divinity School** in 1835. He was a fellow divinity student with T. Parker,* J. F. Clarke,* E. Channing,* and C. P. Cranch.* Before coming to Cambridge, he was already acquainted with the Idealism** of Plato,** Berkeley,** and Kant**; but at the Divinity School, he came to know the transcendental thought of Coleridge* and the heterodoxy of R. W. Emerson.* Before leaving Cambridge, his faith in intuition, the organic** nature of the universe, and the immanence** of God had been formed. After Harvard, he preached for a year in Cincinnati, where he was regularly in touch with the Transcendentalist editors of *The Western Messenger.*** Upon returning to Boston in 1836, he became a regular member of the Transcendental Club,** beginning with its first formal meeting on 16 September 1836. He attended at least 14 of the 30 meetings of the club between September 1836 and June 1840, 6 of which were held in his home. Like most of the Transcendentalists, he desired to infuse vitality and Spirit into the Unitarian Church and free it from the bonds of forms and rituals. His whole life, as it turned out, became a search for a higher religion of Spirit, but his Transcendentalism, which generally tended to be of the conservative kind, was often at variance with that of the other Transcendentalist ministers. He found the radical directions of some of the reformers, especially Emerson and Parker (both of whom he liked), unacceptable and before the middle of the 19th century distanced himself from them. The principal belief that separated him from Emerson and Parker, and likewise from the Unitarian denominationalists like his friend the Rev. Henry W. Bellows, was his belief in personal theism, an idea he got mainly from A. B. Alcott.* The admiration of B and Alcott was mutual and enduring, as is attested in B's laudatory sermon "Amos Bronson Alcott: His Character" (1888) and Alcott's "Sonnet XXI" in *Sonnets and Canzonets* (1882), in which he praises B as "Poet of the Pulpit." In the 1840s, B and Emerson were not always on the best of terms, but in later times, while arguing to open the Lord's Supper** at the West Church to those of all faiths and even thinking about leaving the ministry, he sought Emerson's advice. Emerson graciously sent him a manuscript copy of his famous sermon of 1832 on the Lord's Supper and advised him to continue preaching. B could not endorse the excesses of Parker's preaching, and when in 1853 the Boston Association of Congregational Ministers excluded Parker, he assented. But later when he encountered the materialistic influences of the denominationalists in the Unitarian Church, he remembered Parker more sympathetically.

In response to a move in the Unitarian Church toward more restrictive denominationalism, B met with a number of radical Unitarians at his home on 5 February 1867 to form the Free Religious Association. The purpose of the organization was "to promote the interests of pure religion, to encourage the scientific study of theology and increase fellowship in the spirit." But his interest in the association soon waned because, with its excessive emphasis upon science and materialism, it failed to create a religion of the Spirit, just as Transcendentalism had failed. But by 1872 he had once again begun to think better of Transcendentalism and in an essay entitled "Transcendentalism" said that there was a present need to vindicate the premise of the Transcendentalists who made intuition and not sense the foundation of truth.

In his older age, B manifested his continuing interest in Transcendentalism in several lectures at the Concord School of Philosophy:** "The Transcendent Faculties in Man" (1881), twice on "The Nature of Knowledge: Emerson's Way" (1882), and "Emerson's Religion" (1883). Many of his views on the Transcendentalists and Transcendentalism appeared in his dozens of published essays, reviews, and sermons in *The Christian Examiner*,** *The Radical*,** *The Index*, *The Unitarian Review*, and other leading periodicals. Much of his thinking on Transcendentalism is also concentrated in a few of his books, especially *Discourse on the Christian Spirit and Life* (1850); *Church and Congregation: A Plea for Unity* (1858); *The Word of the Spirit to the Church* (1859); *Radical Problems* (1872); and *The Rising Faith* (1874).

B was the last of the original New England Transcendentalists to die; and of the second generation, he was outlived only by M. D. Conway,* T. W. Higginson,* E. Channing, and F. B. Sanborn.* He neither effected major reforms in religion nor contributed anything new to any philosophical system, but his intuitive bent of mind freed him from enslavement to the senses and human creeds and caused him to see and proclaim, as Charles Ames said, "the Real Presence in nature,** in history, in humanity, and in the Silent Order of the world."

References: There is no complete biography of B. Charles G. Ames has a good sketch of his life in *Heralds*, 3: 17–22. B's religious and philosophical thought are closely studied by William G. Heath in "CB: An Early Critic of Emerson" (Diss., Univ. of

Minnesota, 1970); and in the introduction to *On Spirit and Personality* (1977), Heath focuses on B's themes of the Church of the Spirit and Personal Theism. Heath deals with B's economic ventures in real estate in ''CB's Transcendentalism,'' *SAR* 1979: 399–408. For B's relationship to church reform, see Hutchison (1959); for B's Transcendentalism, see William R. Hutchison, ''To Heaven in a Swing: The Transcendentalism of CB,'' *HTR* 56 (October 1963) : 275–95. B is placed in his Transcendental milieu in Cooke* (1902) and in Frothingham* (1876). The most complete bibliographies of B are those by Heath in *On Spirit and Personality* and in Myerson (1984), 97–99.

Guy R. Woodall

BLAKE, HARRISON GRAY OTIS (1816–1898), admirer of R. W. Emerson* and disciple of H. Thoreau,* was born and died in Worcester, Massachusetts. Like many other figures in the Transcendental movement, he was trained for the Unitarian** clergy. Entering Harvard College at 15, he graduated in 1835 and proceeded to the Harvard Divinity School.** Near the end of his theological studies, B, with two classmates, was delegated to invite the commencement speaker. They chose Emerson to deliver the ''customary discourse, on occasion of [the graduates'] entering upon the active Christian ministry'' (*L* 2:147n). As the committee knew, the discourse would be far from customary: Emerson's iconoclastic oration drew immediate support from partisans of the religious newness and a sustained counterattack from defenders of Unitarian orthodoxy. The first printing of the Divinity School Address also owes something to B, who promptly joined four fellow graduates in soliciting the manuscript for private issue or formal publication.

These contacts initiated a lifelong friendship and correspondence between Emerson and B, who was a guest in Concord** in November 1838 and was perhaps then first introduced to Thoreau. The next summer B informed Emerson that his views on the clerical vocation had altered under Emerson's and Carlyle's* influence; and indeed he abandoned the ministry, becoming a teacher instead. He taught in his own private schools and in others', in the Boston area and in Worcester, with interruptions, from 1839 until the 1860s. His pupils (usually girls) received tutorial and group instruction ''in ancient and modern languages and in the common and higher English studies.'' In 1840 he married Sarah Chandler Ward, who died in 1846 after bearing their second child. In 1852 he wed Nancy Pope Conant of Sterling, Massachusetts, a former student, who brought him considerable property and died in 1872.

Worcester in the late 1840s and 1850s was both a burgeoning industrial-commercial center and a hotbed of religious liberalism, Free Soil sentiment, and abolitionism.** T. W. Higginson* gathered a Free Church there in 1852; another Worcester church was led by E. E. Hale.* Despite sharp contentions with conservative residents about political offices and the control of cultural organs such as the Lyceum,** the reform party flourished. Emerson was in frequent demand as a lecturer, and B, active in the intellectual community, took charge of arrangements for his friend's appearances at public halls like Mechanics' and

Brinley's or in the parlors of the like-minded. In March 1848, Emerson being overseas on a lecture tour, B's Concord interests swung toward Thoreau; Emerson later remarked half seriously that Thoreau had monopolized B's devotion. Some remarks of Thoreau's during his last visit, B wrote, had made a "sublime" impression on him, an impression renewed when B reread Thoreau's July 1840 *Dial*** essay on Persius. He tried to summarize Thoreau's essential attitude: "You would sunder yourself from society, from the spell of institutions, customs, conventionalities, that you may lead a fresh, simple life with God" (*Corr*, 213). Voicing thus the Transcendental shibboleths of self-reliance, the primacy of the individual soul, and the immanence** of the Divine, B enlisted Thoreau as a spiritual counselor (as he had earlier enlisted Emerson) and began what would become Thoreau's largest and most consistently philosophical correspondence. That exchange included 51 surviving letters by Thoreau, letters often approximating the most elevated thought and most ebullient rhetoric of his books, lectures, and essays. Until Thoreau's death, the two men regularly exchanged visits. When a letter from Thoreau arrived, B would assemble Thoreau's other Worcester adherents for a reading and discussion. Thoreau presented his idealizing essays on "Love" and "Chastity & Sensuality," in manuscript, to B in September 1852, as gifts and guides for B's impending second marriage. He delivered at least nine lectures in Worcester, some in halls and some in B's hospitable parlor.

While not a keen naturalist, B delighted in outdoor influences and owned stout legs, which served him well on hikes with Thoreau in Concord and central Massachusetts. He was a welcome companion on Mount Monadnock in June 1858, and the next month, at Thoreau's invitation, he and another Worcester devotee, the philosophical tailor T. Brown,* followed Thoreau and E. S. Hoar* over the summit of Mount Washington for an extended rough camp in Tuckerman's Ravine and climbs elsewhere in the White Mountains. He could not accept a proposal (3 May 1861) to accompany Thoreau to Minnesota when the writer's lungs began to fail. During Thoreau's final illness, B several times chose to walk from Worcester to Concord and once even skated down the Sudbury River from Framingham to see his dying friend.

Emerson's and A. B. Alcott's* first idea for publishing Thoreau's letters was a collection centering on the aphoristic missives to B, edited by the recipient; eventually, Emerson himself assembled *Letters to Various Persons* (1865). After Thoreau's sister Sophia edited *Excursions, The Maine Woods, Cape Cod*, and *A Yankee in Canada* (1863–66), she guarded Henry's journal** notebooks against the editorial aspirations of F. B. Sanborn* and E. Channing.* But she had given Emerson, Alcott, and B ready access to them, B sometimes carrying a volume home. When in 1873 she moved to Bangor, to spend her last years with her Thatcher cousins, she left the 40-odd journal volumes, the Indian Books and other extract notebooks, all of Thoreau's drafts of lectures and published works, and the voluminous manuscripts of unfinished natural history** projects in the care of the aging Alcott, specifying that they should not leave his house.

Learning that this charge had been neglected, she deposited the papers in the town library, their safety to be verified by Emerson. Sophia died in 1876, assigning, by the final clause of her will, all Henry's manuscripts (except his maps and surveys) to ''Harry'' B. No more dedicated and conscientious a custodian among Thoreau's acquaintances could have been chosen. B had been the ideal disciple: intelligent, enthusiastic, high-minded, devoid of selfishness and egotism, a man of gentle bearing, great precision, and legendary probity. He was not slow in reviewing the journal notebooks, determining an editorial approach, and transcribing selected passages. He settled on a day-book plan—entries would be arranged under the same dates for various years, so as to give a ''calendar'' of Thoreau's observations and reflections; and the comprehensive scheme would be seasonal. (The sequential structure of Thoreau's incomplete botanical projects, and his chronologies of leafing, flowering, bird arrivals, and meteorological phenomena, offered a loose authorial model.) A handwritten preliminary table of extracts survives for the first volume B edited, *Early Spring in Massachusetts* (1881), which presented between four and nine entries for each date; the book publication was anticipated by journal extracts thus arranged in the April, May, and June 1878 *Atlantic Monthly*.** B knew the manuscripts were priceless: He deposited them with the American Antiquarian Society on departing for Europe—his second trip—in 1882. The next volume of journal selections was *Summer* (1884), followed by *Winter* (1888) and *Autumn* (1892). By way of variety, B in 1890 compiled *Thoreau's Thoughts*, 365 passages drawn from previously published works by Thoreau and printed under topical headings. He attended regularly the Concord School of Philosophy** (1879–88), where he also gave readings.

After four years of infirmity, B died of a stroke in 1898, bequeathing the Thoreau manuscripts to his younger Worcester friend and fellow educator E. Harlow Russell. Russell was soon negotiating with Houghton, Mifflin and Co. about publication of the journal in extenso, for $3,000 and a further sum for several hundred autograph leaves to be mounted as keepsakes in the new ''Manuscript Edition.'' His right to such revenues was unsuccessfully contested in 1903 by a Thatcher representative and B's executor. The next year, with Russell's sales to dealer George Hellman, the grand diaspora of Thoreau's manuscript remains commenced.

References: Besides the standard Thoreau and Emerson biographies, letters, and journals, Alcott's journals, and the published correspondence among B, S. Thoreau, T. Brown, D. Ricketson,* and H. Salt,* the following are valuable sources of information about B: obituaries in the (Worcester) *Daily Spy* and *Evening Gazette*, 19 April 1898; two articles by Ruth H. Frost in *Nature Outlook* 3 (May 1945) : 116–18 and 4 (November 1946): 16–18 (rpt. *ARLR* 6 [1992]); Daniel Gregory Mason, ''H G. O. B, '35, and Thoreau,'' *HMo* 26 (1898):87–95; Kenneth W. Cameron, ''The Thoreau Family in Probate Records,'' *ESQ* 11 (2d Q 1958):22; Cameron's checklist of B's correspondence, in *ARLR* 5 (1991):150–71; ''The Will of H. G. O. B,'' *TSB*, no. 68 (summer 1959):2–3;

and Edmund A. Schofield, ''Time Recovering Itself: E. Harlow Russell's Thirty Years (and More) with Henry D. Thoreau,'' *CS* 17 (August 1984):14–48.

Joseph J. Moldenhauer

BOWEN, FRANCIS (1811–1890), a conservative Unitarian,** was a leading critic of Transcendentalism through his essays in *The Christian Examiner*** and the *North American Review*,** the latter of which he edited from 1843 to 1853. B became the spokesman for the Common Sense** School, attacking the speculative philosophy of the Transcendentalists. In R. W. Emerson's* *Nature*, he saw ''beautiful writing and sound philosophy . . . , but the effect is injured by occasional vagueness of expression, and by a vein of mysticism.'' B's complaint with the Transcendentalists was their emphasis on intuition over reason: ''They profess to look not only beyond facts, but without the aid of facts, to principles'' (*ChEx* 21 [January 1837]: 371, 384). For B, this a priori reasoning could only lead to abstraction and atheism.

Aside from the philosophical differences, B also disliked Transcendentalism for its German influence and the arrogance of its followers. In ''Locke** and the Transcendentalists'' he saw the movement as ''abstruse in its dogmas, fantastic in its dress, and foreign in its origin'' (*ChEx* 23 [November 1837]: 175). B felt that by introducing German philosophy to the American public the Transcendentalists were ''contaminating'' the English language ''by admixture of words of foreign derivation'' (181). He also complained that the Transcendentalists wrote obscurely in order to separate themselves from their fellow men: ''Men do not usually understand what is intentionally made unintelligible'' (184). In his review of B's article, O. Brownson* saw ''a striking want of clear discernment of the difference between philosophy and common sense'' (*BoQR* 1 [January 1838]: 88). He condescendingly called B's article ''obviously the production of a mind which has not yet grappled, very closely, with the real problems of metaphysics'' (83).

B, however, was a leading philosopher of his day. After graduating from Harvard in 1833 and tutoring there from 1835 to 1839, he was named the Alford professor in natural religion,** moral philosophy,** and civil polity in 1853, a position he held until 1889. His *Modern Philosophy from Descartes** to Schopenhauer and Hartmann* (1877) was an important contribution to his field. By the time of its publication, however, B had embraced Hegelian* idealism,** rejecting the Scottish Common Sense philosophy that he had defended against the Transcendentalist attack.

References: Much of B's writings can be found in *ChEx* and *NAR*. His most important essays on Transcendentalism appear in *Critical Essays on a Few Subjects Connected with the History and Present Condition of Speculative Philosophy* (1842). Other works include *The Principles of Metaphysical and Ethical Science Applied to the Evidences of Religion* (1855) and *A Layman's Study of the English Bible Considered in Its Literary and Secular Aspect* (1885). For other bibliographic information, see Monica Maria Grecu's entry on B in *DLB*, vol. 59, ed. John W. Rathbun and Grecu (1987). The best delineation of B's position in Unitarian philosophy is Howe (1970). See also Bruce Kuklick, *The Rise of American Philosophy: Cambridge Massachusetts 1860–1930* (1977).

John P. Samonds

BRADFORD, GEORGE PARTRIDGE (1807–1890), although not a doctrinaire Transcendentalist, exemplified the highest Transcendental ideals of character and manner of life. He was a companion of R. W. Emerson,* B. Alcott,* and H. Thoreau* and a teacher at Brook Farm,** where he established an enduring friendship with N. Hawthorne.*

Despite two Harvard degrees (baccalaureate in 1825, theology in 1828) and expertise in languages, astronomy, and botany, B never distinguished himself professionally, earning his livelihood by teaching small classes of young women or by gardening. Because of inveterate wanderlust, he seldom remained in one place over three years.

During the 1840s and 1850s, B did some lyceum** lecturing, with two documented appearances in Concord,** and the manuscripts of his lectures in the Houghton Library indicate a broad, if not a deep, knowledge of English literature, particularly Shakespeare.** B's students, especially those at Brook Farm (1841–42 and intermittently 1842–44), praised him highly for his affinity with nature,** his gentleness, and his ability to motivate. B's publications were sparse, composed of one book, *Thoughts on Spiritual Subjects Translated from the Writings of Fénelon*** (1843), and a few articles, including revising and completing the late G. Ripley's* ''Philosophical Thought in Boston'' in volume 4 of *The Memorial History of Boston*, edited by Justin Winsor (1881), and the posthumously published ''Reminiscences of Brook Farm by a Member of the Community'' (*CM* 45 [November 1892]: 141–48).

B's associates respected him for his intellect, high principle, and modesty. Emerson confided to his journal** that ''I can better converse with G. B. than with any other'' and wrote Carlyle* that ''he is a far better scholar than I, & is one of the three companions I find in Concord.'' Hawthorne in *English Notebooks* judged him ''a scholar, with true cultivation; he has independence of thought, and keeps his own thoughts distinctly, against whatever other man's.'' Alcott described him as ''an old acquaintance and the more valued since through his kindness I made Emerson's acquaintance more than forty years ago. . . . A kindly man with a mystic tinge. Scholarly, though never having published himself save by teaching the classics, and in conversation with his friends, of whom Emerson is one'' (Diary, 28 October 1877, 778, ms. in Houghton Library).

References: Perceptive assessments by other contemporaries can be found in G. W. Curtis,* ''Editor's Easy Chair,'' *Harper's Monthly* 80 (May 1890): 965–66; and Ora Gannett Sedgwick, ''A Girl of Sixteen at Brook Farm,'' *Atl* 85 (March 1900): 395–96, 399, 402. Lindsay Swift's sketch is derivative but informative (*Brook Farm* [1900], 187–

94). A more recent, comprehensive portrait is James W. Mathews, "GPB: Friend of Transcendentalists," *SAR* 1981: 133–56.

James W. Mathews

BRISBANE, ALBERT (1809–1890), a social reformer originally from Batavia, New York, who studied with many reformers and social philosophers in Europe, was the major spokesman for Fourierism* in the United States between 1840 and 1844. Responsible for convincing the community at Brook Farm** to become a phalanx, he was blamed by many for the community's eventual failure.

In his *L, JMN*, and essay "Historic Notes of Life and Letters in New England," R. W. Emerson* often refers to B, whom he met in New York in 1842. Emerson is particularly sarcastic when he says that Fourier (and, by implication, B) "treats man as a plastic thing, something that may be . . . moulded, polished, made into solid or fluid or gas . . . —but [he] skips the faculty of life, which spawns and scorns system and systemmakers." Nevertheless, Emerson grants that Fourier's and B's scheme for prospective phalanxes is one of "bold and generous proportion" and admires, with reservations, B's drive and enthusiasm.

Other commentators were not so generous. O. B. Frothingham* agrees with Emerson's negative comments and states that B's Fourierism is antithetical to true Transcendentalism. In *Pedlar's Progress: The Life of Bronson Alcott,** Odell Shepard calls B a Lockean** with a "shopkeeping morality, and a philosophy merely prudential."

The Brook Farmers were more cordial; although never a member of the community, B persuaded them to embrace Fourierism in 1844. He often visited the farm, once staying for several months. Despite feeling that Brook Farm was not the ideal Fourieristic community, he considered it the most successful in America.

In *The Flowering of New England*, Van Wyck Brooks blames B and Fourierism for the failure of Brook Farm. In *George Ripley,** Frothingham, too, commented on how "helplessly astray" was the attempt "to reconstruct the social order" at Brook Farm and elsewhere. However, Frothingham grants that the undertaking revealed "a loftiness of sentiment and a vigor of thought." B himself, in his *Mental Biography*, says that Brook Farm broke up because its members needed a "satisfying field of action" where they could "[apply] principles concretely." Richard Francis, in one of the best articles on the development of ideology at Brook Farm, sees the adoption of Fourierism as a logical extension of earlier Transcendentalism: The phalanx put into action the beliefs of the more individualistic Transcendentalists, such as Emerson and H. Thoreau.* It recognized that the harmony of the phalanx was dependent on the harmony within the individual and between individuals.

B sailed for Europe in May 1844, thus leaving Fourierism without its most prominent American spokesman. After his return to America, he never regained the prominence as a public figure that he had had between 1840 and 1844.

Boston became the center of American Fourierism, but the movement soon lost its appeal.

Nevertheless, B has left his legacy as a prolific writer of books, letters, and columns for the New York *Tribune* under H. Greeley's* editorship. His journal *The Phalanx* (1843–45) was succeeded by *The Harbinger*** (June 1845–February 1849), both important documents of U.S. intellectual—and, the latter, of Transcendental—thought. In his sixties, B seems to have become more ''Transcendental.'' He felt that he had been diverted from his true vocation—to teach a new religion rather than to promote the ''low, practical idea'' of industrial reform. B devoted his later years to study, to travel, to his inventions, and to his last book on Fourierism.

References: Most of B's biographers have relied heavily upon the autobiographical *AB: A Mental Biography, with a Character Study by His Wife Redelia Brisbane*, ed. Redelia Brisbane (1893; rpt. 1969). More objective, with an evaluation of the autobiography, is Arthur E. Bestor, ''AB—Propagandist for Socialism in the 1840's,'' *NYH* 28 (1947): 128–58. See also *Letters of the American Socialist AB to K. A. Varnhagen von Ense*, ed. Terry H. Pickett and Françoise de Rocher, part of the series *Anglistische Forschungen* (1986), and the B entry in *DAB*, vol. 3. B's other books include *Social Destiny of Man; or, Association and Reorganization of Industry* (1840); *Association: or, A Concise Exposition of the Practical Part of Fourier's Social Science* (1843; rpt. 1975); and *General Introduction to Social Science* (1876; rpt. 1976).

Discussions of B's relationship to Transcendentalism and Brook Farm are in Frothingham (1876) and in O. B. Frothingham, *George Ripley* (1883; rpt. 1970), 173–76. Helpful studies are Sterling F. Delano, *'The Harbinger' and New England Transcendentalism* (1983), and Richard Francis, ''The Ideology of Brook Farm,'' *SAR* 1977: 1–48. Anne C. Rose, *Transcendentalism as a Social Movement, 1830–1850* (1981), discusses why Fourierism appealed to Brook Farmers (and to other utopians) and why it failed there. On Brook Farm's ''unnatural union of Transcendentalism and Fourierism,'' see Myerson (1984), 56–68. Noteworthy is B's (much shortened) piece ''Means of Effecting a Final Reconciliation Between Religion and Science,'' *The Dial*** (July 1842), in conjunction with Emerson's essay ''Fourierism and the Socialists,'' as well as Emerson's ''Historic Notes.''

April Selley

BROOKS, CHARLES TIMOTHY (1813–1883), was a Newport, Rhode Island, Unitarian** minister and a poet. An important translator of German literature, B brought foreign writers to the attention of American readers, including Transcendentalists. He contributed *Songs and Ballads: Translated from Uhland, Körner, Bürger, and Other German Lyric Poets* (1842) to G. Ripley's* *Specimens of Foreign Standard Literature.*** B's choice of verse appealed to New England Transcendentalists for literary as well as moral, nationalistic, and theological reasons.

Buell ranks B as a second-tier Transcendentalist, citing Emersonian* ideas in his teachings, although B tended not to use Transcendentalist rhetoric. Elizabeth R. McKinsey notes his reputation ''as a man of childlike purity, impracticality, humor, and deep propriety.'' Besides his translations of German literature (including minor poets, the prose of Auerbach, Schefer, Goethe,* Richter,** and Rückert, and a popular translation of *Faust*) and theological writings, B also wrote a biography, *William Ellery Channing:* A Centennial Memory* (1880), and occasionally published in Transcendentalist periodicals, including *The Dial.***

References: See George W. Wendte's biographical sketch in B's *Poems*, ed. W. P. Andrews (1885). Major works, bibliographies, manuscripts, editions, and criticism are found in Elizabeth R. McKinsey, ''CTB,'' in Myerson (1984). On B's scholarship and translations, see Stanley Vogel, *German Literary Influences on the American Transcendentalists* (1955), and Pochmann (1957). Cooke* (1902) comments on B's Harvard ties and Transcendentalist friendships. See also Buell (1973), *NET*Dial, and Camillo von Klenze, *CTB: Translator from the German and the Genteel Tradition* (1937).

Doni M. Wilson

BROWN, JOHN (1800–1859), was emphatically, in the words of R. W. Emerson* himself, ''a representative of the American Republic'': An idealist** as well as a practical abolitionist,** he ''believed in his ideas to that extent that he existed to put them all into action.'' As a 35-year-old sheep farmer of fluctuating fortune in Ohio, B proposed helping fellow men in bondage by procuring a slave and raising him as a son in his own household and by establishing a school for ex-slaves. But his assault on slavery was to become much more forceful. In 1855, he moved part of his extensive family to North Elba, New York, and joined the rest in Osawatomie, Kansas, where he became captain of a company of Free Soilers devoted to preserving Kansas as a free state. After the sacking of Lawrence by Border Ruffians, B led his men—including four of his sons—on a retaliatory raid along the Pottawatomie River during which five proslavery men were brutally executed.

In the partisan warfare that erupted in Kansas, B sought and gained the support of six prominent Northerners: George L. Stearns, Gerrit Smith, F. B. Sanborn,* T. W. Higginson,* T. Parker,* and Samuel G. Howe. After B's bloody beginning, there could be no doubt as to the nature of his business: Part of their support was a cache of Sharps' breech-loading rifles. But as the Kansas business subsided, B and the rifles seemed to go underground.

On 16 October 1859, B and 18 men, black and white, assaulted the town of Harpers Ferry, now West Virginia. When B had discussed his plan with F. Douglass,* the latter had told him that he was walking into ''a perfect steel trap.'' Nearly all of B's men were captured or killed, and B himself, though dangerously wounded, was held captive and tried for treason and leading a slave revolt. Although he was executed within two months, in the time between his capture and hanging, he became an international cause célèbre. Even those who had disagreed with his methods saw his value as a martyr. The Transcendental community was nearly unanimous in its support of B. H. Thoreau,* whom one would not usually associate with such tactics, rose in defense of the old man:

''We made a subtle distinction, forgot human laws, and did homage to an idea.'' As Brown awaited martyrdom, J. Redpath* assembled a collection of essays to be sold for the support of B's family, *Echoes of Harper's Ferry* (1860). Headed by one of Thoreau's lectures, the work focused commentary by W. Phillips,* Emerson, Parker, and Victor Hugo, along with poetry by Whittier,* L. M. Alcott,* L. M. Child,* and W. D. Howells. In the subsequent congressional inquiry, Stearns testified, ''I believe JB to be the representative man of this century, as Washington was of the last.'' After the ensuing Civil War, which certified B as a folk hero, H. Melville,* in ''The Portent,'' called him ''the meteor of the war.''

References: The standard biography remains Oswald Garrison Villard's *JB 1800–1859: A Biography Fifty Years After* (1911). A more recent view is Stephen B. Oates, *To Purge This Land with Blood* (1984).

R. D. Madison

BROWN, THEOPHILUS (THEO) (1811–1879), a Worcester, Massachusetts, tailor, belonged to an informal literary salon that took an interest in the work of B. Alcott,* R. W. Emerson,* and H. Thoreau,* inviting them to lecture in Worcester and offering them hospitality during their visits. B and his wife, Sarah Ann Brown, sometimes hosted Thoreau and Alcott (though not concurrently) and allowed Alcott to use their home for his Conversations.** B and his friends, including H. G. O. Blake,* T. W. Higginson,* E. E. Hale,* and D. Wasson,* were particularly interested in Thoreau; Blake would invite the group to his home for breakfast in order to share his most recent letter.

B was born in Seekonk (then Rehoboth), Massachusetts, the youngest of six children. From age 12 until he was 16, he lived in Attleboro with the Universalist Asa Allen, a man who, B later wrote, ''hammered away on the virtue of industry, in the most emphatic way man ever hammered.'' Opportunities for leisure and recreation were rare, and B remembered (perhaps with some exaggeration) that the Bible, the almanac, and the *Universalist Trumpet* were the only reading material available in Allen's home. In 1828, B moved to Worcester, where he began an apprenticeship in the tailor shop of his brothers, Albert and William Brown.

Over time, the shop became a meeting place for chess and conversation among B's literary friends. Though he had less formal education than many of his circle, B seems to have held his own among them intellectually. Higginson said that B had ''the freshest and most original mind in Worcester'' and described him as ''rather the wit of the city.'' Although he did not attempt to launch a serious literary career, B had some interest in writing and in his later years wrote light verse, some of which appeared in *Harper's* ''Editor's Drawer.''

In addition to his work and his active social life, B involved himself in community organizations. Along with Blake, Higginson, and George Frisbie Hoar, he was a member of the Young Men's Library Association and served on the executive committee of Worcester's lyceum** from 1852 until 1855; he was probably responsible for that organization's first (and apparently its only) invitation to Thoreau to lecture in January 1855. (Thoreau's many other lectures in Worcester were arranged without the lyceum's sponsorship.) B also belonged to Higginson's Free Church and supported the antislavery cause, contributing to the "Aid to Kansas" campaign in 1856.

B was one of 75 people to whom Thoreau and his publisher sent copies of *A Week on the Concord and Merrimack Rivers*, and he received one of the three daguerreotypes that Thoreau had made of himself during an 1856 visit to Worcester. However, B knew Thoreau primarily through Blake; Thoreau often asked Blake in his letters to "remember" him to B and invited the two of them for visits and excursions, but he rarely corresponded with B directly. Blake and B met Thoreau and E. S. Hoar* in the White Mountains in 1858 for what turned out to be a rather wet and uncomfortable journey and visited Thoreau in Concord** many times as well, especially during his last illness. B continued to think of Thoreau after his death. In 1868 he wrote to D. Ricketson* that in Concord "the river still runs and the birds still sing . . . but to my eye nature** somehow looked bereft of her lover. The loss [of Thoreau] seemed so great that one could easily fancy that the river would henceforth run only tears, and that the bobolinks even, if they sung at all, would sing in the minor key." He added that he considered it "no small achievement to so live as to raise the value of one's surroundings," as he felt Thoreau had done.

REFERENCES: Portions of B's correspondence have been published. Two of his letters appear in *Corr*, 562, 634; three are included in *Daniel Ricketson and His Friends*, ed. Anna and Walton Ricketson (1902), 213–18. For a larger selection, see *Extracts from the Letters of TB* (1879) or *Letters of TB, Selected and Arranged by Sarah Theo. Brown* (1898). A brief but useful biographical entry on B appears in *American Authors, 1600–1900: A Biographical Dictionary of American Literature*, ed. Stanley J. Kunitz and Howard Haycraft (1938). See also Ruth H. Frost, "TB, Friend of Thoreau," *Nature Outlook* 2 (May 1944): 15–19. Brief mentions of B appear in Milton Meltzer and Walter Harding, *A Thoreau Profile* (1962); Harding (1965); and Edmund A. Schofield, "Time Recovering Itself: E. Harlow Russell's Thirty Years (and More) with Henry D. Thoreau," *CS* 17 (August 1984): 14–48.

Susan M. Ryan

BROWNSON, ORESTES AUGUSTUS (1803–1876), an editor and reviewer, was both a leading defender and critic of Transcendentalism as he progressed through various religious beliefs. His greatest contributions to Transcendentalism were his journal essays, especially those in *The Christian Examiner*** and later in his own *Boston Quarterly Review*,** which he published between 1838 and 1842. He defended the other Transcendentalists from outside attack, even when he did not agree completely with their views.

B's life reveals a religious quest. Raised a Congregationalist, he became a Presbyterian at age 19. In 1824, however, B turned to Universalism and was ordained as a preacher in 1826. After a period of agnosticism, B became, in 1832, a Unitarian** preacher. Moving in 1834 to Canton, Massachusetts, to be closer to the "New School" of Unitarian ministers, he was one of the founding members of the Transcendental Club** in 1836. By 1842, however, B had rejected the Transcendentalists, and was rejected by them, as he began to convert to Roman Catholicism.

During his Transcendental phase, B was most influenced by B. Constant* and V. Cousin.* From Constant, B received validation of his views that each age must develop its own religious tenets and that social reform must come through Christianity. More important was Cousin's eclecticism, which gathers the positive elements of various philosophies and "attempts to mould them into one grand whole" ("Cousin's Philosophy," *ChEx* 21 [July 1836]: 38). According to B, Cousin also believed that man's consciousness has three faculties: sensibility of the external world; activity, or phenomena that we ourselves create; and reason, from which we receive "all our ideas of the Absolute, the Supersensible" (42–43). B disagreed, then, with the other Transcendentalists, whom he felt equated man with God by seeing reason, or intuition, as a human ability.

In 1836, as the organizer of the Society for Christian Union and Progress in Boston, B preached his eclectic views, emphasizing the need to address the concerns of the masses who were avoiding church. At the same time, he published *New Views of Christianity, Society and the Church*, a history of Christianity in which he claimed that "we must realize the atonement" between Catholic spiritualism and Protestant materialism. In "The Mediatorial Life of Jesus" (1842), B saw Jesus as this atonement, being both spiritual and material, God and man. The other Transcendentalists, however, saw Jesus as a man more attuned to the spirit.

B wrote primarily for periodicals, and his reviews of other works, both by Transcendentalists and their antagonists, were his greatest contribution to the movement. While others vilified B. Alcott* for his *Conversations with Children on the Gospels*, B claimed that "there was no man in our country who so well understands the art of education" than Alcott, although he does not "admit the identity between Man and God, and God and Nature,** which [Alcott] does. God is in his works; but he is also separate from them" (*BoQR* 1: 418, 431). R. W. Emerson* received similar treatment. While praising him for encouraging "men to be men," B disagreed with Emerson's belief in the Divinity School Address that we can become God if we follow our higher instincts: "This were deification of the soul with a vengeance. It were nothing but a system of transcendental selfishness" (*BoQR* 1: 513, 503–4).

Perhaps B's greatest defense is his July 1840 review of A. Norton's* *Two Articles from the Princeton Review*. B claimed that Norton's reliance on Lockean** sensualism denies man the ability to attain spiritual knowledge without the aid of a teacher, which B saw as undemocratic. B agreed with G. Ripley* that "we may have . . . a direct perception of the truths of religion." Therefore, ''the real aim of the Transcendentalist is to ascertain a solid ground for faith in the reality of the spiritual world'' (*BoQR* 3: 278, 272).

Ironically, this defense was published in the same issue as the first part of ''The Laboring Classes,'' where he argued against both property inheritance and the clergy. This essay caused an uproar that both aided the Whig victory in the November presidential election and contributed to B's break with Transcendentalism. In *The Convert*, B lamented that there was ''not a voice raised in my defence.'' B also resented the other Transcendentalists for starting *The Dial*** in July 1840 instead of using his journal as their messenger. In reviewing *The Dial* in January 1841, he identified it as the ''organ of the Transcendentalists,'' radicals ''who would *radicalize* in kid gloves and sattin [*sic*] slippers'' (*BoQR* 4: 131–32). In this period, then, B lost faith in the Transcendentalist tenets that championed ''the divinity of the people.''

The other Transcendentalists' views of B varied. After hearing Emerson's lecture on ''The Present Age,'' T. Parker* wondered whether B's ''Democracy and Reform'' was not the more original. Ripley, with whom B was most closely affiliated, said of Brook Farm:** ''If I had never known you, I should never have engaged in this enterprise.'' However, Emerson felt that B ''never will stop and listen, neither in conversation, but what is more, not in solitude.''

As he progressed toward Catholicism after 1840, converting in October 1844, B's critiques of Transcendentalism intensified. In 1842, when E. P. Peabody* corrected his interpretation of Parker's ''Discourse of the Transient and Permanent,'' B claimed that he was attempting ''to check the growth of . . . an incipient but fatal heresy'' (*BoQR*, 5: 199). His review of Parker's *A Discourse of Matters Pertaining to Religion*, which comprises the final issue of the *BoQR*, first praises Parker for searching for truth, but ''we make no professions of regard, of sympathy, or of tenderness for his feelings and the like'' (5: 387). B returned to Parker's *Discourse* in the early issues of *Brownson's Quarterly Review* (publ. 1844–64, 1873–75), chastising all the Transcendentalists for championing man over God. By this time, he even felt that Ripley was ''worse than an infidel.''

During his own time, B was seen as a leading intellectual. However, his shifts from one religion to another, especially his rejection of Transcendentalism, has caused his reputation to wane. Only recently has he become a subject of serious study.

References: Some of B's writings are collected in [Henry Brownson, ed.,] *The Works of O A. B*, 20 vols. (1882–1907); see also *Selected Writings*, ed. Patrick W. Carey (1991). For his view on Ripley, see *The B–Hecker* Correspondence*, ed. Joseph F. Gower and Richard M. Leliaert (1979), 115. For biographies, see Henry F. Brownson, *O A. B's Early, Middle, Latter Life*, 3 vols. (1898); Arthur M. Schlesinger, Jr., *O A. B: A Pilgrim's Progress* (1939, 1966); and Thomas Richard Ryan, *OB: A Definitive Biography* (1976). On B and Transcendentalism, see Alvan S. Ryan, ''OB: The Critique of Transcendentalism,'' in Harold C. Gardiner, ed., *American Classics Reconsidered: A Christian Appraisal* (1958), 98–120, 290–91; R. W. B. Lewis, *The American Adam* (1955); and

Russell Kirk, "Two Facets of the New England Mind: Emerson and B," *Month* 8 (October 1952): 208–17. See also Leonard Gilhooley, *Contradiction and Dilemma: OB and the American Idea* (1972), and Gilhooley, ed., *No Divided Allegiance: Essays in B's Thought* (1980). Other bibliographical information appears in Gilhooley, "OAB," in Myerson (1984).

John P. Samonds

BRYANT, WILLIAM CULLEN (1794–1878), newspaper editor and poet, was born into a devout and cultivated New England family. A precocious child, B published his first poem, a political satire, at the age of 13 and entered Williams College at 15. Trained as an attorney, B found the legal profession to be unprofitable and uninspiring. In 1826, he became an editorial assistant at the *New York Evening Post*, a position that better suited his temperament. He remained active in journalism for the rest of his life, assuming the editorship of the *Evening Post* in 1829.

A primarily Romantic poet, who published several works before New England Transcendentalism emerged, B was influenced by Wordsworth* and by the critical works of Pope, Dryden, Alison, Johnson, and others. Transcendentalism, as a philosophical construct, he did not fully grasp. When R. W. Emerson* visited New York in 1842 to deliver a series of six lectures, B reported on the elusiveness of his new doctrine in the 4 March *Evening Post*: "We cannot say that we precisely apprehend what [the doctrines] are. Now and then, in listening to his discourses, or reading his essays, we have fancied that we caught glimpses of great and novel truths—truths that seemed to reveal to us an entirely new existence, and that certainly gave a fresh impulse and elevation to our moral nature." Following Emerson's final lecture, B summarized his observations in the 16 March *Evening Post*: "His doctrines, original and profound as they are, seem to us wanting in coherence and completeness. . . . He seems to feel that his best and deepest sayings, to borrow the peculiar phrase of his own doctrine, are only the spontaneous and unobstructed utterance of the *one soul* which dwells in *all men*, and that thus whenever they are authentic, they must, of necessity, be recognized and received." More pragmatic than spiritual or intuitive, B found little appeal in the Transcendentalist movement.

Although they never formed a friendship and occasionally professed dislike for one another, Emerson and B nevertheless practiced mutual respect. Making an appearance at B's seventieth birthday party, Emerson paid tribute to the "native, sincere, original, patriotic poet" (*Evening Post*, 7 November 1864). After B's death in 1878, Emerson praised his poetry as "some of the very best . . . that we have in America" (*Evening Post*, 12 June 1878). Despite his dismissal of Transcendentalism, B, like Emerson, was profoundly interested in the relationship between man and death and nature,** a theme he explored in his most famous poem, "Thanatopsis," written at 17 or 18 and subsequently revised. A meditation on death, the poem offers consolation by appealing to man's conscious, rational understanding of the natural and universal aspects of the death experience. Denounced as a pagan poem by Henry Ward Beecher because of the absence from the verse of allusions to God or an afterlife, ''Thanatopsis'' focuses not on religion but on the anxieties and perceptions of man as he faces death.

References: Though nature was a common theme in B's writing, his oeuvre included translations, hymns, and prose works. See G. W. Curtis,* *The Life, Character, and Writings of WCB* (1879). The most authoritative biography is Charles H. Brown, *WCB* (1971). Also of interest is Stanley Brodwin et al., eds., *WCB and His America: Centennial Conference Proceedings, 1878–1978* (1983).

Denise D. Knight

BURROUGHS, JOHN (1837–1921), nature** lover and essayist, observed and wrote with remarkable clarity, willing to take people on their own terms, seeing those terms, and expressing them. About W. Whitman* he wrote, ''I have studied him as I have studied the birds,'' and this is invariably the formula that leads to B's best writing: He always looked for the person first, the ideas second: ''A man reaches and moves you, not an artist''; ''It is not truth alone that makes literature; it is truth plus a man.'' It is hard to emphasize strongly enough how literally B meant this. His most insightful writing is about his contemporaries whom he knew personally—the farther away in time and distance B finds himself, the less interest he seems to show and the less convincing his commentary. His book *John James Audubon* (1902), for instance, is strained and artificial, as is, to a certain extent, the essay on H. Thoreau* in *Indoor Studies* (1889). Seeing Thoreau only through his writing, B was led to write impatiently, ''He was more intent on the natural history** of his own thought than on that of the bird.''

Strongly influenced by the British writers Gilbert White, Wordsworth,* Carlyle,* and Arnold, he learned his craft from imitating R. W. Emerson* and T. W. Higginson.* Remarkably, his literary judgment has been borne out by time to be extremely accurate: B seemed to back winners just as certainly as Higginson almost uniformly failed to recognize genius.

B's most important associations and writing deal with Whitman, whom he knew personally and with whom he was familiar from 1863 to 1892. In fact, B's early Whitman writings were collaborations between the two. His first book, *Notes on Walt Whitman as Poet and Person* (1867), was superseded by *Walt Whitman: A Study* (1896) after the poet's death; the latter remains a solid introduction and valuable personal analysis. In his own right, B became perhaps the most well-known and best-loved nature writer of his time. He traveled afield with J. Muir* and Theodore Roosevelt and was historian of the Harriman Alaska Expedition of 1899, a veritable who's-who of naturalists at the turn of the century.

References: The writings of B have appeared in several editions by Houghton Mifflin Company, and his life and writings have been fully chronicled in three major works by his secretary Clara Barrus: *Our Friend JB* (1914), *The Life and Letters of JB* (1925), and *Whitman and B: Comrades* (1931). A good autobiographical sketch is ''An Egotistical Chapter'' in *Indoor Studies*, 243–59. Edward J. Renehan, Jr., *JB: An American Naturalist* (1992) is a recent evaluation.

R. D. Madison

C

CABOT, JAMES ELLIOT (1821–1903), served as R. W. Emerson's* official biographer and literary executor, publishing the family-authorized *A Memoir of Ralph Waldo Emerson* in 1887. C published (anonymously) an essay, "Immanuel Kant,**" in the last number of *The Dial*** (April 1844); the next year, he met Emerson, and the two corresponded, shared books and ideas, and met occasionally for over 30 years before C began working as a sort of secretary to the aging Emerson in 1875. For the next 20 years, C compiled essays and lectures for Emerson; supervised publication of the 11-volume *Complete Works* (1883–93), including compiling and editing three new volumes; organized and cataloged Emerson's manuscripts (letters, lectures, essays, and journals**); and wrote the 2-volume *Memoir*, the first study of Emerson to use unpublished manuscripts, correspondence, and journals. In all of this work, C served as the major link in the transmission of Emerson to the 20th century.

Chapter 7 of the *Memoir* places Transcendentalism in the larger context of European Romanticism, contained by "the Puritan** spirit," and sums up the movement as "a deeper way of feeling and an enlarged way of thinking about all subjects"—which describes C's experience as much as Emerson's. Despite his solidly affluent Boston background and conservative and shy nature, he shared many tendencies of the Transcendentalists, especially their interest in German idealism** and post-Kantian philosophy and their revolt against the "commonplace." He disproves Stanley M. Vogel's claim that "Concord** men of letters were not profound students of any language, philosophy, or science." After graduating from Harvard in 1840, C spent three years in Europe, including a winter in Berlin, where he mastered German and read *The Dial* and Emerson's *Essays* (1841) and attended lectures by F. W. J. Schelling* and Heinrich Steffens. In Germany the lackluster Harvard collegian became a lifelong student of philosophy, the subject of most of his more than 50 essays and reviews, published in the years when he moved from lawyer to architect to family man and patron of the arts.

One result of his studies in Germany was a manuscript translation of Schelling's "Essay on Freedom," which Emerson kept for almost two years and probably loaned to other Transcendentalists, such as E. Peabody.* Though Emerson sought a publisher, the translation was never printed. C assisted Swiss scientist L. Agassiz* in his work and wrote the "Narrative" of Agassiz's 1849 expedition to Lake Superior (published 1850). With T. Parker* he edited *The Massachusetts Quarterly Review*,** where he published at least 11 pieces, including "The Philosophy of the Ancient Hindoos" (1848), a wide-ranging review of Sanskrit literature that helped introduce people like H. Thoreau* to "oriental"** thought.

References: Pochmann (1957) provides a brief but solid discussion of C in the context of German thought (253–55). Vogel's comment is in *German Literary Influences on the American Transcendentalists* (1955), 106. See Nancy Craig Simmons, "Man Without a Shadow: The Life and Work of JEC" (Diss., Princeton Univ., 1980); Simmons has published C's "Autobiographical Sketch," *HLB* 30 (1982): 117–52, and two articles detailing his work for Emerson: "Arranging the Sibylline Leaves: JEC's Work as Emerson's Literary Executor," *SAR* 1983: 335–89, and "Philosophical Biographer: JEC and *A Memoir of Ralph Waldo Emerson*," *SAR* 1987: 365–91.

Nancy Craig Simmons

CARLYLE, THOMAS (1795–1881), British essayist and biographer, was a significant influence on Transcendentalism from the late 1820s through the 1840s. C introduced American readers to German literature and philosophy, and his highly rhetorical style stimulated writers like H. Thoreau,* Whitman,* and Melville* to find their own distinctive voices.

C was born in Ecclefechan, Scotland, to Calvinist parents. While he later cast off the doctrines of Calvinism, C retained its moral seriousness and prophetic temperament. In the early 1820s, he was drawn to the works of German writers, particularly Goethe,* whom C considered his moral mentor, and Schiller,* whose biography he published in 1825.

C's anonymous essays in the *Edinburgh Review*,** notably his "State of German Literature" (1827), "Signs of the Times" (1829), and "Characteristics" (1831), and several in the *Foreign Review*,** attracted American readers. His essays on German writers and philosophers introduced Americans to Schiller, Goethe, de Staël,** Kant,** Richter,** Novalis,** among others. In his topical essays, C offered his cultural criticism: The powers of invention and rationality have conquered nature** but have left humanity bereft of deeper spiritual wisdom. C called for the revaluation of intuitive knowing, a new religious sense of awe and wonder.

To young New Englanders chafing under the rationalism of Harvard Unitarianism** and worrying about the shift in American economy from agriculture** to manufacture, C's essays were tonic. J. F. Clarke* recalled that "there was a freshness and unworn life in all he said, new and profound views of familiar truths, which seemed to open a vista for endless reflection.'' Clarke and M. Fuller* began to study German as a result of these essays, while G. Ripley* felt he had discovered ''the untold treasures of German thought'' through C's ''State of German Literature.'' Not all the responses to C's anonymous essays were favorable, however; T. Walker* responded to ''Signs of the Times'' with a defense of mechanism and rationality: ''[I]n plain words, we deny the evil tendencies of Mechanism, and we doubt the good influences of his Mysticism. We cannot perceive that Mechanism as such, has yet been the occasion of any injury to man'' (*NAR*,** July 1831).

R. W. Emerson,* too, had been reading this anonymous writer, copying passages from C's translation of Goethe's *Wilhelm Meister* into his journal** in 1830, and reading the Scot's essays in 1831. In October 1831 he wrote, ''I am cheered and instructed by this paper on Corn Law Rhymes in the Edinburgh by my Germanick new-light writer, whoever he be. He gives us sympathy in our principles.'' Emerson appreciated C's attack on practicality and rationality and applauded the Scot's view that reformation of society required reformation of the self.

In August 1833 during his first European trip, Emerson visited C and his wife, Jane Welsh C, at their remote farm house Craigenputtock, near Glasgow. Both men were pleased with the brief but crucial encounter. C described Emerson as ''a most gentle, recommendable, amiable, whole-hearted man,'' admiring ''his unity with himself,'' while Emerson called the visit ''a white day in my years.''

For the next 14 years, Emerson was involved in publishing and promoting C's work in the United States. He arranged for the first publication of *Sartor Resartus* (1836), which had appeared earlier in serial form, for the first edition of *The French Revolution* (1837), and for the four-volume *Critical and Miscellaneous Essays* (1838, 1839).

By the early 1840s, C's reputation and influence were immense in the Transcendentalist circle. E. Peabody* read *The French Revolution* to her great satisfaction; N. Hawthorne* read *On Heroes and Hero-Worship* while at Brook Farm.** Together with his critique of the modern machine age, C offered a model of redemption, borrowed from German idealism,** that was equally appealing to avant-garde Americans. Echoing Schiller, C argues that the individual's growth into consciousness parallels the history of the human race and is the psychic equivalent of the Fall. The fact of alienation is painful for the individual but is necessary for the reconciliation of individuals and of the entire race. Seen most clearly in the work of artists and in men of action, this synthesis of fall and redemption involves seeing the material world as symbolic of the spiritual.

While many Transcendentalists approved of C's theses, not all were so charmed by his hyperbolic style. Writing of the installments of *Sartor Resartus* then appearing in *Fraser's Magazine*,** Emerson wrote to C in 1834, ''I comprehend not why you should lavish in that spendthrift style of yours Celestial truths.'' In his preface to the American edition of *Sartor*, Emerson distanced himself from C's style: ''It is his humor to advance the gravest speculations upon the gravest topics in a quaint and burlesque style.''

The enemies of Transcendentalism seized upon C's style as a sign of the decline of respect for authority and reason. In ''The New School in Literature and Religion,'' A. Norton* made the link explicit: ''[T]he rejection of reasoning is accompanied with an equal contempt for good taste. All modesty is laid aside . . . unmeaning, but coarse and violent metaphors abound, and withal a strong infusion of German barbarisms. Such is the style of C, a writer of some talent.''

Thoreau, however, defended C's style in ''TC and His Works'' (written at Walden** and first published in 1847): ''He utters substantial English thoughts in plainest English dialects. . . . [I]f you would know where many of those obnoxious Carlyleisms and Germanisms came from, read the best of Milton's** prose . . . or go and listen once more to your mother's tongue.'' C helped Thoreau find his own rhetorically fluid voice. Melville, too, was probably influenced by C. Throughout 1850 Melville borrowed many of C's works from E. Duyckinck,* and the power of language to express the full range of emotion is apparent in *Moby-Dick* (1851).

In 1847–48 Emerson made a second trip to England, visiting C several times between lecture tours. During the 1840s, C had moved away from his earlier philosophical idealism and toward a new respect for fact and history, reflected in his biographies of Cromwell and others. Equally, C had become more harshly critical of social reform and of democracy, preferring an organic hierarchical society in which charismatic men of power and vision took command. These views strained, but did not break, the friendship between C and Emerson. The latter expressed the new distance between them in this journal passage written in 1848: ''Carlyle is no idealist in opinions, but a protectionist in political economy, aristocrat in politics, epicure in diet, goes for murder, money, punishment by death, slavery, and all of the pretty abominations, tempering them with epigrams.'' C for his part was growingly impatient with Emerson's hazy idealism, repeatedly describing his American friend as ''moonshiny.'' The differences between the two and between their two nations are reported in Emerson's *English Traits* (1856). Despite their disagreements, C's influence on Emerson is still apparent in the latter's *Representative Men* (1850). Prompted in part by C's *On Heroes and Hero-Worship* (1841), Emerson's book is nonetheless strikingly different, moving away from a Carlylean stress on ''great men'' and toward a celebration of the heroic in each person.

In the later 1840s and throughout the 1850s, the gap between C and American intellectuals grew rapidly. His 1849 essay ''Occasional Discourse on the Nigger Question'' attacked the notions of racial equality and economic freedom, alienating Americans who had moved into more radical forms of antislavery. C ridiculed America (in his 1850 *Latter-Day Pamphlets*) as a nation of ''Eighteen Millions of the greatest *bores* ever seen in this world before.'' During the Civil

War, C refused to state his views, although it was clear he preferred a Southern victory. After the war, he continued his assault on democracy and racial equality, notably in *Shooting Niagara, and After* (1867).

Despite C's political authoritarianism, his influence on American Transcendentalists was vast. He helped them break out of their cultural isolation by encouraging a critique of Unitarian rationalism. He introduced them to German writers and philosophers. His literary style freed several prominent writers of the stiff 18th-century prose they had inherited, encouraging them to find their own voices. In the 1830s and early 1840s, the years of his greatest influence, C wielded, in T. Parker's* words, "a strong and . . . healthy influence on old and young."

References: C's published works are available in the *Centenary Edition of the Works of TC,* 30 vols., ed. H. D. Traill (1896–1901). The Univ. of California Press has initiated a new edition of C's writings. Central to understanding C's impact on American Transcendentalism is *The Correspondence of Emerson and C*, ed. Joseph Slater (1964). Several of the most important responses to C, including those of Walker, Norton, Clarke, and Parker quoted here, are found in Miller (1950). A useful modern biography that treats C's American connection is Fred Kaplan, *TC* (1983). Two relevant works are Kenneth Marc Harris, *C and Emerson: Their Long Debate* (1978), and Robert Weisbuch, *Atlantic Double-Cross. American Literature and British Influence in the Age of Emerson* (1986).

Bruce A. Ronda

CHANNING, EDWARD TYRREL (1790–1856), brother of the Rev. W. E. Channing,* was the third Boylston Professor of Rhetoric and Oratory at Harvard (1819–50). Many of his students became important to Transcendentalism, among them R. W. Emerson,* H. Thoreau,* J. F. Clarke,* and J. Very;* others were prominent literary figures, including O. W. Holmes,* J. R. Lowell,* Richard Henry Dana, Jr., and T. W. Higginson.* A Unitarian,** C is linked to Transcendentalism in practical rather than in philosophical terms: Both Emerson and Thoreau considered him a primary influence on the evolution of their rhetorical styles. Emerson was likely among the crowd who heard or at least read C's inaugural address at Harvard, "The Orator and His Times," collected in *Lectures Read to the Seniors in Harvard College* (1856). In that speech, C praises classical oratory but cites it as insufficient for a modern audience who would be more intrigued by quality of reasoning than passionate appeal. In so doing, C departed from precedents established by earlier Boylston Professors, including John Quincy Adams, who had based their instruction on classical models. Emerson may also have heard C's 1818 Phi Beta Kappa address, "Literary Independence," in which he uses the term "American Scholar" (rpt. from the original manuscript by Richard Beale Davis, *Key Reporter* 26.3 [1961]: 1–4, 8). C thereby anticipates Emerson's later call for men who could speak of and to their own time.

Although he believed speech to be the most powerful means of affecting human action, C offered his greatest contribution to American letters not as an orator but as an instructor. He selected for his classroom lectures such topics as "A Writer's Habit" and "Clearness of Expression and Thought." As a college senior, Emerson, like his classmates, submitted weekly themes to the professor for his comments. C worked more closely with Thoreau; according to Walter Harding and Robert Richardson, Jr., Thoreau readily credited C with having taught him to write. Yet in an earlier biography of Thoreau, Henry Seidel Canby asserts that C's rigorous demands for a correctly composed theme actually stifled Thoreau's intuitive approach to writing. Nevertheless, Thoreau's emphasis on precision in word choice and the careful crafting of individual sentences suggests a debt to C, if for no other reason than that C provided him with a regular opportunity to write for an audience. In his introduction to the posthumously published *Lectures Read to the Seniors*, Dana observed that because of C's "influence over the taste and judgment of the men who learned from him, it would not be easy to estimate his indirect contributions to the literature and eloquence of America."

References: *Lectures Read to the Seniors in Harvard College* was rpt. in 1968, ed. Dorothy I. Anderson and Waldo W. Braden, with a foreword by David Potter. Anderson and Braden set C's attitudes toward rhetoric and teaching in the context of his own time, particularly as those ideas relate to Scottish Common Sense philosophy.** This volume includes the most thorough bibliographic information available for varied references to C. Howe (1970) classifies C as one of Harvard's 12 "Unitarian moralists" and discusses his rhetorical theories in relation to Unitarianism. Scattered references to C surface in works about his brother, W. E. Channing, and in the biographies of contemporaries and famous students. See Canby, *Thoreau* (1939); Harding (1965); *DLB*; and Robert D. Richardson, Jr., *Henry Thoreau* (1986). C's papers, including notes taken by students in his class, are housed with other faculty manuscripts in the Harvard University Archives.

Kathryn B. McKee

CHANNING, WILLIAM ELLERY (1780–1842), was the spiritual and intellectual leader of the Unitarian** movement in early 19th-century New England and one of the most potent influences on R. W. Emerson* and the Transcendentalists. C's early development included an intense period of soul-wrestling and an engagement with the doctrines of Calvinism, which he gradually discarded in his early years. He would later describe his life as a "process of conversion," implying that the process of spiritual development was never complete. C was educated at Harvard (A.B., 1798), serving as a tutor in Virginia (1798–1800) before assuming the pastorate of the Federal Street Church in Boston in 1803. The clergy of the Churches of the Standing Order in Boston and Eastern Massachusetts had a generally liberal bent at this time, and though they were cool to many points of the Calvinist orthodoxy, they retained a secure sense of themselves as members of the New England Protestant tradition. Their liberal views became a public issue in 1815, however, when Jedidiah Morse and Jeremiah Evarts attacked them by linking them to the Unitarian movement in England and argued that the orthodox should deny them Christian fellowship.

C and the liberals had in fact been less concerned about the doctrine of the Trinity than other Calvinist doctrines such as innate depravity and election to grace, which conflicted with their views of human dignity and human freedom. But in his 1819 sermon ''Unitarian Christianity,'' C accepted the name of Unitarianism for the liberal movement, attacking Calvinism directly as a theological system that distorts both the nature of God and of humanity, and defining the movement as one that emphasized the human capacity for reason and moral judgment. C's powerful polemics and eloquent presentation of the Unitarian theological perspective constituted a key factor in coalescing the Boston liberals into a denomination, even though he remained somewhat skeptical of the value of sectarianism. His preaching in the 1820s and 1830s continued to exert enormous influence. His 1821 Dudleian Lecture at Harvard, ''The Evidences of Revealed Religion,'' defended the necessity of supernatural revelation for the religious life, and its oratorically powerful exemplification of the moral imagination impressed the young Emerson, who took it as model of his aspirations as a preacher. C's 1828 sermon ''Likeness to God'' portrayed the religious life as a continual movement of the soul toward a greater realization of divinity, a program for religious growth that typified the moral ethos of early Unitarianism, and was a major influence on the theories of self-culture propounded by Emerson, H. Thoreau,* and M. Fuller.* His 1838 lecture ''Self Culture'' proposed a life of strenuous effort at constant self-improvement, offering self-culture as both a spiritual goal and a social good.

C's ''Self-Culture'' indicates his growing orientation toward social ethics, a significant element of which was expressed through his antislavery writings. His 1835 treatise *Slavery*, influenced by L. M. Child,* added to the growing antislavery sentiment in New England. His last public work, the ''Address Delivered at Lenox'' (1842), used the anniversary of the British emancipation of the slaves in the West Indies to call for an end to slavery in the United States by legal and peaceful means.

C was revered by the younger generation of Unitarians, including those inclined toward Transcendentalism, for his rhetorical brilliance and the moral elevation of his thinking and preaching. Although he remained a Lockean** in his epistemology, while Emerson and the Transcendentalists embraced Coleridge's* version of religious intuitionism, he shared with the Transcendentalists the fundamental emphasis on the culture of the soul, based on its innate divinity, as the essential work of religion. Most of Emerson's essential doctrines can be found in incipient form in C's works, and C's presence and the example of his imaginative and deeply spiritual preaching were probably a more important influence on Emerson.

References: See *The Works of WEC D.D.*, 6 vols. (1841–43), and W. H. Channing,* ed., *Memoir of WEC, with Extracts from His Correspondence and Manuscripts*, 3 vols. (1848). For a review of scholarly work on C, see David Robinson, ''WEC'' in Myerson (1984), 310–16. John White Chadwick, *WEC: Minister of Religion* (1903), and Jack Mendelsohn, *C: The Reluctant Radical* (1971), are important biographical studies. For

C's work on antislavery, see Andrew Delbanco, *WEC: An Essay on the Liberal Spirit in America* (1981). On C's Unitarian context, see Howe (1970). C's influence on Emerson is discussed in David Robinson, "The Legacy of C," *HTR* 74 (April 1981): 221–39, and *Apostle of Culture: Emerson as Preacher and Lecturer* (1982).

David M. Robinson

CHANNING, W. ELLERY (1817–1901), Transcendentalist poet and the first biographer of his friend H. Thoreau,* was born in Boston, Massachusetts, the son of Walter Channing, a Harvard University Medical School professor and himself a minor poet. E is often confused with his uncle W. E. Channing* (1780–1842), the Unitarian** divine. (To distinguish the two, it is common practice to refer to the poet as "Ellery" or "WEC the Younger.")

Because his mother died when he was about five, E spent an unhappy childhood farmed out to live with relatives. He entered Harvard College in 1834 but dropped out after only a few months, not being willing to submit himself to its discipline. Since his father supplied him with a small regular income for his entire life, he felt no need to do anything as prosaic as earning a living and, except for working briefly on newspapers in New York and New Bedford, devoted his life to writing poetry, reading, and observing nature.** In 1839 he experimented briefly with pioneer farming in Illinois. In 1842 he married M. Fuller's* sister Ellen and the next year settled down in Concord, Massachusetts,** to be near R. W. Emerson,* remaining there most of the rest of his long life.

C's most important contribution to literature was his biography *Thoreau, the Poet-Naturalist* (1873). C became acquainted with Thoreau when he moved to Concord, and they rapidly became bosom friends, spending many a day wandering together in the woods and fields and on the ponds and rivers of Concord. (C is the otherwise unidentified "C" of Thoreau's Journal.) He himself occasionally made attempts at journal** keeping, but they are very fragmentary and of little worth but for the occasional light they shed on his friendship with Thoreau. C started his biography of Thoreau shortly after the latter's death in 1862 and began serial publication of it in the Boston *Commonwealth* in 1863 but soon quarreled with the editor, F. B. Sanborn,* and withdrew the manuscript with only a small portion of it in print. In 1873 Roberts Brothers of Boston offered to publish it, but finding it too brief, they insisted he enlarge it. This he did by arbitrarily inserting into its middle two chapters of excerpts from the unpublished journals of Thoreau, B. Alcott,* Emerson, and Channing without bothering to identify which speaker was which. The resulting book is weird, erratic, and often confusing. There is astonishingly little biographical detail—the Walden** experiment and the jail incident being hardly more than mentioned. But he does include many of the anecdotes that have become standards in the Thoreau legend. His critical comments on Thoreau's writings are sharp and to the point, and his warm portrayal of Thoreau's personality serves as an excellent antidote to the cold, inhuman, Stoic image that Emerson portrayed in his eulogy over Thoreau. The excerpts from Thoreau's unpublished journal that

C included served to whet interest in them and helped to set the stage for their eventual publication. Students should, however, be aware that a 1902 edition of the biography, this time edited by Sanborn, suffers from the vagaries of Sanborn's editing eccentricities and is not always to be trusted.

C was one of the most prolific of the Transcendentalist poets and, in fact, contributed more writings to *The Dial*** than any other. He published seven volumes of his poetry in his lifetime—*Poems* (1843), *Poems, Second Series* (1847), *The Woodman* (1849), *Near Home* (1858), *The Wanderer* (1871), *Eliot* (1885), and *John Brown* (1886)—as well as many individual short poems scattered through various newspapers and magazines. The best of his poems are probably those written in tribute to his friend Thoreau appended as ''Memorial Verses'' to his Thoreau biography. More polished than most of his other works, they give a warm picture of their friendship. His most successful book-length poem is *The Wanderer*, which gives thinly veiled sketches of his Concord friends, particularly Thoreau and Emerson. His *Collected Poems* fill more than a thousand pages. Unfortunately, he was much more interested in quantity than quality and refused ever to polish or work over his poetry. Thoreau hit the nail on the head when he said C's poetry was written in the ''sublimo-slipshod'' style. He sometimes wrote memorable lines such as, ''If my bark sinks, 'tis to another sea,'' which his fellow Transcendentalists loved to quote, but he virtually never wrote an entire poem that any anthologist found worthy of reprinting. His most devastating critic was E. A. Poe,* who said of C's first volume, ''His book contains about sixty-three things, which he calls poems, and which he no doubt seriously supposes them to be. They are full of all kinds of mistakes, of which the most important is that of their having been printed at all.''

Much of C's prose is little, if any, better than his poetry. His one other book-length prose work was *Conversations in Rome Between an Artist, a Catholic, and a Critic* (1847), a series of commentaries on art, religion, architecture, and poetry cast into the conversational form. Although some portions of it still have life, it is for the most part too formalized and like so much of his poetry would have benefited from heavy editing. ''The Youth of the Poet and Painter,'' a semiautobiographical satire published serially in letter form in the last volume of *The Dial*, was left unfinished when *The Dial* itself died. It gives some general idea of the lives and interests of the younger Transcendentalists.

References: Two biographies—Frederick T. McGill, Jr., *C of Concord* (1967), and Robert N. Hudspeth, *EC* (1973)—effectively complement each other, for the former emphasizes biographical detail, while the latter's emphasis is critical.

Original editions of C's works are difficult to find, for they were printed in very small editions and sold very poorly. There is even a legend—surely apocryphal—that one of his volumes of poetry sold only one copy. But all the volumes of poetry and most of the scattered individual poems have been gathered together in *The Collected Poems of WEC the Younger*, ed. Walter Harding (1967). Francis B. Dedmond has superbly edited ''The Selected Letters of WEC,'' *SAR* 1989–92, and several of C's unfinished satires.

The largest collection of C manuscripts, including that of his journal, is in the Houghton Library of Harvard University. Other manuscripts may be found in the Concord Free Public Library, the Pierpont Morgan Library, the Massachusetts Historical Society, Brown University Library, the Boston Public Library, and the Henry Huntington Library.

Walter Harding

CHANNING, WILLIAM HENRY (1810–1884), minister, editor, and (according to Emerson's* famous "Ode") the "evil time's sole patriot," was among those first-generation Transcendentalists whose primary aim was applying the "new views" to social and political affairs. Wide-ranging in his interests, he sampled a variety of projects, leaving his lasting mark on few of them, during the long odyssey that he himself termed the "spiral ascending path" of his life.

The nephew of Dr. W. E. Channing,* the revered Unitarian** divine, WH was graduated from Harvard in 1829 and concluded his divinity studies there in 1833. For several years he preached in New York City and toured Europe; then, in 1838, he went west, accepted a Unitarian pulpit in Cincinnati, and in 1839 assumed the editorship of the monthly *Western Messenger.*** Always more interested in reform than in speculations, he turned the magazine toward economic and social criticism. After the magazine's demise in 1841, he returned to preaching in New York, visiting prisons and editing *The Present*** (1843–44), a journal of Fourierism.* A frequent visitor at the Brook Farm** community, he founded the Religious Union of Associationists in Boston in 1847 and launched another journal, the aptly named *Spirit of the Age*,** which folded in 1849 after less than a year. In 1854 he left for England, serving radical Unitarian societies there for the rest of his life, with frequent extended visits to the United States.

C's intellectual wanderlust was anchored by a Transcendentalist's faith in the innate divinity of the individual, what C later would call "the splendour of the Divine Presence over, & through, & in Humanity." In addition to his work as a magazine editor, his literary legacy to American Transcendentalism resides in his work on two biographies: *Memoir of William Ellery Channing* (3 vols., 1848) and *Memoirs of Margaret Fuller* Ossoli* (2 vols., 1852).

REFERENCES: The only full-length biography is O. B. Frothingham,* *Memoir of WHC* (1886), which includes excerpts from essays and letters. For C's work with periodicals, see Sterling F. Delano, *"The Harbinger" and New England Transcendentalism* (1984), and Robert D. Habich, *Transcendentalism and the "Western Messenger"* (1985). David M. Robinson analyzes C's reformist activity in "The Political Odyssey of WHC," *AQ* 34 (summer 1982): 165–84, and Habich has edited "The 'Spiral Ascending Path' of WHC: An Autobiographical Letter," *ESQ* 30 (1st Q 1984): 22–26. A bibliographical essay by Elizabeth R. McKinsey is in Myerson (1984), 108–11. Many of C's manuscripts were destroyed by fire; the best remaining collections are in the Houghton Library, Harvard University; the Massachusetts Historical Society; and the Henry E. Huntington Library.

Robert D. Habich

CHAPMAN, JOHN JAY (1862–1933), was a lawyer, reformer, and cultural critic dedicated to Emersonian individualism. Deeply involved with the social and political issues of his day, he wrote wide-ranging critical essays on R. W. Emerson,* W. L. Garrison,* and J. W. Howe,* among others.

C's father, Henry Grafton Chapman, was a founder of the Knickerbocker Club and president of the New York Stock Exchange. His mother, Eleanor Jay Chapman, and grandmother, Maria Weston Chapman, were active in the abolition** movement. This legacy of public service strongly influenced C. After graduating from Harvard College and Harvard Law School, he began practicing law in New York City and subsequently became interested in political reform, joining the City Reform Club and the Good Government Club. In 1897, C founded *The Nursery* (later titled *The Political Nursery*) as a forum for political and cultural criticism. In both essays and poetry, C targeted the "moral cowardice" that he believed was undermining American democracy. In "Bismarck," his most famous poem, he argued that "Enlightened public thought in private men" was the only solution to the political upheaval in Europe. C came to believe that social and political reform were not enough; reform must start with the individual and private life. Although he became increasingly conservative in his later years, C often warned about the potential for democracy to lead to the homogenization of the individual.

C's ideas about individualism and the dangers of moral cowardice clearly stem from his study of Emerson, whose life and works he discusses in his essay simply entitled "Emerson" (orig. pub. in two parts, *Atlantic Monthly*** [1897]). Although C criticized Emerson's lack of understanding of human emotion and his ideas about the fixed nature of character, he believed Emerson was a true prophet for America. C claimed that Emerson's two central themes are the "unfathomed might of man" and the dangers of "moral cowardice." Although C himself believed in the efficacy of reform movements as long as they were linked to change within the individual, he understood Emerson's dislike of the methods of reform movements. C claims that Emerson "saw in [the reform movements] people who sought something as a panacea or as an end in itself" rather than "the development of the individual."

C also wrote a number of favorable essays on social activists such as Garrison and Howe. C singled out Garrison for particular praise, claiming that while Emerson dealt in abstractions, Garrison was "devoted to the visible and particular evils of his times." Garrison, C believed, epitomized Emerson's "influential individual." Although ultimately critical of Transcendentalism for its failure to make itself relevant to the rest of America, C celebrated the reformers of the 19th century and helped keep alive Emerson's ideas about the importance of the individual.

References: C's work may be found in several different collections. Jacques Barzun, *The Selected Writings of JJC* (1957), includes C's most important essays on Emerson and Garrison. *The Collected Works of JJC*, 12 vols. (1970) reprints his book-length works, as well as all issues of *The Political Nursery*. The most complete biography is Richard B. Hovey, *JJC—An American Mind* (1959). M. A. DeWolfe Howe, *JJC and His Letters* (1937), is also useful. Both biographies quote extensively from C's private, unpublished papers, at the Houghton Library, Harvard University. On Emerson's radicalism, see Nancy C. Simmons, ''Speaking of Emerson: Two Unpublished Letters Exchanged Between JJC and James Elliot Cabot,*'' *HLB* 31.2 (1983): 181–87. Critical views of C's work include Edmund Wilson, *The Triple Thinkers* (1948), 133–64; Stuart Gerry Brown, ''JJC and the Emersonian Gospel,'' *NEQ* 25 (June 1952): 147–80; Alfred Kazin, ''A Leftover Transcendentalist: JJC,'' *Contemporaries* (1962), 64–69; and Sherman Paul, ''The Identities of JJC,'' in *Transcendentalism and Its Legacy*, ed. Myron Simon and Thornton H. Parsons (1966), 137–49.

Karen A. Weyler

CHEEVER, GEORGE BARRELL (1807–1890), was a vocal orthodox Congregationalist minister, abolitionist,** and critic of the Unitarians** in the 1830s. A college friend of N. Hawthorne's* at Bowdoin, C contributed to the Calvinist critique of liberal ''unbelief,'' characterizing Unitarianism as ''shifting as the sands, having no stability, no permanent creed, no grounds of certainty, nothing fixed but a mortal aversion to the evangelical scheme'' (*Spirit of the Pilgrims* 6 [December 1833]: 703–26). However, as an outspoken critic of slavery, C shared a degree of common ground with some Transcendentalist positions on the Civil War. He also wrote a popular and controversial temperance** allegory, *Deacon Giles' Distillery* (1835), as well as an essay on Coleridge* for the *North American Review*** (40 [April 1835]: 299–351). His writings reflected his interests in literature and theology and include a biographical description of J. Marsh.*

References: The most complete biographical and bibliographical study is Robert M. York, *G B. C: Religious and Social Reformer, 1807–1890,* in *University of Maine Studies, Second Series* 69 (1955). C's criticism of Unitarianism is briefly discussed in C. H. Faust, ''The Background of the Unitarian Opposition to Transcendentalism,'' *MP* 35 (February 1938): 297–324. See C's *Characteristics of the Christian Philosopher: A Discourse on the Virtues and Attainments of Rev. James Marsh* (1843). Robert C. Albrecht briefly discusses C's similarities with Transcendentalists in ''The Theological Response of the Transcendentalists to the Civil War,'' *NEQ* 38 (March 1965): 21–34. See also Margaret B. Moore, ''Hawthorne and 'The Lord's Anointed,' '' *SAR* 1988: 27–36.

Doni M. Wilson

CHENEY, EDNAH DOW LITTLEHALE (1824–1904), was a social activist, a lecturer at the Concord School of Philosophy,** and the editor of L. M. Alcott's* letters and journals.** As a young woman, C was strongly influenced by M. Fuller* and T. Parker* and as a result later became active in the woman's rights** movement and antislavery work.

C explains her debt to the Transcendentalists in her *Reminiscences* (1902), particularly recalling the influence of Fuller: ''I absorbed her life and thoughts, and to this day I am astonished to find how large a part of 'what I am when I am most myself' I have derived from her.'' C regularly attended Fuller's Conversations,** and in 1895, C delivered a biographical lecture based upon her personal knowledge of Fuller to the Congress of American Advancement of

Women. This impressionistic, anecdotal address explores the reasons for Fuller's continued influence on American thought. C concludes that Fuller's devotion to the "individual right for freedom and development" and for "natural equality and political rights" explains her enduring significance in American feminist thought.

C had numerous other connections among the Transcendentalists, including a long-standing friendship with the Alcott family. At B. Alcott's* invitation, she was a regular lecturer at the Concord School of Philosophy from 1879 until 1888. C later claimed that she "owed this invitation rather to the wish to do honor to women by giving them an equal position than to [her] own individual merits," and for this reason, she labeled herself "a representative woman." Most often she lectured on art and literature, but she also delivered a number of lectures on R. W. Emerson,* including "Emerson and Boston," published in *The Genius and Character of Emerson* (1885). This biographical essay explores the importance of Boston and its literary culture in Emerson's education and the development of his thought.

In 1889, C edited and annotated *Louisa May Alcott: Her Life, Letters, and Journals*. C intersperses Alcott's writings with a memoir of her life, but she attempts to allow Alcott to speak for herself "without disguise." She therefore opens each chapter by sketching a general outline of Alcott's life during a particular time period and then printing long excerpts from her journals and letters, with annotations interspersed throughout. C ultimately portrays Alcott as torn between her vocation as a writer and her need to support her family. Although numerous other biographies have supplanted C's, her work on Alcott remains important because it reprints several documents that are no longer extant.

C also participated in a number of reform movements. Influenced by Parker, C was active in antislavery work as well as the education of freed slaves. After the Civil War, she lobbied for women's rights and the suffrage movement as an active member of the New England Women's Club, the Massachusetts School Suffrage Association, and the New England Woman Suffrage Association. C also joined the Free Religious Association** and participated in that organization's lecture series.

References: There is no biography of C, but her autobiographical work *Reminiscences* is useful in exploring her connection to Transcendentalism, and her *Memoir of Seth W. Cheney* (1881) provides additional biographical information, as does J. W. Howe's* *Representative Women of New England* (1904) and Evelyn Shakir, "EDC: 'Jack at All Trades'," *ATQ* 47–48 (summer/fall 1980): 95–115. C's personal papers are located at the Boston Public Library, the Massachusetts Historical Society, Smith College, and Radcliffe College. The two volumes of *Concord Harvest* (1970), ed. Kenneth W. Cameron, provide reprints of a number of essays and lectures C delivered at the Concord School of Philosophy, as well as information about her activities with the school. *Gleanings in the Fields of Art* (1881) reprints several lectures not included in *Concord Harvest*.

Karen A. Weyler

CHILD, LYDIA MARIA (1802–1880), author and editor of more than 40 books, was also an abolitionist** whose outspoken humanitarianism won supporters and detractors alike. Introduced to Transcendentalism in 1824, when she moved to Watertown, Massachusetts, to board with her recently married brother, she frequently participated in parlor discussions attended by R. W. Emerson,* Whittier,* G. Ripley,* M. Fuller,* T. Parker,* and others. Intellectually curious and predisposed to write, LM had already published several books by the time she married her husband, David Lee Child, in 1826.

Although a student of Transcendentalism, C did not embrace all of its tenets, nor did she consider herself a Transcendentalist in the popular sense. Rejecting its passive spiritual contemplation in favor of conscious action, she confessed with some amusement in *Letters from New-York* that ''there are people, very intellectual ones too, who mystify me in the strangest fashion. After talking with them, my spirit always has to bite its finger, to know whether it exists or not.'' Emersonian Transcendentalism, in particular, she found irrelevant to contemporary life, and although she admired the man tremendously, she was keenly disappointed by his reluctance to lend more visibility to the antislavery movement.

C's *Philothea, A Romance* (1836) has been characterized by some critics as a Transcendentalist novel. Appearing the same year as Emerson's *Nature*, it is generally considered C's best fictional work. Set in Greece in the Age of Pericles, *Philothea* employs Transcendentalist concepts in depicting nature** and emphasizing intuition. *Philothea*, however, is also an oblique commentary on the 19th-century American political arena: The issues of slavery, woman's rights,** and Jacksonian democracy** are all suggested by the novel's subtexts. C's earliest work, *Hobomok, A Tale of the Times* (1824), is a story of miscegenation between an Indian man and a white woman. Set in Puritan** New England, *Hobomok* also addresses many of C's moral concerns: religious zealotry, social hypocrisy, and racial intolerance.

Generally remembered for her antislavery activism, most notably for *An Appeal in Favor of That Class of Americans Called Africans* (1833) and for her editorship of the *National Anti-Slavery Standard* (1841–43), C also authored a domestic handbook, *The Frugal Housewife* (1829); two volumes of *Letters from New-York* (1843 and 1845); and several other works.

REFERENCES: On her biography, see *Letters of LMC* (1883); Helene G. Baer, *The Heart Is Like Heaven: The Life of LMC* (1964); Milton Meltzer, *Tongue of Flame: The Life of LMC* (1965). Useful for its focus on C's literary contributions is William S. Osborne, *LMC* (1980).

Denise D. Knight

CHOLMONDELEY, THOMAS (1823–1863), an English aristocrat, world traveler, and onetime New Zealand colonist, was a friend and correspondent of H. D. Thoreau.* He met Thoreau on his first visit to Concord** in 1854, while a dinner guest of the Emersons,* and subsequently boarded with Thoreau's family for several weeks. During his stay, C hiked with Thoreau and H. G. O. Blake* to the top of Mount Wachusett and went on to spend part of the winter in Boston. On a second visit in 1858, he asked Thoreau to travel with him to the West Indies, but Thoreau declined the invitation and C eventually abandoned the trip as well. The two met for the last time in January 1859 but continued their correspondence until 1861.

In a letter to Blake, Thoreau described C as " 'a good fellow,'—a man of principle, and quite reliable; but very peculiar." His peculiarities included an unusually high voice and a tendency to travel with more fanfare than most Americans: On his first visit to Concord, he brought a tremendous quantity of luggage and his own bathtub. C's extravagance extended beyond his personal effects, however. In fall 1855, he sent Thoreau a collection of Oriental** books—21 separate works in 44 volumes—including works on Indian literary history and criticism and translations of the *Viṣṇu Purāṇa*,** the *Mandukya Upaniṣads*, and the *Bhagavadgītā*.** The gift pleased Thoreau enormously, but it arrived too late in his career to have had much influence on his writing; indeed, it is unclear how much of the collection he read. When C. Dall* asked him why he would not learn Sanskrit so that he could read certain of the volumes, Thoreau answered, "Now this box holds everything; then I might find it very empty."

Thoreau later sent C a number of books, including *Walden*, R. W. Emerson's* *Poems*, and Whitman's* *Leaves of Grass*. C seemed not to know how to take Whitman, writing that *Leaves* was the first truly "*new*" book he had ever seen but adding that Whitman appeared "not to know how to behave himself." In his letters, he often assessed the books he had encountered and asked Thoreau for his literary recommendations. These letters touched on political issues as well; calling himself a "thorough English conservative," C confessed that he dreamed of "a *glorious commonwealth*" and supported his country's involvement in the Crimean War, writing that he "*would rather see the country decimated* than an unglorious or even accomodating [*sic*] peace." However, in an 1861 letter—written well after his brief tour of duty in that war—C expressed far less militaristic sentiments, wishing that "we had got done with this brutal stupidity of war altogether."

C believed that Thoreau was too solitary and wrote to encourage him to seek "society," adding that he thought Thoreau's love of nature** would prove to be "ancillary to some affection" that he had "not yet discovered." He often tried to convince Thoreau to visit England; these entreaties were unsuccessful, though Thoreau did write that he would "think seriously" of making the trip if he were "ever rich enough." Because Thoreau developed few international (or even extraregional) friendships, C merits attention as an exception. Though he was far more politically and culturally conservative than Thoreau, and far more worldly, C's extensive travels and knowledge of literature, his class position and values, and his magnanimity attracted Thoreau's attention.

References: The information available on C is limited and largely anecdotal. F. B. Sanborn* discusses him in *The Life of Henry David Thoreau* (1917), 301–13, giving both 1863 and 1864 as the year of his death. See also Harding (1965), 346–50. Much of the Thoreau-C correspondence has been published in *Corr.* For C's literary efforts, consult his *Ultima Thule: or, Thoughts Suggested by a Residence in New Zealand* (1854). Robert D. Richardson, Jr., discusses the work briefly in *Henry Thoreau: A Life of the Mind* (1986), 329–30.

Susan M. Ryan

CLARKE, JAMES FREEMAN (1810–1888), Unitarian** minister, author, and editor, was one of the original members of the Transcendental Club** and helped spread the influence of Transcendentalism throughout a long and active life that seemed inextricably intertwined with the leaders and currents of the time. C attended Harvard (1825–29) and the Harvard Divinity School** (1829–32), moved to Louisville, Kentucky, immediately after graduation, then returned to Boston in 1841 to live the rest of his life as a Unitarian preacher, social activist, and literary man.

In Cambridge, C encountered the radical new ideas that, to the dismay of the administration, were floating around campus. By reading Coleridge* he discovered Kant,** through whom C realized that he ''was born a transcendentalist'' (*Autobiography*, 39). He also formed a close friendship with M. Fuller,* who encouraged his interest in German literature. C continued his close study of German works, especially Goethe,* and his translation of *Theodore or the Skeptic's Conversion* by W. De Wette* appeared in G. Ripley's* *Specimens of Foreign Standard Literature*** (1842). Although C's friendship with Fuller waned over the years, mainly because of her demanding personality, he continued to acknowledge her genius and personal support through his early years of searching for an appropriate niche in life. After her death, C, R. W. Emerson,* and W. H. Channing* edited the *Memoirs of Margaret Fuller* (1852).

C went to Louisville to help establish liberal religion in the West, to preach ''comfort to the sorrowful, making God seem near, dwelling on the duties of human life and the blessed help that comes from divine love'' (*Autobiography,* 72). In addition, he helped found *The Western Messenger*,** a liberal religious magazine that was the first Transcendental periodical and gave the movement a Western voice. As editor from April 1836 to April 1839, C used the *WM* to defend German literature, to publish important Transcendental works including the first of Emerson's poems to see print, and to support the liberal tradition in thinking and religion.

C attended the first two meetings of the Transcendental Club in 1836 and continued the association after permanently returning to Boston. He supported the Transcendentalists' idealism,** desire for social betterment, devotion to God within themselves, and beliefs in innate ideas, self-direction, and self-development. But C demonstrated the looseness of the movement by never fully endorsing the more radical of the Transcendental notions. Just as he later owned the Brook Farm** property without ever having joined or even visited the Utopian enterprise, C avoided such Transcendental excesses as the denial of miracles** and the divinity of Jesus. He lived by the principle of taking the good from a variety of liberal positions and then synthesizing a workable compromise between those ideas and the more conservative background given him by his stepgrandfather, James Freeman. This unique combination of radical and conservative made him a popular and successful minister and citizen. His Church of the Disciples, formed in 1841 on the principles of congregational participation in governance and worship, served as a model of liberal Christianity in Boston. During his long and respectable ministry, C preached funerals for many famous citizens, including N. Hawthorne* and Emerson.

Throughout his later years in Boston, C served as a spokesperson for numerous reform causes, such as temperance,** peace, poverty, education,** capital punishment, and especially antislavery; but his speeches and leadership tended to be moderate. C, who in a *WM* article had defended Emerson's Divinity School Address against the criticism of his former teacher A. Norton,* defended J. Brown's* dedication to reform—though not his raid on Harpers Ferry—and T. Parker's* right to free speech during his confrontation with the Boston Ministerial Association—though not some of Parker's views. As a member of the Board of Overseers of Harvard University, C supported the study of modern languages, an expansion of the college observatory, coeducation, and tolerance of broader theological teaching at the Divinity School.

C gave Transcendentalism an early boost through his enthusiasm for some of its tenets, his published defense of its ideas and leaders, and his friendship with its guiding lights. Later he added respectability and moderation, by his example and such actions as editing J. Very's* *Poems and Essays* (1886).

References: For biographical details, see *JFC: Autobiography, Diary and Correspondence*, ed. E. E. Hale* (1891); John Wesley Thomas, *JFC: Apostle of German Culture to America* (1949); and Arthur S. Bolster, Jr., *JFC, Disciple to Advancing Truth* (1954). Elizabeth R. McKinsey's *The Western Experiment: New England Transcendentalism in the Ohio Valley* (1973) provides useful insights into the role of the *WM* in the 1830s. See also *The Letters of JFC to Margaret Fuller*, ed. John Wesley Thomas (1957).

Larry R. Long

CLOUGH, ARTHUR HUGH (1819–1861), English poet, was a close friend and correspondent of R. W. Emerson.* A sensitive intellectual who struggled with the doubts of the age, C found in Emerson not only a kindred spirit but a source of hope and inspiration at a time when many had lost faith in established truths of society and religion. C, who had read Emerson's *Essays* as an undergraduate at Balliol College, Oxford, initiated the relationship by inviting Emerson, late in 1847, to be a guest at Oxford, where C was then a tutor. The friendship lasted until C's death.

Emerson admired both C's intellectual capabilities and his poetry. Upon learning of his death, Emerson wrote to C's widow, "He interested me more than any other companion, when I first knew him, in 1848, by his rare freedom & manliness. . . . [His] intellectuality . . . seemed so little English,—that I wrote home to my friends that I had found in London, the best American.'' Emerson especially praised C's poem *The Bothie*. Through Emerson's efforts and encouragement, C came to America in 1852 in search of work as a tutor, a venture that was not lucrative. Within a year he returned to England to assume a position in the Education Office; however, while C was in America, Emerson introduced him to intellectual and literary members of Boston and Concord** such as N. Hawthorne,* H. Greenough,* H. W. Longfellow,* T. Parker,* and E. Channing.*

In Emerson, C saw an individual who, like himself, had struggled with his religious beliefs and had followed his higher conscience. As Emerson had followed his inner voice and resigned from his ministry, so, too, had C resigned from his post as tutor at Oxford in 1848 for reasons of conscience. Oxford demanded that tutors subscribe to the Thirty-nine Articles of the Anglican Church; C had doubts about Christianity and could no longer swear to his belief in the Articles. Although C was not Emerson's disciple and did not subscribe to his mysticism, he found Emerson's idealism* and his stress on intuition as a mode of (or substitute for) epistemology attractive.

The friendship between Emerson and C endured, despite long silences in their correspondence and the distance between America and England. A story often recounted about the two has it that while C was seeing Emerson off after a visit to England in 1848, he said to the American, ''What shall we do without you? Carlyle* led us all out into the desert and he has left us there!'' Emerson, the story continues, placed his hand on C's head and said, ''I consecrate you Bishop of all England. It shall be your part to go up and down through the desert to find out these wanderers and to lead them into the promised land.''

REFERENCES: A good biography is Robindra K. Biswas, *AHC* (1972); Evelyn Barish Greenberger, *AHC, The Growth of a Poet's Mind* (1970), is a useful biography and critical work. Standard editions are *The Poems of AHC*, ed. F. L. Mulhauser (1974); *Selected Prose Works*, ed. Buckner B. Trawick (1964); *The Correspondence of AHC*, ed. Frederick L. Mulhauser, 2 vols. (1957); and *Emerson-C Letters*, ed. Howard F. Lowry and Ralph Leslie Rusk (1968). An early edition of C's prose and letters that includes an unreliable biography is *Prose Remains of AHC*, ed. Blanche Clough (1888). For C's early development, see *The Oxford Diaries of AHC*, ed. Anthony Kenny (1990).

Kathleen M. Healey

COLERIDGE, SAMUEL TAYLOR (1772–1834), British Romantic poet and philosopher, was one of the major influences on the development of American Transcendentalism. To the Americans, educated in the sensationalist** school of Locke,** C's philosophical writings, with their emphasis on humankind's spirituality and intuition, were like water in an intellectual desert. While Locke seemed to divorce humankind from the spiritual, C fused the material and spiritual. Although some of C's works were available in American libraries and [illegible]y Transcendentalists were familiar with them, it was publication of J. Marsh's* edition of C's *Aids to Reflection* (orig. pub. 1825) in 1829 that sparked their minds and enthusiasm. According to F. H. Hedge,* soon after publication of Marsh's edition, those who would later be named ''Transcendentalists'' began to meet regularly. Marsh also edited C's *The Friend* in 1833, another work important to the Transcendentalists. (Serially published in 1809 and 1810, *The Friend* was reissued in book form in 1812. Marsh used a different edition published in 1818.)

C's influence is incalculable. Not only did his writings offer an alternative to Locke; they were a vehicle through which Transcendentalists received German philosophy, especially that of Schelling.* W. E. Channing* was to say that he owed more to C than to other philosophers. B. Alcott* found in C what Lockean psychology had obscured—the spiritual component of the mind—and soon concluded that what was in the mind was God. C was preeminent among R. W. Emerson's* teachers; between 1825 and 1836 C's volumes were always on his working table, and the ideas of no other author appear so frequently in his early journals.** C's influence is evident in Emerson's sermons, ideology, and philosophic writings, such as *Nature* and ''The American Scholar.''

One of C's most important concepts to the Transcendentalists, especially Emerson, was his distinction between Reason and Understanding, which is central to *Aids to Reflection* and *The Friend.* C believed that the mind possesses two faculties and ways of knowing: Reason is universal and absolute, the source of ideas and universal, fixed truths. It is intuitive, and the regenerate individual is capable of communication with the Divine Spirit. For C, Reason is equivalent to the spirit. Understanding is the faculty of reflection, in which the individual attains knowledge and makes judgments through the senses. C argued that animals possess Understanding but not Reason, and this is what distinguishes humans from animals. In *The Friend* C argued, ''Thus, God, the Soul, eternal Truth, &c. are the objects of Reason; but they are themselves reason. We name God the Supreme Reason; . . . Whatever is conscious Self-knowledge is Reason; and in this sense it may be safely defined the organ of the Super-sensuous; even as the Understanding . . . may be defined the conception of the Sensuous . . . that faculty, the functions of which contain the rules and constitute the possibility of outward Experience.'' Akin to Understanding and Reason are Talent and Genius, for Talent lies in Understanding and is inherited, while Genius is produced by Reason and therefore is rare.

C's distinction between Reason and Understanding was important to Transcendentalism because it affirmed humankind's spirituality and intuition and revealed that the individual has access to higher truths. Marsh believed that Reason is akin to faith and enables humankind insight into moral and spiritual truths. For Emerson, this meant that the individual should be self-reliant and depend upon the voice of Reason, which in *Nature* he called the ''universal soul.'' Emerson later echoed C's definition of Genius in ''The American Scholar'': ''Genius looks forward: the eyes of man are set in his forehead, not in his hindhead: man hopes: Genius creates. Whatever talents may be, if the man create not, the pure efflux of the Deity is not his;—cinders and smoke there may be, but not yet flame.''

Vital also to Transcendentalism, especially in relation to poetics, was C's definition of the Imagination, which he addresses in the *Biographia Literaria* (1817). C distinguishes between two levels of Imagination: the Primary and the Secondary. The Primary Imagination is intuitive; it is ''the living Power and prime Agent of all human Perception, and as a repetition in the finite mind of the eternal act of creation in the infinite I AM.'' The Secondary Imagination ''is an echo of the former, co-existing with the conscious will. . . . It dissolves, diffuses, dissipates, in order to re-create; or where this process is rendered impossible, yet still at all events to idealize and unify.'' C stresses the inspirational quality of the Primary Imagination—that which springs from the Divine—which was of foremost importance for the Transcendentalists. Poetry, like any created work, should be inspired.

Despite C's intellectual impact on the Transcendentalists, not all of the Americans were impressed when they actually met him. While Channing enjoyed meeting C, Emerson was disappointed, a feeling that C reciprocated. Although C did not live up to Emerson's expectations, Emerson and the other Transcendentalists still admired C's work—one of the major forces in shaping American Transcendentalism.

References: For philosophical and critical writings, see *The Collected Works of STC*, 16 vols., ed. Barbara E. Rooke (1969–); for poetry, *The Complete Poetical Works of STC*, 2 vols., ed. Ernest Hartley Coleridge (1912). A useful biography is Oswald Doughty, *Perturbed Spirit: The Life and Personality of STC* (1981). J. Marsh's ''Preliminary Essay'' in *Aids to Reflection* (1829) is invaluable in understanding C's impact on the American Transcendentalists, as are F. H. Hedge, ''Coleridge,'' *ChEx* 14 (March 1833): 109–29; Harold Clarke Goddard, *Studies in New England Transcendentalism* (1908); Alexander Kern, ''The Rise of Transcendentalism, 1815–1860,'' in *Transitions in American Literary History*, ed. Harry Hayden Clark (1953); and Kern's ''C and American Romanticism: The Transcendentalists and Poe,'' in *New Approaches to C*, ed. Donald Sultana (1981). For C's influence on Emerson, see Frank T. Thompson, ''Emerson's Indebtedness to C,'' *SP* 23 (1926): 55–76; Kenneth Cameron, *Emerson the Essayist*, 2 vols. (1945); and Barry Wood, ''The Growth of the Soul: C's Dialectical Method and the Strategy of Emerson's *Nature*,'' *PMLA* 91 (May 1976): 385–97. On Marsh's edition of *Aids to Reflection*, see Marjorie Hope Nicholson, ''James Marsh and the Vermont Transcendentalists,'' *PhR* 34 (1925): 28–50; and John J. Duffy, ''Problems in Publishing C: James Marsh's First American Edition of *Aids to Reflection*,'' *NEQ* 43 (June 1970): 193–208.

Kathleen M. Healey

COMBE, GEORGE (1788–1858), was a Scottish education reformer and moral philosopher** who based his ideas on the phrenology** of Viennese physicians Franz Joseph Gall and J. C. Spurzheim.* His *The Constitution of Man* (1829) and 1837–38 lectures in the United States helped popularize phrenology as the basis for a system of moral improvement and education reform.** C's most important American follower was H. Mann,* who advocated his system in his Secretarial Reports to the Massachusetts Board of Education, in his editorship of the *Common School Journal,* and in his influence at the Massachusetts State legislature, which made the teaching of physiology a state law in 1850. C's ideas also appealed to B. Alcott,* T. Parker,* and R. W. Emerson,* though Emerson and Alcott later cooled toward phrenology.

C appealed to 19th-century reformers and Transcendentalists because he emphasized the perfectibility of human nature and made the individual responsible for the process. If people would only make self-knowledge a high priority, by studying their own physiology and corresponding temperament, they could direct their own improvement. "So many hours a-day should be spent in the sedulous employment of the knowing and reflecting faculties. The leading object should always be, to find out the relationship of every object to our own nature," declared C. C believed that the quest for knowledge, particularly scientific knowledge, was too often a debased secular pursuit, rather than a more noble search for connections between nature** and human spirituality. C believed the discovery of these connections must precede any improvement of education or any "regulation of individual and national conduct." C pleased Transcendentalists and conservative Christians by integrating scientific inquiry with a reverence for spiritual truth, writing a special chapter "to convince conscientious, evangelical Christians, that there is nothing in Phrenological Science, in the least at variance with the Oracles of Inspired Truth." On first reading *The Constitution of Man* in 1830, Emerson called it "the best sermon I have read for some time."

C gave Alcott a conceptual framework for beginning his own investigation of the relationship between the development of human nature and physical circumstances of the body. What interested Alcott was not a particular phrenological map of the human mind but rather the idea that human nature could be mapped through study and observation and then regulated. For his study Alcott kept journals** of the development of his children, recording his observations of Anna "obeying the great laws, by which nature is expanding her faculties, for her future use and happiness," as when her "organs which indicate intellectual and moral attributes" began "protruding themselves."

Emerson cooled to C and to phrenology after the once-serious field of investigation degenerated into a fad science in the hands of Orson and Lorenzo Fowler, who traveled the country with measuring tapes and plaster casts examining heads. But while Emerson lamented that "the attractive depths of nature" had been "vulgarized by the foot of ignorant conjurers, mesmerisers** & phrenologists," he also believed that the pseudoscience "affirmed unity and connection between remote points, and as such was excellent criticism on the narrow and dead classification of what passed for science; and the joy with which it was greeted was an instinct of the people which no true philosopher would fail to profit by." Alcott, too, realized that the new moral and physiological science had its limitations for a Transcendentalist who believed that the soul transcends all things. After hearing C lecture in 1838, Alcott felt that phrenologists subordinated the soul to the body in claiming that human nature develops in response to physiological circumstances.

References: C's ideas on education reform are collected in *Education, Its Principles and Practice*, ed. William Jolly (1879), which includes a short biography and a chronology of advancements of his theory. The only complete biography is Charles Gibbons, *The Life of GC*, 2 vols. (1878). Madeleine B. Stern discusses the reaction of Emerson to phrenology and of phrenology to Emerson in "Emerson and Phrenology," in *SAR* 1984: 213–28. Miller includes a contemporary review of *The Constitution of Man* by I. Ray,* as well as comments by Emerson and Parker about phrenology. For Alcott's interest in C and in phrenology, see Dahlstrand (1982).

D'Ann Pletcher-George

CONSTANT DE REBECQUE, HENRI BENJAMIN (1767–1830), was a French eclectic philosopher, political philosopher, and novelist. In *De la Religion, Considérée dans sa Source, ses Formes et ses Développements* (5 vols., 1824–31), he professed a philosophy that stressed the distinction between a universal religious sentiment in mankind and the transitory forms it assumed in particular religious sects. C saw religion as historically evolving in external form, from primitive fetishism to polytheism to the more "advanced" monotheism, but static, profound, and universal in essential content. Based on this hypothesis, he argued for a personal religion unhampered by priestly domination and rejected as inadequate a purely rational attitude toward life. For C, religion at large and Christianity in particular were central elements in human life and the source of man's highest moral aspirations and achievements. A purified and "reasonable" Christianity manifested the final stage of human endeavor and aspiration.

Transcendentalists found the notion of a universal religious sentiment complementary to that of the common moral sense, one of the cornerstones of Transcendentalism. It was also the chief source of its quarrel with the prevailing religious institutions, which Transcendentalists regarded as temporary and probably distorted manifestations of this vast underlying religious instinct. O. Brownson* was attracted to C's position that religion originates in a natural human sentiment and that access to truth is possible without supernatural divine revelation, as well as by C's theory that man seeks to embody religious ideas in institutions. These institutions ultimately serve as the concrete instruments of progress (a point at which Brownson diverges from major Transcendentalists). He recommended C's *De la Religion* in the preface to *New Views of Christianity, Society, and the Church* (1836). G. Ripley* compiled the first two volumes of *Specimens of Foreign Standard Literature*** with selections of V. Cousin,* his student T. Jouffroy,* and C. H. Thoreau* first encountered C's writings in 1835 while teaching school in Canton, Massachusetts, and boarding with Brownson's family.

References: See John Cruickshank, *BC* (1974). There is no complete edition of C's works, in French or in English.

Leigh Kirkland

CONWAY, MONCURE DANIEL (1832–1907), Unitarian** and freethought minister, historian, biographer, abolitionist,** and American disciple of Hegelianism,* is unique among those associated with Transcendentalism because he was born in Stafford County, Virginia, to a slave-owning family. He described his life as "[a] pilgrimage from pro-slavery to anti-slavery enthusiasm, from Methodism to freethought." After graduation from Dickinson College in 1849, C became a circuit-riding Methodist minister in Montgomery County, Maryland (1851–53). He read R. W. Emerson's* essays and fell under the influence of a settlement of Hicksite Quakers** in Sandy Spring, Maryland. These influences eventually led him away from Methodism and to Boston, Concord,** and the Harvard Divinity School,** where T. Parker* soon became his role model and Emerson his friend and mentor. When he graduated from the Divinity School in 1854, C was briefly a pastor of the Unitarian church in Washington, D.C., where he became acquainted with W. Whitman.* In 1856 he became pastor of the First Congregational Church in Cincinnati. As editor of *The Dial* (1860), a Cincinnati-based magazine for "literature, philosophy and religion" that took its name from the Transcendentalist journal of the 1840s, C pressed his increasingly radical religious and political views in nearly 30 articles and 70 book reviews. After the start of the Civil War, he published two books of abolitionist propaganda, *The Rejected Stone* (1861) and *The Golden Hour* (1862), and in August 1862, he accepted coeditorship of the Boston antislavery weekly, *The Commonwealth*.

In March 1863 C sailed for England, where he apparently intended to supply the role of an abolitionist presence in London. In June 1863, in a letter to Confederate emissary James Murray Mason, he proposed that if the Confederacy would emancipate its slaves, abolitionists in the North would oppose further prosecution of the war, leaving the South a de facto independent nation. Perhaps sensing C's lack of authority to make such a proposal, Mason rejected it, but C's unilateral action drew considerable scorn from patriotic abolitionists in America. The Lincoln administration chose to ignore the incident, which otherwise might have resulted in C's being charged with treason. In 1864 he published a third abolitionist tract, *Testimonies Concerning Slavery*, which was aimed at a British audience, and he accepted a call to the pulpit of South Place Chapel, London's most radical religious institution. C held that position until 1885 and again from 1893 to 1897.

In addition to his duties at South Place Chapel, C spent the decades following the Civil War on his prolific journalism; works of scholarship, notably *Demonology and Devil Lore* (1879) and *Solomon and Solomonic Literature* (1899); biographies such as *Emerson at Home and Abroad* (1882), *Life of Nathaniel Hawthorne** (1890), and the still-important *Life of Thomas Paine* (1892); and two novels, including the autobiographical *Pine and Palm* (1887). He was also important in publishing the work of American authors, notably Emerson, Mark Twain, and Whitman, in Britain. Always a believer in the Emersonian notion of evolution toward the good, C's optimism diminished near the end of his life with the death of his wife, Ellen Davis Conway, in 1897, and his bitter opposition to the Spanish-American War.

REFERENCES: Any study of C should begin with his memoir, *Autobiography, Memories and Experiences*, 2 vols. (1904). The best introduction to C's life and work is John d'Entremont, *MC, 1832–1907* (1977), and the most authoritative treatment of C's early life is d'Entremont, *Southern Emancipator, MC: The American Years, 1832–1865* (1987). Bibliographical information can be found in Robert E. Burkholder, ''MDC,'' in Myerson (1984), 117–22.

Robert E. Burkholder

COOKE, GEORGE WILLIS (1848–1923), was a Unitarian** minister and critic who helped make the ideas and writings of the Transcendentalists accessible to late 19th- and early 20th-century audiences. His biographies of R. W. Emerson* and J. S. Dwight* remained standards for decades, as did his work on *The Dial*,** and his well-received anthology of Transcendentalist poetry preserved many important documents that would have been otherwise lost. C also made a major contribution to the study of Transcendentalism with his *Bibliography of Ralph Waldo Emerson*, a thorough compilation of primary and secondary material that remains a valuable aid to scholars.

C found in Transcendentalism a set of ideas that, despite the acknowledged influence of European sources, remained distinctly American, and he traced these ideas to the first generation of Puritans and Jonathan Edwards. In this he anticipated the scholarship of such later critics as Perry Miller and Sacvan Bercovitch. C defined Transcendentalism as ''democracy in contact with Puritanism,''** the grafting of such ideas as freedom and liberty onto a base of profound religious faith. This ''movement of inquiry'' was a powerful combination of humanism and idealism,** asserting ''the worth and dignity of man'' made manifest through its ''numberless movements for social amelioration and practical reforms.'' Much like T. W. Higginson,* C emphasized the social dimensions of Transcendentalism and traced his own political liberalism to this heritage. While he disapproved of the atomizing individualism and mysticism that tinged so much of Transcendentalist thought, C believed that Transcendentalism was responsible for the best writing and thinking produced in the 19th century and would serve as the foundation for the most important work to be done in the 20th.

REFERENCES: The most useful account of C is Robert Burkholder's ''GWC,'' in *DLB* 71: 50–57. C's work on the Transcendentalists includes *Ralph Waldo Emerson: His Life, Writings, and Philosophy* (1881); *John Sullivan Dwight, Brook Farmer,** Editor, and Critic of Music: A Biography* (1898); *An Historical and Biographical Introduction to Accompany* The Dial (1902), reissued as *Memorabilia of the Transcendentalists in New*

England (1973); ''Thomas Wentworth Higginson,'' in *Authors at Home*, ed. J. L. and J. B. Gilder (1889), 119–62; *The Poets of Transcendentalism: An Anthology* (1906); and ''Emerson and Transcendentalism,'' *NEMag* 28 (May 1903): 264–80.

Charles Mitchell

COUSIN, VICTOR (1792–1867), was a prolific and wide-ranging French philosopher who for some time wielded considerable influence in Latin Europe and New England. The Transcendentalists found C appealing for two reasons: His revolt against 18th-century materialism, mechanism, and sensationalism** supported their idealistic tendencies; and his elegant popularizations of German philosophical thought made Kant** and Hegel,* among others, much more accessible. C's famous eclecticism, however, had little effect because the Transcendentalists soon perceived its indefiniteness (C later called it, even more vaguely, ''spiritualism'') and its speculative poverty. For all its pretensions, eclecticism turned out to be little more than mere syncretism.

Although several Transcendentalists read C in the original, he became more generally available through such translations as Henning G. Linberg's *Introduction to the History of Philosophy* (1832), C. S. Henry's* *Elements of Psychology: Included in a Critical Examination of Locke's** Essay on the Human Understanding* (1834), and G. Ripley's* *Philosophical Miscellanies* (1838), which inaugurated the latter's *Specimens of Foreign Standard Literature*** series. Ripley was C's chief advocate, praising him as the thinker most adequate to America's philosophical needs since his clarity of thought and style and his respect for humanity's deep-seated prephilosophical convictions showed that philosophy could be democratized and be made an instrument of social cohesion, while his demolition of the claims of sensationalism would help promote idealism** among a new generation of American thinkers. Ripley went so far as to embrace eclecticism. Reviewing C's *Fragments philosophiques* (2d ed., 1833) and the Linberg and Henry translations, he concluded, ''We must be eclectics . . . accepting and melting all into one vast system,'' thus fusing the truths to be found ''in all schools, in all creeds, in all ages, and in all countries'' (*ChEx*** 21 [September 1836]: 61). T. Parker* was more cautious, praising C for having ''helped to free'' the American mind from ''gross sensationalism'' and ''grosser supernaturalism'' but finding his ''brilliant mosaic'' ultimately ''not satisfactory.'' R. W. Emerson,* after some initial enthusiasm, proved the most telling critic of eclecticism, declaring in ''Literary Ethics'' (1838): ''It looks as if they [C and his disciples] had got all truth, in taking all the systems, and had nothing to do, but to sift and wash and strain, and the gold and diamonds would remain in the last colander. But, in fact, this is not so. . . . Translate, collate, distil all the systems, it steads you nothing; for truth will not be compelled, in any mechanical manner.''

References: C is the dominant figure in Walter L. Leighton's still-useful survey *French Philosophers and New-England Transcendentalism* (1908; rpt. 1968). Georges J. Joyaux, ''VC and American Transcendentalism,'' *FR* 29 (December 1955): 117–30, examines the American and especially the Transcendentalist reception of C as reflected in the periodicals of the day. Emerson R. Marks, ''VC and Emerson,'' in *Transcendentalism and Its Legacy*, ed. Myron Simon and Thornton H. Parsons (1966), 63–86, situates the relation between the two men in a wider religious and philosophical context. C's role as an intermediary between German and American thought is clarified by Pochmann (1957), 102–9 and passim.

Gustaaf Van Cromphout

CRANCH, CHRISTOPHER PEARSE (1813–1892), was a talented Unitarian** minister, editor of *The Western Messenger*,** poet, author of children's books, and landscape** painter. Never having worked at any one of these occupations for very long, he appears the dilettante or dabbler among Transcendentalists. Biographers defend him against this charge by calling attention to his struggle to reconcile his artistic inclination with his Unitarian conception of religious duty. C's father, a staunch Federalist and conservative Unitarian, taught him to define religious duty as action and art as inaction or leisure, making it impossible to devote to any artistic inclination until Transcendentalism allowed C to find an active devotion to Christian duty through artistic expression.

After graduating from Harvard Divinity School** in 1835, C briefly served as assistant pastor to F. H. Hedge* before following J. F. Clarke* to the Ohio Valley, where he preached in Clarke's pulpit and edited the *WM* from 1837 to 1839. The magazine defended liberal Unitarianism against the attacks of orthodox Calvinists and occasionally, conservative Unitarians. C praised R. W. Emerson's* ''The American Scholar'' as ''beautiful and masterly'' and defended the speech against the condemnation of Harvard faculty members. C and Clarke qualified a defense of the Divinity School Address, however, supporting the ''honest seeker'' though not necessarily the results of the search. They also identified W. E. Channing,* and not Emerson, as the leader of ''the New School,'' whose members ''look, and hope, and labor for something better than now is, who believe in progress, who trust in future improvement, and are willing to spend and be spent in bringing forward that better time.'' C further asserted his critical distance from Emerson through caricatures he and Clarke drew illustrating lines from Emerson's works, such as the ''transparent eye-ball'' passage from *Nature*: C drew a cartoon figure of an eyeball attached to two spindly legs, looking out over the New England landscape.

Emerson's definition of art as a method of perceiving higher truth, rather than a secular endeavor, did help C gain the confidence he would need to ''sink the minister in the man,'' as he told Emerson he planned to do. His interest in Transcendentalism grew on his return to Boston, as he submitted poems to *The Dial*** and *The Harbinger*,** entertained Brook Farmers** with his musical talents, and attended meetings of the Transcendental Club.** By 1841, C felt comfortable asserting that if ''in the remotest degree'' his poetry or painting ''bring the thoughts of nature** and the dreams of paradise into a single soul,'' he has done good. But C's poems provide evidence that a struggle to reconcile artistic expression with religious duty continued in his art. The five poems published in *The Dial* are all rather blunt and uninspired attempts to turn Transcendental philosophy into poetry. Claiming to have reached a synthesis between the ''Inworld'' and ''Outworld,'' the speaker in poems of those titles states mechanically and unconvincingly that ''he felt that voices twain/ Had come from different spheres with different truths,/ That seemed at war and yet agreed in one.''

If C failed in his early poetry to find symbols to integrate an outer world of activity with an inner world of spirituality, his later poetry improved. The speaker in ''The Garden,'' published in his 1875 collection *The Bird and the Bell with Other Poems*, learns by immersing himself in the very real, very material atmosphere of nature that ''Repose and Beauty preach a gospel too,/ Deep as that sterner creed the Apostles knew.'' The collection also contains ''The Spirit of the Age,'' one of the best expressions of the excitement Transcendentalists felt at being at the center of ''The prophesy of coming change'' while others ''sleep heedless of the electric gleams.'' Ironically, the poem was written 35 years after its author ceased to believe in Transcendentalist philosophy.

C quickly turned from poetry to painting. He went to Europe to study the masters and painted in the style of the Hudson River School. While praised for serenity and a true relation with nature, C's paintings also were criticized for vagueness, lack of emphasis, and lack of firmness in drawing. During the 1850s C wrote and illustrated children's stories in which he continued to explore the conflict between a life of dutiful action and one of artistic leisure. Dwarves in *Kobboltozo* listen to an obscure prophesy that convinces them to shamefully abandon their villages, shops, gardens, and entire society in a failed attempt to become giants. If C felt secure that his own authorship counted as action, he made it clear that a life spent in pursuit of a prophesy was egotistical and passive.

REFERENCES: The best source of biographical information is Leonora Cranch Scott, *The Life and Letters of CPC* (1917). C's caricatures of Emerson, his best-known works, are collected in F. DeWolfe Miller's *CPC and His Caricatures of New England Transcendentalism* (1951). Lindsay Swift discusses C's visits to Brook Farm in *Brook Farm: Its Members, Scholars, and Visitors* (1900). Julie Norko finds in the prose of C's ministry period a conflict between duty to vocation and inclinations as an artist, in ''CC's Struggle with the Muses,'' *SAR* 1992: 209–27. J. C. Levenson finds the weakness of C's poetry to be an understanding of the symbol limited to one-to-one correspondences, while Emerson saw quadruple meanings, in ''CPC: The Case History of a Minor Artist in America,'' *AL* 21 (January 1950): 415–26. Miller (1950) finds C a dilettante though ''one of the most futile and wasted talents'' among the Transcendentalists.

D'Ann Pletcher-George

CURTIS, GEORGE WILLIAM (1824–1892), author of a number of once widely read travel books, novels, and volumes of essays, is important to the

American experience not as a man of letters but as one of the late 19th century's two or three most influential ''liberal reformers.'' More than any other political activist of his day, perhaps, the prominent New Yorker frankly embraced and embodied the Emersonian ideal of the gentleman-intellectual as man of action. ''Though not usually classed as a transcendentalist,'' observed G. W. Cooke,* ''C was one of its most legitimate products.''

C was born in Providence, Rhode Island, to a prosperous entrepreneurial family. He pursued his higher education for 17 months as a student boarder at Brook Farm.** His skepticism of its communitarian principles together with the attraction of R. W. Emerson's* philosophical individualism prompted his removal to Concord,** where he stayed for another two years, exploring ideas with the leading Concord writers. He was, for example, a member of Emerson's short-lived discussion club, and he helped build H. Thoreau's* famous cabin at Walden Pond.**

In 1853, C commenced his long career as a lyceum** speaker, in time becoming one of the most popular lecturers of the day. And beginning as an occasional columnist for *Harper's Weekly*, by 1863 he was its editor, a position he held for the rest of his life. Through his hundreds of columns and public appearances, he shaped the opinions of thousands of middle-class Americans and through his private correspondence enjoyed personal access to such imposing notables as Presidents Grant and Hayes.

''I feel that our evils are entirely individual, not social,'' the youthful C explained, echoing Emerson: ''What is society but the shadow of the single men behind it?'' But C's definition of citizenship demanded an attention to politics. In 1856, energized by the slavery issue, he gave his well-known oration ''The Duty of the American Scholar to Politics and the Times,'' signaling his turn from a strictly literary career to reform. After the Civil War he remained a loyal Republican until becoming one of the most prominent ''Mugwump'' defectors to the Democrats in 1884.

C's postwar Emersonian individualism is hard to disentangle from the tenets of laissez-faire economics so prevalent among Gilded Age intellectuals. Thus, his negative outlook regarding such ''collective'' remedies as a federal income tax, inflationary currency, the eight-hour day, labor unionization, and socialism is not unusual. Yet his steady insistence on individual moral accountability seemed to set him apart. While demanding strict government regulation of the railroads, for example, C held that what was *essentially* wrong was individual rather than institutional—''the covetousness, want of good faith, and low moral tone'' of corporate managers.

His acknowledged leadership of the liberals' crowning endeavor, civil service reform, must to some extent be ascribed to its Emersonian appeal for him. It was at base an individualist solution to an institutional dilemma—how to obtain honest, efficient government in an era of extravagant official corruption. The answer was a professional meritocracy created by filling federal jobs through competitive examination rather than ''spoils system'' patronage. Among some of his colleagues, this emphasis on competency reflected a crude elitism, but to C the task was always a principled search for individual integrity and administrative talent.

In the end, passage of the 1883 act setting professional standards for many federal jobs owed more to President Garfield's death at the hands of a disappointed office seeker than to C. But his National Civil Service Reform League (1881), of which he was a founder and first president, was ready with model legislation, once an outraged public finally called for it.

References: Gordon Milne, *GWC and the Genteel Tradition* (1956), and "GWC," in Myerson (1984), 317–19, emphasize C's literary career. C's concerns as a postwar political activist are embedded in Ari Hoogenboom, *Outlawing the Spoils* (1968), and John Sproat, *"The Best Men"* (1968). Still useful is Cooke (1902), 2:170–75.

Jo Ann Manfra

D

DALL, CAROLINE WELLS HEALEY (1822–1912), author, lecturer, reformer, was one of the most prolific and colorful contemporaneous historians of the Transcendentalist movement. She was, in her own words, "a Transcendentalist of the old New England sort" both by philosophy and by lifelong association.

At the age of 12, C, whose wealthy father, Mark Healey, was eager to provide her with intellectual stimulation, was a member of R. W. Emerson's* lecture audience. Thus began her education by the Transcendentalists, who were to help set her life's course on a track of idealism,** independence, and reform. When she was 18 C came under the influence of E. P. Peabody,* who arranged for her to attend M. Fuller's* Conversations** in spring 1841. Despite being a newcomer to the group, C boldly entered into the talk; Peabody, Fuller, and perhaps Emerson were dismayed at her presumption. Her assertiveness, in fact, was throughout her life to alienate her from many associates. Though her relationship with Fuller was limited to this one experience and though she felt that Fuller did not like her, she took Fuller as a role model and proved to be one of the most effective heirs and defenders of her legacy of independence.

T. Parker* opened C's eyes to the "newness" on the theological front; by age 19 she was a convert to his radical views. When she expressed to Parker her criticism of his shock tactics, he addressed her concerns seriously, treating her as an equal, and she became his devoted defender. For Parker she supplied the kind of support that he badly needed in the face of attacks from the conservatives and defections from his friends. As Parker later moved into social reform, he was again an example for her.

C married in 1844 Charles Henry Appleton Dall, a Unitarian** minister who 11 years later left his wife and two young children to become a missionary to Calcutta. In his absence C, who had already been active in the antislavery and women's** movements, became a full-blown reformer. Her lecturing and writing on the woman question culminated in the pioneering feminist work *The*

College, the Market and the Court; or, Woman's Relation to Education, Labor, and Law (1867). D, building upon Fuller's model, provided a basic theoretical foundation, with more specific applications than Fuller's, for the women's movement in Victorian America. She was, after Fuller, the primary Transcendentalist voice on this issue. Later in the century, she turned her energies (in collaboration with F. Sanborn* and others) to the American Social Science Association, advocating a variety of social reforms, including improvements in prison conditions, the treatment of the insane, public health, and education.**

Herself a second-generation Transcendentalist, D maintained long-term relationships with many of the older generation. With Peabody, the always rocky relationship continued only until the mid-1860s. Peabody disapproved of D's open discussion of such topics as prostitution. Her views on the woman question were ultimately too radical for Peabody, and following a personal dispute, for the last several decades of their lives, they did not speak to each other.

Among the other Transcendentalists with whom she was closely associated, B. Alcott* for a time gained her enthusiastic support: She wrote that the city of Boston should pay him simply to live there (Journal, 13 January 1851, CD Papers, Massachusetts Historical Society). She participated in his Conversations in the 1850s and recorded invaluable "abstracts" of them, but looking back on the movement 40 years later, D flatly dismissed him, concluding that "he had no significant influence." To F. H. Hedge,* who as he grew older was an increasing favorite of hers, she assigned the central role in initiating the movement that became Transcendentalism. J. F. Clarke,* whose preaching she always admired and at whose Church of the Disciples D served for a time as Sunday School superintendent, sustained the longest close relationship with her of any of the Transcendentalists, acting as her personal and spiritual counselor.

Though her relationship with Emerson was never close, D was a persistent audience for his lectures and writings and had the pleasure of receiving many compliments from him on her own work. When she spoke before a joint committee of the Massachusetts legislature on women's legal rights in 1858, Emerson read the address, he told her, and took heed (Journal, 11 April 1858, CD Papers). In her journals,** she records her poignant observations of the ravages of age on Emerson and indeed on many of the original Transcendentalists, all of whom she outlived.

As a historian of the movement, D left three major published records. *Margaret and Her Friends* (1895), her reconstruction of Fuller's Conversation series that she attended in 1841, is interesting for its insights into the interactions of the group. *Historical Pictures Retouched* (1860) includes D's defense of Fuller. *Transcendentalism in New England* (1897) presents her reminiscences of the broader circle and suggests a philosophical link between the Transcendentalists and another intuitionalist, Anne Hutchinson. D's unpublished journals (covering more than three quarters of a century) remain, like Alcott's, a vivid and priceless chronicle of her long association with the other Transcendentalists.

References: No published monograph on D exists. Gary Sue Goodman, ''All About Me Forgotten: The Education of CHD (1822–1912)'' (Diss., Stanford Univ., 1987) is a good account of her early life, through 1840. Rose Norman, '' 'Sorella di Dante': CD and the Paternal Discourse,'' *A/B: Auto/Biography Studies* 5 (fall 1990): 124–39, treats D's depiction of herself in certain autobiographical writings. Joel Myerson traces the history of *Margaret and Her Friends*: ''CD's Reminiscences of Margaret Fuller,'' *HLB* 22 (October 1974): 414–28; and ''Mrs. D Edits Miss Fuller: The Story of *Margaret and Her Friends*,'' *PBSA* 72 (2nd Q 1978): 187–200. See also Helen R. Deese, ''Alcott's Conversations on the Transcendentalists: The Record of CD,'' *AL* 60 (March 1988): 17–25; and Deese, ''A New England Women's Network: Elizabeth Palmer Peabody, CHD, and Delia S. Bacon,'' *Legacy: A Journal of American Women Writers* 8 (fall 1991): 77–91. A useful treatment of D as a reformer is William Leach, *True Love and Perfect Union: The Feminist Reform of Sex and Society* (1980), 263–91.

Helen R. Deese

DANA, CHARLES ANDERSON (1819–1897), is important to the Transcendentalist movement primarily due to his association with Brook Farm.** D, a descendant of one of the early settlers of the Massachusetts Bay colony, was born in New Hampshire. After his business failed, D's father often sent his children to live with relatives for long periods, and at 12, D became a clerk at his uncle's store in Buffalo, New York; in his spare time, he educated himself by extensive reading, including study of Latin and Greek. Although academically prepared to begin at Harvard in 1839, he was forced to leave college in his junior year due to failing eyesight from overstudy. He was awarded an honorary degree 20 years later.

After leaving college, D became interested in G. Ripley's* Brook Farm experiment. In a letter to his sister, he announced his intention of ''living purely and justly and of acting from higher principles than the world recognizes. . . . the excellent society into which I should here be thrown, and a warm sympathy with the peculiar views of my friends decided me to come here.'' A cousin of Sophia Ripley,* D was one of the founding members who signed the Articles of Association for Brook Farm in September 1841, and he contributed $1,500 (the amount necessary to buy three shares) to the enterprise at its outset. His sister Anne also joined the community in 1844.

The young man listed his occupation as ''student'' but was soon to be known around the community as ''the Professor.'' D taught Greek, German, and occasionally Spanish, and when not occupied in intellectual labor, he worked on the farm. Due to his prior experience as a clerk, others considered him somewhat of a business expert, and he quickly became Ripley's right-hand man in most matters. He served in one or more executive offices in every year of Brook Farm's history. D also lectured and published in *The Dial*** and *The Harbinger*.**

Although initially hesitant about the conversion of Brook Farm to a Fourierist* phalanx contemplated by its leaders in the winter of 1843–44, he supported the community until it dissolved in 1847 and worked actively during that period to promote the cause of Fourierism in the United States. On the eve of the disastrous fire at Brook Farm, D married Eunice Macdaniel, another member of the community; at the conclusion of the Brook Farm experiment, he turned to journalism, serving for a short time on the Boston *Daily Chronotype.* He worked with H. Greeley* on the New York *Tribune* until a disagreement over the Civil War alienated him from his editor. Before he acquired the New York *Sun* in 1867, he worked with the U.S. War Department. D remained interested in government and reform movements, and his growing cynicism about politicians and labor unions colored the pages of his newspaper; the *Sun* led the opposition against President Grant's third-term reelection and took vociferous stands on most other issues.

References: Early accounts on D focus on his role as journalist. Charles J. Rosebault, *When D Was the* Sun (1931), Candace Stone, *D and the* Sun (1938), Alfred H. Fenton, *D of the* Sun (1941), and most recently, Janet E. Steele, *The* Sun *Shines for All: Journalism and Ideology in the Life of CA.D* (1993), briefly treat D's life at Brook Farm. The *Life of CA.D* (1907) by James Harrison Wilson discusses D's involvement in more detail. See also John Thomas Codman, *Brook Farm: Historic and Personal Memoirs* (1894); Lindsay Swift, *Brook Farm* (1900); Marianne Dwight, *Letters from Brook Farm: 1844–1847* (1928); and Henry W. Sams, *Autobiography of Brook Farm* (1958). Carl J. Guarneri, *The Utopian Alternative: Fourierism in Nineteenth Century America* (1991), treats D's involvement in Fourierism at some length.

Julie M. Norko

DARWIN, CHARLES (1809–1882), was known to the Transcendentalists first as the British naturalist and explorer of South America, then for proposing the notorious theory of evolution by natural selection. The earlier D was represented by the *Journal of Researches* (rev. ed., 1846), his account of the voyage of the *Beagle*, which H. Thoreau* read and annotated heavily in his journal** in 1851. For Thoreau, D was the wise and humane scientific traveler,** a model for his own activities. The evolutionary theories in *The Origin of Species* (1859) were generally assimilated by the Transcendentalists as scientific proof of the metaphysical law of organic** progress.

Thoreau first encountered D's *Journal* during an intensive period of reading in the works of scientific explorations. He responded enthusiastically to D's mixture of alert and detailed observation and humane response, noting after several days buried in D's book, "There would be this advantage in travelling in your own country even in your own neighborhood, that you would be so thoroughly prepared to understand what you saw." He went on to read many of the books mentioned by D, journeying vicariously to the earth's far corners, collecting information in his *Fact Book.*

The controversy over *Origin* attracted R. W. Emerson's* attention, though he was inclined to sympathize with his friend L. Agassiz* (who opposed D) and to read D as already adequately anticipated by the progressive and developmental theories of such as L. Oken.* Protoevolutionary theories had indeed been proposed before; D's innovation lay in proposing that species were related by lineal descent and in proposing a mechanism for evolutionary change. Although D's "descent with modification" did come to be widely accepted, few accepted Darwinian natural selection without meliorating its amoral materialism.

Thoreau read *Origin* immediately upon its arrival in Concord** in January 1860 and proceeded to argue with Emerson about it. His own scientific studies of seed distribution and forest succession proved deeply compatible with D's ideas, and his late work extends and applies much of D's reasoning. He also found joy in the vision of nature** thus revealed: "The developmental theory implies a greater vital force in nature, because it is more flexible and accommodating, and equivalent to a sort of constant *new* creation." While the contemporary Victorian imagination seized on the Malthusian cruelty of a nature in which only the fittest survive, it was characteristic of both D and Thoreau to express exhilaration and awe before the prodigious energy and proliferation of life, finding in it a fascination that could only be satisfied by further study.

References: The literature on D is immense. The first edition of *The Origin of Species* has been usefully reprinted by Harvard Univ. Press (1964). A. Gray's* reviews are collected in *Darwiniana*, ed. A. Hunter Dupree (1963). An excellent introduction to current D studies is *The Darwinian Heritage*, ed. David Kohn (1985). For D and the Transcendentalists, see references in Myerson (1984); and John B. Wilson, "D and the Transcendentalists," *JHI* 26 (1965): 286–90. Discussion of Thoreau and D may be found in John Aldrich Christie, *Thoreau as World Traveler* (1965), 74–82; Robert Sattelmeyer, *Thoreau's Reading* (1988), 80–90; Robert D. Richardson, Jr., *Henry David Thoreau* (1986), 242–45, 376–84; and Laura Dassow Walls, *Seeing New Worlds* (1995).

Laura Dassow Walls

DE WETTE, WILHELM MARTIN LEBERECHT (1780–1845), was a German theologian who sought to reconcile modern philosophy and biblical criticism with Christian faith and traditional piety. His efforts made him attractive to the Transcendentalists, who were struggling with the same issues. T. Parker* could write to D that "your works are more read & appreciated among us, than almost any of your theological contemporaries." Even A. Norton* had to admit that no theologian of "the German school" had had "more direct influence on opinion out of Germany."

Inside of Germany, his reputation as a reconciler contributed to his rapid rise in the academic world. After he presented his doctoral dissertation at the University of Jena in 1807, he taught at Heidelberg and then, beginning in 1810, at Berlin, where he associated closely with F. Schleiermacher.* But in 1819, his fortunes reversed. He was dismissed from his post by the Prussian authorities, who accused him of espousing subversive (liberal) political opinions. In 1822, he took a professorship at Basel, in Switzerland, where he taught until his death.

D has been called the father of modern biblical criticism; it was in the field of Old Testament criticism especially that he made his most original and lasting contributions to theology. He effectively discredited the surface history of the

Old Testament and made possible the first scholarly historical reconstruction of the development of Israelite religion. He himself believed that the first Jews had worshipped freely but that a priestly class had arisen and, with it, centralized religious control. The oldest Old Testament texts reflected the original Judaism, but as the religion was changed, so were the Scriptures. New texts were written, while the old ones were rewritten or redacted, all to justify the new order. Although D thought the Old Testament of no value as an actual history of the Jews, and in fact made up largely of myths, he held that it had great theological value. Its myths, he argued, could be appreciated aesthetically, as poetry. They were genuine expressions of ancient Jewish faith and set out in a symbolic way great religious truths. D always expressed reverence for the Hebrew Scriptures, and his translations of the Psalms were valued for their poetic beauty.

To the Transcendentalists, D's example served to counter the accusation of their opponents that theological radicalism inevitably led to irreligion. The high esteem in which the Transcendentalists held him can be measured in a concrete way: They translated and published four of his most important works. Parker produced the most substantial of these translations, the *Critical and Historical Introduction to the Canonical Scriptures of the Old Testament.* G. Ripley,* meanwhile, published two more as part of his *Specimens of Foreign Standard Literature*** series: the treatise *Human Life; or Practical Ethics* (trans. S. Osgood*) and what was probably D's most popular book, the autobiographical, didactic *Bildungsroman, Theodore; or a Skeptic's Conversion: History of the Culture of a Protestant Clergyman* (trans. J. F. Clarke*). All three of these translations, which appeared in the early 1840s, went through multiple editions. Finally, in 1858, Frederick Frothingham put out an English-language version of D's *Historico-Critical Introduction to the Canonical Books of the New Testament.*

REFERENCES: The starting point for further research on D is John W. Rogerson, *W. M. L. de Wette, Founder of Modern Biblical Criticism: An Intellectual Biography* (1992), which contains a comprehensive bibliography. Also useful are Ernst Staehelin, *Dewettiana. Forschungen und Texte zu Wilhelm Leberecht De Wettes Leben und Werk* (1956), and Andreas Staehelin, *Geschichte der Universität Basel, 1818–1835* (1959). The most thorough account of D's influence on American Transcendentalism remains Siegfried Pucknat, "D in New England," *PAPS* 101 (1958): 376–95; see, too, Pochmann (1957); and Perry Miller, "Theodore Parker: Apostasy within Liberalism," in *Nature's Nation* (1967), 134–49.

Dean David Grodzins

DEWEY, JOHN (1859–1952), prolific American philosopher and social theorist whose philosophy of Pragmatism—in which knowledge grows out of common human experience and serves, in turn, as an instrument for guiding future endeavors—represents an important transformation of certain Transcendentalist ideas. Ironically, D found Transcendentalism itself to run contrary to his own efforts, and his commentary on it is consistently negative. He identified Transcendentalism with a species of antiempiricism that grew out of Kantian notions of a priori knowledge. Such ideas, when taken to the extreme by some of Kant's** successors, led to the regrettable conclusion that knowledge and reality are independent of actual experience. In *Experience and Nature* (1925), D lamented that Transcendentalism, through its emphasis on the "supra-empirical self," had promoted a general lack of respect for the value of concrete experience and served to isolate the community of selves from natural existence. Similarly deleterious was the influence of Transcendentalism on education.** For D, the Transcendental theory of "pure rationalism" promoted knowledge as an end in itself, thus leading to a system of education the primary aim of which was to train gentlemen and other members of "the ruling class."

D was nonetheless careful to distinguish Kantian Transcendentalism from the thought of "Emerson,* etc." These New Englanders were Transcendentalists only "in a loose sense," emphasizing the intuitive, the spiritual, and the supersensuous not in opposition to empiricism but as a way of breaking through social, moral, and religious conventions. Such a view was consistent with D's own in that it challenged inflexible traditions by appealing to the variety and mutability of human experience. D saw Pragmatism as reaffirming the primacy of individual experience without isolating the individual from the community. Like W. James* before him, he found Emerson to be a worthy precursor in this endeavor.

In an address delivered in 1903 as part of the celebration of the centenary of Emerson's birth, D praised Emerson for asserting the dignity of individual experience in the face of impersonal intellectual systems that looked to transcend the details of real life. He also admired Emerson's commitment to demonstrating the connection between individual experience and the community that nurtures it. For D, Emerson's greatest contribution was his belief that the private insight achieves its fullest significance only through the medium of public communication. It was for this that D dubbed Emerson "the philosopher of Democracy," and it was this qualification of Transcendental individualism that formed the foundation of Pragmatism.

References: D wrote two brief articles on "Transcendentalism," one reprinted in JD, *The Middle Works* (1976), 2:258, and the other in *The Middle Works* (1979), 7:357–58. D's comparison of Pragmatism with Transcendentalism may be found in "The Bearing of Pragmatism upon Education," *The Middle Works* (1977), 4:178–91. "Ralph Waldo Emerson: Philosopher of Democracy" is in *The Middle Works*, vol. 3 (1977). For a discussion of the common heritage of Emerson and D, see Cornel West, *The American Evasion of Philosophy* (1989), and Giles Gunn, *Thinking Across the American Grain* (1992).

Charles Mitchell

DEWEY, ORVILLE (1794–1882), was a Unitarian** minister much admired for his eloquence and leadership in the church. Listed by R. W. Emerson* in his journal** as one of his benefactors, D was married to Emerson's cousin,

Louisa Farnham, and maintained an agreeable relationship with Emerson, who preached for him at his New Bedford church for three weeks in November 1827, before Emerson had his own church, and again in 1833, after Emerson had resigned from Second Church. While in New Bedford, Emerson became acquainted with Quakers,** most notably Elizabeth Rodman and Mary Rotch, who were to have some influence on his stand on the Lord's Supper.**

Though first ordained as a Congregational minister in 1819, within a year D connected himself with the Unitarian Church and became, in O. B. Frothingham's* words, "perhaps the greatest" preacher "that the Unitarian communion has produced" (*Recollections and Impressions*, 186). D ministered to the New Bedford church for ten years before ill health compelled him to resign and seek rest in Europe. Upon his return to the United States, he took over the pastoral reins of the Unitarian Church of the Messiah in New York City until 1849, when ill health again forced him from the pulpit. In addition to his ministerial duties, D served as president of the Unitarian Association (1845–47) and contributed articles for such journals as *The Christian Register*, *The Christian Examiner*,** and *North American Review*.** He published several volumes of sermons (1835, 1841, 1846) and was often engaged as a speaker, delivering the Phi Beta Kappa Address at Harvard in 1830 and the 1836 Dudleian Lecture and in 1851 conducting a course of lectures on "The Problem of Human Destiny."

D's reputation as a conservative is based on his politics; he was criticized for his stand on "gradual emancipation" and by Emerson for supporting the 1850 Fugitive Slave Law. But as a philosopher of religion and orator he was more liberal, making some of the same points that Emerson would about the natural theology** of the soul. In "On Human Nature" (1835), he speaks of the individual's "own capacious and unmeasured understanding," and in "The Moral Significance of Life" he states, "Man stands before us, visibly confined within the narrowest compass; and yet from this humble frame, stream out, on every side, the rays of thought, to infinity, to eternity, to omnipotence, to boundless grandeur and goodness" (1841). As this quote demonstrates, D well deserved his reputation for eloquence. Like others of his time, D understood the power of eloquence, and like Emerson he understood that true eloquence emanates from the soul. In an essay for the *NAR* (July 1829), D asserts, "The voice is the principal organ of the soul." In his Phi Beta Kappa Address, prefiguring Emerson's own Phi Beta Kappa Address, he insists that true genius is derived from study, not just from books, and that it must be put into action and stand "forth embodied in the form of living, commanding, irresistible eloquence."

References: For D's best sermons, see *Discourses on Various Subjects* (1835) and *Discourses on Human Life* (1841). See also *The Works of OD, D.D.* (1883) and *Autobiography and Letters of OD, D.D.*, ed. Mary E. Dewey (1883). For a modern appraisal of D's sermons, see Buell (1973); and Lawrence Buell, "The Unitarian Movement and the Art of Preaching in Nineteenth Century America," *AQ* (May 1972): 166–90.

Susan L. Roberson

DICKINSON, EMILY (1830–1886), may well be both the best- and least-known major American author. A recluse for most of her adult life and thereafter as mysterious a figure in the imaginations of later readers as she was to her small-town neighbors, D shared poems with her sister-in-law and other friends including T. W. Higginson,* who, with Mabel Loomis Todd, edited and promoted them in posthumous publications of the 1890s. In the 20th century, the startling brilliance of her tersely experimental verse has firmly established D as one of this country's preeminent poets—equivalent in stature to W. Whitman* though very different both in form and in tone. Like Whitman's, D's writings (letters as well as poems) show affinities to the Transcendentalists despite points of significant difference.

Born a generation after R. W. Emerson* and raised in an Amherst, Massachusetts, environment of Congregational orthodoxy, D found inspiration in his call to fresh vision, although her darker perspective and continuing impulse toward religious faith prevented full acceptance of his message. Emerson remained a suspect, radical figure in her community, drawing small numbers for his lectures. Whether D heard him speak on "The Beautiful in Rural Life" during his October 1857 visit remains uncertain. No record exists of her attendance or of their meeting when he visited on that occasion with her brother and sister-in-law. Yet Susan Dickinson's rapturous recollection of her houseguest expresses the poet's enthusiasm as well: "When I found he was to eat and sleep beneath our roof, there was a suggestion of meeting God face to face, or one of the Patriarchs of Hebrew setting, or, as 'Aunt Emily' says, 'As if he had come from where dreams are born.' " D read Emerson early and appreciatively, especially in the decade when she first committed herself to her poetic vocation. Benjamin Newton, her father's law clerk, presented her with *Poems* in 1850, and her letters feature direct allusions to the "Concord Hymn" and "Fable," among other poems. Her family library included copies of *The Conduct of Life*, *Society and Solitude*, *May-Day*, and *Essays*, along with books by H. D. Thoreau* and T. Parker.* Comments in her letters demonstrate her familiarity with these writers and her favorable response to what they had to say. Of Parker's *The Two Christmas Celebrations* she wrote, "I heard that he was 'poison.' Then I like poison very well." Describing an Amherst fire, she remarked, "The fire-bells are oftener now, almost, than the church-bells. Thoreau would wonder which did the most harm." Yet it was Emerson to whom she recurred most often, sending *Representative Men* to an ill friend as "a little Granite Book you can lean upon" and describing Holmes's* biography as "sweetly commended" to her Norcross cousins who—living in Concord**—mixed in the great man's literary circle. To the bewilderment of modern scholars, there is no evidence that Fanny and Lou Norcross made any effort to introduce D's poetry to Emerson in his old age any more than Susan Dickinson had shared manuscripts when he was her guest at the Evergreens. For literary counsel, D turned to Higginson but ignored his invitation to hear Emerson address a ladies' reading group in Boston. Geographically, intellectually, and emotionally, she kept her distance despite evident admiration. In April 1882, she grieved that "the Ralph Waldo Emerson—whose name my Father's Law Student taught me, has touched the secret Spring."

Public ascription to Emerson of D's "Success," which appeared anonymously (and without its author's consent) in Helen Hunt Jackson's 1878 anthology *A Masque of Poets*, calls attention to resemblances between her habit of seeking "consolation upside down" and his theory of compensation.** There is a kind of tragically Transcendentalist quality to D's haunting theme of "sumptuous Destitution," analogous to the grim vision of Emerson's "Fate." For her, value gained immediacy from loss.

Parallels may also be drawn between D's riddling assertion that "My Business is Circumference" (with all the imagery of circles, orbs, crowns, diadems, and diameters by which she worked out the implications of that assertion) and Emerson's "Circles"—especially when she applied that imagery to her "Flood subject" of immortality. "Circumference," a key word in D's private lexicon, loomed larger in her metaphoric imagination than it did in Emerson's, and in her case, it constricted rather than expanding the circle. She found barriers protective of consciousness, identity, sensory stimuli, and love even as they excited her curiosity about whatever fulfillment or abyss beckoned beyond the inevitable circumference of death.

D's poems reflect agreement with Emerson's pronouncement that "the eye is the first circle," though D (threatened at the height of her creativity in the early 1860s by some alarming disorder of her eyes) characteristically directed her gaze inward to reflect conditions of consciousness—often at points of psychic extremity. When looking outward and upward, however, she remarked skeptically: " 'Faith' is a fine invention/When Gentlemen can *see*—/But *Microscopes* are prudent/In an Emergency."

When optical vision afforded insight, it often did so by directing her attention to nature** as discovered in the cycles of the botanical year, the slant of winter light, and the behaviors of creatures she observed through her windows. D responded with romantic delight to all manifestations of life—bats as well as flowers and birds—and her most ebulliently playful poems often focused on her garden. Surging, metamorphosing, regenerative biological life assured her of creative energy ever at work within and around her. Yet she found it as hard to read nature's revelation in the comforting Transcendental sense of Thoreau's swelling, sympathetic pine needles as in the emblematic Christian sense. "Nature is a stranger yet," D declared. "The ones that cite her most / Have never passed her haunted house, / Nor simplified her ghost." Hers is a poetry of doubt, honestly confronted.

D's orphic, aphoristic, economical style in letters as well as poems links her to Emerson; yet one could argue that the austere life choices of this woman who celebrated her voluntary self-obliteration with the insouciant irony of "I'm Nobody! Who are you?" actually reflected Transcendental influences even more than did her writing. It would be as fatuous to trace her seclusion to reading of

Walden as to disappointment in love, but Concord writers may have fortified D for the radical simplification of life she achieved by closing the doors to her father's house and opening her spirit to empowerment that expressed itself in artistic creation. When this soul selected her own society, she made a rigorous, lonely, but fruitful choice that resulted in "the power and the glory" to which she looked forward as "post mortuary gifts."

REFERENCES: Scholarly editions of D's writing include *The Letters of ED* (1958) and *The Poems of ED* (1955), both sets edited by Thomas H. Johnson. Principal biographies are Richard B. Sewall, *The Life of ED* (1974), and Cynthia Griffin Wolff, *ED* (1986). For perspective on D's mixed response to Transcendentalism, see Albert J. Gelpi, *ED: The Mind of the Poet* (1965); Hyatt H. Waggoner, *American Poets from the Puritans to the Present* (1968); Joanne Feit Diehl, *D and the Romantic Imagination* (1981); and Evan Carton, *The Rhetoric of American Romance: Dialectic and Identity in Emerson, D, Poe, and Hawthorne* (1985).

Jane Donahue Eberwein

DOD, ALBERT B. (1805–1845), a professor of mathematics at Princeton from 1830 until his death, participated in the attack on Transcendentalism. Although ordained by the Presbytery of New York in 1828, and associated with Princeton theologians C. Hodge* and J. W. Alexander, D was known by the Princeton students for his success and power as teacher of mathematical science. But he is best known to students of Transcendentalism for his attack on it, V. Cousin,* and R. W. Emerson.* Dismayed by the "emptiness and fatuity" of "the German insanity," D, together with Hodge and Alexander, wrote two articles analyzing the New England religious situation. First published in *The Biblical Repository and Princeton Review*, Alexander and D's article on "Transcendentalism" (January 1839), and Hodge's "The School of Hegel*" (January 1840) were subsequently published together by A. Norton* as *Two Articles from the Princeton Review, Concerning the Transcendental Philosophy of the Germans and of Cousin and Its Influence on Opinion in This Country* (1840). This salvo against Transcendentalism and Emerson was later met by O. Brownson* in *The Boston Quarterly Review*** (July 1840).

A confirmed Calvinist, D (and his coauthor) complains of the new wave of philosophy acquired by "a double transportation, from Germany *via* France" that preaches skepticism and subjectivity. Tracing the influence of Kant** on the new thought, D complains that Cousin's brand of subjectivity is an "uncertain path for arriving at certainty" and criticizes Cousin for rejecting the God of Scriptures for "a shadowy abstraction." D also finds fault with the distinction made by Cousin and the Transcendentalists between Reason and Understanding and warns of "the dark and hopeless bewilderment" into which Cousin's thought is sure to plunge young Americans. D is no less critical or satirical of Emerson and his 1838 Address to the Harvard Divinity School.** He calls the address "nonsense and impiety" and Emerson an "imitation of Carlyle* . . . but without his genius." D's essay is consistently learned and his position founded on theological conservatism.

The only other essays published by Dod, reprinted in *Essays, Theological and Miscellaneous* (1847), give further evidence of his staunch Calvinism, the rational organization of his argument, and his biting sarcasm.

References: Excerpts from Norton's reprint of *Transcendentalism of the Germans and of Cousin* are included in Miller (1950), 231–40. D's only other work appears in *Essays, Theological and Miscellaneous, Reprinted from the Princeton Review, Second Series. Including the Contributions of the Late Rev. AB.D, D.D.* (1847).

Susan L. Roberson

DOUGLASS, FREDERICK (1818–1895), born a slave on the eastern shore of Maryland, became a leading abolitionist** orator. Though D was reviewed kindly by M. Fuller* and incorporated into sermons by T. W. Higginson,* his life paralleled rather than intersected with the lives of American Transcendentalists. Although D's life and writing bear the hallmarks of Transcendentalism—one of his most popular lectures was "Self-Made Men," written in 1855—D espoused communal rather than individualistic values.

If the defining event in his life as a slave came when he fought Edward Covey's sadistic abuse, the defining moment as an orator occurred at a church meeting in 1839 where D had passionately and eloquently denounced shipping slaves to Africa. W. L. Garrison* praised this speech in the *Liberator*, and D was invited to speak at the Massachusetts Anti-Slavery Society meeting in Nantucket.

In 1845, D published the *Narrative of the Life of FD*, which was widely circulated and enthusiastically received by abolitionists. That same year, D began an antislavery lecture tour in Ireland, Scotland, and England, where Anna Richardson, a Quaker,** purchased his freedom. Upon returning to the United States in 1847, D moved with his family to Rochester, where he began his own antislavery newspaper, the *North Star*. He thereby distanced himself from Garrison's organization, a necessary step in D's independence from the subtler forms of white control. In 1851, he published his only work of fiction, "The Heroic Slave," and renamed his newspaper *Frederick Douglass' Paper*, later continued as *Douglass' Monthly*. In 1855, D published his second autobiography, *My Bondage and My Freedom*.

D did not endorse violence generally nor J. Brown's* raid on Harpers Ferry in particular. Nonetheless, association with Brown cast suspicion on D, who fled to England in 1859. On returning to the United States and the Civil War, D recruited soldiers—including his sons Lewis and Charles—for the black regiments from Massachusetts. A respected public figure, D labored during and after the war for the enfranchisement of blacks, sometimes finding himself at odds with advocates of the vote for women.

In 1881 he published *The Life and Times of FD*, hoping to keep the nation focused on the story of slavery. Shortly after the death of his wife in 1882, D married Helen Pitts, a white woman previously hired as his secretary. D held several public offices in Washington, D.C., and, in 1889, became U.S. minister and consul to the troubled regime of President Hyppolite in Haiti, thus continuing his life's work of negotiating racial and political issues.

References: D has become increasingly the subject of scholarly biographical and critical studies. Two excellent biographies are Benjamin Quarles, *FD* (1968), and William McFeeley, *FD* (1991). Edited by William L. Andrews, *Critical Essays on FD* (1991) provides varied critical approaches to D's writings as well as Andrews's succinct overview of research on D in the introduction. Andrews's own essay in that volume, "*My Bondage and My Freedom* and the American Literary Renaissance of the 1850's," helps to situate D's life and accomplishments within the currents of the New England Transcendentalists.

Patricia Dunlavy Valenti

DUYCKINCK, EVERT (1816–1878), was a leading editor, anthologist, and literary journalist of the antebellum generation whose influence as a promoter of American letters was at its peak during the high years of American Transcendentalism. D, however, was personally removed from the intellectual sources of the movement, distanced from it by background, and suspicious of its temper. In fact, given his breeding and temperament, it is a curiosity that D became a prime supporter of some of the leading figures in the movement, including R. W. Emerson,* H. Thoreau,* and M. Fuller.*

Born and raised in New York City, D attended Columbia College and made the grand tour of Europe before settling down in New York, his home to the end of his life. Freed by his father's legacy from the necessity of committing himself to a professional career, D devoted himself instead to the cause of letters. During the 1840s, he became a leading figure among the cultural nationalists of the city and nation and an ardent supporter of international copyright as a basis for securing due protection to both American and foreign authors. It was within this context that around 1840 he began encouraging and promoting the work of various Transcendentalists, as well as other New England writers (such as Hawthorne*) on the movement's fringe. Then, in 1845, when he assumed the literary editorship of the New York publishing house of Wiley and Putnam, he actively sought to include the work of various New England writers in the firm's new Library of American Books. Though personally repelled by the pantheism** of Emerson and Transcendentalism generally, D worked hard to entice Emerson (unsuccessfully) and Hawthorne (successfully) to write for the series, agreed to publish in book form the uncollected reviews Fuller had originally written for the New York *Tribune*, and accepted Thoreau's unsolicited *A Week on the Concord and Merrimack Rivers* (although Thoreau was unable to come to acceptable terms with Wiley).

Under D's editorial guidance, Wiley and Putnam became a primary address in the mid-1840s for New England Transcendentalism, as well as for works important to the Transcendentalists by Carlyle* and Goethe.* A decade later, D and his brother George compiled the fullest anthology to date of American letters, their *Cyclopaedia of American Literature* (1855), which furthered the important cultural work D had been doing for 15 years of opening up and promoting the field of American letters.

References: The modern biography of D has yet to be written. When it is, it will mine the important D collection at the New York Public Library, which includes his unpublished diary and a rich trove of private papers and letters. Nor is there in print a book-length study of D, who has typically been treated parenthetically in studies of other, better-known literary figures. Useful modern sources on D include John Stafford, *The Literary Criticism of ''Young America''* (1952); George Edwin Mize, *The Contributions of E A. D to the Cultural Development of Nineteenth-Century America* (Diss., New York Univ., 1954); Perry Miller, *The Raven and the Whale* (1956); and Ezra Greenspan, ''ED and the History of Wiley and Putnam's Library of American Books, 1845–1847,'' *AL* 64 (December 1992): 677–93.

Ezra Greenspan

DWIGHT, JOHN SULLIVAN (1813–1893), was born in Boston and graduated from Harvard College (1832) and Harvard Divinity School** (1836). Though briefly and unhappily a Unitarian** minister in Northampton, Massachusetts, before joining the Brook Farm** community (1841), he was accepted by notables in the movement, but always with a hint of condescension, perhaps reflective of his own insecurities both intellectual and social. His lifelong interest was in music, early evidenced in his music criticism in the Fourierist* *Harbinger*** (1845–48) but most effectively demonstrated in his editorship of *Dwight's Journal of Music* in Boston (1852–81). Indeed, this landmark body of music criticism remains our primary source for the history of music in New England from the earliest concerts (orchestral) to the founding of the Boston Symphony Orchestra.

This quintessential Transcendentalist musician, however, evidences both the strengths and weaknesses inherent in approaching music from this orientation. As music critic he boldly made provocative assumptions: ''imagination . . . give[s] form and figure to invisible *felt* realities. It moulds its recognition of a divine essence into an image. . . . Music . . . hints of what cannot be uttered'' (''Music in Boston,'' *The Harbinger*, 1:155). Yet at the same time this completely amateur musician—he was his own flute and piano instructor with almost no knowledge of harmony and counterpoint—could freely make rash judgments about the most brilliant composers of Europe: ''We look upon him [Meyerbeer] as the musician who of all others has done the most to pervert and demoralize the art of music in our day. He is the founder . . . of the whole school of 'effect.' Berlioz, and Liszt, and Wagner, and Verdi, . . . all take after this false prophet'' (''Meyerbeer's Inspirations,'' *Dwight's Journal of Music* 28 [26 September 1868]: 286). He defended ''pure'' music, praising particularly Beethoven's *Sixth [Pastoral] Symphony*, and attacked Wagner's music, which utilizes words, with the admonition: ''No, Herr Wagner! The great tone poet does not need the word poet to impregnate his creative genius, or to furnish him the wherewithal to express himself'' (''Richard Wagner,'' *Dwight's Journal of Music* 30 [30

July 1870]: 286). At the same time, he preferred the *Ninth Symphony* of Beethoven above anything that Wagner wrote, despite its use of a text; and he unabashedly embraced Mozart's *Don Giovanni* and Handel's *Messiah* as music of the highest order.

The last 20 years of D's life were spent as resident librarian and president of the Harvard Musical Association, but though he was the recognized "grand old man" of music in late 19th-century Boston, he was bypassed in the opening of the new Music Hall and the founding of the emerging Boston Symphony Orchestra. He was a man who had served Boston music with great dignity yet lived to see his own obsolescence as "professional" music critics began to emerge on the scene.

References: The best biography remains G. W. Cooke,* *JSD: Brook-Farmer, Editor, and Critic of Music* (1898; rpt. 1969), though it is blind to many of D's human (and intellectual) weaknesses. Walter L. Fertig, "JSD, Transcendentalist and Literary Amateur of Music" (Diss., Univ. of Maryland, 1952), gives a good balance to Cooke's biographical data; and William A. Call, "A Study of the Transcendental Aesthetic Theories of JSD" (Diss., Univ. of Illinois at Urbana-Champaign, 1971), is particularly useful in his analysis of D's approach to utilizing Transcendentalism in music criticism. A bibliography by William G. Heath appears in Myerson (1984), 131–34.

David P. McKay

E

ECKERMANN, JOHANN PETER (1792–1854), was the author of *Conversations with Goethe* in the Last Years of His Life* (pts. 1 & 2, 1836; pt. 3, 1848). By presenting a well-integrated, harmonious portrait of the old Goethe and providing a treasury of Goethean wisdom, E defined, more than anyone else, posterity's image of Goethe as the Sage. E's *Conversations* also made Goethe more accessible and more palatable to many Transcendentalists who were troubled by the master's own works for reasons aesthetic as well as moral.

M. Fuller's* first published book was her translation of E's *Conversations with Goethe* (1839). By 1839, only the first two parts of E's work were available, and even these Fuller did not translate completely, leaving out, for instance, all material concerning works of Goethe not yet available in English. Fuller nevertheless captured the spirit and richness of the *Conversations* so well that John Oxenford found her text very useful when preparing his own complete and long-standard translation (1850). Fuller's translation not only was an important chapter in her long endeavor to come to terms with Goethe intellectually and psychologically, but it also introduced many Transcendentalists to aspects of Goethe's personality and thought not to be found in any of his works. T. W. Higginson's* response to Fuller's translation is enlightening: ''[I]t brought [Goethe] nearer to me than any other book, before or since, has ever done'' (*Margaret Fuller Ossoli* [1884], 189).

R. W. Emerson,* who read the *Gespräche mit Goethe* in the original before he acquired a copy of Fuller's translation, found that ''Eckermann was full of fine things & helps one much in the study of Goethe.'' In his journal,** he copied passages presenting Goethe's opinions on such matters as the qualities that make a poet, the realism of the ancients, the spiritual limitations of the French, the symbolic nature of life, the historical superiority of ''objective'' to ''subjective'' epochs, and the virtues of Homer's epics. Goethe's extraordinary range and profundity of thought as displayed in the *Conversations* were a major factor in Emerson's appreciation of him as the only man able to cope with the modern world's "multiplicity . . . this rolling miscellany of facts and sciences"; Goethe's status as "the philosopher of this multiplicity" made him, in Emerson's view, *the* representative of the modern age, "the soul of his century."

References: Russell E. Durning, *Margaret Fuller, Citizen of the World* (1969), 109–14, discusses in considerable detail Fuller's translation of E's *Gespräche mit Goethe*.

Gustaaf Van Cromphout

ELLIS, CHARLES MAYO (1811–1878), Boston lawyer and reformer, is generally thought to be the author of the anonymously published *An Essay on Transcendentalism* (1842), published by Crocker & Ruggles in Boston. Although the authorship has been variously attributed to Henry Winsor, William Dexter Wilson, and even to R. W. Emerson,* the preponderance of evidence points to E.

E grew up on the farm in West Roxbury that eventually became Brook Farm.** He was graduated from Harvard in 1839 and was admitted to the bar in Boston in 1842. He became active in the antislavery movement, serving for the defense in the famous Anthony Burns case and helping to defend T. Parker* when he was cited for contempt of court in that case. He and Parker were lifelong friends, and he was long active in Parker's church. E also wrote *The History of Roxbury Town* (1847) and numerous political and legal pamphlets. According to his obituary in the 25 January 1878 *Boston Advertiser*, he had by the time of his death quite un-Transcendentally "accumulated considerable property."

The *Essay* discusses such topics as "Principles," "Progress," "Criticism," "Art," "Government," "Religion," and "Moral Obligation," giving comprehensive summaries of the most commonly held beliefs of the Transcendentalists as a group. It, however, must be kept in mind that the Transcendentalists were all extreme individualists and that therefore one cannot assume that any of the precepts set forth in this pamphlet would necessarily be accepted by any particular individual in the group. Yet it also must be added that the author of this pamphlet was remarkably astute in setting forth the principles so that there is surprisingly little in it that any particular Transcendentalist would not accept. The fact that there is a highly favorable review of it in *The Dial*** (3 [January 1843]: 406–11), by C. Lane,* indicates its general acceptance by the group.

References: While the original pamphlet is now extremely rare, it has been reprinted in facsimile by Scholars' Facsimiles & Reprints (1954), with an introduction by Walter Harding that discusses the various authorial attributions and gives further details of E's life and publications.

Walter Harding

EMERSON, CHARLES CHAUNCY (1808–1836), Ralph Waldo's* youngest brother, was also the sibling with whom he was most intimate. C followed three of his brothers—William,* Waldo, and Edward—to Harvard, graduating in 1829 as valedictorian. Lacking Edward's brilliance, he was nonetheless more successful academically than Waldo; at Harvard, he received the Boylston Prize for elocution and the Bowdoin Prize for his senior thesis. Upon earning his undergraduate degree, C commenced the study of law and earned grand praise from D. Webster.* Shortly after announcing his engagement to E. Hoar* in 1835, he took over the law office of his prospective father-in-law, S. Hoar,* who had been elected to Congress the previous November. That C held more traditional religious views than Waldo is apparent in his teaching Sunday school with Elizabeth in E. Ripley's* church during the period of their engagement.

In spring 1831, he and Waldo traveled to Vermont, where they met university president J. Marsh,* whose edition of Coleridge's* *Aids to Reflection* (1829) was soon to become a primary influence on the development of American Transcendentalism. Because Waldo and C had been discussing the writing of Coleridge together in recent years, they would have taken special pleasure in this meeting with his foremost proponent in the United States. During their travel into the ''wilds'' of New Hampshire and Vermont that summer, the brothers had much time for the type of literary discussion they both relished. In addition to their interest in Coleridge, they found common ground in their admiration of Shakespeare.** On this topic C seems to have reached the deeper appreciation first and led Waldo to reread Shakespeare more sensitively and sympathetically. In 1840 he published C's short essay on Shakespeare in the opening issue of *The Dial*.**

Waldo's closeness to C has often been noted by biographers and critics, but its significance in his aesthetic development has been generally underestimated. Jonathan Bishop characterized C as Waldo's ''alter ego.'' More than any of the Emerson siblings, Waldo could, and did, turn to C for counsel and solace. Upon his brother's death, Waldo lamented to Lidian* over the loss of ''my ornament my wisdom & my pride.'' He acknowledged to H. Martineau,* too, that C ''was my philosopher, my poet, my hero, my Christian,'' and Martineau herself praised him for his courageous advocacy of free speech when she was confronted by hostility during her visit to Boston. During the first year of her marriage, when C would dine with them at the Old Manse** in Concord,** Lidian admitted to her sister that sometimes she was astonished over being ''housed with these two wonderful beings,'' Waldo and C, whose conversation so impressed her.

Waldo recognized much to admire in the short life of his youngest brother, who had embodied ''the fourfold perfection of good sense, of genius, of grace & of virtue.'' The depth of his grief is universalized in two passages of *Nature*, which become more poignant with the reader's awareness that ''the dear friend'' lost to death in the closing sentences of chapters one and five are anonymous references to C.

References: The best sources for the limited scholarship on C are the major biographies and biocritical studies of R. W. Emerson, which should be consulted in conjunction with *L*. See Jonathan Bishop, *Emerson on the Soul* (1964), 175.

Sanford E. Marovitz

EMERSON, EDWARD WALDO (1844–1930), edited the works of his father, R. W. Emerson,* and commemorated American Transcendentalism in his own works. As a young man, he accompanied H. Thoreau* on many nature** outings. After graduating from Harvard College in 1866 and the Medical College in 1874, he served as physician in Concord, Massachusetts,** until his father's death in 1882, when he turned his attention to full-time writing. He was also a painter and instructor at the Boston Museum of Fine Arts, a fellow of the American Academy of Arts and Sciences, and a member of the Massachusetts Historical Society.

Reported to be of frail health, he was unable to serve in the Union Army. He married Annie Shepard Keyes of Concord on 19 September 1874. All of their six children, except a son Raymond, predeceased them.

REFERENCES: E's works include ''Memoir of Ralph Waldo Emerson'' (1888; rpt. as *Emerson in Concord,* 1889); *Life and Letters of Charles Russell Lowell* (1907); *Henry Thoreau as Remembered by a Young Friend* (1917); and *Early Years of the Saturday Club*** (1918). Editions include the annotated Centenary Edition of his father's works (1903–04) and the *Journals of Ralph Waldo Emerson* (1909–14) with Waldo Emerson Forbes. He collaborated with Moorfield Storey on *Ebenezer Rockwood Hoar* (1911).

Karen L. Kalinevitch

EMERSON, ELLEN TUCKER (1839–1909), was the first daughter of Ralph Waldo* and Lidian Jackson Emerson.* She was named after Emerson's first wife, Ellen Louisa Tucker Emerson, and on the day of her birth, Emerson wrote in his journal,** ''Lidian, who magnanimously makes my gods her gods, calls the babe Ellen.'' Miss E, for she never married, devoted her adult life to caring for her parents, the often ill Lidian and the aging Emerson. In Emerson's mature years she was his traveling companion, accompanying him to Egypt in 1872 after their home burned, and general assistant—his memory, judgment, and manager of his literary compositions. She helped J. E. Cabot* edit her father's literary remains. As Emerson's mind deteriorated, she stood by his side to prompt him when he gave a lecture, as she did on 6 February 1878, when he read ''Education'' at the Concord** Lyceum.**

Her own literary endeavors consist of a biography of her mother, *The Life of Lidian Jackson Emerson* (not published until 1980) and her many letters, collected by Edith Gregg. In both cases, E provides an intimate look at the Emerson household, its members and many visitors, and at social life in Concord until her mother's death in 1892, when both records close. The biography of her mother not only brings to light the woman behind the man but illuminates 19th-century middle-class domestic and religious life, education, medical care, and attitudes toward death. *The Letters of ETE* spans nearly half a century of her experiences as the daughter of Ralph and Lidian Emerson, from age 15 to her mother's death. Though her brother Edward* recognized their worth and urged her to publish the letters, their chief value lies in their closeness to the Emerson household. Most of the letters are in the nature of a ''journal,'' recounting what she did and the people she met. She was devoted to her family and relished her role as sister and aunt; most of the letters collected are addressed to her younger sister, Edith.

E was known for her kindness, modesty, and Christianity. Mrs. Daniel Chester French said of E that she "lived in the realm of the Beatitudes." E was well educated, attending schools headed by L. Agassiz* and F. Sanborn,* and was quite adept at foreign languages. When she was not taking care of her parents, she was busy with community and church organizations; she was the first woman elected to serve on the Concord school committee, and for many years, she taught Sunday School for the First Parish Church. She was not, however, an advocate of Women's Suffrage, differing here with her mother. Indeed, she seemed to be a woman of the 19th century more than one about to announce the 20th. People often remarked about her quaint style of clothes; Engel notes that "she dressed as she had in about 1860 and never changed with the varying styles."

References: For a personal glimpse at Miss E, see *I Remember the Emersons*, by Mary Miller Engel (1941), and the introductions to *The Life of Lidian Jackson Emerson*, ed. Delores Bird Carpenter (1980), and *The Letters of ETE*, 2 vols., ed. Edith E. W. Gregg (1982).

Susan L. Roberson

EMERSON, LIDIAN JACKSON (1802–1892), of Plymouth, Massachusetts, became R. W. Emerson's* second wife in 1835. She was, at this time, a devout Christian; an avid gardener and animal lover; a witty conversationalist and feisty debater; a woman dedicated to good works, including antislavery activities; and withal a shrewd commentator on contemporary foibles.

Though a busy housekeeper and the mother of four children, L was no meek helpmate. Her generous but rigorous insights delighted such luminaries as H. D. Thoreau,* M. Fuller,* A. B. Alcott,* W. Phillips,* and E. P. Peabody.* But L never considered herself a Transcendentalist; on the contrary, she found many of the movement's tenets repugnant and heretical. Her spiritual orientation was based on a Swedenborgian** reading of evangelical Christianity and sanctioned by a vision of Christ she was granted as a young adult.

Resistant to the Congregationalism of her youth, L became a Unitarian** and found her faith a comfort during the hectic period she mocked as "Transcendental Times." When her husband left off family prayers, and preached that Jesus was only an exceptional young man, L suffered, grieved, and held on to her belief in a personal God. It is hard to know how Emerson utilized his wife's belief system. He claimed to appreciate her loyal opposition: "My wife L is an incarnation of christianity," he told T. Carlyle,* "& keeps my philosophy from Antinomianism." And he did try out his fledgling speeches and essays on her combative intellect. But his journals** reveal no remorse about L's painful disillusionment concerning her husband's philosophy.

With the possible exception of Abby Alcott, Waldo's circle found L attractive.

Thoreau admired her deeply—some have thought he fell in love—and J. Very* was even less discreet. Fuller and L enjoyed a cautious friendship; and when Fuller died, L mourned her, recalling, ''She did me the honour and it was truly an honour to care for me somewhat.'' Concord** neighbors would have protested that L underrated her importance: ''[T]he world little knew,'' one source reported, ''how much Mr Emerson owed to his wife, that he would have been a different man with another woman.''

Though L left few records apart from personal letters, one short text indicates the astringent wit cherished by her family and friends. In the text daughter E. Emerson* called ''the Transcendental Bible,'' L satirized her husband's intellectual circle. ''Never confess a fault,'' reads one of the new commandments. ''You should not have committed it and who cares whether you are sorry?'' Another sanctions selfishness: ''Loathe and shun the sick. They are in bad taste, and may untune us for writing the poem floating through our mind.'' A few commend reformers' complacent elitism: ''Despise the unintellectual, and make them feel that you do by not noticing their remark and question lest they presume to intrude into your conversation.'' Finally, a want of compassion is adduced as characteristic of the Newness: ''It is mean and weak to seek for sympathy; it is mean and weak to give it. Great souls are self-sustained and stand ever erect, saying only to the prostrate sufferer 'Get up, and stop your complaining.' '' This short essay pleased Emerson mightily: Swarmed by radicals, visionaries, and downright cranks, he was delighted that his ''Queenie'' had distilled their excesses into a creed.

L held strong views. She believed, for instance, that marriage to an unfit mate was slavery, a noose that childless women should feel free to slip. Yet when her aid was requested, she would debate with Shaker** elders on the propriety of godly marriage. In time, she would campaign vigorously, though within her own social circle, for women's suffrage, and she supported antislavery activities before her husband did. A sheet anchor and doughty fighter, generous opponent and pragmatic wit, L remains one of the least known of the American Transcendentalists.

References: The two best sources of information are Delores Bird Carpenter, ed., *Selected Letters of LJE* (1987), and Ellen Tucker Emerson, *Life of LJE*, ed. Delores Bird Carpenter (1980).

Barbara Ryan

EMERSON, MARY MOODY (1774–1863), was a vital forerunner of Transcendentalism and a primary source of nephew R. W. Emerson's* thought and language. She has long been seen as a religious guide to his childhood and an aged, ''eccentric'' figure in the movement. Waldo himself offered a more far-reaching interpretation in his 1869 portrait of M, calling her life a ''fruit of Calvinism and New England'' that marked ''the precise time when the power of the old creed yielded to the influence of modern science and humanity.'' But only in the 1980s and 1990s, as her letters and ''Almanack'' (diary) are edited and interpreted, have the range of her voice and extent of her influence been emerging.

She was the "fruit of Calvinism" because raised apart from her Concord** siblings in the household of a grandmother and aunt in Malden, Massachusetts, who had directly experienced the First Great Awakening. Intellectually precocious in an impoverished setting, M knew Milton's** *Paradise Lost* from a coverless copy long before learning its author or title. She also read and reread Jonathan Edwards, finding his defense of God's sovereignty in *Freedom of the Will* her own best opening to become "*an agent*." Her grounding in orthodoxy was expressed in a lifelong preoccupation with sin and grace, redemption through Christ, and fervid, intuitive experience of divinity.

M's intuitionism incorporated a strain of Liberal and Enlightenment thought, however, when as a young woman (now reconnected to her Concord family) she read books available in their Harvard-based intellectual world. From Samuel Clarke she learned of post-Newtonian "natural religion,"** from Richard Price and Joseph Butler a Platonic** view of the mind's ascent to God, from Mark Akenside and Edward Young an affirmation of imaginative and sublime perception. Her own views of the religious imagination and of natural history** as means "to infer the operations of divine wisdom" were published in the *Monthly Anthology*** in 1804, despite the fundamental disagreement of her editor-brother William. But such philosophic understanding justified her experiences of inward dancing to "the music of [her] own imajanation" at a dull church service and savoring the "sublime in perception" during a solar eclipse, both reported in her contemporary Almanack. These printed and manuscript texts together amount to an unparalleled proto-Transcendentalist viewpoint within the *Anthology*'s cultural world. Consciously bypassing Locke,** M was translating New Light pietism into a naturalized, individualistic "enthusiasm." By 1820 she called herself a Unitarian** but was finding deepest affinity to Staël's** *Germany* and Wordsworth's* *Excursion*.

A single woman by choice, M was also intensely devoted to shaping protegés of both sexes to heights of intellect and spirit. After William Emerson's death in 1811 she played a direct role in the nurture and education of his sons, including Waldo. M and Waldo's exchange of letters in the 1820s, now available from both sides, is the crucial dialogic text through which his Transcendentalism took form. M recommended Price, Plato,** Staël, and Hindu scripture to him before he knew them elsewhere; she urged solitude and retirement, "sentiment" over "sense"; she believed in his Muse and vocation as priest and poet. "We love nature**—to individuate ourselves in her wildest moods—" she wrote in 1821, in a stunning 15-year anticipation of his manifesto *Nature*," . . . but we better love to cast her off and rely on that only which is imperishable." Waldo copied this letter among others into his journal** as the wisdom of "Tnamurya," anagram for "Aunt Mary."

M stopped short of a fully Romantic epistemology, dissenting from any "real or pretended idealism"** that produced doubt rather than confirmation of God.

But by 1830 she had adopted Coleridge's* terms *Reason* and *Understanding* into her sense of God-centered human life. In 1832, amidst disappointment at Waldo's humanized divinity and resignation from the ministry, she also admired the ''extravagance'' with which he questioned institutions and predicted that ''free from ties to forms & instruction [he] . . . may find in the religion of a solitary imajanation that nearer to the heart.'' The thought was both characteristic of her utterance and prophetic of his.

Though her major adult home was a farm near the White Mountains in Maine, she participated often in Concord's formal and informal conversations.** Usually she played an antagonistic role, but on much narrower grounds of dispute than the polarities of Transcendentalist ''heresy'' and Calvinist orthodoxy that generations of critics have asserted. Casting herself in the position of learner, she devoted passionate energy to the antislavery cause, sought Fuller's* *Woman in the Nineteenth Century*, corresponded about theology with Peabody,* and conversed with H. Thoreau* when he was in his thirties and she her eighties. Her last Concord conversation was an 1858 defense of B. Alcott's* view of the Moral Law against the attacks of H. James, Sr.* In her rebuttal to James, she invoked the authority of Samuel Clarke, so appearing to those gathered as a relic of the past but also showing the real affinity between her own natural religion and Transcendentalist views.

References: Primary sources include M's manuscript letters and Almanacks (Houghton Library) and contributions to the *Monthly Anthology* (1: 453–54, 456–57, 646–47; 2: 140–41, 342–44). See *The Selected Letters of MME*, ed. Nancy Craig Simmons (1993), and R. W. Emerson's four ''MME'' notebooks (Houghton), printed essay (*W*, 10: 397–433), and many letters to and journal entries about her. Evelyn Barish began the reinterpretation of Waldo and M's relationship in ''Emerson and 'The Magician': An Early Prose Fantasy,'' *ATQ* 31 (1976), then incorporated a reading of their early letters into *Emerson: The Roots of Prophecy* (1989). David R. Williams delved into Waldo's transcriptions of M in ''The Wilderness Rapture of MME: One Calvinist Link to Transcendentalism,'' *SAR* 1986: 1–16. Phyllis Cole studied the diary in ''The Advantage of Loneliness: MME's Almanacks, 1802–1855,'' in *Emerson: Prospect and Retrospect*, ed. Joel Porte (1982), and traced the longer family lineage in ''From the Edwardses to the Emersons,'' *CEA Critic* 49 (1986): 70–77.

Phyllis Cole

EMERSON, RALPH WALDO (1803–1882), was a lecturer and an essayist whose power to stimulate through language that was bold and at the same time elusive made him a central figure in the Transcendentalist movement. Ordained a Unitarian** minister at Boston's Second Church, E loved preaching but quickly became frustrated at the rigidities of ''historical Christianity,'' as he called any religion that tried to derive its authority from past events. He resigned his position at the Second Church and, after a tour of Europe, returned to Boston to make a career as a lecturer and writer. His essays spread his fame beyond Boston and drew to him younger admirers, inspired by his call to trust their intuitions to lead them to greatness. Though his writings were initially denounced as nonsense by some, as heresy by others, E gradually won acceptance at home and abroad as America's foremost man of letters, the man whose private meditations, recorded faithfully in his journal** and then made public in his writings, were marked by such candor and originality of expression that they began a new era in American literature.

Born in Boston, E was the son of a liberal clergyman who found time during his ministry at the First Church in Boston to encourage literary enterprises like the *Monthly Anthology*.** In later life when E was called upon for memories of his father, he could remember only "a rather social gentleman, but somewhat severe to us children." The father died in 1811, when E was only eight. Ruth Haskins Emerson, his widow, was left with five sons and few sources of income. Her struggle to keep the family together was successful, though their poverty was sometimes severe. The family's cohesiveness was strong, and the love E felt for his brothers remained all his life the standard by which he measured the strength of other human ties.

In 1812 he entered the Boston Latin School, and in 1817 he enrolled as a freshman at Harvard. His career there was undistinguished, though he did win second prize in the Bowdoin competition for an essay on the character of Socrates. He also began while at Harvard to keep a journal. The habit of depositing his meditations in the notebooks he came to call his "savings bank" gave him practice in writing, which he badly needed, and made his intense self-scrutiny productive. The paragraphs he wrote in the journals were fully formed blocks of text he could copy out when he wanted to construct a longer discourse—a sermon, lecture, or essay. They also came to seem the natural repositories of his thought, the form into which his ideas most easily flowed. Freed from the obligation to connect ideas discursively or to reconcile them with one another, E could express each idea with a vividness that places the journals of his maturity among great monuments of English prose in the 19th century.

After graduating from Harvard in 1821, E spent several unhappy years as a schoolteacher, helping to finance the education of his younger brothers, while he tried to decide on a career. Shortly before his twenty-first birthday in 1824, he dedicated himself to the Church. He began studying divinity at Harvard in 1825, though poor health prevented him from taking a degree, and was approbated to preach in 1826. For the next few years, he supplied pulpits in a number of Massachusetts and New Hampshire cities and towns; on one of these visits he met his future wife Ellen Tucker. Though offers of pastorates were made to him, he refused permanent settlement until his health should improve and his supply of written sermons increase. In 1828 he was suddenly called to supply the pulpit of the Second Church in Boston when its pastor, H. Ware, Jr.,* was forced to retire because of poor health.

Formally ordained as junior pastor on 11 March 1829, the 25-year-old E in fact had full responsibility for Second Church. The discipline of weekly sermon writing gave E habits of regular composition that lasted throughout his life and partially compensated for the discontinuity of inspiration he complained of frequently in his journals. More important, the act of preaching taught him what he later called the capital secret of the orator's art—to convert life into truth.

The Unitarian tradition of preaching was hospitable to the kind of intensity E valued, and its emphasis on self-culture, its belief in the moral sense as God's voice within the individual, formed the core of his mature faith. But Unitarianism still clung to Christian traditions that to E seemed outmoded, if not indeed superstitious. Chief among these was the Lord's Supper.** E felt so strong an antipathy to the rite that he requested to be allowed to celebrate it as a commemorative service only, without the bread and wine, and preached a sermon explaining both his theological and personal reasons. When the church declined to accept the proposed changes, E resigned his pastorate, though he remained on affectionate terms with his church and, for several years afterward, continued to serve as a supply preacher in various Unitarian pulpits.

The years of his ministry (1829–32) coincided with the years of his brief marriage to Ellen Tucker (1829–31), whose death from tuberculosis was only the first of the bereavements the disease was to cause E in the next few years. Ill himself, E set out for Europe after his resignation from the Second Church on a tour that succeeded in restoring his health and introducing him to a wider world. He admired Catholic architecture and monastic simplicity in Italy. A visit to the Jardin des Plantes in Paris, where specimens were arranged in a cabinet of natural history,** gave him a new sense that Nature** was a huge, interconnected organism upheaving with life, whose most savage and grotesque forms nevertheless corresponded to something in "man the observer." The disappointment he felt when he discovered that the writers who had seemed all-wise to him in America—Landor, Coleridge,* Wordsworth*—proved to be ordinary mortals when he called on them in person made him more confident ever afterward that the new aspirant for greatness need not feel overawed by men already called great. (The friendship he began with Carlyle,* however, proved to be richly satisfying, if sometimes stormy.)

When he returned to Boston, E was fortunate enough to discover that his need to find a new profession coincided with the rise of the adult education movement in America. The appetite for lectures on a variety of topics was great, and a competent lecturer who provided a course of winter lectures to a city or country lyceum** could earn an income from his writing. E's income from lectures, from his supply preaching, and from his first wife's legacy was enough to allow him in 1834 to leave Boston for Concord,** his family's ancestral home. He married Lydia Jackson (Lidian Emerson*) of Plymouth, a woman whose spirituality seemed to him Asiatic in its largeness but who also exhibited a gift for satire, as his journal accounts of her trenchant comments on people and affairs make clear.

E's lectures and lecture series covered a variety of topics: natural history, Italy, English literature, biography. His titles for series were often as general as "Human Culture" or "The Present Age," but the pungency of his language and the originality of his ideas, delivered in a "rich baritone" (as J. R. Lowell* remembered it), kept people returning year after year. "There are some of us who would hardly consent to be young again," Lowell wrote in 1868, "if it were at the cost of our recollection of Mr. Emerson's first lectures during the consulate of Van Buren."

In spring 1836 E began work on a longer project, this time destined for print rather than for the lecture hall. He had long enjoyed tracing evidences that nature was a mute scripture, that particular natural objects had correspondence** to moral ideas. Now he tried to work out a more ambitious scheme, destined to show that the key to the riddle of nature lay in man. Man is the final cause of nature, the reason for her existence. She feeds and clothes him, satisfies his sense of beauty, gives him a richly metaphoric language with which to express his ideas, and disciplines him through tragedy to a detachment from her outward forms. Finally, she delivers him to the realm of ideas, of which her forms are merely representations.

E had nearly completed this prose rhapsody (later published as *Nature*) in June 1836, when his beloved younger brother Charles* died suddenly of tuberculosis. For a while E's grief was paralyzing. Then, suddenly, in the closing days of June, he wrote in his journal passages that he would fashion into two new chapters for the book he had been working on, chapters that reject philosophic idealism** as inadequate and instead demand something "progressive" in nature and man that will heal their current separation. A fable sung by an "Orphic poet" tells of a time when nature emanated from men and women, until they became forgetful of their own divinity and allowed themselves to be dwarfed by their own creation. But the time is not far distant when the timid human race will remember its divinity, and the "kingdom of man over nature" will, like the kingdom of God in the Gospels, come "without observation," driving away all evil and suffering from the world. The completed, eight-chapter version of *Nature* was published in September 1836.

The confidence born of successful creation suffuses the pair of famous addresses E delivered at Harvard in the next two years. In August 1837 he was invited to deliver the annual address to the Phi Beta Kappa Society during the Harvard commencement week. Speaking on the traditional topic, "The American Scholar," E launched an attack upon the spiritual timidity he saw as responsible for the woeful state of American letters. American authors look at European ones with fear and trembling. "Meek young men grow up in libraries, believing it is their duty to accept the views which Cicero, which Locke,** which Bacon have given, forgetful that Cicero, Locke, and Bacon were only young men in libraries when they wrote those books." Imitation dooms the imitator to mediocrity. Despite what humanists might say of the beneficence of great art, experience proves the reverse—at least for those who would be artists themselves. "Genius is always the enemy of genius by over-influence."

"The American Scholar" was favorably received. E's next graduation address called forth a different response. In 1838 the seven members of Harvard's Divinity School** graduating class asked him to speak at their commencement. E was still serving regularly as a supply preacher, and his impatience with the petrification he saw everywhere within Unitarianism was just as strong as it had been when he resigned his pastorate. In the Divinity School Address, E pointed with dismay to the faults of the church the graduates were about to enter. The sermons they hear are frigid and traditional, the parishes they might hope to serve are dwindling in size, and the theology they have just finished studying is an incongruous mixture of true faith in man's moral nature with superstitious reverence for merely historical facts, pinning all its hopes for everlasting life upon empirical proofs that a man 1,800 years ago performed certain miracles.** Christ himself ordered his followers to let the dead bury their dead, and E encourages his young colleagues to do likewise, even if it means trusting their own consciences more than Scripture. ''Dare to love God without mediator or veil.''

The scandal caused by this address was considerable, and E suddenly found himself an object of hostile scrutiny. He was denounced in the newspapers, called a heretic and an atheist in the religious periodicals. Though the experience shook him, he remained silent in public. E continued his lecturing and slowly began collecting material for a book. E's *Essays* were published in 1841. The 12 essays asserted the authority of the soul against the combined voices of society, tradition, and the soul's own timidity. In a series of epigrams that were meant to sting as well as to uplift, E urges his readers to scorn conformity and trust themselves, for only in themselves will they find the faith that others vainly search for in historical records or theological debates. ''Nothing can bring you peace but yourself,'' he asserts at the end of his most famous essay, ''Self-Reliance.'' ''Nothing can bring you peace but the triumph of principles.''

E's fame had already begun to draw younger admirers into his circle of acquaintances. Their demands on his time and emotional energy both exhilarated and alarmed him. H. D. Thoreau* and M. Fuller* both, in their different ways, offered him an adoration that could turn quickly into resentment when E's habitual reserve frustrated their wishes for greater intimacy with him. The ''coldness'' he often lamented in himself was intensified when, early in 1842, he lost his dearly beloved firstborn son, Waldo, to scarlet fever. The unreal haze caused by grief came to stand in his mind for the distance that separates all perception from reality, all selves from other selves. In *Essays: Second Series* (1844) E explores the dark side of Transcendentalist self-sufficiency in essays like the devastatingly honest ''Experience'' or the subtly malicious ''Gifts.''

Still, E had never lost his interest in heroic character, and if his mature sense of human imperfection made him realize that the greatest men were always cursed by some debilitating flaw, he nevertheless hoped to compose a kind of composite portrait of human greatness by choosing heroes representative of different strengths and admitting their weaknesses honestly. *Representative Men* (1850) first glorifies and then debunks figures as diverse as Napoleon and Montaigne** in essays that celebrate human genius even as they lament human imperfection.

The 1850s drew E out of his scholarly retirement and involved him in events. The passage of the infamous Fugitive Slave Law (part of the Compromise of 1850**) and the subsequent capture of two fugitive slaves in Boston filled him with fury at the betrayal of the moral law, and he denounced the law in two separate public addresses. Privately, however, he was troubled by doubts about the capacity and even the humanity of the African race, whose sad history seemed to suggest some malignant fate or natural inferiority. The conflict between the moral law and the brutal, limiting side of natural law preoccupied him more and more as the decade drew on. But pessimism ultimately yielded to reaffirmation of moral absolutism. In the essay "Fate" from *The Conduct of Life* (1860), E tries to resolve the contradiction between freedom and necessity by arguing that the moral freedom of the human race is the final stage in nature's upward evolution and so is part of nature even when apparently fighting against it. "Our freedom is necessary."

There was another side to E as well, one frequently visible in the journals, in books like *English Traits* (1856), the account of his visits to England, and *Society and Solitude* (1870). Low-key, amused, tolerant of human compromises and affectionate toward eccentricities, E's voice here belongs to the "mid-world," that highway of human existence where all of us pass our lives as best we can. His love of the ordinary is one of the things that makes his zeal for the transcendent credible and his pursuit of it safe. As he wrote in "Musquetaquid," published in his *Poems* of 1846:

> All my hurts
> My garden spade can heal. A woodland walk,
> A quest of river-grapes, a mocking thrush,
> A wild-rose, or rock-loving columbine,
> Salve my worst wounds.

Toward the end of his life, E suffered a progressive loss of memory that put an end to his work. His daughter Ellen,* together with a younger friend, J. E. Cabot,* helped collect the essays in *Letters and Social Aims* (1876). His influence upon his contemporaries was profound, not only within the Transcendental movement but among poets, essayists, philosophers, and religious thinkers of all kinds.

References: *W*, the standard edition of E's writings since 1903–04, is being superseded by *CW*. Standard editions include *JMN, L, Sermons, EL, PN,* and *TN. E's Antislavery Writings* (1995) have been edited by Len Gougeon and Joel Myerson, and Myerson and Ronald A. Bosco are editing the later lectures. The vast and daunting literature by and about E is helpfully surveyed by Robert E. Burkholder and Joel Myerson in Myerson (1984), 135–66. The indispensable primary bibliography is *EBib*. Secondary bibliographies are B&M and B&M2. *An E Chronology*, comp. Albert J. von Frank (1994), is a useful guide to E's daily life. Rusk (1949) remains the standard biography, though see

Robert D. Richardson, Jr.'s impressive intellectual study *E: The Mind on Fire* (1995). An annual E bibliography is published in *ESP*.

Barbara L. Packer

EMERSON, WILLIAM (1801–1868), R. W. Emerson's* two-years-older brother, studied theology at the University of Göttingen in Germany intending to return home as a Unitarian** minister—a course of action that Waldo also intended to pursue. W. E. Channing,* aware of Harvard's strong basis in Unitarianism and Göttingen's more radical beliefs, protested. E sent home advice and information on German Higher Criticism,** including textual examination of the Scriptures, scientific explanation of the miracles,** and theories on man's blindness to his own divinity. For example, a 27 June 1824 letter to his younger brother Edward anticipates R. W.'s Divinity School Address: "I do not find it needful to seek for proofs of the being and omnipresence of God in my metaphysical subtleties, for I find them in my own thoughts, in my own moral history . . . to convince me that I too am a Son of God, and that I need but throw off my shackles, these bonds of habit, and early perverted nature, to attest my relation to the Divinity."

Rusk says of WE, "[T]he example of the older brother, prying into the mysteries of the new German school of theologians and historians, could not have been without influence on [Ralph Waldo]." When young, E worked as a waiter while at Harvard. He and Waldo taught school during vacation time to supplement their mother's income. On 26 August 1818 he graduated and established the School for Young Ladies.

On 5 December 1823 E set sail for Cork, Ireland, and toured Europe before beginning his theological studies at Göttingen on 5 March 1824. After his studies, he could no longer pursue the ministry. He now felt that all men were divine and that churches throughout the ages had misinterpreted Christ's words, that Christ spoke not only of his but of all men's divinity and relationship to God (all people were sons and daughters of God). E consulted Goethe,* who advised preaching to the people what they wanted to hear and keeping his personal beliefs private. E resolved to follow this advice. On his voyage across the Atlantic, however, the ship entered a terrific storm, and E made his last account with the Deity. Realizing that he could not in good conscience die and face his maker if he followed Goethe's advice, he renounced the ministry and studied law after his return home.

By 1827 E joined the law offices of Ketchum and Fessenden in New York City. On 3 December 1833 he married Susan Woodward Haven of Portsmouth, New Hampshire. A successful lawyer, William became county judge of Richmond Court. He and Susan named their Staten Island home "Snuggery." Three sons survived to adulthood: William, Junior, called Willie (1835–64); John Haven, called Haven (1840–1913); and Charles (1841–1916). All three married, but only Haven had children.

E retired to Concord, Massachusetts.** After his wife's 6 February 1868 death, he returned to live at 33 East 19th Street, where he died on 13 September. He was buried beside his wife and near their eldest son in Concord's Sleepy Hollow Cemetery.**

References: For a complete account of E's life and philosophies, see ''Ralph Waldo Emerson's Older Brother: The Letters and Journal of WE'' (Diss., Univ. of Tennessee, 1982), by Karen Kalinevitch. Information on E may also be found in the biographies of his famous younger brother, such as Gay Wilson Allen, *Waldo Emerson: A Biography* (1981); Rusk (1949); Van Wyck Brooks, *The Life of Emerson* (1932); and G. E. Woodberry,* *Ralph Waldo Emerson* (1907). H. Thoreau,* who served as tutor for E's children in their Staten Island home, refers to the household in his journals.**

Karen L. Kalinevitch

EVERETT, ALEXANDER HILL (1790–1847), like his younger brother E. Everett,* combined politics and literary endeavors. His easy acquaintance with European languages, literature, and politics, derived from a long and varied diplomatic career, enabled him through his own writings, his editorship of the *North American Review,*** and personal friendships to bring to the attention of Americans the riches of European thought and literature.

Though he did much to expose American readers to European thought, his literary and philosophical stance was infused with a conservative politics that celebrated democracy, progress, and prosperity. In his ''History of Intellectual Philosophy'' (1829), E argues that once the philosophical reaction to the French Revolution has passed, a reaction that shrouds reality with the theory of Idealism,** then ''the enlightened opinion of the public will quietly settle down again to the conclusions of Locke** and Aristotle.'' Understanding the political motive behind Idealism as well as its appeal, he nonetheless dismisses it as ''an unsubstantial dream.'' In *New Ideas on Population* (1826), he disarms Malthus's theory that population is the source of evil by proposing that population increase, as in America, is a ''symptom and a cause of public prosperity.'' He also takes Godwin to task for proposing ''the destruction of government, religion, property, and marriage,'' arguing that the institutions of society promote personal happiness. He continues this line of thinking in *America* (1827), where again he holds up as exemplary the American condition, finding that American democracy promotes prosperity and progress.

As editor of the *NAR* from 1830 to 1835, E was instrumental in bringing the latest in thought and literature to the attention of American readers, if not always favorably. His own essays—on Byron, Staël,** Schiller,** Mackintosh, Carlyle,* French drama, and Spanish poetry—demonstrate his appreciation of the European tradition. At the same time that he encouraged Americans to broaden their reading, he also called for a ''national emancipation'' from the ''mechanical and intellectual workshops of Europe'' in his 1830 ''Review of American Literature,'' participating in the emerging literary nationalism and prefiguring R. W. Emerson's* own position in ''The American Scholar'' oration. Though Emerson was pleasantly surprised by E's ''friendly notice'' of Carlyle's work, his assessment of E was not always favorable; he wrote in his journal** that his brother ''Charles* says that to read Carlyle in N A Review is like seeing your brother in jail; & A Everett is the sheriff that put him in.''

References: Of the publications by E, those mentioned here include his essay on ''History of Intellectual Philosophy,'' *NAR* (1829), and in Miller (1950); ''Review of American Literature,'' *NAR* 31 (July 1830); *New Ideas on Population with Remarks on the Theories of Malthus and Godwin* (1826); and *America: or A General Survey of the Political Situation of the Several Powers of the Western Continent, with Conjectures of Their Future Prospects* (1827).

Susan L. Roberson

EVERETT, EDWARD (1794–1865), is remembered primarily as an orator and public servant, yet it was he who, as professor of classics at Harvard (1819–25), ignited one of the first sparks of the New England Renaissance. After graduation from Harvard (1811) and brief service as minister of the Church in Brattle Square, he spent the years from 1815 to 1819 studying in Europe, principally at the University of Göttingen, where in 1817 he received the first Doctor of Philosophy degree awarded to an American. E wrote the first substantial American commentary on Goethe,* which was published in the *North American Review*** for January 1817. From 1820 to 1823 he was chief editor of that journal.

Strong encouragement to American literary initiative came in E's Phi Beta Kappa Address at Harvard in 1824, in which he decried subservience to the past, noted the unique materials and opportunities for creativity in a democracy, and urged potential scholars and poets to be active and not reclusive. E's conviction that the gifted person should not neglect practical matters is perhaps one of the reasons he abandoned scholarship for politics in 1825, when he was elected to Congress. Subsequently, he became governor of Massachusetts (1835–39), minister to the Court of St. James (1840–45), secretary of state (1852–53), and U.S. senator (1853–54). He served as president of Harvard (1846–49) in an undistinguished tenure. Beginning in the late 1820s E became more and more conservative philosophically, and by the 1850s he had developed a strong antipathy for R. W. Emerson* and liberal Unitarianism.**

References: Still the standard biography of E is Paul Revere Frothingham, *EE, Orator and Statesman* (1925; rpt. 1971). Studies of E as scholar and critic are William K. Christian, ''The Mind of EE'' (Diss., Michigan State Univ., 1952), and Monica Maria Grecu, ''EE,'' in *American Literary Critics and Scholars, 1800–1850*, ed. John W. Rathbun and Monica M. Grecu, *DLB* 59: 135–41. The evolution of the tension between E and the Transcendentalists is the subject of James W. Mathews, ''Fallen Angel: Emerson and the Apostasy of EE,'' *SAR* 1990: 23–32; the dichotomies of E's entire career are treated in Paul A. Varg, *EE: The Intellectual in the Turmoil of Politics* (1992).

James W. Mathews

F

FELTON, CORNELIUS CONWAY (1807–1862), was a prominent writer and Harvard classicist. Miller characterizes him as a moderate Unitarian** capable of appreciating the Transcendental position in a limited way; F criticized T. Parker* and R. W. Emerson* but appreciated Emerson's gifts. F also illustrates the growing awareness of German thought even among mainstream (Harvard) thinkers and educators: He taught German, wrote reviews on German topics in the *North American Review*** and *The Christian Examiner*,** and translated Wolfgang Menzel's *German Literature* (1840) for G. Ripley's* foreign literature series.

Parker and M. Fuller* attack Menzel's text in *The Dial*** (1 [January 1841]). F's introduction acknowledges Menzel's uneven treatment of German literature, discounting in particular the harsh assessment of Goethe.* Parker argues, "Mr. Menzel does not give us a faithful picture of things. . . . He carries with him violent prejudices, which either blind his eyes to the truth, or prevent him from representing it as it is" (331–32). Toward Goethe, Parker accuses Menzel of "hostility [that] amounts to absolute hatred, we think, not only of the works but of the man himself" (332). Fuller's article, "Menzel's View of Goethe," begins with the words "is that of a Philistine" (340). Parker, incidentally, praises the "fidelity" of F's "idiomatic" and "fresh" translation.

F graduated from Harvard in 1827. Unlike colleagues G. Ticknor* and E. Everett,* he could not afford a German study tour; instead, he taught Latin and finally in 1834 became Eliot Professor of Greek. Among his students was H. D. Thoreau.* In 1855 he gave a Concord** Lyceum** lecture; starting in 1856 he attended Saturday Club** meetings with Emerson, J. R. Lowell,* H. W. Longfellow,* L. Agassiz,* and others. F was made president of Harvard in 1860, reportedly due to Agassiz's machinations, but died in 1862.

F criticized Emerson in his May 1841 *ChEx* review of the *Essays* for his "point-blank contradictions," and although Emerson "has given us fair warning,'' F notes that ''a writer, whose opinions are so variable, cannot wonder if they have but little value in the eyes of the world'' (30: 254). He dislikes Emerson's irreverence: ''With many of Mr. Emerson's leading views we differ entirely, if we understand them; if we do not, the fault lies in the author's obscurity''(255). At the same time, F argues that ''some of the best writing of late years has proceeded from the pens of . . . Transcendentalists'' and calls Emerson ''an extravagant, erratic genius, setting all authority at defiance, sometimes writing with the pen of an angel, (if angels ever write,) and sometimes gravely propounding the most amazing nonsense. To subject his writings to any of the common critical tests, would be absurd''(30: 254). F views American artists generally the same way; reviewing Raczynski's *Modern Art in Germany*, F states, ''Our countrymen have shown remarkable aptitude for the fine arts; but they need educators, they want learning'' (*NAR* 57 [October 1843]: 425). F concedes Emerson's genius but finds him insufficiently grounded.

References: For more on Menzel's minimal influence in America, see Pochmann (1957). On F, see Miller (1950).

Stephen N. Orton

FOLLEN, CHARLES (1796–1840), emigrated to America in 1824 to escape political persecution in Europe and became the first professor of German at Harvard and a fervent abolitionist.** Although his life ended prematurely in a tragic ship explosion, F and his wife, Eliza,* befriended current and future Transcendentalists such as R. W. Emerson,* T. Parker,* and H. D. Thoreau.* Active in religious, intellectual, and abolitionist circles in and around Boston, F at his death was widely admired both as a fiery Unitarian** preacher and as a moral leader who spoke out vociferously against human bondage.

Through numerous essays, lectures, and sermons on issues ranging from slavery to psychology, F in his two decades in the United States became popular with important writers and thinkers. Not all were impressed with F's talents, including Emerson, who wrote of the German emigre's ''singularly barren and uninteresting intellect.'' By 1834, however, F had gained the respect of fellow abolitionists with the publication of the vehemently antislavery ''Address to the People of the United States.'' In the January 1843 issue of *The Dial*,** Parker published a tribute to F that not only outlined the late abolitionist's life and work but also praised him as a leader of ''the cause of the oppressed and downtrodden African.'' Although these abolitionist activities led to F's ouster from his Harvard professorship, he continued to press for liberal reforms, especially abolition.

References: F's writings were edited by his wife, E. C. Follen, and preserved in the five-volume *The Works of CF* (1841–42). The first volume consists of a well-written and informative biography of F by his wife. Edmund Daniel Spevack's recent ''CF's Search for Nationality and Freedom in Germany and America, 1795–1840'' (Diss., Johns Hopkins Univ., 1993) should add significantly to our understanding of the antebellum scholar and activist.

Jonathan Wells

FOLLEN, ELIZA CABOT (1787–1860), was a Massachusetts writer and abolitionist** who together with her husband, Charles,* worked tirelessly to end slavery. F assumed a position of intellectual and social prominence in Boston and consequently was acquainted with important Transcendentalists such as R. W. Emerson.* In addition to her abolitionist activities, F authored numerous books, poems, and stories for children.

F began her literary career with works such as *The Well-Spent Hour* (1827) and continued throughout the antebellum period to write essays and books including *The Skeptic* (1835). From 1843 to 1850 she also edited a popular children's periodical, *Child's Friend.* While F's writings for children drew the attention of many Americans, it was her writings on slavery that gained the respect of leading Transcendentalists. T. Parker,* whose wife was related to F, claimed that ''she has long been my parishioner, neighbor, and friend.'' As a member of the American Anti-Slavery Society and the Boston Female Anti-Slavery Society, F edited the abolitionist magazine *The Liberty Bell* and authored well-received abolitionist essays. After her husband's untimely death, F devoted herself to the publication of *The Works of Charles Follen* (1841–42). She recovered from the sudden, tragic end of her marriage to continue her crusade on behalf of abolition until her own death on the eve of the Civil War.

REFERENCES: Biographical information on F can be found in the first volume of *The Works of Charles Follen* (1841–42) and Elizabeth Bancroft Schlesinger, ''Two Early Harvard Wives: Eliza Farrar and EF,'' *NEQ* 38 (June 1965): 147–67. F's most notable works include *The Skeptic* (1835), *Poems* (1839), and *Sketches of Married Life* (1839).

Jonathan Wells

FOURIER, FRANÇOIS MARIE CHARLES (1772–1837), a major influence on Transcendentalist reform, was born in Besançon, France. Despite his provincial bourgeois origin and scanty education, he became a brilliant radical theorist. Shocked by Revolutionary violence and the ensuing reaction, disgusted by a life of stockjobbing and commerce, F experienced a vision in 1799 that took him the rest of his life to explicate. In countless self-published books and pamphlets read by no one, he propounded a total reshaping of society. Some have classified F as a ''utopian socialist''—along with Owen* and Saint-Simon**—but he knew he was unique. Yet he lived alone in a series of hotels and rented rooms with his flowers and cats. The few who knew him, like Balzac, considered him an amusing eccentric.

Like near-contemporaries William Blake and De Sade (less religious than the former, more genial than the latter), F was a maker of imaginal worlds and systems—and a mystic sensualist. His vision was rooted in rejection of ''Civilisation'' and in radical ''doubt'' concerning all received ideas. All contemporary relations and institutions failed to measure up against F's ideal of ''divine Providence,'' the boundless generosity of the material world and its becoming. All ''philosophy'' was but a mask for oppression, all ''morality'' a cause of misery. F alone (such was his quasi-messianic role) had discovered the true law of Nature,** that ''Attractions are proportional to Destinies''; that is, that human ''Passions'' are innate. While orthodox religion scorns desire as sin, F elevated it as the sole possible principle of social organization. If everyone followed their passions, even ''manias,'' to the fullest, all desires would harmonize in their very fulfillment. If all were thus free to enjoy sensuality, love, wealth, luxury, art, fine food, then all cause for social discord would evaporate. This utopia was possible because by nature each human also feels passion for freely chosen economic activities. This theory of ''Attractive Labor'' was F's most famous contribution to socialist thought.

To organize humanity for the next and utopian stage of becoming, called ''Association'' or ''Harmony,'' F proposed large communes (''Phalanxes''), each with exactly 1,620 members, the minimum number for the expression of all 12 major Passions. Members would live in vast ''unitary'' palaces called Phalansteries and engage in gardening, arboriculture, light industry, operas, and orgies.

F englobed his social theory within an amazing imaginal cosmology, which proved an embarrassment to his earnest disciples—although we may now appreciate its wonderful surrealism. F believed Civilization a menace to the Earth itself, which has been literally thrown out of cosmic alignment. Planets and stars are living beings, which make love through space via ''aromal rays'' (Earth's ray would be the Aurora Borealis, were our sexual links with other systems restored). Once Harmony is attained, Earth will again receive aromal rays from other worlds; the climate will change (the oceans will turn to lemonade); wild animals will become benign; Terra will acquire five new living moons to replace its single dead satellite; the whole solar system will crowd closer together in an aromal orgy, and we shall be able to communicate with aliens; indeed, we shall become ''alien'' ourselves, changing our very form, for example, growing useful tails, each with an extra hand and eye at the tip.

Such ideas—and F's intense sexuality (he even condoned fetishism and homosexuality), ''feminism'' (he coined the word), insistence on luxury and ''gastrosophic'' cuisine, bizarre numerology, occult theory of ''Analogies,'' and most delightful science-fictional texts—were suppressed or forgotten by the Fourierist movement. ''Fourierism'' was reduced to the theory of Attractive Labor, conceived as ''cooperation,'' and to certain advanced educational practices. F had envisioned these as transitional stages between Civilization and Harmony, not as ends in themselves.

Late in life, F finally acquired some disciples, including a few dissident Saint-Simonians and men of talent like Just Muiron and Victor Considerant (who later tried to found a Phalanx in Texas); but the long-awaited millionaire patron never appeared. During F's lifetime, only one attempt was made to organize a phalanstery in France, F himself denouncing it as falling short of minimum requirements for capital and membership. But after the Founder's death, the movement acquired momentum. In the mid-19th century hundreds of phalansteries were founded, from Russia (Dostoevski went through a Fourierist period) and eastern Europe to Algeria, to South America—to France and North America. Not one experiment ever attained the 1,620 members or amount of start-up capital F himself deemed necessary.

In the early 1830s an idle young American seeker-after-wisdom met F in Paris and was instantly converted. The adoption of Fourierism usually involved a kind of religious enthusiasm, and A. Brisbane* was no exception. Back in America by the late 1830s, he convinced H. Greeley* to give him a column in the New York *Tribune*. By this propaganda organ, Brisbane spread the doctrine with astonishing success. By 1844 the first experiment—the North American Phalanx (NAP) in Red Bank, New Jersey—had been launched. Over the next decade or so, nearly 30 phalansteries sprang up in America. Most failed within a year or two. The NAP outlasted them all, surviving till 1855; the Wisconsin Phalanx was also quite successful. But Fourierism was short-lived, one of many wildfires that burned over reform-obsessed mid-19th-century America.

In adapting Fourierism to America, Brisbane and others soft-pedalled or even censored some of F's more radical notions. The bizarre cosmology was played down; labor theory was played up. The attack on marriage and the orgiastic sexuality proposed by F would not have harmonized with the puritanical** heritage of American reformism. F's scathing critique of Christianity was suppressed. Several authentic works of F appeared in English (*The Passions of the Human Soul* in 1851; *Theory of the Four Movements* in 1856); Brisbane's translation of the latter, however, omitted the chapters on "Gastrosophy," presumably because American radicals tended to be vegetarian teetotalers. Even the F-influenced Free Love** movement remained fairly timid by F's exalted standards.

Among Transcendentalists, however, who tended to be better educated and more genuinely radical than most American communitarians, the doctrines of Association found sympathy and understanding. F's strange blend of anarchic freedom and intense socialization appealed to New England taste, while his apparent practicality seemed to solve the problem of Transcendentalism's largely literary and too lofty idealism.** Brook Farm** founder G. Ripley* read F and met Brisbane, and in 1844–45 Brook Farm rewrote its constitution to embrace Fourierist organizational ideas. Some condemned the transformation (O. Brownson*), some remained skeptical (Emerson*), but most shared the enthusiasm to some degree (T. Parker,* W. H. Channing,* M. Fuller*). Brook Farm's school, its most successful operation, adopted some Fourierist practices, and the other work groups now became "Series" devoted to Attractive Labor. Much borrowed money was invested in a large phalanstery, which burned to the ground in 1846. The fire killed Brook Farm, not its venture into utopian socialism.

A myth persists that Brook Farm was somehow ruined by its conversion to

Fourierism. N. Hawthorne's* cruel caricatures in *The Blithedale Romance* and Emerson's witticisms in "New England Reformers" have weighed against the voices of less-famous Brook Farmers. But a different story emerges out of the Farmers' letters, diaries, journalistic pieces, and memoirs. Not only Ripley, C. Dana,* and the "leaders" were swept up in the Fourierist enthusiasm but also such attractive figures as Marianne Dwight, her husband the Associationist lecturer John Orvis, and her brother, musician J. S. Dwight.* In their eyes Brook Farm reached its high point only after the phalanx was inaugurated, and the vague but lofty values of Transcendentalism given definition by the practical utopianism of Harmonial Association. In their memories, they returned again and again to the Brook Farm years as the high point of their lives, even Hawthorne declaring, "I feel we struck upon what ought to be a truth. Posterity may dig it up and profit by it."

Of course there were solid and specific economic and social reasons for the failure of Brook Farm and the phalansterian movement in general. But in the end, none of the reform movements was equipped to survive the rise of modern capitalism. The contradiction between the freedom of humanity and the "freedom" of expansionist monopoly and imperialism proved fatal to all forms of radicalism. The Civil War put a temporary end to progressive reform and made the world safe for "progress" as *economic growth*. Only one reform goal—abolition of slavery—was allowed. The rest were doomed, and even the freed blacks were forgotten and abandoned by the industrial North. Such delicate blooms as Transcendentalist Fourierism were crushed beneath history's boot heel and consigned to the dustbin of mere literature.

Nevertheless, the Brook Farm hybrid of utopianism and "high thought" made a lasting but secret donation to American culture. In the post–Civil War era, such figures as S. P. Andrews* passed on reform enthusiasms to a new generation. So did such younger Transcendentalists as Whitman* (he probably adopted his butterfly symbol from F, who called one of the Twelve Passions "the Butterfly") and artists like Frederick Law Olmsted, designer of New York's Central Park, who had experienced the Fourierist enthusiasm in his youth. In the later 19th and 20th centuries, F was rediscovered countless times—first by Marx and Engels, then by the Surrealists, by Walter Benjamin, R. Barthes, the Situationists who launched the Paris "Events" of May 1968, and by contemporary "post-ideological" theorists and proponents of a "utopian poetics." F and his Transcendentalist adherents were perhaps a century ahead of their time—and the time may have come (again) to dig up their truth, and profit by it.

References: See F, *The Passions of the Human Soul and Their Influence on Society and Civilization*, 2 vols., trans. H. Doherty (1851; rpt. 1968); John Humphrey Noyes, *Strange Cults & Utopias of 19th Century America* (1966; orig. publ. as *History of American Socialisms*, 1870); Alice Felt Tyler, *Freedom's Ferment* (1944); Henry W. Sams, ed., *Autobiography of Brook Farm* (1958); Jonathan Beecher, *CF: The Visionary and*

His World (1986); and Carl J. Guarneri, *The Utopian Alternative: Fourierism in Nineteenth-Century America* (1991).

Peter Lamborn Wilson

FRANCIS, CONVERS (1795–1863), Unitarian** minister, biographer, and historian, was born in West Cambridge, Massachusetts, the fifth of six children. The family moved to Medford in 1800, where F showed an interest in literature and was prepared at a local academy for entrance to Harvard College. He was graduated from Harvard in 1815, after which he studied divinity, preaching his first sermon in 1818. His ordination on 23 June 1819 represented an auspicious beginning to his career: Among those who helped were President Kirkland of Harvard, the Rev. E. Ripley* of Concord** and his son, the Rev. Samuel Ripley* of Waltham, and J. G. Palfrey.* F was installed at Watertown at an excellent salary of $1,000 per year. On 15 May 1822, he married Abby Bradford Allyn, and by 1834, they had four children, two of whom died in infancy. F took time from his pastoral duties to contribute to religious periodicals and to write *An Historical Sketch of Watertown* (1830) and a *Life of John Eliot* (1836), the apostle to the Indians, for Jared Sparks' Library of American Biography. His house in Watertown was frequented by his friends, including his sister, L. M. Child,* R. W. Emerson,* and T. Parker,* whom F tutored prior to his entering the Harvard Divinity School.** In 1836, F became a member of the Transcendental Club** and, as the eldest member, its moderator. F left Watertown in 1842 to become Parkman Professor of Pulpit Eloquence at Harvard, a post he held until his death. F never approached the social radicalism of Parker or the intellectual radicalism of Emerson because he was more interested in working from within existing institutions than in attacking them from without.

References: See J. Weiss,* *Discourse Occasioned by the Death of CF, D.D.* (1863); Mosetta I. Vaughan, *Sketch of the Life and Writings of CF, D.D.* (1944); Guy R. Woodall, "The Journals of CF (Parts One and Two)," *SAR* 1981: 265–343, *SAR* 1982: 227–84; Woodall, "CF," in Myerson (1984), 167–70; Woodall, "Selected Sermons of CF (Parts One and Two)," *SAR* 1987: 73–129, *SAR* 1988: 55–131; and Woodall, "CF and the Concordians: Emerson, [A.B.] Alcott,* and Others," *CS* New Series 1 (fall 1993): 23 58.

Joel Myerson

FRENCH, DANIEL CHESTER (1850–1931), an American sculptor born in Exeter, New Hampshire, completed busts of R. W. Emerson,* B. Alcott,* and E. A. Poe.* F also sculpted the monumental figure of Abraham Lincoln seated in Washington, D.C.'s Lincoln Memorial; and he created *The Minute Man* statue, on the base of which is engraved Emerson's poem "Concord Hymn."

At age 15, F moved to Concord, Massachusetts,** with his family and studied art and the rudimentary elements of sculpture with May, the youngest sister of L. M. Alcott.* In 1873 at the urging of F and with the support of Emerson, the people of Concord and Lexington commissioned F to create a monument celebrating the one hundredth anniversary of the first battle of the Revolutionary War. Emerson discussed the commission in a letter written 4 September 1874: ''DF has made a statue of the *Minute-Man*. . . . He is a good sensible youth.'' The 19 April 1875 centennial observation was attended by 10,000 people.

The bust that brought F the most acclaim was that of Emerson, completed in 1879. According to several accounts by the sculptor's daughter, Margaret French Cresson, F apologized for putting Mr. Emerson to so much trouble during the actual sitting. Emerson replied that he found the experience ''as easy as sleeping'' and added, ''You know, Dan, the more it resembles me, the worse it looks.'' When F completed the bust, Emerson conceded, ''Yes, Dan, that's the face I shave.'' When Emerson died in spring 1882, the bereaved family sent for F, who draped the philosopher in white cloth.

References: On F's relationship with Emerson, see *The Life of DCF. Journey into Fame*, by Margaret French Cresson (1947). The chapter titled ''Italy'' includes a lively account of the unveiling of *The Minute Man*. Cresson's other book, *DCF* (1947), contains a good sampling of photographs of F's sculptures including *The Minute Man*, the life-size bust and statue of Emerson, and the portrait bust of Poe. See esp. Michael Richman, *DCF: An American Sculptor* (1976), and Wayne Craven, *Sculpture in America* (1984).

Heidi M. Schultz

FROST, BARZILLAI (1804–1858), has enjoyed dubious fame since Conrad Wright identified him in 1956 as the model for the ''formalist'' preacher R. W. Emerson* demolished in the Divinity School Address. Born in Effingham, New Hampshire, F graduated from Harvard College (1830) and the Divinity School** (1835). On 1 February 1837 he became associate pastor to Emerson's stepgrandfather, E. Ripley,* at First Parish Church in Concord.** F busied himself in public service as school committee member, local lyceum** curator, library proprietor, and Middlesex Sunday-School Society secretary, and he took part in the temperance** and antislavery movements.

Liked and respected, F loved ''an earnest talk.'' But even Henry A. Miles had to admit, in his funeral sermon for his close friend, that F was an unexceptional preacher: He showed ''neither flexibility of voice, nor play of imagination, nor gush of emotion''; he did, however, possess ''discriminating good-sense.'' F reflected his own proclivities when he eulogized Ripley as a ''*rational*'' preacher who ''excelled'' ''in the devotional and pastoral duties of his office'' (*A Sermon Delivered at the Funeral of the Rev. Ezra Ripley, D.D.* [1841]). But as Emerson proclaimed to the Divinity School graduates on 15 July 1838, the high calling of the preacher is not to serve as custodian of institutional traditions but to ''convert life into truth.'' Converting his experience with F into an image of dryasdust sermonizing, Emerson complained, ''I once heard a preacher who sorely tempted me to say, I would go to church no more. . . . A snowstorm was falling around us. The snowstorm was real; the preacher merely spectral. . . . If he had ever lived and acted, we were none the wiser for it.'' F, according to Emerson's indictment, could not express the ''grandeur'' of the divinity within.

An uninspiring preacher, F espoused conventional Unitarian** theology. He conveyed a blandly optimistic hope, for example, that Christianity had outgrown the violence of darker ages and that ''This is the dawn, as we believe, of a brighter and fairer day'' (*A Discourse Delivered at the Dedication of the New Church of the First Parish in Concord, Mass., December 29, 1841* [1842]). Just as Emerson had F in mind in his address three and a half years earlier, F in this discourse seems to be chastizing Emerson, both in his defense of the Scriptures, ''religious ordinances and institutions,'' and ''public worship and instruction''—and in this striking footnote: ''This [orthodox] view of the discovery of new truth, from the enlargement of the spiritual powers and progress in holiness, is very different from the 'emanation from God,' the 'inner light[,]' 'intuition,' the 'teachings of the spirit,' as explained by the Mystics, the Swedenborgians,** the Quakers,** and many sects of the present time. According to these, every individual is made the subject of a special revelation.'' ''New revelation'' should indeed be the message of preachers, Emerson had declared at Cambridge—but F seemed to cling to routinized purveyance of historical Christianity instead of dealing out ''life passed through the fire of thought.''

Though Emerson preferred walking in the woods to hearing F preach on Sundays, they were cordial in social meetings. Consumption forced F to resign his pastorate on 3 October 1857. That November he journeyed to Fayal Island in search of health, but his ten-year-old son was killed in a climbing accident. F returned to Concord, where he died on 8 December 1858.

References: Conrad Wright's classic essay ''Emerson, BF, and the Divinity School Address'' (*HTR* 49 [January 1956]: 19–43) is reprinted in Wright's *The Liberal Christians* (1970), 41–61. For biographical information, see two sketches by Henry W. Frost, in *H[arvard]. U[niversity, Class of 1830] Memoirs* (1886), 39–40, and in *Memoirs of Members of the Social Circle in Concord*, Third Series (1907), 54–59; and *Heralds*, 1: 173–74. See also Henry A. Miles, *A Sermon Preached in the First Parish Church, Concord, December 10, 1858, at the Burial of Rev. BF* (1859). A third published discourse by F is *A Sermon, Preached in the First Church, Concord, November 9th, 1856, being the Sunday Succeeding the Death of Hon. Samuel Hoar, L.L.D.** (1856).

Wesley T. Mott

FROTHINGHAM, NATHANIEL LANGDON (1793–1870), was the minister of the First Unitarian** Church of Boston from 1815 to 1850, succeeding R. W. Emerson's* father. A close friend of the Emerson family and the father of the ''younger generation'' Transcendentalist O. B. Frothingham,* F chaired T. Parker's* ''Heresy Trial'' in January 1843, representing the conservative Unitarians.

However, Buell maintains that F's imagery and range of reference prefigure those of the most accomplished Transcendentalists. Noting a passage that Emerson copied into his journal** from a F sermon, Buell remarks that although

F writes more clearly and conventionally than the Transcendentalists, his sentiments sometimes resemble Emerson's and H. Thoreau's.* Nevertheless, most commentators agree with Miller, who considers F "the most stalwart of the Unitarian rationalists." Certainly F and his son O. B. differed significantly on the Parker issue and on Free Religion.** Yet the elder F once said, "I am perfectly satisfied with my son" (Nichols, *Memorial Paper*, MS in Unitarian Library, 25 Beacon Street, Boston).

O. B. praised his father in *Boston Unitarianism*, saying that he owed F his idealism,** imagination, devotion to literature, and freedom of intellectual movement, as well as his conservatism (232). However, O. B. judged F more harshly elsewhere: "[W]hen the question was . . . one of custom and institution and social tranquility, [he] left the ranks of the pioneers, and fell back upon the old guard" (William White Chadwick, *Theodore Parker, Preacher and Reformer* [1901], 120).

Although F was never a "convert" to Transcendentalism, he and Emerson corresponded between 1827 and 1867. F once politely declined Emerson's invitation to a Transcendental Club** organizational meeting. Frequent references to F appear in *L* and *JMN*, nearly all of a personal or social nature, including an 1864 invitation to F to be a guest of the Saturday Club,** which he accepted. Emerson includes F on the list of people to be sent a copy of *Nature*, but no record exists of F's reaction to the work. Emerson remarks in "Historic Notes of Life and Letters in New England" that F is "an excellent classical and German scholar" who had acquainted others "if prudently, with the genius of Eichhorn's** theologic criticism."

Only in three instances does Emerson deal with F's ideas: the example referred to above by Buell; a brief comment on a sermon dealing with the parting of Elijah and Elisha; and the following: "Nothing vulgar is connected with [F's] name but on the contrary every remembrance of wit & learning & contempt of cant. In our Olympic Games we love his fame. But that fame was bought by many years' steady rejection of all that is popular with our saints & as persevering study of books which none else reads & which he can convert to no temporary purpose." George Harvey Genzmer (*DAB*, vol. 7) considers this proof of Emerson's admiration for F, but Miller's evaluation of the latter part of the quote as flippant seems more accurate.

References: O. B. F's ambivalence toward his father, particularly NF's role in the Parker controversy, is evident in *Boston Unitarianism 1820–1850: A Study of the Life and Work of NLF* (1890); *Recollections and Impressions 1822–1890* (1891); and *Theodore Parker: A Biography* (1874). J. Wade Caruthers, *Octavius Brooks Frothingham: Gentle Radical* (1977), is indispensable on the father-son relationship. Caruthers also discusses the NF-Emerson correspondence in the Houghton Library at Harvard. Brief references to F appear in Buell (1973); Hutchison (1959): and Myerson (1984). F's review of Carlyle's* *Sartor Resartus* is excerpted in Miller (1950). For a contemporary biographical article, see *PAAAS* 8 (1873): 226–28. F's published sermons are listed in J.

Sabin, *Dictionary of Books Relating to America*, vol. 7 (1875), and E. A.* and G. L. Duyckinck, *Cyclopedia of American Literature* (rev. ed., 1875).

April Selley

FROTHINGHAM, OCTAVIUS BROOKS (1822–1895), was a second-generation Transcendentalist, organizer and first president of the Free Religious Association** (FRA), member of the Transcendental Club,** first historian of Transcendentalism, and biographer of several major Transcendentalists. In his biography of F, J. Wade Caruthers establishes F as "the major figure in the development of radical religious ideas in the post-Parker era of nineteenth-century America."

F was ordained a Unitarian** minister. However, his ideas became too radical for his parishioners at The North Church of Salem. His theology evolved partially under the influence of T. Parker* (an influence F had difficulty acknowledging in some of his writings, perhaps because his father, N. F,* presided at Parker's "Heresy Trial"). F was also uncomfortable with celebrating the Lord's Supper.** He had considered leaving his parish already when the capture and reenslavement of Anthony Burns inspired him to deliver the controversial sermon "The New Commandment," which attacked Christianity, especially for tolerating slavery.

A year later, F accepted an invitation from a new Unitarian Society to go to Jersey City. However, the church was not so much Unitarian as Transcendental theist. When F grew unhappy there, he moved to New York, where he was instrumental in the evolution of the Third Congregational-Unitarian Society into the Independent Liberal Church.

During 20 years in New York, F established himself as one of the most impressive preachers of the time. His theology eventually found its fullest expression in the FRA, of which F served as president from 1867 to 1878. In his essay "Why Am I a Free Religionist?" he describes his theology as "absolute freedom of thought in the study of religious literature, perfect freedom of movement among all religious phenomena, a pure fellowship of religious intention and purpose, a frank confession of the superiority of practical morality to dogma." Although vague, this theology concurs with R. W. Emerson's* own remarks on Transcendental religion, referred to by F in "Some Phases of Idealism** in New England": "[I]n his [Emerson's] view, Transcendentalism . . . was simply a protest against formalism and dogmatism in religion; not a philosophical, but a spiritual movement, looking toward a spiritual faith."

Emerson and F also agreed that spirituality must be combined with good works, as shown when Emerson, an old friend of N. and OBF, spoke at the Organizing Meeting (30 May 1867) and Second Annual Meeting (28 May 1869) of the FRA. At the first meeting, Emerson noted that free religion must have practical applications: "It is only by good works, it is only on the basis of active duty, that worship finds expression." Emerson repeated this sentiment two years later when he praised the advent of "a more realistic church" where people would have "the ambition to excel each other in good works." Later, in *Transcendentalism in New England: A History* (1876), F took pains to point out the practical accomplishments of the Transcendentalists: "They achieved more practical benefit for society, in proportion to their numbers and the duration of their existence, than any body of Baconians of whom we ever heard."

F astutely recognized that New England Transcendentalism was a philosophical, religious, literary, and social reform movement and that many different voices, attitudes, and actions composed it. His history, which deals with all aspects of the movement, remains one of the most comprehensive. Recent scholars have criticized it as outdated, and some have accused F of being too close to his subject, since he personally knew most of the people about whom he writes and had difficulties dealing forthrightly with the clash between his father and Parker. Yet all critics have acknowledged the work's importance.

F traces the development of Transcendentalism through Kant's** *Critique of Pure Reason*, the works of other German and French philosophers, and the works of Coleridge,* Carlyle,* and Wordsworth.* He sees the American roots of Transcendentalism already in Jonathan Edwards's "Treatise on the Religious Affections." He devotes only four pages to the Unitarian bases of Transcendentalism and has this to say for the denomination in which his father remained a minister: "This profession of free inquiry [within Unitarianism] . . . opened the door to the speculation which carried unlooked-for heresies in its bosom; and before the gates could be closed the insidious enemy had penetrated to the citadel."

F's history devotes a chapter apiece to those he considered the major Transcendentalists: Emerson, B. Alcott,* M. Fuller,* Parker, and G. Ripley.* Generously quoting from their works as well as secondary sources, F also evaluates the Transcendentalists as human beings. He comments briefly on their ideas, but his aim was "to write . . . not a critical or philosophical history, but simply a history." He also deals with "Minor Prophets"—W. H. Channing,* William F. Channing, C. Bartol,* J. F. Clarke,* S. Johnson,* D. Wasson,* T. W. Higginson,* and J. Weiss.* F's only major omissions are H. Thoreau,* who is mentioned once in passing, and himself.

As for F's own Transcendentalism, he says: "The writer was once a pure Transcendentalist. . . . His ardor may have cooled . . . later studies and meditation may have commended to him others' ideas and methods; but he still retains enough of his former faith to enable him to do it justice." Both his contemporaries and later critics have debated whether F recanted his Transcendentalism later in life. F seems to have agreed with Emerson that "a foolish consistency is the hobgoblin of little minds." After spending a lifetime protesting against dogmatism in religion, he has received criticism precisely for remaining to the end true to his undogmatic, and so not easily summarized, "becoming," evolving religious views.

References: F's works are cited in Myerson (1984) for biographical information on many Transcendentalists. The F section in Myerson, by J. Wade Caruthers, is a useful overview of F's thought. The most complete bibliography of primary and secondary sources is in Caruthers's *OBF, Gentle Radical* (1977). Although oversimplifying F's ideas, Sydney E. Ahlstrom's "Introduction" in the 1972 reprint of *Transcendentalism in New England* is a useful overview that lists several older sources on F. Ahlstrom believes that F's *The Religion of Humanity* (1872) substantiates F's later "scientific theism," influenced by Darwin* and Spencer. However, Caruthers believes that the issue is complex and deals with it at length. See also Edmund Clarence Stedman, *OF and the New Faith* (1876), and the list of eulogies and memorials in Myerson. Several brief references to F appear in Hutchison (1959) and in Buell (1973). Robert D. Habich focuses on a letter to F, "The 'Spiral Ascending Path' of William Henry Channing: An Autobiographical Letter," *ESQ* 30 (January 1984): 22–26. Besides Caruthers, the most useful sources on F are those he wrote himself. His important works on Transcendentalism include *Transcendentalism in New England* (1876; rpt. 1972), *Theodore Parker: A Biography* (1874), *George Ripley* (1883), *Memoir of William Henry Channing* (1886), and *Boston Unitarianism 1820–1850: A Study of the Life and Work of Nathaniel Langdon Frothingham* (1890).

April Selley

FULLER, SARAH MARGARET (1810–1850), was an intellectual, a feminist, and a leading Transcendentalist who also served as a catalyst to other Transcendentalists. Her Transcendental concepts developed and strengthened during the various stages of her life until they expressed themselves in feminist concern and, toward the end of her life, in political activism. Every phase of her extraordinary career reflects her developing Transcendentalism as well as its impact upon those who interacted with her.

F's intellectuality grew with what it fed on. Her early studies at the Misses' Prescott school in Groton (1823) and the Cambridgeport Private Grammar School (1826) were supplemented by a self-imposed program of studies in music, Greek, and readings in Sismondi's *Literature of the South of Europe* and Thomas Brown's *Philosophy*. F's acquaintance with F. H. Hedge,* J. F. Clarke,* and W. H. Channing* helped stimulate her interest in metaphysics, the philosophy of poets, and especially German thought. Goethe's* dictum "Das ewig weibliche zieht uns hinan" (The ever womanly draws us forward) eventually played a role in the shaping of her feminism and her persona. In 1832 F began the study of German; in 1839 she published her translation of Eckermann's* *Conversations with Goethe* and began work on a biography of Goethe that she would never complete. She had initiated herself in the German counterpart of Transcendentalism and already personified Kant's** principle of the fidelity of the mind to itself.

Meanwhile F had in 1836 assisted at B. Alcott's* Temple School** in Boston, which itself might be characterized as a pedagogical Transcendental experiment, and in 1837 taught at the Greene Street School in Providence, Rhode Island. In 1836 she paid her first visit to R. W. Emerson* in Concord** and the next year attended a few meetings of the Transcendental Club.** Her attitude toward an ideology that sought to transcend the real for the ideal was acceptable to the Transcendental coterie, and in 1839, when a Transcendental periodical was projected, she was invited to become its editor.

The first number of *The Dial: A Magazine for Literature, Philosophy, and Religion*** (July 1840) reflected not only the leanings of the Transcendental Club, whose organ it was, but those of its editor. It included a lengthy essay on the divine element in man, ''Man in the Ages'' by T. T. Stone;* a short essay on woman by Sophia Ripley,* who asserted that in the present society woman possesses not but is possessed; Emerson's musings on nature** and art: ''Nature paints the best part of the picture. . . . The mind that made the world is not one mind, but the mind. Every man is an inlet to the same, and to all of the same.'' Alcott's ''Orphic Sayings'' set the axe at the tree of idolatry: ''The trump of reform is sounding throughout the world for a revolution of all human affairs.'' To all this F added her essay on Wolfgang Menzel's view of Goethe in which she wrote of Goethe: ''See how he rides at anchor, lordly, rich in freight, every white sail ready to be unfurled at a moment's warning.''

The editor implemented the purposes of the new periodical: to search for principles, to discuss principles rather than promote measures, to mold the magazine into the freest expression of thought by soliciting contributions from the like-minded, Hedge, Clarke, Channing, T. Parker,* Alcott, Emerson, E. Hooper,* C. Sturgis (Tappan).* H. Thoreau* would achieve in *The Dial* his first appearance in print, and a later issue (July 1843) would carry F's article ''The Great Lawsuit—Man Versus Men, Woman Versus Women,'' the nucleus of *Woman in the Nineteenth Century*. While the reception of *The Dial* was far from favorable, the editor had opened channels for the expression of Transcendental thought, and she continued her editorship until March 1842, when Emerson took her place.

Meanwhile she had completed her translation of the correspondence between Bettina von Arnim and the canoness Günderode, which was published in 1842 by E. P. Peabody* under the simple title *Günderode*; and she had drafted ''A Credo'' in which she sought to establish her relationship to the universe.

While *The Dial* served as a printed conduit for Transcendental thinkers, F used the spoken word to enunciate her thoughts and stimulate others, especially women, to cerebration. Between 1839 and 1844, during and following her editorship of *The Dial*, she held at the Peabody bookstore, 13 West Street, Boston, four series of Conversations.** In most of these her audiences consisted of women, participants including L. M. Child,* Sarah Freeman Clarke, L. Emerson,* Elizabeth Hoar,* E. Littlehale (later Cheney),* Mary and Sophia Peabody (Hawthorne),* Ann (Mrs. Wendell) Phillips, and Sophia Ripley.* F made it clear that the purpose of her Conversations was not to teach but to provoke thought. Subjects centered upon Grecian mythology, fine arts, education,** creeds, literature, demonology, ethics, the ideal, society, Goethe, Spinoza.** Through the force of her dynamic personality as well as her intellectuality, F summoned forth the thoughts of listeners upon a variety of subjects of interest to Transcendentalists: the interrelations of matter and spirit, freedom, the infinite, life, creativeness. In the course of interchanges with participants, F succeeded also in crystallizing her own thoughts on such topics. Especially she sought to demonstrate the intellectual equality of men and women at a time of political and social inequality—a subject she would address in what would be considered her major work.

In the course of her Conversations and her *Dial* editorship, F acquainted herself with ways of life that differed from her own but were expressions of her times. At Brook Farm,** the community founded in West Roxbury, Massachusetts, by G. Ripley,* she was an observer, never a member. The philosophy of Association practiced there in 1841 resulted in a combination of farming and meditation that she found inadequate. Transcendentalism seemed incompletely applied at Brook Farm, and life in fraternity was not, in F's eyes, a necessary step to a perfect society.

''To woo the mighty meaning'' of yet another scene, ''perhaps to foresee the law by which a new order, a new poetry is to be evoked from this chaos,'' F in the summer of 1843 journeyed west with J. F. Clarke and his sister, artist Sarah Freeman Clarke. It was a Midwest in transition that F witnessed when, Hoosier-style, she viewed the Great Lakes and the prairies of Illinois, Michigan, and Wisconsin Territory. She charged both missionary and white settler with guilt for the palpable degradation of the native Indians, and her views were clearly expressed in her first authored book, *Summer on the Lakes in 1843*, published the following year by Little and Brown. In it she wrote: ''Let me stand in my age with all its waters flowing round me. If they sometimes subdue, they must finally upbear me, for I seek the universal—and that must be the best.'' Reviews were favorable. One critic was deeply impressed—H. Greeley,* who regarded the book as ''one of the clearest and most graphic delineations . . . of the Great Lakes, of the Prairies, and of the receding barbarism, and the rapidly advancing, but rude, repulsive semi-civilization, which were contending . . . for the possession of those rich lands.'' His admiration induced him to offer to the author a post on his newspaper, the *New-York Daily Tribune*.

Before she took up her new work as journalist, F spent seven weeks in Fishkill, New York, where she expanded, modified, and revised her *Dial* article on ''The Great Lawsuit'' and produced the first American feminist landmark, *Woman in the Nineteenth Century*.

In that work F marshaled world opinion, past and present, on woman, encapsulating her readings in literature and the classics, Greek mythology, Scandinavian sagas, German philosophy. As a result, *Woman in the Nineteenth Century* is a compilation. At the same time it is a manifesto. The intellectual expansion of woman was supremely significant to her. She held, ''In proportion as a nation is refined, women *must* have an ascendancy.'' She recognized the androgynous nature of men and of women: ''Man partakes of the feminine in the Apollo, woman of the masculine as Minerva.'' ''By Man I mean both man and woman:

these are the two halves of one thought.'' And she understood all too personally that '' '[t]is an evil lot to have a man's ambition and a woman's heart.'' In F's view, there could be no interdependence without independence; the free unfoldment of the inner woman was every woman's birthright. In the language of Transcendentalism she set forth her demands: ''What woman needs is not as a woman to act or rule, but as a nature to grow, as an intellect to discern, as a soul to live freely and unimpeded, to unfold such powers as were given her when we left our common home.'' F sought specifically legal, educational, and economic rights for women, and she sought these as rights, not as concessions, as she sought the rights of black men and red men. At the base of her egalitarianism was her humanitarianism. ''And so,'' she wrote, ''the stream flows on; thought urging action, and action leading to the evolution of still better thought''—surely a codification of Transcendentalism.

Published in February 1845 by *Tribune* editor Greeley and his partner Thomas McElrath, *Woman in the Nineteenth Century* was greeted by some with abuse, by others with respect. Poe* considered it ''a book which few women in the country could have written, and no woman in the country would have published, with the exception of Miss Fuller.'' Greeley believed it ''the ablest, bravest, broadest, assertion yet made of what are termed Woman's Rights.''** It remains a book less timely than timeless, less particular than universal, a distillation of world thought on woman and a feminist manifesto.

Both F's feminist concerns and her Transcendental beliefs found a voice in her work on the New York *Tribune*. Her first review in the 7 December 1844 issue was a criticism of Emerson's second series of *Essays* and his interpretation of the spiritual laws by which we live. Among the two or three articles a week that she contributed before she sailed abroad 1 August 1846 were a number that introduced German thought and culture to American readers. In the *Tribune*'s pages appeared F's numerous articles on social welfare, from her discussion of the Bloomingdale Asylum for the Insane to her account of the Asylum for Discharged Female Convicts, from her surveys of city charities and the slavery question to her relations of prison discipline, Sing Sing, and Blackwell's Prison. She was rounding the arc that led from spiritual Transcendentalism to practical Transcendentalism.

In 1846 an opportunity arose that would plant her firmly in a political arena. Marcus Spring, merchant-philanthropist, and his wife, Rebecca, invited F to accompany them abroad. Greeley gave her an advance payment of $125 for such articles as she would send from Europe, and Emerson gave her a letter introducing to Carlyle* ''our citizen of the world by quite special diploma.''

It was in Rome, where Fuller lived between 1847 and 1850, that she attained that status. There, on 5 September 1848, she bore a son to a young Italian, Giovanni Angelo Ossoli, whom she married secretly, and there she identified herself with the great movement for Italian liberty and unity. She was present when, in February 1848, Rome was declared a Republic, and she witnessed Garibaldi's entrance into the city at the head of his legion. While Giovanni

Ossoli mounted guard, F assisted with the wounded, serving in the hospital of the Fate-bene Fratelli in Rome. Between April and June 1849, when Rome was besieged by the French, F identified with the Romans, and when the revolution failed, in July, she mourned with the Romans. Through the American envoy, she obtained a passport for Mazzini, whom she had met during his London exile and whose belief that moral man cannot be sundered from practical man she shared.

Throughout the struggle, F had kept a journal,** recording the events of the Italian revolution and planning to write its history—a book that promised to be the culmination of her other published works, which now included *Papers on Literature and Art* (1846). That history would never be written. After the fall of Rome, F, with her husband and child, sailed for home on 17 May 1850 aboard the barque *Elizabeth*. On 19 July 1850 the barque foundered in a hurricane off Fire Island, and all three perished.

MF had come full circle. She had voyaged from the life of the mind to political and social involvement, and the events of her own life personified that Transcendental progress. As she was never orthodox, her Transcendentalism was not orthodox; but it enriched the movement, as she enriched its followers.

REFERENCES: The first attempt to record F's life was *Memoirs of MF Ossoli*, ed. by R. W. Emerson, W. H. Channing, and J. F. Clarke (1852). About a dozen biographies of varying merit have subsequently aimed at interpretations of F's life and career, her mind and personality, among them Paula Blanchard, *MF: From Transcendentalism to Revolution* (1978); Charles Capper, *MF: An American Romantic Life* (1992–); T. W. Higginson,* *MF Ossoli* (1884); J. W. Howe,* *MF (Marchesa Ossoli)* (1883); and Madeleine B. Stern, *The Life of MF* (1942; rev. 2d ed., 1991). Primary sources include Bell Gale Chevigny, *The Woman and the Myth: MF's Life and Writings* (1976; rev. and expanded ed., 1994). Especially valuable is Robert N. Hudspeth, ed., *The Letters of MF*, 6 vols. (1983–94), and *''These Sad but Glorious Days'': Dispatches from Europe, 1846–1850*, ed. Larry J. Reynolds and Susan B. Smith (1991). Bibliographies have been compiled by Joel Myerson: *MF: A Descriptive Bibliography* (1978) and *MF: An Annotated Secondary Bibliography* (1977). See Hudspeth's bibliographical chapter in Myerson (1984), 175–88. Also valuable is Myerson's edition of *Critical Essays on MF* (1980). F papers, manuscripts, and letters are deposited in the Houghton Library of Harvard University, Boston Public Library, and Massachusetts Historical Society.

Madeleine B. Stern

FURNESS, WILLIAM HENRY (1802–1896), Unitarian** clergyman, theologian, reformer, and author, was called, without qualification, by O. B. Frothingham,* ''a Transcendentalist of the most impassioned school.'' The characterization fits best if it means that he had a passion for the humanity of Christ, the naturalness of the biblical miracles, and a great faith in intuition. F's involvement in the New England Transcendental movement was mainly related to his position on the miracles of the Bible, especially those of Christ. Most Unitarians believed that the miracles were supernatural interruptions of natural laws and were performed as proofs of the teachings of Christ. F never denied the miracles but contended that they were not necessary as evidences since the truth could be known by intuition. His special conception of the miracles was that they were wholly natural, and if they appeared to violate natural laws, this was only because of one's lack of spirituality to comprehend them.

F was born and early educated in Boston. He graduated from the Harvard Divinity School** in 1823 and settled as pastor over the Unitarian Church in Philadelphia in 1825, where he was an active and emeritus minister for over 70 years. Though away from the Boston area when the Transcendental movement began, he was very much a part of it. The Transcendental Club** began in September 1836 as an assemblage mainly of young Unitarian preachers (A. B. Alcott,* R. W. Emerson's* "God-ordained priest," and a few scholarly women—M. Fuller,* E. Peabody,* and S. W. D. Ripley,* excepted). F, an invitee, lived too far away to attend the meetings, but he stayed au courant with the members' activities. In 1836—the "Annus Mirabilis" of the Transcendentalists—Alcott, O. A. Brownson,* Emerson, C. Francis,* Peabody, and G. Ripley* all published books philosophically at variance with Lockean** empiricism. From Philadelphia, F joined in the Transcendentalist revolt with his *Remarks on the Four Gospels* (1836).

The *Remarks* placed F in the front ranks of those who were in conflict with the Unitarian establishment on the nature and purpose of the miracles and set him upon a lifelong mission of humanizing Christ by explaining Christianity by natural rather than supernatural phenomena. The book became a part of the Miracles Controversy** beginning in 1836 that raged for several years in the Unitarian fellowship between the liberal ministers—led by Ripley, T. Parker,* and Emerson—and the conservative Boston Association of Congregational Ministers and Harvard Divinity Professors, whose most prominent spokesman was A. Norton.* F was not nearly so conspicuous in the Miracles Controversy as Ripley, Emerson, and Parker, but his presence was always felt, and he, as they, bore the stigma of heresy. Long before the *Remarks* appeared, H. Martineau* lamented in December 1834 that F was being branded as a heretic by some in the Boston community. M. L. Hurlbut* soundly condemned the book in *The Christian Examiner*** (22 [March 1837]: 101–24). F reaffirmed in the *ChEx* (22 [July 1837]: 283–321) all that he had said before about the miracles. Norton perhaps had F and Ripley in mind when he fulminated in *The Latest Form of Infidelity* (1839) against those ministers who admitted the miracles were true but were to be explained as "exaggerated and discolored relations of natural events." Some who were kindly disposed toward F but were not convinced by his arguments were his revered friends Dr. W. E. Channing,* H. Ware, Jr.,* F. H. Hedge,* and Emerson. Some who found F's ideas agreeable were C. P. Cranch,* C. Francis, and J. F. Clarke* in his *Western Messenger*** (21 [December 1836]: 341–49).

Throughout his life F maintained a friendship with the early group of New England Transcendentalists, all of whom he outlived. He and Emerson had a long and affectionate relationship, which has been traced in over 90 Emerson-

F letters in Horace Howard Furness's *Records of a Lifelong Friendship* (1910). They were childhood schoolmates and playmates in Boston and over the years followed each other's careers through correspondence and visits. In Philadelphia F was often Emerson's apologist and literary liaison with the publishers in the city, and F was, as Emerson said to Fuller, "my dear gossip." At the death of Emerson, F was called to conduct a private funeral service at Emerson's home. F and Alcott, likewise, enjoyed a long and special friendship. Alcott paid him a high compliment by including a verse portrait of him in "Sonnet III" (Part 2) in *Sonnets and Canzonets* (1882). With several other of the Transcendentalist ministers—Francis, Hedge, Parker, Clarke, M. D. Conway,* and Cranch, F remained in close touch throughout the years. He strongly protested Parker's exclusion by the conservative Unitarians in Boston and was an able collaborator with Hedge in translating the prose and poetry of major German writers.

References: There is no complete biography of F. Two of several substantial accounts of his life are John White Chadwick's necrology in the *ChReg* (6 January 1896): 84–86; and "WHF," in *Heralds*, 3: 133–38. Good historical and critical treatments of Unitarianism by G. W. Cooke* (1902), O. B. Frothingham* (1876), Conrad Wright, and Robinson (1985) place him in his denominational milieu, as does his own autobiographical sermon *Recollections of Seventy Years* (1895); and in matters of church reform and aesthetics he is cited, respectively, in Hutchison (1959) and in Buell (1973). F's involvement in the Miracles Controversy and his personal views on the miracles and Christ are treated in R. Joseph Hoffmann, "WHF: The Transcendentalist Defense of the Gospels," *NEQ* 56 (1983): 238–60; and Guy R. Woodall, "WHF's *Remarks on the Four Gospels* in the 'Annus Mirabilis' (1836)," *ATQ* 3, NS (September 1989): 233–44. References to him are numerous in the published letters and journals** of Emerson, Alcott, Conway, Cranch, Francis, and other Transcendentalists. For Cranch's opinion, see Francis P. Dedmond, "Christopher P. Cranch's Journal. 1839," *SAR* 1983: 131.

Guy R. Woodall

G

GARRISON, WILLIAM LLOYD (1805–1879), was among the most notable of the leaders of the abolition** movement. In Boston on 1 January 1831 he founded *The Liberator*, which was destined to become one of the most influential antislavery journals of the time. In 1832, G, with E. G. Loring* and others, founded the New England Anti-Slavery Society. G was committed to the philosophy of "immediate emancipation," and he eschewed political action as a means to achieve this end. His evangelical fervor in pursuing the goals of abolition, as well as his sometimes abrasive attacks on those holding different opinions, irritated many of Boston's social elite and also many prominent Transcendentalists.

While R. W. Emerson,* at times, clearly shared this irritation, his journals** show that eventually he came to feel considerable admiration for the man. Indeed, some of his earliest comments on G (1839) describe him as "a man of great ability in conversation, of a certain longsightedness in debate which is a great excellence . . . and an eloquence of illustration which contents the ear & the mind." Later, in 1846, his estimation of the man had grown, and he came to see G as one of "the five or six personalities that make up . . . our American existence." B. Alcott* was also impressed with G since first hearing him lecture on slavery in 1830, and his brother-in-law, S. J. May,* became one of G's earliest and strongest supporters.

G was also highly regarded in the Thoreau household. A Women's Anti-Slavery Society was formed in Concord** around 1837 and counted the Thoreau women, as well as L. Emerson* and her daughters, as members. While H. Thoreau,* like Emerson, felt strong reservations about G's emphasis on organized efforts at reform, he also was eventually drawn into a virtual alliance with G's organization. Thus, it was at a mass meeting called by G on the 4th of July 1854, to protest the rendition of the fugitive slave Anthony Burns, that Thoreau delivered what is probably his most virulent address, "Slavery in Massachusetts'' (*RP*, 91–109). G further outraged conservatives when he ceremoniously burned a copy of the U.S. Constitution at the same meeting.

As agitation on the antislavery issue became more heated from the mid-1840s on, Emerson often responded positively to requests from G that he speak on the subject. Thoreau, T. Parker,* W. H. Channing,* and others would do the same. Parker was impressed with G from the first, and they soon became united in the cause of antislavery. It has been suggested that Parker was converted to abolitionism largely by the example of G and his followers. Emerson's opinion of G throughout this tumultuous time is probably best summed up in the statement, ''I cannot speak of that gentleman without respect.''

References: Good modern biographies of G are Walter M. Merrill, *Against Wind and Tide: A Biography of WLG* (1963), and John L. Thomas, *The Liberator: WLG* (1963). For an early view on the relationship between Emerson and G, see J. J. Chapman,* *WLG* (1913); for a later view of this relationship, see Gougeon (1990). Also useful are Wendell Phillips Garrison, *WLG, 1805–1879, The Story of His Life Told by His Children*, 4 vols. (1885; rpt. 1969), and Walter H. Merrill and Louis Ruchames, eds., *The Letters of WLG*, 6 vols. (1971–81). For a study of philosophical influence, see James Duban, ''Thoreau, G, and Dymond: Unbending Firmness of the Mind,'' *AL* 57 (May 1985): 273–86.

Len Gougeon

GÉRANDO, JOSEPH MARIE, BARON DE (1772–1842), historian of philosophy, legal and educational theorist, before 1789 intended to enter the priesthood, but after a series of exiles, he returned to France for good in 1798 with his wife, Annette de Rathsamhausen. After his 1799 paper on signs and the formation of ideas took first prize at the Institut de France, he prepared it for publication as *Des Signes et de l'art de penser, considérés dans leurs rapports mutuels* (1800). His appointment to the Ministry of the Interior began a distinguished career of administrative service in France, Italy, and Catalonia. He lectured on moral philosophy** at the Lycée de Paris, and his 1802 paper on the genesis of human knowledge won the prize of the Academy of Berlin. This led to his influential *Histoire comparée des systèmes de philosophie, considérés relativement aux principes des connaisances humaines* (3 vols., 1804). In 1819 he began lecturing on administrative law in Paris and was also actively engaged in several educational and philanthropic projects. This resulted in *Le visiteur du pauvre* (1820), *Du perfectionnement morale, ou de l'éducation de soi-même* (1824), and *De l'éducation des sourds-muets de naissance* (1827). Other important texts include his classic ethnographic advisory *Considérations sur les diverses méthodes à suivre dans l'observation des peuples sauvages* (1800) and the *Traité de la bienfaisance publique* (1839).

E. Peabody* translated in Boston the 1820 and 1824 works as *The Visitor of the Poor* (1832) and *Self-education: or, The Means and Art of Moral Progress* (1830), the latter also appearing in revised editions in 1832 and 1860. G. Ripley* wrote a long review essay, ''Degerando on Self-Education,'' in *The Christian Examiner*,** and B. Alcott* drew on it for his early writings about education.**

G should be given a place along with Pestalozzi** and others as theorist for the Temple** and Brook Farm** schools. Important as G's thinking on education and moral development was for Transcendentalists, his *Histoire comparée . . . de philosophie* may have had more impact. A frequently consulted guide to philosophy, its correctness of detail and comprehensive view was virtually unequaled in its time. R. W. Emerson* began reading it in January 1830, ''beginning on the best recommendation'' (Peabody? A. Murat?* V. Cousin?).** G intended his critical exposition of philosophic systems to present the strengths of each, in effect announcing the principle of eclecticism before Cousin. The *Histoire*'s introduction to the pre-Socratic philosophers, gnostics, and Neoplatonists** in the implicit context of modern philosophic systems influenced Emerson, who commented extensively in his journal** on G's writing as support for his own search for a ''First Philosophy.'' In 1837–38 H. D. Thoreau* outlined parts of the first two volumes, although he might have had to compete for reading time with M. Fuller,* who had two volumes of Emerson's Degerando in May 1837. As a critical historian of philosophy and as a social reformer, G was a significant influence on the Transcendentalist movement.

References: Ripley's ''Degerando on Self-Education'' appeared in *ChEx* 9 (1830): 70–107; Peabody's ''Joseph Marie de G'' in *NAR* 92 (1861): 391–415. William Girard, ''Du Transcendentalism consideré essentiellement dans sa definition at ses origines françaises,'' *UCPMP* 4 (18 October 1916): 351–498, recognizes G among important French influences. Kenneth Cameron, ''The Pre-Platonic Philosophers Through the Eye of Baron G,'' in *Emerson the Essayist* (1945), 17–36, and Carl F. Strauch, ''G: A Source for Emerson,'' *MLN* 58 (1943): 64–67, discuss Emerson's use of G. See Cameron, *Transcendentalists and Minerva* (1958), 248–61, for Thoreau's interest.

Frank Shuffelton

GODDARD, MARTHA LE BARON (1829–1888), lived for over 15 years in Worcester, Massachusetts, and participated in a literary circle influenced by the concepts and the writings of the Transcendentalists (T. W. Higginson,* H. G. O. Blake* T. Brown*). During that period, she wrote a series of ''Home Letters'' for the *Worcester Evening Transcript* (1860). In 1868 when her husband, Delano A. Goddard (1831–1882), became editor of the *Boston Daily Advertiser*, she became its review editor as well as Boston correspondent for the *Worcester Spy*. Comments on literary figures (H. Thoreau,* B. Alcott,* N. Hawthorne,* G. W. Curtis,* Higginson, Holmes*) are scattered among her periodical writings. She corresponded in the 1870s and 1880s with the educational theorist Thomas Davidson (1840–1900), with whom she shared discussions of Transcendentalism. With H. W. Preston, she edited a collection, *Sea and Shore* (1874), including poems by Thoreau and R. W. Emerson.*

References: *Letters of MLG* (1901) is a selection by Sarah Brown, wife of T. Brown. Ruth H. Frost's biographical sketch, ed. K. W. Cameron, *ARLR* 6 (1992): 130–47, is updated in Kent P. Ljungquist, ''MLG: Forgotten Worcester Writer and Thoreau Critic,'' *CS* 2 (1994): 149–56.

Kent P. Ljungquist

GODWIN, PARKE (1816–1904), was not a Transcendentalist. However, his interest in social reform and the works of C. Fourier* connect him to the Brook Farm** experiment and to the Transcendentalists involved in that enterprise. G was born into a wealthy and relatively prominent New Jersey family with Federalist leanings. Earlier generations of the family had fought in the Revolution, and his father had served in the War of 1812. After his graduation from Princeton in 1834, G studied law in Paterson, New Jersey, and then moved to Louisville, Kentucky, where he planned to start a practice. According to many accounts, the institution of slavery in the Southern states disturbed him and prompted his return in 1836 to New York, where he met W. C. Bryant.* Bryant helped G see a future in journalism when he offered him a position on the New York *Evening Post*. The association lasted for over four decades, and in 1842 G married Bryant's daughter, Fanny. During this same period, he also contributed to J. L. O'Sullivan's *United States Magazine and Democratic Review*.

G's articles in these journals demonstrate his early commitment to Jacksonian democracy** and the promise of free enterprise capitalism. He became, however, increasingly disillusioned with the Democratic Party's notions of government and converted to Fouricrism. He was one of a group of reform-minded New Yorkers who viewed the Brook Farm experiment with interest. Although he never lived at the community, he did visit and gave the enterprise his complete verbal support, especially when the community began plans to convert the ''Association'' to a ''Phalanx'' based on Fourier's model.

As a leading American advocate of Fourier, G edited and contributed to *The Harbinger*** as well as the *Phalanx*. He also wrote *Democracy, Constructive and Pacific* (1843) and *A Popular View of the Doctrines of Fourier* (1844). In the latter, he defended Fourier against charges of immorality, a common criticism based on Fourier's views on marriage. G was one of the New York Fourierists who helped to create a national organization that, for a short time, united the existing Fourier societies in the United States. In the constitution of the American Union of Associationists,** announced in *The Harbinger* in 1846, G was named as the foreign corresponding secretary.

While national enthusiasm for *The Harbinger* and the American Union of Associationists waned in the following few years, G remained active in social reform movements, focusing on issues like labor reform and slavery. He is primarily known as an editor, a position he held on a variety of magazines and newspapers until he retired from public life. He edited *Putnam's Monthly Magazine,*** the New York *Evening Post* (after the death of Bryant in 1878), and the *Commercial Advertiser*. His works demonstrate the diversity of his interests; they include a translation of the first section of Goethe's* *Autobiography* (1846–47), *Vala: A Mythological Tale* (1851), a biography of his father-in-law (1883), and a study of Shakespeare's** sonnets (1900).

REFERENCES: Substantial treatments of G do not exist, but Carl J. Guarneri, *The Utopian Alternative: Fourierism in Nineteenth Century America* (1991), treats G in detail. Also useful are W. W. Clayton's *History of Bergen and Passaic Counties, N.J.* (1882) and William Nelson and C. A. Schriner's *History of Paterson and its Environs* (1920).

Julie M. Norko

GOETHE, JOHANN WOLFGANG VON (1749–1832), the preeminent figure in German literature and by virtue of the range and brilliance of his accomplishments the prime instance of a universal genius in the history of European culture, confronted the Transcendentalists with a cultural and moral challenge that some found disturbing and others liberating. G's all-embracing humanism and his cultured broad-mindedness were bound to make him suspect or morally offensive to representatives of a movement informed, to a degree, by New England's religious and moral idealism;** at the same time, G's dominant ideal of *Bildung* (the complete and harmonious development of the individual) enriched and supported the Transcendentalist understanding of and aspiration to self-culture.

G was the Continental writer most extensively discussed in American periodicals in the heyday of Transcendentalism. Many of his works were available in translation, the most famous of these being Carlyle's* versions of *Wilhelm Meister's Apprenticeship* (1824) and *Wilhelm Meister's Travels* (1827). Several Transcendentalists produced translations of their own, for example, M. Fuller,* *Torquato Tasso* (1834; publ. 1860); J. F. Clarke,* "Orphic Sayings. From G" (1836); and S. G. Ward,* *Essays on Art* (1845). G had become increasingly available in German since 1819, when he presented a 30-volume edition of his works to Harvard. For Transcendentalist readers the most complete G was the 55-volume edition published by J. G. Cotta in Stuttgart (1827–33); R. W. Emerson,* for example, had a complete set by 1836.

Almost every Transcendentalist had something negative or positive to say about G. The attitudes of the two most significantly affected by G—Fuller and Emerson—also embody the ambivalence toward him characteristic of the Transcendentalist response as a whole. More than anyone else, however, Fuller and Emerson succeeded in making constructive use of what G uniquely had to offer. Although Fuller complained of G's hyperintellectualism and artistic formalism, she became his most fervent defender in a New England all too ready to condemn him and many of his works for "immorality." She honored G as a true liberator of the human spirit, the champion of self-culture, and an ally in her feminist aspirations. G was not only "the great apostle of individual culture," but he "always represent[ed] the highest principle in the feminine form." In his portrayal of the remarkable women that people his oeuvre, G "aims at a pure self-subsistence, and free development of any powers with which they may be gifted by nature" (*Woman in the Nineteenth Century; The Dial*** 2 [July 1841]: 26). Fuller's most ambitious scholarly project was a biography of G, which she was not able to complete. Emerson—though troubled by G's "immorality," courtier's lifestyle, and preference for the real rather than the ideal—considered G the crucial figure in modern literature. G's naturalistic pantheism,** his theories of art and literature, his concepts of metamorphosis and polarity, and his commitment to individual culture profoundly affected Emerson's views. Emerson was also impressed with G's symbolic theory of history. G treated selected persons, events, or objects from the past as symbolic in two senses: (1) as embodying a given idea and (2) as signifying, through the very intensity and concreteness of their particularity, many similar persons, events, or objects. For ''symbolic'' in this second sense, G often substituted the term ''representative.'' G's biographical works best exemplify his symbolic theory of history, and they especially demonstrate the various implications of his concept of representativeness. These works not only were a major influence on Emerson's historical thinking but also became the chief conceptual and formal model for *Representative Men*. Finally, Emerson the ''philosophical poet'' (as Frost called him) learned much, technically and methodologically, from G's *Gedankenlyrik* (poetry of ideas).

References: Stanley M. Vogel, *German Literary Influences on the American Transcendentalists* (1955), and Pochmann (1957) provide detailed surveys of the Transcendentalist reception of G. Frederick Augustus Braun, *Margaret Fuller and G* (1910) is still useful. Russell E. Durning, *Margaret Fuller, Citizen of the World* (1969), 89–120, examines in detail Fuller's writings on G and her translations of several of his works. David M. Robinson, ''Margaret Fuller and the Transcendental Ethos: *Woman in the Nineteenth Century*,'' *PMLA* 97 (January 1982): 83–98, contains a perceptive discussion of G's role in Fuller's personal and intellectual development. Frederick B. Wahr, *Emerson and G* (1915), studies Emerson's critical response to G. Gustaaf Van Cromphout, *Emerson's Modernity and the Example of G* (1990), examines the impact on Emerson of the man he considered the pivotal figure in modern literature.

Gustaaf Van Cromphout

GOODWIN, HERSEY BRADFORD (1805–1836), was colleague pastor to the Rev. E. Ripley* at First Parish Church in Concord, Massachusetts.** Though only 30 when he died, he touched the Emerson family in important ways and impressed R. W. Emerson,* who had resigned his own pulpit in 1832, as an exemplary minister. Born in Plymouth, Massachusetts, G graduated from Harvard College in 1826, then entered the Harvard Divinity School.** At his installation in Concord on 17 February 1830, the Right Hand of Fellowship was offered by Ripley's stepgrandson the Rev. R. W. Emerson, who attended with the delegate from Second Church in Boston—his brother and parishioner C. C. Emerson.*

Though frail and self-effacing, G as student and minister was immediately and widely popular for his keen intelligence, character, and personal warmth. B. Frost* recalled his sermons as ''clear, graceful, sententious, and direct,'' his social views as not ''radical'' but ''progressive.'' Emerson enjoyed hearing him preach as late as October 1835, and Cazneau Palfrey thought his delivery had the pleasing ''effect of extemporaneous speaking.'' Interested in history and reform of public education,** G lectured at the Concord Lyceum,** served on the school and town library committees, and was an early practitioner of total abstinence from alcohol. His first wife, Lucretia Ann Watson of Plymouth, died in 1831 after 17 months of marriage; in 1834 he married Amelia Mackay of Boston.

After C. C. Emerson died suddenly on 9 May 1836, G preached the eulogy, earning the gratitude of the Emersons for his depiction of Charles and moving them with his message of consolation: Even ''when the child of bright promise is taken from earth,'' we may be assured that ''he is now as a treasure that is laid up in heaven.'' The fragility of life, he had admonished his listeners, is a lesson not just for the old but for the young ''who have high hopes and bright prospects.'' Yet it came as a shock when on 9 July young G, who suffered from heart disease, died two days after being stricken while visiting Plymouth. Grieving over his double loss, R. W. Emerson eulogized G as ''an amiable and devout spirit'' who ''loved truth,'' selflessly served others while maintaining ''the independence of his character,'' and exhibited ''no mean gifts as a writer and public speaker.'' As a strawman for Emerson's own ongoing vocational struggle, G represented the ministerial virtues of the emerging new age, just as his successor in the Concord pulpit, the unfortunate B. Frost, would embody dryasdust formalism in the Divinity School Address two years later.

References: On G's life and career, see [Cazneau Palfrey,] ''A Memoir of the Rev. HBG,'' *ChEx*** 21 (January 1837): 273–91 (includes selections from a sermon, school committee report, a ''discourse on Atheism,'' and the conclusion to his eulogy for C. C. Emerson); and William B. Sprague, *Annals of the American Pulpit* (1865), 8: 548–52. Personal accounts are by G's college classmate Andrew Preston Peabody, *Harvard Reminiscences* (1888), 155–57, and by Frost, ''Memoir of HB.G,'' *Memoirs of Members of the Social Circle in Concord. Second Series, From 1795 to 1840* (1888), 276–85. On Emerson's connection, see Kenneth Walter Cameron, ''Emerson's Ideal Clergyman—HBG,'' *ESQ* 12 (3d Q 1958): 39–44; the texts of Emerson's ''Right Hand of Fellowship'' (*Sermons* 4: 262–64) and his eulogy of G (*Sermons* 4: 244–50); and analysis of the eulogy in Wesley T. Mott, *''The Strains of Eloquence''* (1989), 174–82.

Wesley T. Mott

GRAHAM, SYLVESTER (1794–1851), was a leading prophet of health, diet, hygiene, and sexual reform in the 1830s—an advocate of vegetarianism, unbolted flour, moderate exercise, loose clothing, cold baths, and strict temperance.** Along with William Andrus Alcott, A. B. Alcott's* cousin, G lectured to large audiences on the need to eschew debilitating stimulants. Their work, called ''Grahamism,''** attracted people involved in temperance movements, physical and moral purity, and the retheorization of sexual mores. By the late 1830s, G's followers included such luminaries as H. Greeley,* the Grimké sisters and Theodore Weld, Mary Gove, and Gerrit Smith; and his ideas on dinner informed the menu at Fruitlands,** Brook Farm,** the Northampton Association, Shaker** villages, the Oneida community, certain colleges, and Seventh Day Adventist circles. R. W. Emerson* apostrophized G as the ''poet of bran bread and pumpkins''; today, a cracker still bears his name.

G, who had served briefly in the Presbyterian ministry, became a temperance agent in 1830. When he added lectures on chastity, the prevention of cholera, and general diet reform to his repertoire, his popularity soared from Philadelphia to Boston, and as far west as Ohio. Published works that added to his fame include *The Young Man's Guide to Chastity. The Aesculapian Tablets of the Nineteenth Century* (1834), and *Treatise on Bread and Bread-Making* (1837). The last-named inspired a riot, on one occasion, when butchers and bakers showed up at a lecture to decry G's allegations about their trades.

The Graham Journal of Health and Longevity spread his views between 1837 and 1839; then G published his magnum opus, *Lectures on the Science of Human Life* (1839). After 1840, his influence and popularity drooped, and G began a large work on the Christian Scriptures. He completed only the first volume, *The Philosophy of Sacred History* (1855).

Scholars have credited William Andrus Alcott with doing more to establish American vegetarianism and related health reforms. But G was the better showman: Contemporaries commented on his histrionic gestures one found ''rather fantastical,'' and another lampooned him as a ''Peristaltic Persuader.'' G's emphasis on sexual ethics probably added to the furor: Following the work of François J. V. Broussais, he believed that excessive stimulation lay at the heart of most diseases and increased vulnerability. He therefore advocated abstinence from unnecessary stimulants, especially alcohol, tobacco, spices, and refined foods—but also sexual intercourse. Believing that even lustful thoughts inflamed and irritated the nerves and tissues associated with sexual pleasure, G proposed that disciples indulge their sexual appetites no more than once a month. Just as food should be chewed thoroughly, and with a merry heart, so sexual relations should be savored, fully digested, and enjoyed with moderation.

With no medical training, G was inevitably mocked by physicians of his own day; nonetheless, he taught Americans to think about diet, exercise, sexual practices, and hygiene, in an early crusade for preventive health care based on self-discipline.

REFERENCES: The best study is Stephen Nissenbaum, *Sex, Diet, and Debility in Jacksonian America: SG and Health Reform* (1980). But see also James C. Whorton, *Crusaders for Fitness: The History of American Health Reformers* (1982), and Mildred Naylor, ''SG, 1794–1851,'' *Annals of Medical History* 4 (1942): 236–40. G's ties to one Transcendentalist are investigated in James Armstrong, ''Thoreau,* Chastity, and the Reformers,'' in *Thoreau's Psychology*, ed. Raymond D. Gozzi (1983), 123–44.

Barbara Ryan

GRAY, ASA (1810–1888), botanist, fought for the acceptance of C. Darwin's* *Origin of Species* in America. A Darwinian theist who was never affiliated with the Transcendentalists, G argued against the mutual exclusivity of evolution theory and natural design. Born in Sauquoit, New York, and raised an orthodox Presbyterian, G took an M.D. degree from Fairfield Medical School in 1831. After serving as curator to the New York Lyceum of Natural History, in 1842 he was appointed Fisher Professor of Natural History** at Harvard College, where he remained until his death. He published widely, most notably *Flora of North America*, with John Torrey (1838–43), and *Manual of the Botany of the Northern United States* (1848).

G met Darwin in London in 1839, and the two began corresponding in 1855. In 1859, upon reading his friend's newly published *Origin of Species*, G began a public campaign to secure an American audience for Darwin, which led to public confrontations, both in debates and in journals, with his Harvard colleague L. Agassiz,* among others. Agassiz's popular position held that nature** progressed according to the design of a supreme power rather than through natural selection, while G argued that evolution does not preclude design in nature and indeed may progress according to it. Hence, G espoused a theory of nature uniting scientific theory with belief in a creative, potentially controlling force. G collected 13 of his articles defending Darwin in *Darwiniana: Essays and Reviews Pertaining to Darwinism* (1876; 1963).

R. W. Emerson* invited G to join the Saturday Club** in 1873; however, there is no evidence of any association between G and the Concord** Transcendentalists.

References: A collection of G's botanical works is *Scientific Papers of AG*, 2 vols., ed. Charles S. Sargent (1889). See also *Letters of AG*, 2 vols., ed. Jane Loring Gray (1893). A full biography that touches on G's lack of contact with the Transcendentalists is A. Hunter Dupree, *AG* (1959). Dupree's introduction to the 1963 Harvard edition of *Darwiniana* is an excellent source on G's Darwinian theism. Also of interest is *Calendar of the Letters of Charles Robert Darwin to AG*, prepared by the Historical Records Survey, intro. Bert James Lowenberg (1959).

Alan D. Brasher

GREAVES, JAMES PIERREPONT (1777–1842), was an English mystic and reformer who was influenced early in his life by J. H. Pestalozzi** and later by A. B. Alcott.* In addition, he was a follower of J. Böhme** and was well read in German transcendentalism. Following a failed career in business, G became interested in education reform** and in 1817 joined Pestalozzi for four years at his experimental school in Yverdun. After another four years during which he taught on the Continent, G returned to England and established the London Infant School Society with the intention of spreading Pestalozzi's pedagogical theories and practices.

During this period, he published *Three Hundred Maxims, for the Consideration of Parents* and *Physical and Metaphysical Hints for Every Body*, both issued in London in 1827 and edited by his friend and fellow educator Edward Biber. The former work, with some additional material, was later published in America under the title *Spiritual Culture; or, Thoughts for the Consideration of Parents and Teachers* (1841). In *Letters on Early Education* (1827) he translated the communications that Pestalozzi had sent him; this book was published in New England as *Letters of Pestalozzi on the Education of Infancy* (1830), which helped disseminate Pestalozzi's ideas among American teachers, including Alcott.

In the early 1830s, G became involved in a scheme in rural England to improve the lot of agricultural workers. Upon his return to London he founded the Aesthetic Institution, or the Syncretics, a philosophical society that numbered among its participants John Abraham Heraud, John Goodwyn Barmby, Francis Foster Barham, and others mentioned by R. W. Emerson* in ''English Reformers,'' *The Dial*** 3 (October 1842): 227–47. In 1837, having received a copy of E. Peabody's* *Record of a School* from H. Martineau,* who had recently visited Boston, G initiated correspondence with Alcott, whose Temple School** he found inspiring, and expressed hope that they could one day meet. Alcott, in response, shipped over *Conversations with Children on the Gospels* as well as other copies of his works.

In 1838, with the help of William Oldham, Henry G. Wright, and C. Lane,* G established in Surrey the Alcott House, a school modeled directly on Alcott's Temple School. There, as Alcott had been doing in America, the staff encouraged self-culture and attempted to nurture the God-like spirituality of the young pupils. As part of his larger reform agenda, G promoted celibacy, water drinking, and vegetarianism among his colleagues and advocated hydrotherapy. Unfortunately, he died several months before Alcott's visit to England in 1842. Despite never having the opportunity to meet his English devotee, Alcott greatly enjoyed the homage he received at Alcott House and was joined on his return voyage with Wright and Lane, the latter of whom became Alcott's partner in the utopian experiment at Fruitlands** in 1843.

REFERENCES: *Letters and Extracts from the MS Writings of JPG*, 2 vols., was published in England in 1843 and 1845. Perhaps the most informative tribute to G is Lane's ''JPG,'' *The Dial* 3 (October 1842, January 1843): 247–55, 281–96, in his introduction to which Emerson wrote: ''Timely and welcome!'' for it reveals ''a certain grandeur about the traits of this distinguished person, which we hardly know where to parallel in recent biography.'' For further information about G, as well as his coadjutors at Alcott House, see Joel Myerson, ''William Harry Harland's 'Bronson Alcott's English Friends,' '' *RALS* 8 (spring 1978): 24–60.

Larry A. Carlson

GREELEY, HORACE (1811–1872), journalist, author, and reform politician, was born in Amherst, New Hampshire, to a poor farm family. Although prodigiously erudite as an adult, he was largely self-educated. Following a four-year apprenticeship as a printer, in 1831, out of work, he moved to New York City and soon graduated into full-fledged journalism. In 1837, still struggling financially but having made a name for himself as a writer and editor, he was invited to join—as a kind of downstate junior partner—with Albany's Thurlow Weed and Auburn's William H. Seward in forming a political triumvirate that dominated New York State's Whig (later Republican) politics for many years.

In 1841, G founded the New York *Tribune*, which promptly became a financial success and within several years was apparently the nation's most influential daily newspaper. By 1860 the paper enjoyed a circulation of nearly 300,000, and a decade later, its editor presided over some 500 employees. G became one of the nation's most respected opinion leaders. He regularly traveled the lecture circuit and was the author of several books.

The Transcendentalists fascinated G. ''Not that I agree with all that is taught and received as Transcendentalism,'' he once explained, ''but I do like its spirit and its ennobling tendencies. Its apostles are mainly among the noblest spirits living.'' He was a member of the Transcendentalist clergyman W. H. Channing's* short-lived ''Christian Union'' congregation in New York; he constantly praised *The Dial*,** the movement's literary organ, in the columns of the *Tribune*, sometimes reprinting extracts; and toward R. W. Emerson* he professed an almost reverential regard, although the philosopher's radical individualism hardly meshed with G's lifelong advocacy of Fourierism* and other communitarian designs for social organization. Indeed, G invested financially in the Brook Farm** enterprise during its phalanx period and wrote for *The Harbinger*.** He also became personally associated with a number of leading Transcendentalists. For several years he acted as H. Thoreau's* unpaid literary agent and is thought to have reviewed the writer's first book in the *Tribune*. At various times, he employed M. Fuller,* founding editor of *The Dial*, and G. Ripley,* organizer of Brook Farm, as resident literary critics. And from 1847 to 1862 he commanded the services of another prominent Brook Farmer, C. A. Dana,* who eventually became G's editorial second-in-command.

''There can be little doubt,'' writes G's principal biographer, ''that the individualism of these members of the Transcendentalist school had a considerable influence in the molding of G's views on social problems.'' Although he was always much more of a consistent believer in collective—even governmental—solutions to public problems than most Transcendentalists, his reforming impulse seems to have been occasionally skewed (as toward the ''labor question'') by an almost Emersonian belief in self-help and private virtue. Be that as it may, G encouraged nearly every popular reform of the day, only woman suffrage and free trade failing to win his ardor. For G personally, being a celebrity was not enough. Like many a reformer before and since, he coveted formal political power. A brief and disputatious term in Congress (1849) seemed to prove him temperamentally unsuited to high office. Thereafter, frustrated by lack of support from Whig and Republican politicos, G increasingly charted an independent course. By 1860 he had broken with Weed and Seward, during the Civil War he supported President Lincoln only sporadically, and in 1871 he openly turned on President Grant. His campaign for the White House in 1872, based on a politically unworkable fusion of Democrats and ''liberal Republicans,'' was a disaster. Grant won the 19th century's largest Republican popular majority, and the great editor, psychologically crushed, died within a month of the election.

REFERENCES: See Glyndon Van Deusen, *HG* (1953); Carl Guarneri, *The Utopian Alternative* (1991); Michael Meyer, "The Case for G's *Tribune* Review of *A Week*," *ESQ* 25 (1979): 92–94; G, *Hints Toward Reform* (1853); G in Walter Harding, ed., *Thoreau* (1962); G, *Recollections* (1869); John Codman, *Brook Farm* (1894).

Jo Ann Manfra

GREENE, WILLIAM BATCHELDER (1819–1878), a West Point–educated army lieutenant and Union colonel, onetime Unitarian** minister, social reformer, mathematician, essayist, and poet, represented a fiercely individualistic strain of Transcendentalism and was thus perceived by some of his more famous peers as a social radical courting controversy. Opinionated and brash, G was apparently nonetheless charming, and his zealous devotion to various reform movements endeared him to his fellow New Englanders.

As a short-term participant at Brook Farm** and as a member of the Town and Country Club,** G was well known to most of the major Transcendentalists. He gained the recognition of New England's intelligentsia by way of the introduction afforded him by E. Peabody,* whom he met in 1841 at her Boston bookstore. Impressed by his formidable intellect, Peabody introduced G to W. E. Channing* and spoke warmly enough of him that he was later invited to Concord,** where he met R. W. Emerson.* Emerson was reportedly "delighted" by the man M. Fuller,* perhaps half-sarcastically, had described in a letter to Emerson as "the material-spiritual-heroic-vivacious phoenix of the day." E. D. Cheney* recorded that during one of the public Conversations** held in Boston on the topic of the "Angelic and Demonic Man," B. Alcott* portrayed the demonic man in his remarks as someone who closely resembled G both physically and temperamentally, and Alcott concluded that the "demonic man is logical, loves disputation and argument." Knowing audience members detected the thinly veiled comparison to G, who, seated in front of Alcott, retorted, "But has not the demonic man his value?" Alcott assented but countered sharply, "[H]e is good to build railroads; but I do not like to see him in pulpits." Undeterred by such criticism and committed to radical causes for the rest of his life, a jocular G later joked with T. Parker* that he was disappointed to discover that Parker, one of the most unorthodox theologians to upset conventional New England clergymen, was "such a rotten conservative." Even among the most progressive, free-thinking minds that the young country had yet produced, G considered himself, and was perceived by others, as a radical nonconformist without peer.

G was an industrious writer whose interests were widely eclectic and whose subjects were almost always controversial. His first publication, "First Principles," is also perhaps his most important, appearing as it did by Emerson's editorial decision in *The Dial*** in 1842. The essay offers G's metaphysical speculations on love, freedom, and destiny and reveals his affinity for deductive reasoning even when applied to abstract thought. In 1849 he published *Transcendentalism,* a pamphlet dedicated to Emerson, but true to his iconoclastic nature, much of what G argued would have been unacceptable to most Transcendentalists. G continued to publish a number of pamphlets throughout his lifetime with such far-flung titles as ''Mutual Banking''; ''The Sovereignty of the People,'' a document that confirms G's aggressive stance on civil liberties; ''Explanations of the Theory of the Calculus''; and ''Socialistic, Communistic, Mutualistic, and Financial Fragments,'' an 1875 text containing G's controversial social theories on labor concerns, free love,** and anarchism. G's contentious personality and extremist positions were at once the cause of his short-lived celebrity among Transcendentalists and also the reason that, owing to his ultraradical views, he never achieved wider, more lasting recognition.

References: For discussions of G by his contemporaries, see Peabody, *Reminiscences of Rev. William Ellery Channing* (1880), and T. W. Higginson,* *Cheerful Yesterdays* (1898). The most detailed and useful modern biographical accounts of G are in Cooke* (1902), 2: 117–28, and *NET* Dial, 155–56.

Layne Neeper

GREENOUGH, HORATIO (1805–1852), an acquaintance of R. W. Emerson,* was born in Boston and was the first American to choose sculpture as a profession. He graduated from Harvard in 1825, sailing toward the end of his senior year for Rome, where he began serious study of his art. Drawn to the artistic wealth and beauty of Florence, G moved to that Italian city in 1828 and there first met Emerson in 1833. Over the next two decades, they exchanged 14 letters that reveal a similarity between their theories of aesthetics. G also visited Emerson twice in Concord.**

In early 1843, Emerson visited G, who was in Washington, D.C. to supervise the placement of his federally commissioned full-length sculpture of George Washington in the rotunda of the Capitol. Experimenting with flares and torches to illuminate the statue in the dim center of the rotunda, G caused a fire on the very evening he showed the statue to Emerson. Recounting the event to M. Fuller,* Emerson wrote that he had seen ''lamps melting & exploding & brilliant balls of light falling on the floor.''

In addition to sculpting, G developed what he termed ''a theory of structure'' based upon the adaptation of forms to their functions. This theory appeared in August 1843 in his most important essay, ''American Architecture,'' which appeared in *United States Magazine and Democratic Review*. G pointed out that no meaningless ornamentation exists in nature,** that color and shape have specific functions: ''The law of adaptation is the fundamental law of nature in all structure.'' He applied this concept to a theory of American architecture that, he believed, should be adapted to American needs and the American climate. By 1852, G had collected his essays in *The Travels, Observations, and Experience of a Yankee Stonecutter*. On 2 September he sent a copy of the book to Emerson for his ''candid opinion.'' Emerson replied, ''[Y]our little book . . . contains more useful truth than any thing in America I can readily remember.'' Emerson's enthusiasm can be traced to his own organic** theory of architecture

(''Thoughts on Art,'' *The Dial*** [1840–41]), which closely parallels G's. And on 25 September, Emerson wrote to G, ''[The poet E.] Channing* & Thoreau,* who are both excellent readers, agree with me in the importance of the book.'' Emerson's assessment of G's book on behalf of Thoreau may indeed be true. However, Thoreau in his journal** earlier that year discounted, in part, G's organic theory of architecture.

Emerson's journal entry seven months after G's death indicates his sense of loss: ''I account that man, one product of American soil (born in Boston), as one of the best proofs of the capability of this country.'' Emerson's assessment of G appeared with his recollection of their 1833 meeting in *English Traits* (1856): ''At Florence, chief among artists I found HG. . . . G was a superior man, ardent and eloquent, and all his opinions had elevation and magnanimity.'' On 15 September 1863 Emerson wrote to G's brother Henry, ''I must think that the country has never met so great an intellectual loss as in that life.'' In 1869, G's widow requested that Emerson write her husband's biography. Even though he was unable to comply, he continued to remember G. Almost 20 years after G's death, Emerson wrote the words *''My Men''* in an 1871 journal entry under which he listed 18 names. G's name was among those listed.

REFERENCES: The most readily accessible text of essays by G is *Form and Function: Remarks on Art by HG*, ed. Harold A. Small, with an introduction by Erle Loran (1947). On G's theory of functionalism, see Edward Robert DeZurko, ''G's Theory of Beauty in Architecture,'' *Rice Institute Pamphlet* 39.3 (October 1952): 96–121, and Theodore M. Brown, ''G, Paine, Emerson, and the Organic Aesthetic,'' *JAAC* 14 (1956): 304–17. Studies linking Emerson and G include Charles R. Metzger, *Emerson and G: Transcendental Pioneers of an American Esthetic* (1954), and Nathalia Wright, ''Ralph Waldo Emerson and HG,'' *HLB* 12 (1958): 91–116, which first printed all correspondence between the two. See also Vivian C. Hopkins, *Spires of Form: A Study of Emerson's Aesthetic Theory* (1951), 89–92, which argues that the similarity between Emerson's and G's theory of architecture can be explained as ''interrelation rather than influence,'' and Matthiessen (1941), 136, 140–55.

Heidi M. Schultz

GRIMM, HERMAN (1828–1901), was the foremost exponent of R.W. Emerson's* writings and ideas in Germany in the 19th century and Emerson's only German correspondent of note. The son of Wilhelm G, the philologist, he was an independent scholar for a number of years, writing biographies of Michelangelo (1860–63) and Raphael (1872); in 1873 he was appointed professor of art history at the University of Berlin. With his wife Gisela von Arnim G, the daughter of Goethe's* correspondent Bettina Brentano von Arnim, he was at the center of artistic and intellectual life in Berlin for several decades.

G's interest in Emerson began when he came across the first volume of Emerson's *Essays* at the house of an American friend. ''I followed his thoughts, word for word,'' he wrote later; ''[E]verything seemed to me to be old and well known, . . . and everything was new as if I was learning it for the first time.''

G translated ''Shakspeare''** and ''Goethe'' from *Representative Men* for the *Morgenblatt für gebildete Leser* in 1856, then wrote an influential essay on Emerson for the same journal in 1859. The correspondence between the two began in April 1856 with a letter from G to Emerson, in which he wrote that he believed that ''of all the writers of our day you seem to me to understand the genius of the time most profoundly''; Emerson's responses in his letters were equally admiring of G's literary accomplishments, which included studies of Goethe and Voltaire. Between 1856 and 1872 there were 14 letters between the two, in addition to a number to and by Gisela von Arnim G and Emerson's daughter Ellen* that extended the correspondence through 1882. Emerson and G met only once, in Florence in March 1873.

References: The relevant sources are *Correspondence Between Ralph Waldo Emerson and HG*, ed. Frederick William Holls (1903); Charles Duffy, ''Material Relating to R. W. Emerson in the G *Nachlass*,'' *AL* 30 (January 1959): 523–28; and Luther S. Luedtke and Winfried Schleiner, ''New Letters from the G-Emerson Correspondence,'' *HLB* 25 (October 1977): 399–465. Emerson as a possible model for a character in G's novel *Unüberwindliche Mächte* (Unconquerable powers [1867]) is discussed in Helmut Kreuzer, ''Ralph Waldo Emerson, HG, and the Image of the American in German Literature,'' *Forum* 14 (spring 1976): 15–23.

Ralph H. Orth

GRISWOLD, RUFUS WILMOT (1815–1857), best remembered as the literary assassin of E. A. Poe,* nevertheless facilitated the growth of American literature in the 1840s. He succeeded Poe in 1842 as editor of *Graham's Magazine*, then the leading literary periodical in America. The same year he published *The Poets and Poetry of America*, which by its sheer exhaustiveness represented the coming of age of American letters: ''I have been censured,'' G wrote, ''perhaps justly, for the wide range of my selections.'' Poe, J. Very,* and C. P. Cranch* appear alongside the Schoolroom Poets and a host of less-well-remembered names. H. Thoreau's* poetry—although urged upon G by R. W. Emerson* himself—is not included.

Unlike authors who complained of a dearth of materials, G saw nearly endless possibilities in the ''local subjects'' available to the American writer, specifically detailing ''the beautiful and poetical mythology of the aborigines,'' ''the witchcraft delusion,'' and a catalog of American geography: ''chains of mountains which bind the continent; the inland seas between Itasca and the ocean; caverns, in which whole nations might be hidden; the rivers, cataracts, and sea-like prairies; and all the varieties of land, lake, river, sea and sky, between the gulfs of Mexico and Hudson''—all this roughly a decade before *Hiawatha*, *The Scarlet Letter*, or *Leaves of Grass*.

He published the companion work, *Prose Writers of America*, in 1847. In 1849 he published in the New York *Daily Tribune* the ''Ludwig'' article, which portrayed Poe as a friendless, erratic, and morbid genius and which he expanded into the 1850 ''Memoir'' in his edition of Poe's *Works*. Called by critic Daniel

Hoffman a ''busybody of letters . . . a failed poetaster fattening on the writings of others as does a moth eating Gobelin tapestries,'' G gave Poe a notoriety that probably drew more attention to the poet than any of his stories or poems ever had.

References: G's letters appear in part in *Passages from the Correspondence and Other Papers of R W. G*, ed. William M. Griswold (1898). Joy Bayless has written *RWG: Poe's Literary Executor* (1943). For Hoffman's remark, see *Poe Poe Poe Poe Poe Poe Poe* (1972), 15.

R. D. Madison

H

HALE, EDWARD EVERETT (1822–1909), was an indefatigable Unitarian** clergyman, author, and editor whose personal relationships and broad humanitarianism ultimately brought him into the orbit of Transcendentalism. H's closest Transcendentalist associates were F. H. Hedge,* with whom he edited the liberalized *Christian Examiner*** from 1857 to 1861, and J. F. Clarke,* whose *Autobiography, Diary and Correspondence* he edited in 1891.

Son of Nathan Hale, proprietor of the *Boston Daily Advertiser*, and nephew of E. Everett,* H was graduated from Harvard College in 1839 and taught in the Boston Latin School while studying theology privately. In 1846 he was ordained by the Church of the Unity, Worcester, moving in 1856 to Boston's South Congregational Church, which he served until 1899. In keeping with the major focus of his ministry—the practical application of the Gospel—H endeavored to alleviate the plight of indigent aliens and, as a solution to two social problems, worked tirelessly on behalf of the Massachusetts Emigrant Aid Company, which was settling destitute antislavery sympathizers in Kansas and Nebraska. To generate harmony and mutual assistance within society at large, he established the Christian Unity Society in 1858, and to promote fellowship and discussion among Boston intellectuals, he, along with Hedge and Clarke, organized the Examiner Club in 1863 and was its president from 1889 until his death.

The author of over 200 publications, including history, biography, theology, and literary criticism, H is best remembered for inspirational fiction such as the antisecessionist parable "The Man Without a Country," published in the *Atlantic Monthly*** in 1863, and the novelette *Ten Times One Is Ten* (1870), which spawned a national benevolent organization for youth. Many of his stories featured his alter ego, "Frederic Ingham." H's most significant editorial work was as founder of the monthly miscellany *Old and New*, which absorbed the *ChEx* and was published from 1870 to 1875.

References: The standard "library edition" of H's writings is *The Works of EEH*, 10 vols. (1898–1900). An exhaustive listing of both collected and uncollected works is Jean Holloway, "A Checklist of the Writings of EEH," *BB* 21 (May–August, September–December, January–April 1954–55): 89–92, 114–20, 140–43. A still useful biography is *The Life and Letters of EEH*, 2 vols., ed. Edward E. Hale, Jr. (1917). The most recent book-length studies are Jean Holloway, *EEH: A Biography* (1956), and John R. Adams, *EEH* (1977).

James W. Mathews

HARRIS, WILLIAM TORREY (1835–1909), educator, administrator, and lecturer, was part of the post–Civil War afterglow of Transcendentalism. Through his support of the public school kindergarten, his devotion to Hegelianism, and his work with the Concord School of Philosophy,** H sought to preserve the philosophical idealism** of the movement into an age dominated by materialist and evolutionary thinking.

H was born near North Killingly, Connecticut. After an intermittent education, he moved to St. Louis, where he began teaching in the public schools in 1857. During that time, he read voraciously in the works of Cousin,* Locke,** and R. W. Emerson;* through the writing of Carlyle* and Parker* he was introduced to Goethe* and Kant.** In that same year, H met the self-taught German scholar Henry Brokmeyer, who introduced him to the philosophy of Hegel.* For H as for other American Hegelians, Hegel became an idée fixe, the dialectic a universal method for solving all human dilemmas.

By 1868 H had become superintendent of schools in St. Louis, a post that required considerable powers of organization. His most noteworthy accomplishment was the establishment in 1873 of a kindergarten as part of public education,** a reform instigated by Susan Blow. Blow had been trained in the kindergarten theory of German educator Friedrich Froebel (1782–1852). During his years in St. Louis H was also instrumental in founding the St. Louis Philosophical Society (1866) and *The Journal of Speculative Philosophy* (1867).

In 1879 H served as faculty member at the first session of B. Alcott's* Concord School of Philosophy and in the following year moved to Concord.** In 1884 he purchased Orchard House and participated in all the summer meetings until the end of the school in 1888. He frequently lectured on Hegel and other philosophical topics. After Alcott's death, H and F. B. Sanborn* published a two-volume memoir, *A. Bronson Alcott: His Life and Philosophy* (1893), based in large part on Alcott's journals** and letters to which they had access.

H's Hegelianism bears some resemblance to Transcendentalism, in the desire to find first causes behind the mask of appearance. Indeed, the American Hegelians, of whom H was an important member, popularized and Americanized German philosophical thought in the mid- and late 19th century much the way Transcendentalism had reinterpreted Kant, Fichte,** and Schelling* in the earlier decades. But there were crucial differences. The Hegelians like H saw collectivity as the fulfillment of selfhood, while Emerson, H. Thoreau,* and other

Transcendentalists focused on the solitary self. To early 20th-century pragmatists like W. James* and J. Dewey,* whom many see as the heirs of Emerson's stress on experience and change, the Hegelian dialectic seemed too rigid and mechanistic.

References: H wrote nearly 500 titles, many of them journal articles in *The Journal of Speculative Philosophy* and *Addresses and Proceedings of the National Education Association*. Selections from H and other American Hegelians, together with an excellent introduction and bibliography, are found in *The American Hegelians*, ed. William H. Goetzmann (1973). Eight H lectures from 1882 are reprinted in *Concord Lectures on Philosophy* (1883). Besides the entry in *DAB* and the biographical information in Goetzmann, the only biography is the impressionistic volume by Kurt Leidecker, *Yankee Teacher: The Life of WTH* (1946). An uneven collection is *WTH, 1835–1935*, ed. Edward Schaub (1936), with several essays on H and American philosophy. For the spread of German culture in the United States, see Pochmann (1957).

Bruce A. Ronda

HAWTHORNE, NATHANIEL (1804–1864), was both attracted to and critical of Transcendentalism, finding the philosophy appealing but seeing a danger in its potential ramifications. Introduced to Transcendentalism in Salem by E. Peabody,* H eventually married her sister Sophia,* herself an R. W. Emerson* enthusiast. Before their marriage H spent several months at Brook Farm** (an experience on which he based *The Blithedale Romance* [1852]). He and Sophia were married by J. F. Clarke* in Concord** and took up residence at the Old Manse** in July 1842.

There, surrounded by Transcendentalist neighbors, in the house Emerson's grandfather built, writing in the study where Emerson composed part of *Nature*, H wrote tales about characters who, in Emersonian fashion, follow the pure Ideas in their minds (''Artist of the Beautiful,'' ''Rappaccini's Daughter,'' ''The Birth-Mark'') and sketches satirizing the Transcendentalists themselves (''The Old Manse,'' ''The Hall of Fantasy''). In his first few months in the Old Manse H dwelled upon the Emerson presence in the house and poked fun at the ''seeker'' in the notebooks his wife read—perhaps to establish himself both as the new object of Sophia's intellectual admiration and as new writer on the block.

In Concord, H acted out his ambivalent attitude toward Transcendentalism: He shunned most visitors—especially B. Alcott*—in this provincial mecca famous for intellectual conversations; attended Club meetings but did not participate; chatted amiably with M. Fuller* yet at times wrote critically of her; conversed with Emerson yet caricatured him (as, for example, ''the great original Thinker'') in his writings. Tellingly, much of H's work of this period raises Transcendentalist issues, often in glorified terms, only to expose their inadequacies—a broader employment of an ironic trope seen in several of his direct criticisms of Emerson: for example (from his notebooks), ''Emerson is a great searcher for facts; but they seem to melt away and become insubstantial in his grasp''; or (from ''The Hall of Fantasy''), ''No more earnest seeker after truth than [Emerson], and few more successful finders of it; although, sometimes, the truth assumes a mystic unreality and shadowyness in his grasp.''

H's attraction to the Transcendentalist philosophy is evidenced by the richness and appeal of such self-reliant characters as Hester and Pearl (*The Scarlet Letter* [1850]), Parson Hooper (''The Minister's Black Veil''), Ethan Brand, and Zenobia (*The Blithedale Romance*). But often he illustrates the incompleteness, futility, or monomania of an Emersonian existence: Hester, Hooper, and Brand are to various degrees driven mad by their alienation; Pearl needs familial recognition for self-identity; Brand and Zenobia commit ghastly suicides. (In *Blithedale*, not only suicide but duality, repression, and hypocrisy result from the characters' attempt to enact the Transcendentalist doctrine.) H may have seen the Transcendentalists as harmless, attractive individuals, especially enjoying his strong friendships with E. Channing* and H. Thoreau;* yet he worried (as indeed Emerson did) that their gospel might be taken too seriously. Now rooting his work in the contemporary rather than the historical, he may have offered his work in part as an antidote to the idealism** of his times.

The Hawthornes lived in Concord again in the early 1850s and 1860s, but the Transcendentalist influence during these artistically formative years (1842–45) is particularly significant. Of the 23 tales and sketches he wrote during this period, 6 refer to Transcendentalists by name, and many others—including the minor tales ''Earth's Holocaust,'' ''A Select Party'' (which depicts Transcendentalists ''on a pleasure-party into the realm of Nowhere''), ''The Celestial Rail-road'' (featuring a ''Giant Transcendentalist'' who appears as ''a heap of fog and duskiness''), ''Egotism,'' ''Buds and Bird-Voices,'' and ''Drowne's Wooden Image''—may be seen as pointed illustrations of the Transcendentalist philosophy put into action. And each of the four novels he wrote in the next decade is informed by his Concord experience.

When H died, Emerson, a pallbearer, reflected on the nature of their relationship, which never developed into the ''unreserved intercourse'' he had long hoped for: He blamed the ''tragic element'' in H, which caused his neighbor's ''painful solitude.'' It was that same quality that prevented H from an unreserved engagement with and approval of Emerson's philosophy.

References: Among critics who have looked closely at H's Transcendental traits are Marjorie Elder, *NH: Transcendental Symbolist* (1969); B. R. McElderry, ''The Transcendental H,'' *MQ* 2 (July 1961): 307–23; and Alfred Rosa, *Salem, Transcendentalism and H* (1980). On H's work as to some degree influenced by Transcendentalism, see Mary Rucker, ''Science and Art in H's 'The Birth-Mark,' '' *NCL* 41 (March 1987): 443–61; Michael Colacurcio, ''A Better Mode of Evidence,'' *ESQ* 54 (1969): 12–22; Carol Marie Bensick, *La Nouvelle Beatrice* (1985); Millicent Bell, *H's View of the Artist* (1962), 95–111; Richard Toby Widdicombe, ''H's 'Celestial Rail-road' and Transcendentalism: Apologia or Caricature,'' *NHR* 17 (fall 1991): 5–8; Larry J. Reynolds, ''H and Emerson in 'The Old Manse,' '' *StN* 23 (spring 1991): 60–81; David van Leer,

"Hester's Labyrinth: Transcendental Rhetoric in Puritan Boston," *New Essays on* The Scarlet Letter, ed. Michael Colacurcio (1985), 57–100; R. A. Yoder, "Transcendental Conservatism and *The House of the Seven Gables*," *GaR* 28 (1974): 33–51; Neal Frank Doubleday, "H's Criticism of New England Life," *CE* 3 (January 1942): 325–37; and Myra Jehlen, *American Incarnation* (1986), 153–84. The standard edition is *The Centenary Edition of the Works of NH*, 20 vols. to date, ed. William Charvat et al. (1962–).

David Hicks

HAWTHORNE, SOPHIA PEABODY (1809–1871), born in Salem, Massachusetts, the third daughter of Dr. Nathaniel and Elizabeth Palmer Peabody, was an artist, writer, and Transcendental thinker as well as the wife and inspiration to N. Hawthorne.*

S's early education was influenced by her sister E. P. Peabody.* When the Peabodys moved to Boston, S began a serious artistic apprenticeship. For S, the visual arts yoked the material with the immaterial. Thus, with the encouragement of R. W. Emerson* and the foremost painters of her day—Chester Harding, Thomas Doughty, and W. Allston*—she enjoyed the most creative period in her life, completing four original paintings by 1832.

Notwithstanding—or perhaps because of—her successes as an artist, her health failed. Under the orders of her physician, Walter Channing, S journeyed to Cuba with her sister Mary, a governess on the Morrell plantation. From the end of 1833 through May 1835, S recorded her Cuban experiences in vivid letters to her mother that were bound into three volumes of almost 800 pages and circulated as the *Cuba Journal* among S's family, friends, and acquaintances in Boston for two decades.

Upon returning to Boston in improved health, S resumed painting. In 1837, she met N. Hawthorne. Although she continued her artwork until their marriage in 1842, S's last canvas, *Endymion*, was completed before the birth of their first child, Una, in 1844. Julian was born in 1846, and Rose, in 1851.

S fostered Nathaniel's ability as a writer by providing him with material, shielding him with understanding, and contributing to the family's finances by making and selling decorative art. Although Nathaniel burned almost all of S's correspondence to him, she recorded their lives in two journals** kept with her husband (his portions appear in *The American Notebooks*) as well as in numerous letters to family and friends. These journals as well as her *Cuba Journal* demonstrate S's Transcendental vision of nature** as an emblem of the divine.

In 1854 Nathaniel accepted the position of consul to Liverpool, and the Hawthorne family moved to England, then toured France and Italy after Nathaniel's resignation from that post. S kept a detailed journal—this time in the form of letters to Una—of her trip in 1857 with Nathaniel and Julian to the English Lake District and Scotland.

Upon their return to the United States, Nathaniel's vigor declined. Widowed in 1864, S avoided bankruptcy by editing and publishing her husband's notebooks with the Hawthornes' longtime friend, James T. Fields. After a falling out with Fields, S published her own *Notes on England and Italy* with Putnam. In 1868, S moved with her children to Dresden, where she believed they could live and be educated less expensively. When this proved untrue, she moved again with Rose and Una to London, where she died in 1871.

REFERENCES: Information, not always reliable, about S's life and work can be found in Julian Hawthorne's two-volume *Nathaniel Hawthorne and His Wife* (1884) and Louise Hall Tharp, *The Peabody Sisters of Salem* (1950). Most of S's voluminous correspondence with family and friends, many of whom were prominent figures in the American Renaissance, can be located using Edwin Haviland Miller, "A Calendar of the Letters of SPH," *SAR* 1986: 199–281. David Hicks, " 'Seeker for He Knows Not What': Hawthorne's Criticism of Emerson in the Summer of 1842," *NHR* 17 (spring 1991): 1–2, examines the possible consequences upon Nathaniel of S's enthusiasm for Transcendentalism.

Patricia Dunlavy Valenti

HECKER, ISAAC THOMAS (1819–1888), was a religious seeker who, like his mentor O. A. Brownson,* fraternized with the Transcendentalists during the eventful 1840s but who never became a believer, his sojourn among them culminating in his conversion to Roman Catholicism.

The strongest personal influence on H was Brownson, whose ideas linking reform and religion impressed H and his two brothers, all reform-minded workers in the New York flour mill and bakery of their German immigrant parents. After experiencing a series of mystical "visitations" in autumn 1842, H expressed his spiritual confusion to Brownson, who introduced him to *The Boston Quarterly Review*,** had him read Kant,** Fichte,** and Hegel,* and arranged his residence at Brook Farm** so that he might sort out his beliefs. At Brook Farm (January–June 1843) H operated the bakery and studied philosophy, French, and music. He left the community because it did not offer the desired ascetic atmosphere. He was then attracted to the renunciatory ideas of B. Alcott* and Lane* at Fruitlands,** but he remained there only about two weeks.

In the spring and early summer of 1844, H studied Latin and Greek under G. P. Bradford* in Concord,** where he made friends with H. Thoreau.* While in Concord he finally decided to become a Catholic, and, with encouragement from Brownson, was baptized in New York on 2 August 1844. In 1849 he was ordained a priest and in 1857 founded the missionary order known as the Paulist Fathers.

H's relations with R. W. Emerson* were always tenuous. On a visit to the Shaker** community at Harvard in June 1844, Emerson and Alcott offended him by their oblique probing into his rationale for embracing the Catholic Church. Nineteen years later Emerson was overtly antagonistic when H, now a priest, asked for his help in securing a hall in Concord for a lecture on Catholicism. Emerson, evidently smarting from H's part in the conversion of A. B. Ward,* discouraged him and would not attend the lecture.

H's seasoned critique of the Transcendental movement can be found in his review of O. B. Frothingham's* *Transcendentalism in New England* in *Catholic World* (23 [July 1876]: 528–37), a journal he founded in 1865. Although he interpreted the impetus of Transcendentalism from a Catholic perspective (the "protest of our native reason in convalescence against a false Christianity for its denial or neglect of rational truths"), he did astutely perceive the movement as strongly sociopolitical and as much native as foreign ("the spontaneous growth of the New England mind, in accordance with the law which we have stated, aided by the peculiar influence of our political institutions").

References: H published several books, primarily on Catholicism in the United States, and numerous articles in his own *Catholic World*. Recent biographical sources are David J. O'Brien, *IH, An American Catholic* (1992), and *IT.H: The Diary, Romantic Religion in Ante-Bellum America*, ed. John Farina (1988). Brownson's influence is detailed in *The Brownson-H Correspondence*, ed. Joseph F. Gower and Richard M. Leliaert (1979). Older biographies include Katherine Burton, *Celestial Homespun: The Life of ITH* (1943); Vincent F. Holden, *The Early Years of ITH* (1939); and Walter Elliott, *The Life of Father H* (1891). The Emerson relationship is documented in Glen M. Johnson, "Ralph Waldo Emerson on IH: A Manuscript with Commentary," *CHR* 79 (January 1993): 54–64.

James W. Mathews

HEDGE, FREDERIC HENRY (1805–1890), Unitarian** minister, denominational leader, German scholar, literary editor and critic, university professor, author, and lecturer, was a dominant force in 19th-century New England cultural life. He stood out especially as a prime mover in the beginning of the American Transcendental movement. His Transcendental beliefs, formed during his studies in Germany between 1818 and 1822, became well known in the Boston and Cambridge religious and academic communities when he published five articles in *The Christian Examiner*** in 1833 and 1834. His review of Coleridge's* *Biographia Literaria* in March 1833 was one of the earliest introductions to America of the metaphysical thought of the German philosophers whose intuitive epistemology was embraced as a central tenet by the American Transcendentalists. Upon reading H's review of Coleridge and later another on E. Swedenborg,** R. W. Emerson* wrote his brother Edward on 22 December 1833, "Henry Hedge . . . has just written the best pieces that have appeared in the Examiner; one was a living, leaping Logos, & he may help me." The Boston Transcendentalists found in H's expositions strong support in their struggle against the Lockean** sensual philosophy that dominated the theology and aesthetics of the time. Despite H's great influence in the embryonic stage of the Transcendental movement, H never made Transcendentalism a consuming cause or a basis for radical religious or aesthetic reform, but he did remain a Transcendentalist throughout life.

H moved from his home in West Cambridge, Massachusetts, to Bangor, Maine, in May 1835 to preach for the Independent Congregational (Unitarian)

Church. Here he served for 15 years. One of the cultural and intellectual ties that he maintained with the Boston and Cambridge area was with the Transcendental Club,** founded in September 1836, mainly by some young Unitarian ministers who gathered informally to discuss new ideas in theology, art, philosophy, and literature. The Transcendental Club went by several names, but since it often met when H was back in the area, Emerson called it the "Hedge Club." H attended at least 23 of the Club's 30 meetings between September 1836 and September 1840. His intimates in the Transcendental Club were Emerson, G. Ripley,* A. B. Alcott,* C. Stetson,* C. Bartol,* J. F. Clarke,* C. Francis,* T. Parker,* and M. Fuller.* After moving to Bangor his interest in the Transcendental movement gradually waned because of the increasing radicalism of Emerson, Parker, and Ripley, who were beginning to repudiate historical Christianity. In the early 1840s H spoke candidly in letters to Fuller and Francis about not wanting to be identified with Alcott, Emerson, and Parker because of their heretical tendencies, and a noticeable indication of his separation from their ranks was his failure to give little more than minimal support to *The Dial*** (1840–44). A further evidence of his desire to distance himself theologically from Emerson and Parker was his refusal to permit them to preach in his pulpit.

Notwithstanding intellectual differences that sometimes tested their patience with one another, H and the radical Transcendentalists enjoyed a long-standing friendship and often even an outspoken mutual admiration. H always shared a faith in intuition with the reformers, but his theism was more personal and transcendent than theirs, he always stood for evolutionary rather than revolutionary change, and he never felt a need to discard ecclesiastical frameworks in religion. Unlike his more heterodox friends, H was able to balance comfortably an intellectual radicalism with ecclesiastical conservatism. H's conservative position was well formed by 1841 when he pleaded for an "enlightened conservatism" in his Phi Beta Kappa oration, "Conservativism and Reform," at Harvard. He held that the current Transcendental philosophy being debated was neither the panacea that its advocates suggested nor the evil force its enemies claimed; it was but another philosophy in the progress of human culture. In a letter to C. Dall,* 1 February 1877, H said of his early connection with the Transcendental movement: "It has no importance, except in so far as I was the first in this country, to the best of my knowledge, to move in that direction" (Dall, *Transcendentalism in New England* [1897], 14–15).

H resigned from his pulpit in Bangor in 1850. Subsequently, he preached for the Westminster Congregational Society in Providence, Rhode Island (1850–57), and the First Parish Congregational Society in Brookline, Massachusetts (1857–72). Besides his pastoral work, he was editor of the *ChEx* (1858–61), president of the American Unitarian Association for four terms (1859–63), and a professor of ecclesiastical history (1858–72) and of German (1872–82) at Harvard. During his Bangor years H published 25 items in the forms of sermons, addresses, reviews, translations, and books; but in his final 40 years he became even more intellectually active and published about 90 items. Scattered through these are matters related to the Transcendentalists and his Transcendental faith, but two of his books are noteworthy for their Transcendental contents: an edition of essays entitled *Recent Enquiries in Theology, By Eminent Churchmen; Being "Essays and Reviews"* (1861), which deals with the faults of Lockean sensual thinking in theology; and *Reason in Religion* (1865), a major work on liberal religion and Transcendental Christianity. After returning from Bangor to the environs of Boston, H met his friends from the early days of the Transcendental movement occasionally at gatherings, among other places, of the Saturday Club,** Examiner Club, Radical Club,** and Concord School of Philosophy.** To the end of his life, H, like his old friends, was an intuitionist, but his conception of Transcendentalism allowed for intuition to be augmented by rationalism and historical Christian evidences.

References: There is not a complete biography of H, but there are several good profiles of his life, one by a contemporary, Howard N. Brown, in *Heralds*. Orrie W. Long, *FHH: A Cosmopolitan Scholar* (1940), treats H as a pioneering German scholar and Transcendentalist; and Ronald Vale Wells presents H as a Christian Transcendentalist in *Three Christian Transcendentalists: James Marsh,* Caleb Sprague Henry,* FHH* (1943; rpt. 1972). Bryan F. Le Beau examines H's metaphysics and theology and confirms him as a Christian Transcendentalist and an intellectual radical but ecclesiastical conservative in *FHH: Nineteenth Century American Transcendentalist* (1985). H's relationship to the Unitarian Church is discussed in scholarly books on that denomination by Cooke* (1902), Hutchison (1959), Howe (1970), and Conrad Wright. Buell (1973) cites H's faith in aesthetic inspiration. Two solid articles that deal with the question of whether H truly defected from mainstream Transcendentalism and became more conservative upon his move to Bangor or remained true to his original moderate Transcendental faith are Joel Myerson, "FHH and the Failure of Transcendentalism," *HLB* 23 (1975): 396–410; and Doreen Hunter, "FHH, What Say You?" *AQ* 32 (1980): 186–201. Good bibliographies and assessments of the scholarship on H are in Le Beau's *FHH* and Leonard Neufeldt's essay in Myerson (1984), 189–94.

Guy R. Woodall

HEGEL, GEORG WILHELM FRIEDRICH (1770–1831), a philosophical predecessor of the Transcendentalists, was born in Stuttgart and educated at the University of Tübingen. After stints as a private tutor, he accepted a teaching position at Jena, where he worked with his former schoolmate Schelling.* His first major work, *Phenomenology of Mind*, was published in 1807. He moved to professorships at Heidelberg (1816–18) and at the University of Berlin (1818–31). Other major works published during his lifetime include *Science of Logic* (1812–16), *Encyclopedia of the Philosophical Sciences in Outline* (1817), and *Philosophy of Right* (1821). After his death, his collected works, including lectures and class notes taken by students, was published in 18 volumes.

H's most important contributions are to be found in his method, his thoughts on the mind, and his work on history. His dialectical method, with its emphasis on contradiction, is the basis of his philosophical system. The triad of thesis, antithesis, and synthesis preserves truth while creating new meaning. Only Mind, or Spirit (*Geist*), is real; it is completely free and self-conscious. All individuals participate in the Mind, but only in a partial way. Mind strives, through its self-exercise, to become absolute. History is the story of the dialectical progression of Mind becoming absolute.

H's influence on American Transcendentalism is seen in his adherents in the United States and through Goethe.* Goethe's writings, informed by H's thoughts on modern culture and individuality, were read by most of the Transcendentalists. R. W. Emerson* first read Goethe in 1832 but did not start reading the philosopher until 1855. He found such systematic thought inaccessible and not particularly useful in its original form. Instead, like most of the American Transcendentalists, he preferred H's philosophy as filtered through German literature.

Henry Conrad Brokmeyer (1826–1906) and W. T. Harris* were prominent figures in the St. Louis Hegelian school. Harris may be seen as a liminal figure, connected to both the systematic philosophy of H and the looser confines of the primarily literary Transcendentalist movement. Along with F. B. Sanborn,* he published *A. Bronson Alcott: His Life and Philosophy*, the first biography of Alcott.* *The Journal of Speculative Philosophy*, which Harris edited, published many American Transcendentalist essays. Alcott and Emerson were closely associated with this journal in the 1860s and 1870s. Emerson was an avid subscriber, going so far as to promote articles for publication.

Alcott bristled at the logical demands of philosophy, and although Emerson was a bit more precise in his thought, he nevertheless did not fully embrace Hegelianism (or any other philosophical ''system''). However, his view of history as the progression of the Over-Soul toward the integration of mind and nature** through human culture owes much to H's thoughts on history, or the process of Absolute Mind becoming itself. The one-to one correspondence** that Emerson looked for between the ''contents of the human soul and everything that exists in the world'' would be achieved through a dialectical process and would result in what H would term the end of the process of history.

Harris's essays on Emerson's thought are among the most insightful published in the 19th century. In ''The Dialectic Unity of Emerson's Prose,'' he argues that Emerson's composition process is based on the Hegelian dialectic method. He also carried on a long correspondence with E. P. Peabody* and published a study on F. H. Hedge.*

References: The earliest collection of H's works, *Werke: Vollständige Ausgabe*, was published after his death and republished in Stuttgart (1927–40). A newer edition is *Werke*, ed. Eva Moldenhauer and Karl Markus Michel, 20 vols. (Frankfurt am Main, 1986). The most succinct distillation of H's thought that is accessible to literary scholars is in H. B. Acton's entry in *EP*. Myerson (1984) points to the major secondary sources on H's influence on Transcendentalism. The most impressive are Pochmann (1957); and Pochmann, *New England Transcendentalism and St. Louis Hegelianism* (1948). Henry A. Brann, ''H and His New England Echo,'' *Catholic World* 41 (April 1885), is also crucial. Stanley Cavell, ''Thinking of Emerson,'' *NLH* 11 (Autumn 1979), and Virginia Moran, ''Circle and Dialectic: A Study of Emerson's Interest in H,'' *NR* 1.5 (spring

1969), may overstate Emerson's reliance on the philosopher, but they are still necessary works. Gustaaf Van Cromphout, *Emerson's Modernity and the Example of Goethe* (1990), charts H's influence (through Goethe) on Emerson.

Joe Pellegrino

HENNELL, CHARLES CHRISTIAN (1809–1850), was a British ribbon manufacturer whose rejection of revelation and miracle as grounds for Christian faith and whose advocacy of a religion whose truths could be ''gathered from Nature''** confirmed the religious beliefs of many Transcendentalists (*Christian Theism* [1839]). H, the son of a merchant, was raised as a Unitarian.** In 1836, however, H's sister Caroline married the freethinker Charles Bray, author of *The Philosophy of Necessity* (1841). Shaken by debates with Bray on religious topics, and by arguments that Bray drew from Helvétius, Volney, and Paine, H began a serious study of the Gospels. H expected his analysis to confirm the beliefs with which he had been raised; instead, careful comparative reading of the Bible, Josephus, and Philo convinced him that Christian belief in revelation and miracle grew out of the culture of ancient Israel and not out of historical truth. To replace revelation and miracle, he argued, Christianity should be viewed as ''the purest form yet existing of natural religion'';** its continuing power would arise, he wrote in *An Inquiry into the Origin of Christianity* (1838), from ''that purer moral spirit, and those higher views of the nature of man, the progress of which, although naturally coincident with the advancement of the human mind, received so vigorous an impulse from the life of Jesus.'' Most of *An Inquiry* is devoted to comparative analysis of the Gospels and to separating history from literary and doctrinal embellishments. In 1839 H published *Christian Theism*, in which he formulated a more extensive positive statement about the possibilities of ''Christian theism'' after ''the relinquishment of . . . belief in miraculous revelation.''

Though H had read little biblical criticism when he wrote *An Inquiry*, he later discovered that his explorations had led him to many of the conclusions reached by German scholars. In fact, D. F. Strauss,* author of *Das Leben Jesu* (1835), was so impressed with *An Inquiry* that he instigated its translation into German and wrote the introduction to that edition. Later, H returned the compliment, convincing Elizabeth Rebecca (Rufa) Brabant to begin translating *Das Leben Jesu* into English. Among *An Inquiry*'s British readers was George Eliot, whose beliefs were unsettled by the book and who sought H's acquaintance. After H and Brabant married, H convinced Eliot to complete the translation of *Das Leben Jesu*.

R. W. Emerson's* letters to T. Parker* reveal his intention to have W. H. Channing* review H's work for *The Dial*.** When Channing declined to write the review, Emerson considered printing Brabant's translation of a German review of H but found it too long. Ultimately, Parker volunteered to write the review, which appeared in the October 1843 issue. Parker was impressed by H's lack of formal education. That he had arrived at his conclusions without instruction in the Higher Criticism** reinforced Parker's belief that his understanding of Christianity was ''natural.'' Parker rejected as ''repulsive'' H's view that Jesus's project was partly political but praised *An Inquiry* as a ''serene and manly'' work, ''marked by candor, faithful research, good sense, and a love of truth.'' Parker concluded his review by quoting at length from *Christian Theism*, calling it ''a work of singular beauty and worth.'' Parker also noted in ''Of the Popular Theology of Christendom, Regarded as a Principle of Ethics'' that ''no man answers H'' (*Theism, Atheism and the Popular Theology, Collected Works* [1907], 179).

Parker's review inspired Moses George Thomas of Concord, New Hampshire, a Unitarian minister and a friend of Emerson's first wife, Ellen Tucker Emerson, to write an article denouncing both H and Parker for ''infidelity.'' Thomas submitted this article to Emerson, who accepted it with revisions but did not print it. Thomas eventually asked for the manuscript back and, following its rejection by *The Christian Examiner*,** published it as a pamphlet entitled *A Rejected Article, in Reply to Parker's Review of ''H on the Origin of Christianity'' Offered First to* The Dial; *Then to* The Christian Examiner (1844). *ChEx*'s editors acknowledged this pamphlet in their ''Notes of Recent Publications,'' calling its author ''sincere'' but unconvincing (36 [March 1844]: 288).

References: H's books were reprinted in *An Inquiry Concerning the Origin of Christianity to Which Is Added Christian Theism* (1870). For biography and selected letters, see Sara Sophia Hennell, *A Memoir of CCH* (1899), and the *DNB*. See also *The George Eliot Letters*, ed. Gordon Sherman Haight (1954–78). For discussion of Parker's review and Thomas's response, see *NET*Dial.

Lisa M. Gordis

HENRY, CALEB SPRAGUE (1804–1884), was an Episcopalian minister who translated into English in 1834 V. Cousin's* ''Critical Examination of Locke's Essay on the Human Understanding,'' a portion of Cousin's longer work *History of Philosophy in the Eighteenth Century*. H called his translation *Elements of Psychology*. Cousin's eclecticism, which H termed in the book's introduction ''a method rather than a system,'' combined sensationalism** and spiritualism.** Cousin offended Unitarians** with his direct challenge to the thinking of J. Locke** but appealed to emerging Transcendentalists like G. Ripley* and O. Brownson,* who defended Cousin and his philosophy on several occasions. H's translation sparked controversy. In the January 1839 *Biblical Repertory and Princeton Review*, three leading professors at Princeton Theological Seminary, J. W. Alexander, A. Dod,* and C. Hodge,* vigorously condemned both Cousin and H. They found Cousin's philosophy repellent because it ''makes sad havoc with Christianity'' (77), while concluding of H: ''We are willing to believe that he knows not what he is doing; that fascinated by the first charms of the new philosophy . . . he is not able to see the end from the beginning'' (99).

H found the personal nature of this attack hurtful, and he was deeply offended by the Princeton writers' accusation that Cousin's theories were fueling Transcendentalism. He first refuted these criticisms in the preface to the third edition of *Elements of Psychology* (dated October 1841) and appended further arguments in his and Cousin's defense to the fourth edition preface, written 14 years later. H accused his opponents of misunderstanding Cousin's philosophy (particularly in their claims that he was a pantheist**) and of ignoring the context for the passages they quoted; he dismissed both the critics and their claims as "pitiable and ludicrous" (4th ed., xxii), the result of little more than "petty sneering" (4th ed, lvi). H resisted any link to the "quality of transcendental cloud and moonshine out of Ralph Waldo Emerson,"* and he referred to the doctrines of Transcendentalism as "banned alike by all reputable persons" (4th ed., lix–lx). Cousin's claim that Lockean sensationalism could not completely account for the human acquisition of knowledge may have attracted H, but his conservative religious views precluded the secular applications of Transcendental thought suggested by Emersonian philosophy.

Although Emerson later minimized Cousin's effect on Transcendentalism, the Frenchman's challenge to Lockean notions did surface in American culture at a philosophically critical moment. H's translation (and that of Henning Gottfried Linberg) made Cousin's philosophy accessible to readers on this continent. *Elements of Psychology*, complete with an introduction and notes by H, was published in four editions and served on occasion as a university textbook. A writer for the *North American Review*** retrospectively referred to H's translation of Cousin as "the harbinger of a brilliant and fruitful career" ("Professor H's Writings," 96 [April 1862]: 531). Following his death in 1884, *The Literary World* concluded that "Dr. H's mind was original in its fiber. . . . There has been no touch exactly like his in American literature" ("CSH," 15 [5 April 1884]: 114).

References: The most comprehensive treatment of H's life and work appears in Ronald Vale Wells, *Three Christian Transcendentalists: James Marsh,* CSH*, Frederic Henry Hedge* (1943). Herbert W. Schneider includes a brief discussion of H's theology in *A History of American Philosophy* (2d ed., 1963). Biographical material and personal recollections appear in E. A.* and George L. Duyckinck, *Cyclopaedia of American Literature* (1856), and in Marshall H. Brown's entry on H in *DAB*. H's writings remain uncollected.

Kathryn B. McKee

HIGGINSON, THOMAS WENTWORTH (1823–1911), called the epoch of change to which the term Transcendentalism has been applied "The Period of the Newness" (*Cheerful Yesterdays*, 69–99). He defined Transcendentalism as an experimental impulse for literary, social, and spiritual independence (H and H. W. Boynton, *A Reader's History of American Literature*, 167). For H the chief literary contribution of Transcendentalism was its call for indigenous expression, its resistance to European artistic models. If H's literary career succeeded that creative outburst that F. O. Matthiessen called the "American Renaissance," he became one of Transcendentalism's most informed chroniclers. He was a mentor to women authors, including E. Dickinson,* Harriet Prescott Spofford, and Helen Hunt Jackson, who emerged in the 1850s and 1860s and looked to him as an apostle of Transcendental culture in refined Victorian guise.

During the 1840s H absorbed ideas from many leading Transcendentalists. For many in his generation, R. W. Emerson* offered an antidote to the perceived conventionalism of literary expression; for H, whose daily regimen included ''a dose of Emerson,'' the essays had ''the effect of a revelation'' (*Contemporaries*, 10). He avidly read *The Dial*** and attended sermons of J. F. Clarke.* More influential was the radical thinking of W. H. Channing,* who replaced Clarke as editor of *The Western Messenger*.** Channing sought to combine the best characteristics of all religions; indeed, his pronounced nonsectarianism served as a model for H's later interest in comparative religion, expressed in ''The Sympathy of Religions'' (1871). Clarke's and Channing's embrace of free religion and reform drew H to antislavery meetings. The writings of L. M. Child* intensified his opposition to slavery, and the example of T. Parker,* whose church was a model for H's Worcester Free Church in the 1850s, caused him to question a spiritual life divorced from social responsibility. As he looked back on his ministerial career, he acknowledged that the radical impulse superseded the sacerdotal (*Cheerful Yesterdays*, 112); in fact, the title of his address at Harvard Visitation Day exercises in 1847, ''The Clergy and Reform,'' reflected a commitment that he sustained over the next decade.

H advocated woman suffrage; he supported the disunion movement; he participated in violent riots designed to rescue the fugitive slave Anthony Burns in 1854; and he never wavered in support of J. Brown* before and after his raid on Harpers Ferry in 1859. Serving in South Carolina from 1862 to 1864, he was colonel of one of the first black regiments in the Civil War, experiences captured in the book often deemed H's masterpiece, *Army Life in a Black Regiment* (1870).

An early admirer of *A Week on the Concord and Merrimack Rivers*, H reviewed favorably *The Maine Woods* and *Cape Cod* and encouraged the publication of Thoreau's* journals.** During his Worcester ministry in the 1850s, he cultivated his interest in flora and fauna in a series of *Outdoor Studies* (*Atl***). If that decade was a high point of the natural history** essay, much credit is owed to Thoreau's example; H's pieces, stylistically more voluptuous than Thoreau's, won more numerous admirers, including Dickinson. H has been chided by literary historians for his imperfect comprehension of her verses; nevertheless, their literary relationship reveals her keen admiration for his work and judgment and his championing of her poetry through critical articles and full-scale editions in the 1890s. In the cases of both Thoreau and Dickinson, H's efforts did much to challenge exaggerated charges of eccentricity applied to them.

H's most sustained commentaries on Transcendentalism are contained in his autobiographical volume *Cheerful Yesterdays* (1898); his treatment of ''The

Concord** Group'' in *A Reader's History of American Literature* (1903); his portraits of individual figures (Emerson, B. Alcott,* Parker) in *Contemporaries* (1899); his treatments of major periodicals of the movement in *Old Cambridge* (1899); and his balanced treatment of M. Fuller* in his biography (1884) in the American Men of Letters series. He sensed in the movement a conflict between contemplation and action, impulses integrated in the career of Fuller, whose intellectual influence he deemed nearly the equal of Emerson and Parker. By no means uncritical of the movement, he acknowledged the short-lived nature of its experiments (e.g., Brook Farm**) and its publications (e.g., *The Dial*). Nevertheless, as one of the movement's most ample historians and memoirists, he gave just dues to Transcendentalism for the exuberant intellectual activity it fostered, its opening vistas of philosophical and theological speculation. In the battle for literary independence, Transcendentalism allowed Americans to forego the perspectives of the Old World, in H's words, to look at the stars themselves.

References: The most scholarly modern biography is Tilden G. Edelstein, *Strange Enthusiasm: A Life of TWH* (1968), though both Howard N. Meyer, *Colonel of the Black Regiment* (1967), and Anna Mary Wells, *Dear Preceptor: The Life and Times of TWH* (1963), provide straightforward narrative. James W. Tuttleton, *TWH* (1978), treats literary matters, as does Barton Levi St. Armand, Ch. 6 of *Emily Dickinson: The Soul's Society* (1984).

Kent P. Ljungquist

HILDRETH, RICHARD (1807–1865), philosopher, historian, abolitionist,** and writer, was an avid proponent of Utilitarianism and was not a Transcendentalist. Nevertheless, he defended Transcendentalist theory in *A Letter to Andrews Norton* on Miracles as the Foundation of Religious Faith* (1840).

Born in Deerfield, Massachusetts, to the Rev. Hosea Hildreth and Sarah McLeod Hildreth, H graduated from Harvard College in 1826 and was admitted to the bar in 1830. He did not remain long in law; within a few years he was writing and publishing articles, pamphlets, and one of the first American antislavery novels, *The Slave: or, Memoirs of Archy Moore* (1836). In 1840, he translated Jeremy Bentham's *Theory of Legislation* from the French, making the work widely accessible in America. In his life and in his writings, H practiced Bentham's positive, Utilitarian thinking.

In 1840, H joined the ongoing controversy regarding the ''true foundation of Religious Faith'' when he wrote *A Letter to Andrews Norton* in response to Norton's *A Discourse on the Latest Form of Infidelity* (1839). H defends Transcendentalist views regarding faith and religion, upholding ''the transcendental and supernatural character which it [religion] has ever borne.'' H stresses that ''transcendental reason . . . presents unseen and supernatural things with the vividness and reality of sensible objects. This perception of the supernatural is essential to piety.''

H does not find this defense of Transcendental reason at odds with Benthamite Utilitarianism; he calls Norton's reasoning ''clerical arrogance and pretension'' and attacks it "in the name of Galileo, of Bacon, of Grotius, of Newton, of Locke,** of Bentham, and of all their followers."

References: H's *Letter to Andrews Norton* is reprinted in Martha M. Pingel, *An American Utilitarian: RH as a Philosopher* (1948). This source also contains a short biography of H as well as several of his polemics and unpublished manuscripts. Overviews of H are Arthur M. Schlesinger, Jr., "The Problem of RH," *NEQ* 13 (June 1940): 223–45; and Alfred H. Kelly, "RH," in *The Marcus W. Jernegan Essays in American Historiography*, ed. William T. Hutchinson (1937), 25–42. A listing of H's books, pamphlets, and letters is in Donald E. Emerson, *RH* (1946); and a listing of H's short articles and collections of poetry is in Louis B. Friedland, "RH's Minor Works," *PBSA* 40 (2d Q 1946): 127–50. Nancy Bentley discusses *The Slave* in "White Slaves: The Mulatto Hero in Antebellum Fiction," *AL* 65 (November 1993): 501–22.

Lesli J. Favor

HOAR, EDWARD SHERMAN (1823–1893), the middle son of a prominent Concord** family, was a friend and traveling companion of H. D. Thoreau.* On one of their expeditions, in April 1844, the two accidentally set fire to the woods near Concord while cooking. Although no legal action was taken against them for their carelessness, presumably owing to the influence of H's father, the incident brought Thoreau the disdain of many of his neighbors. Years later, in 1857, H accompanied Thoreau on an expedition to Maine and is the author's unnamed companion in the "Allegash and East Branch" section of *The Maine Woods*. H also went with Thoreau to the White Mountains in 1858 and occasionally "botanized" with him along the Concord River.

H seems to have been far more committed than Thoreau to personal comfort. He complained that the "price" of accompanying Thoreau on his outings was "to walk long and far; to have wet feet, and go so for hours. . . . If you would do that with him he would take you with him. If you flunked at anything he had no more use for you." Ironically, when Thoreau's tuberculosis robbed him of his stamina, he accepted H's offer of the use of a horse and carriage so that he could continue his excursions.

Thoreau and H shared a fascination with the natural world and spent much of their time together observing and discussing plants and wildlife. H commented that although he knew the "natural history** side" of Thoreau quite well, he was "wholly unaware then of the moral side that appears so strongly in his books." After 1878, H devoted himself almost entirely to reading and the study of nature,**, developing friendships with prominent scientists such as L. Agassiz* and the botanist Walter Deane. His daughter Florence donated a large collection of his plant specimens, including some collected by Thoreau, to the New England Botanical Club in 1912.

The H family was quite influential in (and beyond) Concord. E was the son of Sarah Sherman Hoar and S. Hoar,* a lawyer, judge, and congressman. He had two older sisters, Sarah Sherman Storer and Elizabeth Hoar* (who had been engaged to C. Emerson* when he died in 1836), and two brothers; the elder,

Ebenezer Rockwood H, became attorney general under Ulysses Grant and a Massachusetts Supreme Judicial Court judge, and the younger, George Frisbie H, served as a U.S. senator for almost thirty years. Though H graduated from Harvard in 1844, became a lawyer, and served as a district attorney for a time in California, he never attained, nor did he apparently seek, the political and social prominence of his father and brothers. Instead, he preferred a more adventurous life in his youth and early adulthood—traveling to California as an adolescent and again during the Gold Rush, and to Peru in 1856—and in his later years, a more contemplative one.

Although H's epitaph describes him as one whose "eye saw the beauty of flowers and the secret of their life," his observations were not limited to natural phenomena. His conversations with Edward Burgess near the end of his life include not only his impressions of Thoreau, whom he described as having had "a great deal of sympathy that people did not know," but of other Concord figures as well, including Hawthorne,* the Emersons, and E. Channing,* whom he admired in some respects but whose mental health he questioned. While H was hardly one of Transcendentalism's central figures, his friendship with Thoreau and his astute commentary on the Concord scene make him relevant to scholars of the movement.

References: Edward S. Burgess's notes of his conversations with H are located in the Concord Free Public Library; Marcia E. Moss has published a transcription with explanatory notes in "E S. H's Conversations on Concord with Edward S. Burgess," *CS* 17 (March 1984): 17–33. The most thorough biographical treatment of H, including a rare photograph, is Ray Angelo, "E S. H Revealed," *CS* 17 (March 1984): 9–16. On H's relationship with Thoreau, see F. B. Sanborn's* *Life of Henry David Thoreau* (1917), 346, 416, 422; Harding (1965); and Harding's brief piece "EH on Thoreau," *TSB* no. 198 (winter 1992): 6–7.

Susan M. Ryan

HOAR, ELIZABETH (1814–1878), the only daughter of Judge S. Hoar,* Concord's** leading citizen, was one of R. W. Emerson's* closest friends, gaining his affection and respect through her warmheartedness and intelligence. She had been engaged to Emerson's brother Charles,* and after his death in 1836, she never married, becoming instead a devoted "sister" to Emerson and "daughter" to his mother, Ruth Haskins Emerson; to Emerson's children she became beloved "Aunt Lizzie." She was also a frequent visitor to the Alcott,* Channing,* Fuller,* Hawthorne,* and Thoreau* households and during trips to Europe became acquainted with such figures as T.* and Jane Carlyle, A. H. Clough,* and Robert and Elizabeth Browning.

She was able to hold her own in such company because, as a member of a well-to-do family, she had an excellent private education, attending the Concord Academy and developing a love for learning that made her the intellectual equal of her three brothers and her male friends. For the 42 years of her life after the death of Charles Emerson, she was Waldo Emerson's closest confidante outside of his immediate family and respected by all who knew her.

EH's success was due not only to her innate abilities but also to the fact that she escaped the twin dangers facing an intelligent woman in the 19th century: the substantial cares and duties involved in being a wife and mother (like S. Hawthorne*) and the ''freakishness'' of being an unmarried woman forced to make an independent living (like M. Fuller). Her comfortable financial position permitted her to follow her interests through reading, social activities, conversation, and correspondence. Emerson called her ''Elizabeth the Wise'' and wrote an (unpublished) poem about her; even Thoreau, sparing with compliments, called her ''my brave townswoman to be sung of poets.''

References: The fullest description of H's life, with a chronology and 158 selected letters, is in Elizabeth Maxfield-Miller, ''E of Concord: Selected Letters of E Sherman H to the Emersons, Family, and the Emerson Circle,'' *SAR* 1984, 1985, 1986. Also see Maxfield-Miller, ''Emerson and E of Concord,'' *HLB* 19 (July 1971): 290–306. For numerous comments by Emerson on EH, see *JMN*, vols. 5–16; his letters to her are printed in *L*, vols. 2–4. Emerson's poem on EH is published in *PN*, 660–61, 780. Her poem ''George Nidiver'' is printed in Emerson's ''Courage,'' *W*, 7: 277–80.

Ralph H. Orth

HOAR, "SQUIRE" SAMUEL (1778–1856), was a lawyer and statesman whose connection with Transcendentalism stems from his daughter Elizabeth's* association with the movement and the family's residency in Concord.** H's veracity was legendary. An anecdote explains that a jury once deadlocked because although the evidence indicated that the defendant was guilty, H had stated that he believed his client to be innocent. As many of the jurors were convinced that H always told the truth, no decision could be reached.

H was particularly interested in the reforms of the era, especially those in education.** He helped to charter the Concord Free Public Library and initiated the establishment of the Concord Academy, where his children became classmates of H. Thoreau.* His best-known service, however, was as moderator of town meetings. Between 1813 and 1820, he was elected to the position 82 times. In 1820 he became a delegate to the state constitutional convention and later was a state senator and U.S. congressman. Always concerned with the public image of Concord, in 1843 H paid the delinquent poll tax of B. Alcott,* who had refused payment in protest against slavery.

In 1844 H became personally involved in the slavery issue. Accompanied by his daughter Elizabeth, he was dispatched to Charleston as a representative of the Commonwealth of Massachusetts. The port authorities of Charleston had been imprisoning, without criminal charge, any free black sailor who had arrived there on Northern ships. Massachusetts protested the policy, and H was engaged to direct legal action against the city in federal court. However, his mission was never realized as the South Carolina legislature demanded H's immediate expulsion. Threats were made against H's life, and an angry mob collected in front of the hotel where he and Elizabeth were staying. Soon, father and daughter were forced to leave Charleston by a delegation that had been instructed to remove them bodily if necessary. Despite the difficulty and the danger of the situation, Squire H remained calm, dignified, and courageous, attempting to the last to fulfill his assignment. This incident deeply affected the residents of Concord and did much to galvanize the antislavery sentiment among them. H's gallantry and popularity earned him election to the Massachusetts Governor's Council in 1845.

Upon his death in 1856, H was praised by many dignitaries and colleagues including R. W. Emerson.* Although Emerson saw H as a symbol of old Concord, he also recognized H's innate Transcendental qualities. In a tribute ''SH'' (*Putnam's Monthly* [December 1856]), Emerson stated that H had a ''natural reverence for every other man'' (645). He valued simplicity and ''the order of the mind,'' said Emerson in another eulogy, ''The Character of SH'' (*The Monthly Religious Magazine and Independent Journal* [January 1857]); ''He was as admirable as any work of nature**'' (7).

References: For insight into H family life, see Elizabeth Maxfield-Miller, ''Elizabeth of Concord: Selected Letters of Elizabeth Sherman Hoar,'' *SAR* 1984, 1985, 1986. Anecdotal material appears in Harding (1965). See esp. Robert Gross, ''Squire Dickinson and Squire H,'' *PMHS* 101 (1989). George Frisbie Hoar edited his father's papers and published *Memoir of SH of Concord by his Son George F. Hoar* (1882). Eulogies are collected in ''Scrapbook on the Death of SH,'' reposed in the George Frisbie Hoar Papers at the Massachusetts Historical Society.

Barbara Downs Wojtusik

HODGE, CHARLES (1797–1878), stands as a stalwart defender of Reformed theology in the United States. A professor of biblical literature at Princeton Theological Seminary from 1822 until his death, H, a prominent Old School Presbyterian, held strictly to the concepts of the infallibility of Scripture and the absolute sovereignty of God and viewed suspiciously excessive emotionalism in the practice of faith. Departing from the Jonathan Edwards/John Witherspoon brand of theology, H sought a Christianity that would not be, as Sydney Ahlstrom describes it, ''an amalgam of folk religion and Americanism.''

Had he not been in his prime as a theology professor at Princeton during the 1830s, H might well have had nothing to say about R. W. Emerson* and Transcendentalism. Theologians of the H ilk had already assaulted their brethren in the Unitarian** faith, believing that these liberals had watered down Christianity. If the Princeton circle and others saw Unitarianism as a shift from orthodoxy, they saw Transcendentalism as being beyond the pale. For them, Transcendental thought, as set forth in Emerson's *Nature*, continued the German higher criticism** of the Bible, which questioned the inspiration and infallibility of Scripture, degraded the position of Jesus, and stressed ''self-reliance.'' Of the Divinity School Address, H remarked: ''If it was not for its profaneness, what could be more ludicrous?'' At issue here was Emerson's alleged pantheism.**

References: Although in large measure Transcendentalism won the battle over H and his fellow Reformed theologians, H retains an important and respected place in evangelical teaching. His *Systematic Theology* (1871–73) remains a basic text. His son A. A. Hodge published a biography of the elder H in 1880. Sydney Ahlstrom's *A Religious History of the American People* (1972) offers valuable information on H, Transcendentalism, and related matters. "Transcendentalism of the Germans and of Cousin and Its Influence on Opinions in This Country," first printed in *BRPR* and written by J. W. Alexander, A. Dod,* and H, is printed in Miller (1950).

E. Kate Stewart

HOLMES, OLIVER WENDELL (1809–1894), was a Boston Brahmin, medical doctor, poet, and satirist. He had personal associations with several Transcendentalists and was, like them, a Harvard graduate, Unitarian** reformer, critic of Calvinism, and contributor to the *Atlantic Monthly*.** H, however, was too much the scientific rationalist to find Transcendentalism congenial. In his biography of R. W. Emerson* (1885) he expressed admiration for his friend's learning and personal qualities but aimed satiric barbs at Emerson's philosophy and disciples.

"Nothing was farther from Emerson himself than whimsical eccentricity or churlish austerity," H wrote, "but there was occasionally an air of bravado in some of his followers as if they had taken out a patent for some knowing machine." Many Transcendentalists, according to H, were pretentious, dreamy, incomprehensible, poor in citizenship, and indolent. "There is no safer fortress for indolence than 'the Everlasting No,' " he wrote. H. Thoreau,* he added, was "the Robinson Crusoe of Walden Pond,** who carried out a schoolboy whim to its full proportions."

Several of his contemporaries considered H temperamentally and philosophically unsuited to write Emerson's biography; others thought him an appropriate mediator between Emerson's supporters and detractors. Modern readers find the biography unsatisfactory as a guide to Emerson's ideas but better on his character and poetry and valuable as a historical document. The book is praised for recognizing that Emerson's *Nature* was indebted to the Book of Revelation; it is criticized for virtually ignoring Emerson's abolitionist** activities.

Although he condemned slavery, H himself was more conservative on abolition than such Transcendentalists as Emerson and T. Parker,* and he criticized the manners and speech of radical abolitionists. On other matters also he differed from Transcendentalists. Where they saw boundless possibility in human beings, H saw people bound by heredity and training; where they found God in the individual soul, he found potential evil, too; where they were mystical, intuitive, earnest, he was rational, skeptical, ironic; where they admired British Romantics, his models were 18th-century neoclassicists; where they studied nature** as a manifestation of the divine, he probed it scientifically; where Transcendentalists claimed that their literature was "inspired," H rarely made that claim, preferring rational discourse and regular, studied poetic form.

As the reputation of the Transcendentalists has grown since the 19th century, that of H has diminished. In his day he was famous, not only for his medical career and scientific essays but also for his witty conversations, stimulating lectures, and writings in many literary genres. His popular essays, published in *Atl* and in collected volumes, include *The Autocrat of the Breakfast Table* (1858). H poked gentle fun at Transcendentalism in an early number in which the Autocrat refers to ''truth, as I understand truth,'' whereupon his companion ''sniffed audibly, and said I talked like a transcendentalist.''

H wrote three ''medicated novels'' including *Elsie Venner* (1861), which takes issue with the Transcendentalist notion of unlimited human potential by depicting a heroine who is shaped by prenatal influences. His poetry, often occasioned by celebrations and reunions, includes ''The Deacon's Masterpiece'' (1858), which targets outmoded Calvinism, and ''An After Dinner Poem'' (1843), which satirizes *Dial*** writers as ''deluded infants.'' ''The Chambered Nautilus'' (1858), perhaps his only work that approaches the philosophy of Transcendentalism, describes a sea creature that builds new and ever larger shells as it grows. The poem's speaker compares this activity to spiritual aspiration and regeneration in human beings and exclaims, ''Build thee more stately mansions, O my soul.''

REFERENCES: H's biography *Ralph Waldo Emerson*, ed. Charles Dudley Warner (1885), is in the American Men of Letters Series. An early and admiring study is John T. Morse, *Life and Letters of OWH* (1896). More recent studies include Eleanor M. Tilton, *Amiable Autocrat: A Biography of Dr. OWH* (1947), which deals well with H's views on slavery, and Miriam Rossiter Small, *OWH* (1962). For critiques of H's biography of Emerson, see Joel Porte, *Representative Man: Ralph Waldo Emerson in His Time* (1979), and Gougeon (1990).

Laura Jehn Menides

HOOPER, ELLEN STURGIS (1812–1848), was widely regarded as one of the most gifted poets among the Transcendentalists. Her poems appeared in *The Dial*** and also in E. P. Peabody's* short-lived *Aesthetic Papers.*** During *The Dial*'s four-year existence, Fuller* and R. W. Emerson* regularly solicited poetry from both Ellen and her sister Caroline (Sturgis Tappan).* In a letter of 21 June 1840, Emerson told Fuller that the sisters' verses would ''enrich & ensoul'' the pages of the newly formed journal.

In addition to the 10 poems published in *The Dial* (or possibly 11; the authorship of 1 poem remains uncertain), many of H's other poems were privately circulated among friends. H's sister Caroline, Peabody, Fuller, Emerson, Sarah Ann Clarke, and J. F. Clarke* regularly read her poetry, and H. Thoreau* used the final stanzas of her poem ''The Wood-Fire'' to conclude the chapter ''House-Warming'' in *Walden*.

Born into a wealthy Boston family, H received the best education Massachusetts then offered its young women. Her father reputedly controlled half of Boston's China trade, and part of the profits provided his five daughters with opportunities to continue their education long after their formal schooling ended. In 1833, H asked Peabody to lead weekly ''reading parties'' for herself and a group of friends. The women met two to three hours a week; their discussions ranged from Peabody's translations of Socratic dialogues to Herder's** *The Spirit of Hebrew Poetry*. Six years later, H participated in the first of Fuller's Conversations** and remained an active supporter in subsequent series. She attended Emerson's Boston lectures, and when Clarke returned to Boston in 1841, she joined the congregation at his Church of the Disciples.

Her poetry presents a divided world in which individuals stand alone, inaccessible to each other. Hers is the Transcendentalism of Emerson's "Experience." Clearly aware of the schism between youth and adulthood, spirit and material, the ideal and its representation, she charts the course of the individual who seeks to move creatively within a world of "dull cares, hot words, hard work." Like her fellow Transcendentalists, H privileged the solitary seer, most often embodied in the poet, as the one individual able to unite the divide between human life and its divine potential. As she wrote in "The Poet," published in the second number of *The Dial*, the poet was "a soul of flame" who transposed earth's "rude air" into "Heaven's tones." The process was difficult and rarely realized. In a poem that appeared only in the private printing of her poems, she lamented that words were only a "trivial sign" of "airy Beauty, undetermined Thought."

H's poems are marked by urgency and register a protest against the model of tranquility endorsed by societal convention. She creates a restive speaker who seeks action in this world yet remains clear-sighted about its effects. Like Emerson, she questioned allegiance to particular social causes, yet like Fuller, she championed the necessity of decided action. In a poem titled "It Profiteth Thee Nothing," she wrote, "I hear the echo of the piercing cry/ And can no more implore the grace divine,/ But turn to serve this poor humanity."

In 1837, H married the doctor Robert William Hooper, whose family, like her own, represented the prosperous elite of Boston. Fuller characterized the marriage as a mismatch of intellects, an observation seemingly substantiated by H's poem "The Tide Has Turned." Developing tuberculosis in her early twenties, H's health was precarious throughout the 1830s and progressively worsened in the 1840s. At her death in 1848, she left 85 poems and assorted letters and prose fragments as her legacy to her three children, the youngest of whom, "Clover," later married Henry Adams.

Shortly after hearing of H's death, Fuller wrote to Sarah Clarke and urged a private printing, if not publication, of H's poems. Nothing came of Fuller's suggestion, and the majority of her poetry remained in manuscript until the early 1870s when her son Edward brought out a limited edition for family members and friends. Copies are held by the Houghton Library, the Boston Public Library, and Brown University.

References: For biographical information, see Cooke* (1902) and *NET*Dial. Biographies of Clover Hooper Adams quote from several of H's unpublished letters. See Otto Friedrich, *Clover* (1979), and Eugenia Kaledin, *The Education of Mrs. Henry Adams* (1981). In addition to the poems published in *The Dial* (listed in *NET*Dial), Cooke reprints seven others. Emerson included ''Wayfarers,'' ''The Chimney-Sweep'' (titled ''Sweep-Ho!'' in *The Dial*), and ''The Nobly Born'' in *Parnassus* (1874). Ten of H's poems, the author identified only by her initials, appeared in *An Old Scrap-Book*, ed. John M. Forbes (1884).

Sarah Ann Wider

HOWE, JULIA WARD (1819–1910), composer of ''The Battle Hymn of the Republic'' (1861), began her life in New York City, where she enjoyed the benefits of a private education. Left motherless at age five, W studied languages, music, and literature under the tutelage of various instructors. An avid reader whose early religious foundation led her to regard the Bible as ''the true passport to salvation,'' she assumed responsibility for the spiritual welfare of her younger siblings after her father's death in 1839. Eventually exchanging the strict Calvinist (see Puritanism**) rule under which she had been raised for a more liberal Christianity, she still vigorously opposed the ''radical'' doctrines of the Transcendentalists. When she met R. W. Emerson* on a train bound for Providence from Boston in the early 1840s, however, she was surprised to find in him a ''gentle, ethereal quality which belied his reputed wickedness'' (H Papers, Houghton Library, Folder #18). The two discussed religion and philosophy, and after Emerson introduced her to M. Fuller,* then editor of *The Dial*,** she began to soften her long-held convictions about the evils of Transcendentalism. In future years, she and Emerson would cross paths frequently.

Following her marriage to Samuel Gridley Howe in 1843, H turned to poetry writing as an outlet for boredom and loneliness. After publication of her first collection of verse, *Passion-Flowers* (1854), she frequently joined or hosted the circle of intellectual elites in Boston composed of Emerson, Holmes,* Longfellow,* Lowell,* T. Parker,* and others. Now sympathetic toward Transcendentalist teachings, but deciding to invest her energies in larger causes, H campaigned tirelessly on behalf of abolition,** woman suffrage (see woman's rights movement**), and international peace.

Best remembered for ''Battle Hymn,'' H was known as a passionate activist with a strong voice and a gentle sense of humor who won the admiration of her contemporaries. In his journal** on 21 July 1870, Emerson praised H's literary contributions: ''I honor the author of the Battle Hymn. . . . I could well wish she were a native of Massachusetts. We have no such poetess in New England.''

H's other primary publications include *Words for the Hour* (1857), *A Trip to Cuba* (1860), *Later Lyrics* (1866), *Margaret Fuller* (1883), *Is Polite Society Polite? and Other Essays* (1895), and *Reminiscences 1819–1899* (1899).

REFERENCES: For biography, see Laura E. Richards and Maud Howe Elliot, *JWH 1819–1910*, 2 vols. (1915), and Louise Hall Tharp, *Three Saints and a Sinner: JWH, Louisa, Annie and Sam Ward* (1956). Very readable is Deborah Pickman Clifford, *Mine Eyes Have Seen the Glory* (1978).

Denise D. Knight

HUMBOLDT, ALEXANDER VON (1769–1859), was a German naturalist and explorer, a ''universal'' scientist in a time of increasing specialization, widely read and reviewed in the United States from the 1810s to 1860s. R. W. Emerson* first encountered H's work while a student at Harvard (probably through E. Everett*), and his journal** often mentions H, several of whose books he owned. In 1869 Emerson called him ''one of those wonders of the world . . . who appear from time to time, as if to show us the possibilities of the human mind, the force and range of the faculties,—a universal man.'' In the opening of ''A Walk to Wachusett'' (1842), H. Thoreau* invoked H as the heroic explorer-observer. After reading *Cosmos* and *Aspects of Nature* around 1850 and *Personal Narrative* soon after, Thoreau put into practice a local version of Humboldtian field science, collecting specimens, field notes, and measurements and endeavoring to connect the information thus gathered into new understandings of nature.**

H was famous as the first European to explore the interior of South America, from 1799 to 1804. Through his explorations and writings, H aimed to establish a science of the interrelationships of all organic** and inorganic phenomena on earth; the results are visible today in geography, geophysics, meteorology, and ecology. *Personal Narrative* (1814–19) was his first popular writing; the publication of *Cosmos* (5 vols., 1845–62), in which he attempted ''a physical description of the universe'' (including a history of the idea of nature), consolidated his reputation as, after Napoleon, the most famous man of his age. His protégé L. Agassiz* honored him by organizing a centennial celebration at which T. W. Higginson,* F. H. Hedge,* Emerson, and C. T. Jackson all spoke, J. W. Howe* and O. W. Holmes* read poems written for the occasion, and to which Whittier* contributed a letter thanking H for his antislavery support.

Though often linked to it, H scorned German idealist** science, arguing that knowledge is fashioned by the collection and comparison of particular facts and observations. Detail thus in service to the whole leads us to new generalizations and ever-wider horizons, in both art and science; for H, the process of knowledge is initiated and sustained by the experience of pleasure or awe before nature's beauty. Thus, we can trace the ''chain of connection, by which all natural forces are linked together, and made mutually dependent upon each other'' (*Cosmos*, 1:1). The Humboldtian universe is a self-organizing, self-creating, and open-ended whole in which man is a full participant; though his radical, progressivist vision was coopted by a variety of conservative, reactionary, and radical movements, one significant legacy survives in Thoreau's later nature writings.

References: H's books remain available only in their 19th-century editions. *Ansichten der Natur* (1808, 1826, 1849) was translated by E. J. Sabine as *Aspects of Nature* (1849) and by E. C. Otté as *Views of Nature* (1850). *Kosmos/Cosmos* was also translated twice, Vols. 1–2 by Sabine (1846–49) and Vols. 1–4 by Otté (1849–58). *Personal Narrative* was translated first by H. M. Williams (7 vols., 1814–19), then by Thomasina Ross (3 vols., 1852–53); Emerson used an abridged edition by W. Macgillivray, *The Travels and*

Researches of AvH (1833). Contemporary discussion of H is found in Agassiz's *Centennial Address* (1869). For a good biography in English, see Douglas Botting, *H and the Cosmos* (1973). Recent critical studies of H may be found in Margarita Bowen, *Empiricism and Geographical Thought* (1981), and in Mary Louise Pratt, *Imperial Eyes* (1992), 111–43; see also Laura Dassow Walls, " 'The Napoleon of Science': H in Antebellum America," *19th-Century Contexts* 14.1 (1990): 71–98, and *Seeing New Worlds* (1995).

Laura Dassow Walls

HURLBUT, MARTIN LUTHER (1781–1842), was a Williams College graduate, teacher, and Unitarian** clergyman in Southampton, Massachusetts, involved in a debate of sorts with W. H. Furness* over the nature of the extraordinary phenomena in the Bible commonly referred to as miracles.**

The editors of *The Christian Examiner*** assigned H the review (published in March 1837) of Furness's *Remarks on the Four Gospels* published in Philadelphia in 1836. Furness argued that people cannot claim that the "extraordinary works" of Jesus were "impossible in the natural order of things," that is, supernatural, because "the nature of the things concerned is but very partially known." Rather, Furness insisted that "we cannot see the miracles of Jesus as natural facts, except as we are ascending that eminence of Faith, from which we look abroad and recognise the supernatural everywhere in the natural."

In his review, H responded vehemently to these attacks on the more traditional Christian view that miracles are supernatural "revelation[s] made by the Father of spirits" (122). Referring to Furness, H says, "There is a class of writers among us who are, consciously or unconsciously, *philosophizing* away the peculiarities of the Gospel" (104). H was "disposed to regret" the publication of Furness's work (104). H maintained that if the miracles of the Bible are not historically miraculous, but simply regarded as " 'natural facts,' " then Christianity ceases to be because "we are thrown back upon *mere naturalism*" (122).

References: See H's review of *Remarks on the Four Gospels*, by W. H. Furness, *ChEx* 22 (March 1837): 101–24; Hutchison (1959); and Miller (1950).

Moumin Manzoor Quazi

J

JAMES, HENRY, JR. (1843–1916), superior American author, admired R. W. Emerson's* personal qualities and H. Thoreau's* writing style but saw Transcendentalism as quaint, provincial, and innocent—a body of thought that was overly idealistic, insufficiently cogent and tough-minded. In characterizing Transcendentalism as "that remarkable outburst of Romanticism on Puritan** ground," or more invidiously as "a kind of Puritan carnival," J indicated his sense of both its cultural occasion—the felt need to shake off the constraints of the New England legacy—and its inherent tensions, the way in which the muted, repressed side of the New England character simultaneously engendered and impeded romantic aspiration.

While not quite subscribing to Poe's* indictment of Transcendentalism as Frogpondism, J maintained that his later generation could not help but "smile" at its insularity and consequent self-importance. "Tradition was . . . not so oppressive," he wrote, "as might have been inferred from the fact that the air swarmed with reformers and improvers": This was merely the famous New England conscience engaged in "its queer search for something to expend itself upon . . . gasping in the void, panting for sensations, with something of the movement of the gills of a landed fish." J's novels—notably *Roderick Hudson* (1875), *The Europeans* (1878), and *The Bostonians* (1886)—frequently satirize this aspect of the New England character.

J judged that "the Dial** and Fruitlands** and Brook Farm** were the amusement of the leisure-class" and that "their criticism produced no fruit." Even in Thoreau, despite his "beautiful pages," J found only a "violent and limited" application of Emersonian principles; the spiritual component of *Walden* was lost on him, and he loftily dismissed its recorded experiments in economy as "prosaic." Other "Concord-haunting** figures," such as B. Alcott,* were "not so much interesting in themselves as interesting because for a season Emerson thought them so."

Indeed, the exception to J's stringent rule was Emerson himself. Partly for reasons of family history, J retained fondness for the Sage even as he subjected his ideas to criticism. In Emerson the defects and narrowness of mind born of regional life and history were at least compensated by powers of concentration and expression. He was "beautiful" for being "altogether passionless" and without egotism; he enjoyed what authority he had for being "*all* the warning moral voice"; he possessed a "direct, intimate vision of the soul . . . in its passive, exposed, yet healthy form" just because he *lacked* a vision of "its emotions, its contortions and perversions."

Thus, J both respected the "luminous . . . nature" and twitted "the placid nerves of the inventor of Transcendentalism." He also noted certain paradoxes in Emerson's doctrines and their reception: that for all of his stress on self-reliance, his "bookishness" was "constantly reminding . . . readers of the conventional signs and consecrations—of what other men have done"; that for all of his preachment of "rudeness," he epitomized and thus advanced a personal style of "gentle amiabilities, curiosities and tolerances"; that for all his effervescent language, he "liked to taste but not to drink—least of all to become intoxicated"; and that for all his society's agitation over his supposed impiety, "he *was* the prayer and the sermon: not in the least a seculariser, but in his own subtle insinuating way a sanctifier."

Finally, it is no accident that J's best-known caveat against Emerson's thought and bearing—namely, that his "high and noble conception of good" thrived on a "ripe unconsciousness of evil"—occurred in a discussion of Emerson's European travels,** for J would dramatize and censure precisely this American liability in his great novels of the international theme, from *The Portrait of a Lady* (1881) to *The Golden Bowl* (1904). Perhaps what J felt most acutely was how history, in the form especially of the Civil War, had interposed a wall between Emerson's period and his own—how the intellectual and social currents of that "primitive" antebellum world had so suddenly vanished: "Transcendentalism has come and gone, . . . and the novelty of the Unitarian** creed, and the revelation of Goethe,* and the doctrine of a vegetable diet, and a great many other reforms then deemed urgent."

References: See HJ, *Literary Criticism* (1984), 233–71; Richard Hocks, *HJ and Pragmatist Thought* (1974); F. O. Matthiessen, *The J Family: A Group Biography* (1947); Ross Posnock, *The Trial of Curiosity: HJ, William James, and the Challenge of Modernity* (1991).

Eric L. Haralson

JAMES, HENRY, SR. (1811–1884), lecturer and writer of social and religious tracts, addressed topics dear to Transcendentalism—the spiritual opportunities of the self, the relation of the self to society and divinity, the prospects of American culture—but quarreled with Transcendentalism as insufficiently cognizant of the operation of evil, the dangers of self-love, and the need for a more theologically based and interdependent model of personal and societal regeneration. Raised in a rigid Presbyterian environment, J attended but dropped out of Princeton Theological Seminary (1835–38). His subsequent efforts to locate a less austere God and fashion a more humane belief system culminated in a nervous collapse in Windsor, England, in 1844, which he came to describe, after fervent study of Swedenborg,** as a ''vastation'' (or conversion experience) that ''saturated [him] with a sense of evil'' and thus paved the way for his moral renovation. Fusing the spirit of Swedenborg's ''divine natural humanity'' to egalitarian-communitarian principles gleaned from John Stuart Mill and C. Fourier,* J went on to issue a series of proposals for the cure of both souls and social organizations, notably *Moralism and Christianity* (1850), *The Nature of Evil* (1855), *The Social Significance of Our Institutions* (1861), and *Society the Redeemed Form of Man* (1879).

J sought to deemphasize—or at least qualify—both parts of the Emersonian** formula ''self-reliance.'' His own troubled experience seemed to teach that God was, so to speak, still Calvinist enough—and *active* enough—to intervene and punish egotistical pride and that achieving the right kind of individualism required purging the self of selfishness. Self-realization occurred only through others in a divinely redeemed collectivity.

Thus, self-reliance, for J, intertwined with reliance on both society and God, who worked with humanity in an attempt to end ''organized inclemency'' between persons and classes and to illuminate ''that fulness of life they shall find in each other as socially constituted.'' His friend Emerson's blindness or theoretical imperviousness to this necessary cycle of sin and collaborative redemption led J to fault him as ''philosophically infirm,'' ''a man without a handle,'' a person with ''no conscience'' who ''lived by perception, . . . an altogether lower . . . spiritual faculty.'' Relatedly, B. Alcott's* orphic bent, his willingness to postulate God as a vague cosmic beneficence rather than ''a weekday divinity, a working God,'' caused J to chide him as ''an egg half hatched.''

J's project, then, was to trace a middle path between his strenuous religious inheritance and Transcendentalism. J agreed with the Transcendentalists in finding *organized* religion an unlikely site of either individual salvation or social change, being the province of a largely ''comatose'' clergy with a ''loutish conception of Deity.'' He also shared the Transcendentalist zeal for candid expression, preferring to hear ''honest sympathy with [one's] sentiment or an honest repugnancy of it'' to a devious politeness. Like H. Thoreau,* whom he met through Emerson and who applauded him for making ''humanity seem more erect,'' J placed a high value on simple and sincere accounts of life as lived.

For all of his sincerity, J could not seem to arrive at simplicity. So metaphysically abstruse was his *The Secret of Swedenborg* (1869) that William Dean Howells was moved to quip: ''[H]e kept it.'' Contemporary opinion found J (much more so than Emerson) a man without a handle, dismissing his works as (in the words of one reviewer) ''mystical and unsound philosophy'' and going increasingly deaf, as the Gilded Age dawned, to his call for ''inward death to self in all its forms.'' Too random and subjective to qualify as philosophy, too quaint to satisfy a secularizing age or to pass as sociology, J's writings failed to find either a generic niche, a following, or a ''school'' with which to affiliate, but they nonetheless engaged in a lively, instructive confrontation with Transcendentalist thought.

References: See Giles Gunn, ed., *HJ, Senior: A Selection of His Writings* (1974); Dwight W. Hoover, *HJ, Sr., and the Religion of Community* (1969); R. W. B. Lewis, *The Jameses: A Family Narrative* (1991); F. O. Matthiessen, *The J Family: A Group Biography* (1961); Katherine Weissbourd, *Growing Up in the J Family: HJ, Sr., as Son and Father* (1985); Alfred Habegger, *The Father* (1994); and Frederic Harold Young, *The Philosophy of HJ, Sr.* (1951).

Eric L. Haralson

JAMES, WILLIAM (1842–1910), preeminent American philosopher, both sustained and transformed the Transcendental lineage in elaborating his doctrine of Pragmatism. It might be said that J was linked with Transcendentalism from birth: R. W. Emerson*—then a new friend of his father, H. James, Sr.*—beamed on the infant W's cradle, and H. Thoreau,* B. Alcott,* and G. Ripley* paid visits to the family during his childhood. Yet W also imbibed some of his father's reservations about Transcendentalism, particularly the charge that it was not adequately grounded in a schematics of active divinity and practical redemption.

Points of contact and continuity between Transcendentalism and J's philosophy include such precepts as self-reliance; the inviolable sanctity of the individual mind and will (J especially praised Emerson for championing the ''indefeasible right to be exactly what one is''); the need to resist the encroachments of institutional life on human development; the transitive potencies (as well as the insecurities) of language; and the utility of intuition as a guide to insight and conduct.

At the same time, J's pragmatism and empiricism led him to anchor intuition in closely reasoned argument and dialogue; to offer less oracular, more clinical counsel on self-empowerment and the reform of institutions; and to issue a running critique of Transcendentalism's tendency to drift into Neoplatonic** mistiness and inefficacy—its risk of ''let[ting] God evaporate into abstract Ideality'' at the expense of a constructive ''practical religion'' and a socially oriented ethics. ''An entire world,'' he contended, ''is the smallest unit with which the Absolute [as a Transcendental category] can work, whereas to our finite minds work for the better ought to be done within this world.'' J's philosophy stressed a more meliorist vision of progress than did much of Transcendentalist thought. When J wrote that ''in communion with the Ideal new force comes into the world,'' he meant to correct several perceived problems with the ultra-idealist strain in Transcendentalism. The latter posited the immanence** of the divine in mundane nature** and projected various modes of mysterious access to the over-soul—and thereby to ''knowledge,'' ''truth,'' and so forth. The effect of such a belief, J feared, was to relegate ''communion with the

Ideal'' to a hermetic transaction continually in danger of ''losing contact with the concrete parts of life''—the ''muddy particulars of experience''—and thus of collapsing (paradoxically) into a ''sterile'' naturalism.

The task, he observed in *Some Problems of Philosophy* (1911), was to strike a balance that would preserve the truth claims of Transcendentalism while combatting its propensity to detach knowledge from the quotidian world of perception and action: ''to join the rationalists [i.e., the proponents of Transcendental Reason] in allowing conceptual knowledge to be self-sufficing, while . . . join[ing] the empiricists in maintaining that the full *value* of such knowledge is got only by combining it with perceptual reality again.'' Or as he elsewhere said, in terms that both rehearse and discipline Emerson, while also recalling something of the spirit of Thoreau's *Walden*: ''[The Pragmatist] turns away from abstraction and insufficiency, . . . verbal solutions, . . . fixed principles, closed systems, and pretended absolutes'' in favor of ''concreteness and adequacy, . . . facts, . . . action, . . . power'' (*Pragmatism* [1907]).

J argued, that is, for a greater capacity for interactive agency in both the divine principle and the historical subject, joined as they were in common cause to bring ''new force'' into the world. This was necessary because, if nature was a site and source of revelation (as in the Transcendentalist view), it was also the object of an ''immemorial human warfare,'' as society went about feeding, sheltering, and advancing the lives of its members. Whatever his strictly scientific sense of the verbal and psychological barriers subsisting between one subjectivity and another (a concern that might also be traced back to Transcendentalism), J's ethical program called for deployments of will and language such that ''existing realities may be *changed*'' in the direction of a pluralism tolerant of multiple views and interests. Perhaps the distinguishing mark of J's Pragmatism, and one that connects it with the activist vein within Transcendentalism (e.g., abolitionism,** feminism), lies in his speaking out on behalf of racial and ethnic minorities, women in the professions, animal rights, health and mental health care, education reform,** and anti-imperialism.

References: See Gay Wilson Allen, *WJ* (1967); Howard M. Feinstein, *Becoming WJ* (1984); Olaf Hansen, *Aesthetic Individualism and Practical Intellect* (1990); Gerald E. Myers, *WJ: His Life and Thought* (1986); Richard Poirier, *The Renewal of Literature: Emersonian Reflections* (1987); Ross Posnock, *The Trial of Curiosity: Henry James, WJ, and the Challenge of Modernity* (1991).

Eric L. Haralson

JOHNSON, SAMUEL (1822–1882), second-generation Transcendentalist and nondenominational minister, made his greatest contribution to Transcendental thought in the field of comparative religions, publishing a three-volume series, *Oriental Religions and Their Relation to Universal Religion: India* (1872), *China* (1877), and *Persia* (1885), which attempts an objective synthesis of the universal aspects of the major Oriental** religions with Christianity.

Born in Salem, Massachusetts, his fascination with the Orient most likely a result of the seaport's then-fading trade with China and India, J became friends with S. Longfellow,* with whom he compiled two hymn books (*A Book of Hymns for Public and Private Devotion* [1846]; *Hymns of the Spirit* [1864]). J declined ordination into the Unitarian** Church upon graduation from the Harvard Divinity School,** choosing instead, in 1853, to serve as minister to the Lynn (Massachusetts) Free Church, which disassociated itself from the Unitarian Church upon his arrival. He remained there until he retired in 1870. Opposed to organized religion, he remained unordained throughout his life.

Preaching social reform to his congregation, J also developed, through sermons, the ideas that would inform his volume on India, which appeared two years after his retirement from the ministry. The volume was not a success, owing probably to J's insistence on objectivity, which, in the eyes of his 19th-century audience, erred in trying to place Hinduism and Christianity on the same level of spiritual purity. J spent the rest of his life attempting to complete his comparative study but left the final volume, *Persia*, unfinished. (It was published posthumously, ed. O. B. Frothingham.*)

Marred by sloppy scholarship and unreliable sources, J's *Oriental Religions* is nevertheless the most comprehensive contemporaneous attempt to express the union of Eastern and Western religion that informed the Transcendental philosophies of such major figures as R. W. Emerson* and H. Thoreau.*

References: There are two posthumous collections of J's works: *Lectures, Essays and Sermons*, ed. and with a "Memoir" by S. Longfellow (1883), emphasizes J's ministry; *Selected Writings*, ed. Roger C. Mueller (1977), reprints excerpts from *Oriental Religions*, an essay on Transcendentalism, and works of religious theory. The most thorough biography is Roger C. Mueller, "SJ, American Transcendentalist," *EIHC* 115 (January 1979): 1–67. Also useful is the "Memoir" by J's friend and collaborator Longfellow in *Lectures, Essays and Sermons*. On the reception of *Oriental Religions*, with respect to other contemporaneous treatments of the Oriental religions, see Carl T. Jackson, "The Orient in Post-Bellum American Thought: Three American Popularizers," *AQ* 22 (spring 1970): 67–81, and Jackson, *Oriental Religions and American Thought* (1981), 129–34. A contemporaneous review of *Oriental Religions*, indicative of its poor reception, is "J's Oriental Religions," *The Nation* 15 (21 November 1872): 338. A bibliography of J by Mueller appears in Myerson (1984), 204–6.

Alan D. Brasher

JOUFFROY, THÉODORE SIMON (1796–1842), was a French Common Sense philosopher** inspired by Fourier* and Cousin.* In turn, he influenced the Brook Farm** and other American communitarian experiments. A follower of the Scottish school of philosophy, J maintained that common sense alone possesses truth. He believed that all individuals should aspire to truth by reason but that they should accept their consequences by "a blind act of fate." He believed, moreover, that if people understood their dependence on individuality, they would no longer fight with one another and would live together in harmony. J argued that the soul's activity is made up of six different faculties: sensitivity to pleasure, sensitivity to pain, intelligence, expression, movement, and volition. These disparate faculties must unite to find "truth," and from this fusion comes common sense. By extension, cooperation among disparate individuals produces a more nearly perfect truth, communal living

This idea of communal living marks J's influence in New England. G. Ripley,* the prime force behind Brook Farm, translated two of J's treatises for *Specimens of Foreign Standard Literature*:** "Preface to Translation of Dugald Stewart"** and "Philosophical Miscellanies." W. E. Channing,* the Unitarian** minister who helped launch the Transcendental movement itself, also translated two essays: "Critical Survey of Moral Systems" and "Introduction to Ethics." Three other essays were translated by Robert N. Toppan.

References: See George Boas, "TSJ," in *EP*; Harold C. Goddard, *Studies in New England Transcendentalism* (1908); Frothingham* (1876); Gohdes (1931); Walter L. Leighton, *French Philosophers and New-England Transcendentalism* (1908); and Myerson (1984).

David J. Sorrells

JUDD, SYLVESTER (1813–1853), is virtually the only novelist of Transcendentalism. L. M. Child* might rival him for the title if her *Philothea* had the smack of the soil that is the distinctive quality of J's *Margaret* (1845).

Margaret is a nine-year-old nature** child, but Wordsworthian* environmentalism alone cannot explain her. Though lake and woods beneficently nurture her, she is also an orphan with attitude, incongruously placed in a foster family of hard-drinking infidels. But Margaret is herself and no other. She has an aura, an inwardness that sings with the birds. One Sunday, curious about what goes on in town, she sets out through the woods, gathering flowers, only to find flowers forbidden in the church. Here, in miniature, is J's whole case against Puritanism:** It is antagonistic to nature, beauty, and childlike spontaneity. After Meeting, Miss Amy, a prototype for Stowe's* and Twain's Puritanical spinsters, takes Margaret in hand: "It is God's day, and he won't let children play." Margaret: "He lets the grasshoppers play." Miss Amy: "But he will punish children." Margaret: "Won't he punish the grasshoppers too?" Miss Amy admits he won't. Margaret declares, "Well, I guess, I an't afraid of God." Religion comes to her anyway. She dreams of Christ and a flowering cross. She has Jungian pipedreams—silver pipes that pour the sky into a cauldron. Sunbeams, rainbows, "snake-like moonbeam appearances," ladled out by silver ladles, come alive as personified Beauty, ideal Woman. Awake, by day, Margaret canoes in the wonderful lake and "sozzle[s] her feet in the foam." By night, she "sniggle[s] for eels." "The sun swims through me," she says. She *is* the lake.

Growing up, Margaret meets Mr. Evelyn one day in the woods. He is a cultured Unitarian** who provides words and doctrines for what she has been feeling. Eventually she marries him. In one of their first talks Margaret is already overflowing with Transcendentalism: "A watermelon seed can say, 'In me are ten watermelons, rind, pulp and seeds, so many yards of vine, so many pounds of leaves.' In myself seems sometimes to reside an infant Universe. My soul is certainly pistillate, and the pollen of all things is borne to me.'' As she continues, her imagery brings together Edwards and Emerson* a century before Perry Miller did so: ''The spider builds his house from his own bowels. I have sometimes seen a wood-spider let off a thread which the winds drew out for him and raised above the trees, and when it was sufficiently high and strong, he would climb up it, and sail off in the clear atmosphere. I think if you only begin, it will all come to you. As you drain off it will flow in.''

Margaret is at its best when it combines such exaltedness of rhythm, idea, and imagery with a firm sense of life's vulgarity, its roots in the soil. Margaret brushes away the dirt from a rhubarb root to reveal its vermilion and gold. She comments, ''Children that germinate with a plenty of mother earth about them, come out in the fairest hues.'' To vulgar, earthy speech J gives a catchy rhythm. When Margaret first meets Mr. Evelyn, her foster brother teases her: '' 'A fox after the goslin, hey? . . . I saw you on the Head.' '' Margaret blushes. Her foster parents keep it up: '' 'She swells like a soaked pea. . . . What's the matter, husy? I should think he had been rubbing your face with elm leaves.' '' Words that jolt punctuate the cascading metaphors: '' 'You are the spider of the woods. Spin a strong web; you are sure to catch something.' 'She looks as if she had been spun, colored and hung out to dry,' said her mother. 'Gall darn it!' exclaimed Hash. 'I smell potatoes. Give us some dinner.' 'Speaking of spinning,' said Pluck . . . 'keep the thread taught [*sic*] and easy in your fingers . . . only if he is a dum spot of a Lawyer or a Priest, weave him into a breeches-piece, and I'll wear him, I be blown if I don't; and when he is past mending, I'll hang him up for a scarecrow, blast him!' '' In recording the real language of real people, J left Wordsworth, Emerson, and Cooper far to the rear. But a few genteel critics attacked *Margaret*'s ''vulgarity''; and in the second edition, J took out some, though not all, of his coarser expressions. For example, ''an't'' was changed to ''am not,'' ''Don't deary me with your dish-cloth tongue'' to ''Don't deary me,'' and ''Gall darn it!'' to ''By time!'' Only in a few libraries can be found the vivid, unsandpapered first edition.

Like the Transcendentalist movement in general, J was torn between utopian longings and love of nature. He had a nostalgia for childhood; for him, ''utopia'' was a way of saying ''home.'' He both loved and hated the remembered village he recreated in *Margaret*. It was coarse, drunken, cruel, and Calvinistic; but as the image grew in his mind the prose took on a vitality that betrayed his love. J did not suspect that Pluck, the drunken father, was the secret hero of the book, just as the Devil was the secret hero of his next book, *Philo*. And though J professed to love the perfected societies that his books ended with—genteel, prosperous, filled with art and music—he could not make them real and they fell dead in his hands.

Richard Edney and the Governor's Family (novel, 1850) and *Philo: An Evangeliad* (dramatic poem, 1850) continue to display J's pacifist, reformist zeal, but they are no longer rooted in the soil and lack *Margaret*'s freshness and tang. In 1850 J, always first and last a Christian, explicitly denied he was a Transcendentalist.

J was raised in Westhampton, Massachusetts, and in nearby Northampton. Planning to enter the Congregational ministry, he attended Yale College (1832–36). In 1837 he shocked his family by converting to Unitarianism and enrolling at the Harvard Divinity School.** He heard Emerson's major addresses there and became a friend of J. Very.* In 1840 he was ordained at the Unitarian church in Augusta, Maine, serving it until his death in 1853.

J. R. Lowell* called *Margaret* "the most emphatically American book ever written"; N. Hawthorne* picked it and [H. Thoreau's*] *Walden* to send to an English friend. In 1871, in the *Atlantic Monthly*,** William Dean Howells said of *Margaret* that we "must peruse it with something of the contented wonder with which we should linger over [Goethe's*] 'Wilhelm Meister' or a play of Shakespeare** if they were as strange to us. The comparison is of kind, not of degree; but if 'Margaret' were compared with any other romance of its own time, excepting the romances of Hawthorne, we should feel that there was no comparison for it save with the masterpieces." In 1986 Lawrence Buell's *New England Literary Culture* ranked J just after Hawthorne, Stowe, and Elizabeth Stoddard among New England regionalists.

REFERENCES: The J papers are at the Harvard University Library. Francis Dedmond, *SJ* (1980), summarizes J's books. Biographies are Arethusa Hall, *Life and Character of the Rev. SJ* (1854), and Richard D. Hathaway, *SJ's New England* (1981).

Richard D. Hathaway

K

KELLEY, ABIGAIL (1811–1887), was a radical abolitionist** and woman's rights** activist. Her active participation in the administration and planning of the abolition platform forced that movement to deal with the question of women's roles within the movement, and she was instrumental in drawing other women into the abolition movement, including Lucy Stone, Susan B. Anthony, and Elizabeth Cady Stanton. K was never a participant in the Transcendentalist movement, preferring activist involvement with abolition and woman's rights, but she was acquainted with many key Transcendentalists and frequently attended meetings of the Radical Club** during the 1870s at the home of Unitarian** minister John T. Sargent and his wife, Mary. During these meetings, K consistently advocated the practical over the abstract and action over metaphysical speculation. Mary Sargent writes that K believed that "whoever went about among men, entirely devoted and self-consecrated to the work of doing them good . . . as Jesus did, would be more sure of growing into sympathy with God's heart and coming to an understanding of his will than by any other process."

Born a Quaker,** K became involved in the abolition movement in 1836 while teaching in Lynn, Massachusetts. Guided by her "inner light," K felt a "call" to lecture; she later broke with the Quakers over her dedication to abolition. K was one of the first women to lecture to mixed-sex audiences; she shared a platform with virtually every other famous abolitionist of the time, including F. Douglass,* Sojourner Truth, and W. L. Garrison.* For many years K was a staunch Garrisonian, favoring nonresistance** and disunion, although she and Garrison later disagreed about the efficacy of political parties, as K had no faith in them. Besides serving as an antislavery lecture agent and holding numerous offices such as general agent and general financial agent with the American Anti-Slavery Society, K also helped begin several regional abolitionist newspapers, including the New York *National Anti-Slavery Standard* and the

Ohio *Anti-Slavery Bugle*. In 1845, K married a fellow radical abolitionist, Stephen Foster. After their marriage, she generally used the name "Abby Kelley Foster," although she continued to be known popularly as Abby Kelley.

Although K devoted most of her work prior to the 1870s to the abolition movement, she had long been a proponent of equal rights for women and spoke at numerous women's rights conventions. In 1851, at the second National Women's Rights Convention in Worcester, Massachusetts, K urged women to take responsibility for instigating social change; she herself believed she had done so, claiming, "[M]y life has been my speech. For fourteen years I have advocated this cause by my daily life. Bloody feet, sisters, have worn smooth the path by which you have come hither." K believed voting rights should be the primary objective of the woman's rights movement. As a personal act of social protest, K and Foster refused to pay either real estate or personal property taxes, claiming taxation without representation since she was not allowed to vote in Massachusetts. They engaged in this protest from 1872 until 1880, when Foster became too ill to continue. Although K remained interested in social issues, she became less active during the last years of her life.

REFERENCES: The only full-length biography is Dorothy Sterling, *Ahead of Her Time: AK and the Politics of Anti-Slavery* (1991). This work draws heavily on the K-Foster Papers, at the American Antiquarian Society and the Worcester Historical Museum. See also Alla Foster's account of her mother in *Sketches of Representative Women of New England*, ed. J. W. Howe* (1904), 22–29. Mary Sargent, *Sketches and Reminiscences of the Radical Club of Chestnut Street, Boston* (1880), provides additional information about K's interactions with the Transcendentalists. Useful for reporting details of K's abolitionist activities are the *Liberator*, the *National Anti-Slavery Standard*, and the *Anti-Slavery Bugle*. The *Women's Journal* is useful for references to K's work as a feminist.

Karen A. Weyler

KNEELAND, ABNER (1774–1844), was a Universalist minister, orthography expert, newspaper editor, radical Jacksonian** democrat, freethinker, and utopian socialist. In Boston in the 1830s K's positions on political, religious, and social issues defined radicalism for many and were anathema to most Unitarians** and Transcendentalists, including R. W. Emerson.* However, K's 1834 conviction for blasphemy and his subsequent imprisonment in 1838 galvanized the support of the liberal Unitarians for the right of free speech and had a direct effect on Emerson's Divinity School Address and the controversy that followed it.

Born in Gardner, Massachusetts, K attended common schools and spent one term at the Chesterfield Academy in New Hampshire. After a brief stint as a Baptist preacher, he became a Universalist in 1803 and was licensed to preach the following year. He served as pastor of the Lombard Street Universalist Church in Philadelphia from 1818 to 1825, during which time he also began his career as editor and propagandist, editing *The Christian Messenger* (1819–21), the *Philadelphia Universal Magazine and Christian Messenger* (1821–23), and the *Gazeteer* (1824). In 1825 he moved to New York, where he served successively as pastor of the Prince Street Universalist Society and the Second Universalist Society. In May 1827 he began editing the *Olive Branch*, a paper that supported the rational religion of ''free enquiry,'' an interest that was intensified by K's association with Robert Dale Owen and Frances Wright.

K's commitment to free thought and to such causes as woman's rights** and workers' rights became incompatible with institutionalized Universalism, and he separated himself from that sect in 1829. He moved to Boston, established the First Society of Free Enquirers, and began editing the *Boston Investigator*. His advocacy of various causes, including birth control and labor unions, and his championing of the rationalism of Voltaire and Thomas Paine and the politics of Andrew Jackson, made him a threat to the Unitarian establishment of Boston. The conservatives denounced him and the liberals positioned O. Brownson,* himself a radical democrat, to argue against K's views and thus possibly to offset their potential damaging effect on the social and political order.

Three articles by K in the 20 December 1833 *Investigator* became the substance of his indictment for blasphemy under the provisions of a 1782 law. He was tried and convicted of the charge in January 1834, and a series of subsequent trials and appeals, the last before the Massachusetts Supreme Court in 1838, resulted in the upholding of the conviction of the lower court. K was ordered to serve a 60-day sentence, beginning on 18 June 1838. Worried that their opponent's jailing would transform him on the national stage to a martyr for liberty and concerned about the implications K's imprisonment had for their own right to free speech, liberal Unitarians, led by E. G. Loring* and W. E. Channing,* drafted a petition to the governor for K's pardon. The document was signed by 168 citizens, including Emerson and other Transcendentalists. For his part, K rejected the petition in the pages of the *Investigator* because he believed accepting a pardon would constitute an admission of guilt. On his release from jail, K defended Emerson's views as expressed in the Divinity School Address, identifying them as ''our own faith and our doctrine, the same that we have taught ever since we have been in Boston.'' Emerson privately rejected K's support. K continued to write and publish in the *Investigator* on those social and political issues of interest to him, including the emergence of Transcendentalism in Boston. In 1840 he moved to Iowa to establish a free-thought, utopian community, which K had named ''Salubria.''

References: The most complete biography is Roderick Stuart French, ''The Trials of AK: A Study in the Rejection of Democratic Secular Humanism'' (Diss., George Washington Univ., 1971). The details and importance of K's conviction are treated by Henry Steele Commager, ''The Blasphemy of AK,'' *NEQ* 8 (March 1935): 29–41; Leonard W. Levy, ''Satan's Last Apostle in Massachusetts,'' *AQ* 5 (1953): 16–30; and most ably by French, ''Liberation of Man and God in Boston: AK's Free-Thought Campaign 1830–1839,'' *AQ* 32 (1980): 202–21. See also Robert E. Burkholder, ''Emerson, K, and the Divinity School Address,'' *AL* 58 (March 1986): 1–14.

Robert E. Burkholder

KRAITSIR, CHARLES V. (1804–1860), Hungarian-born linguist and professor of languages, contributed to the discussions of linguistics and philology carried on by New England Transcendentalists. Through his pamphlet *The Significance of the Alphabet* (1846) and his longer work *Glossology: Being a Treatise on the Nature of Language and the Language of Nature* (1852), K generally influenced the discussion about the origin and meaning of language and specifically influenced H. Thoreau's* attitude toward language and wordplay.

Educated in medicine at the University of Pesth, K studied philology with J. F. Blumenbach at Göttingen University. Caught up in the Polish Revolution in 1830, K led a group of exiled Poles to France and England and then in 1833 to the United States. K's fluency in English and other languages led to his appointment as professor of modern languages and history at the University of Virginia in 1840, but his horror at slavery caused him to leave that post in 1844 for the more congenial atmosphere of Boston.

In 1845 K gave a lecture series in Boston on his philosophy of language. He had already met E. Peabody,* who had agreed to serve as assistant at K's language academy. Attending his lectures, Peabody developed her notes into a pamphlet of some 50 pages and, with K's approval, published this in the following year as *The Significance of the Alphabet*.

K's impact on the Transcendentalists is situated in the context of decades of argument over the origins and meaning of language. As students of Locke,** conservative Unitarians** argued that language was an artificial system, a cultural agreement that certain sounds carry certain meanings. Having no universal or transcendent meaning and bearing no organic relation to the ideas being expressed, words are best understood when we determine their singular and unambiguous meanings.

Against this view several generations of writers launched critiques. J. Marsh* and Horace Bushnell proposed that the deepest religious truths can only be approached through imaginative language. In *Nature* (1836), following the lead of S. Reed,* among many others, R. W. Emerson* proposed that nature** itself is a vast symbolic language. Peabody, too, commented on the language question. In an 1834 review of J. G. Herder's** *The Spirit of Hebrew Poetry*, she proposed that primitive, or poetic, language derives from nature itself, and thus all languages at their origin share a common bond.

K showed Peabody and others just how, in his view, languages were related. He distinguished between language, the cultural development of syntax and vocabulary, and speech, the physical production of sound. An experience of the natural world results in a vocalization, or ''explosion of reason,'' as K put it. These primal sounds are universal and can be classified as gutterals, labials, and dentals. Ignoring other sounds like palatals and avoiding semantic and grammatical distinctions, K offered what he thought was a scientific basis for a belief in the unity of language and thus the unity of humanity.

Peabody was fascinated by K's ''proof.'' She took the occasion of reviewing Bushnell's ''Preliminary Dissertation on Language'' from his *God in Christ*

(1849) in her one-issue *Aesthetic Papers*** to criticize Bushnell for saying that language is arbitrary. K had proved to her satisfaction that the same basic sounds are found in all languages and convey the same kinds of foundational experiences, and she devoted several pages of the Bushnell review to a summary and defense of this position.

Arguably, it is Thoreau, who owned a copy of *Significance of the Alphabet* and whose notebooks reveal a careful reading of the 1852 *Glossology*, who makes the most inventive use of K's notions. From his earlier readings and conversations, Thoreau had absorbed the insights of many writers and thinkers regarding the metaphoric qualities of language. More than Emerson or Peabody, Thoreau was fascinated by the connections between the definitions of words and their origins in physical acts or natural phenomena. Throughout *Walden* (1854) and particularly in the chapter "Spring," Thoreau reveals his debt to K: The sound of words, based on the physical act of their production, reenact the moment of creation at the famous sandbank.

In 1848, with money raised by Peabody, K returned to Europe, prompted by revolutionary activity there. But his services were not needed, and he returned to Boston only to find he had lost control of his language academy. In 1851 he moved to New York City, where his *Glossology* was published the following year. In the last years of his life, K wrote articles for G. Ripley's* *New American Cyclopedia* and gave private language instruction.

References: None of K's works is in print. The best secondary treatments of him are Philip Gura, *The Wisdom of Words: Language, Theology, and Literature in the New England Renaissance* (1981); Gura, "Elizabeth Palmer Peabody and the Philosophy of Language," *ESQ* 23 (1977): 154–63; and Michael West, "CK's Influence on Thoreau's Theory of Language," *ESQ* 19 (1973): 262–73. Peabody's commentary on K is found in her essay "Language" in *Aesthetic Papers*.

Bruce A. Ronda

L

LANE, CHARLES (1800–1870), an English reformer, is best known as the cofounder, with A. B. Alcott,* of the utopian community in Harvard, Massachusetts, Fruitlands.** Little is known about the first 30 years of his life. During the 1830s, he worked as a commercial journalist and as editor and manager of the *London Mercantile Price Current.* During this period, L met J. P. Greaves* and became part of his reformist circle interested in spiritual affairs and communal education. In 1838, Greaves opened Alcott House, an experimental school at Ham Common in Surrey, and by 1841, L had settled there. With the school's director, Henry Gardner Wright, he edited a tract called ''The Healthian,'' which focused on the connection between proper diet and spiritual renewal. L had begun corresponding with Alcott, and their similar ideas, and L's encouragement of Alcott at a low point in his career, led Alcott to travel to England in 1842. Alcott was greatly impressed by L, describing him as ''the deepest, sharpest intellect'' he had ever met. The two agreed that the time was ripe for putting into practice all the reform theories talked about abstractly on both sides of the Atlantic. With a plan to create a ''true harmonic association,'' Alcott, L, and Wright returned to America together. The ''New Eden'' they visualized would be based on the belief that only by the full intellectual, physical, and moral development of the individual could society be reformed.

L's young son William accompanied him, and the group returned to the Alcott household in Concord** in October 1842. They immediately put into practice their plans for a simple vegetarian diet and individual spiritual development. The following spring, a suitable property for their new communal experiment was found on the western slope of Prospect Hill in Harvard. L purchased the 90-acre farm and signed a year's lease for the use of the house and barn, and the ''Consociate'' family began there on 1 June 1843. Fruitlands was to embody the highest ideals of human nature, a place where ''Universal Love'' would prevail, without the regulation of church or government. L contributed letters and essays to several newspapers and journals describing life at Fruitlands and even wrote H. Thoreau* on Staten Island in an effort to recruit him, but his and Alcott's efforts yielded few new members or supporters.

L was not well liked by the Alcott children, whom he had responsibility for teaching. Nor did Abigail Alcott find it easy to accept him as part of her family, and L's writings of this period reveal his low regard for her. As the summer passed, and L and Alcott went on frequent lecture and recruiting trips, Mrs. Alcott found herself carrying nearly the whole burden of tending and harvesting crops and managing the household. L's influence with her husband began to threaten her own family's harmony, and she profoundly resented the despotic and difficult outsider.

L's views on celibacy were a particular source of tension for the married Alcotts. Formulated from the Pythagorean leanings of his early teacher, Pestalozzi,** and finding support in the example of the nearby Shaker** community, L believed that a true community life could be lived only by celibates. He expressed his admiration for the Shaker way in a *Dial*** article, "A Day with the Shakers" (October 1843), foreshadowing his eventual decision to join them. When the Fruitlands experiment ended in January 1844, the Alcotts went to rented quarters at a neighbor's, and C and William L joined the Harvard Shakers. Mrs. Alcott noted their departure in her journal** (6 January 1844), adding that their care "has been at times exceedingly arduous."

L's move to the Shakers appears to have been a calculated opportunity to advance his own beliefs from within the framework of an established communitarian setting. Earlier that fall, when tensions were building at Fruitlands, he had considered Brook Farm** but had found it lacking in a sense of community purpose. But the Shakers were a well-ordered and strictly regulated sect, and they enthusiastically welcomed L and his persuasive manner of proselytizing. L shared their pious devotion only briefly, however, then became disaffected with the undue influence he felt their leaders exerted over individual members. He quit the Shaker community in August 1845, leaving his son behind as an apprentice to a shoemaker in their village. From this point on, L's whereabouts are not well documented, although Alcott's journals indicate that L stayed for a few weeks in Concord with his family at their new home, Hillside.

In summer 1846, L was back in Harvard, where he and J. Palmer* formed the Leominster and Harvard Benevolent Association. Palmer was paying off a mortgage from L on the Fruitlands property, and with the newly laid tracks of the Worcester and Nashua Railroad line within a hundred yards of the house, Palmer envisioned a refuge where individuals could receive room and board in exchange for labor on lands owned by the association. L quickly grew impatient with this social experiment, and September 1846 found him in New York, ready to set sail for Alcott House in England, where he planned to write a short history of Fruitlands. He resumed his career in journalism and in 1850, abandoning the celibate life, married Hannah Bond. In 1870, L died, leaving behind his wife and three children. His son William left the Shakers in July 1848 to return to London and may have eventually emigrated to Australia.

References: Accounts of the Fruitlands experiment almost universally relate the Alcotts' point of view; L's history, if one was ever written, has never come to light. L. M. Alcott* may have been the most influential in shaping contemporary perceptions of L. In *Transcendental Wild Oats* (1873) she portrays L as Timon Lion, the tyrannical partner of Abel Lamb. Undoubtedly reflecting her family's bias, she paints an unflattering picture of him as the disrupter of a devoted and harmonious family. L's own writings, in *The Dial* and a series of articles on voluntary government in *The Liberator*, show him to be a rational intellectual with little tolerance for others' human shortcomings and sentiments. William Henry Harland, "Bronson Alcott's English Friends" (typescript at Fruitlands Museums), is perhaps the best biographical source on L, as are selected letters also held at Fruitlands. Dahlstrand (1982) is the best modern source on L. Clara Endicott Sears, *Bronson Alcott's Fruitlands* (1915), compiles many primary sources relating to L's involvement. Only one photograph of L is known, which shows him to be a stern and rather forbidding-looking character.

Maggie Stier

LONGFELLOW, HENRY WADSWORTH (1807–1882), the most popular American poet of the 19th century, remained remarkably untouched by Transcendentalism, despite his lifetime acquaintance with R. W. Emerson* and extensive knowledge of German Romantic literature. L likewise exerted little influence on the Transcendentalists, although he inadvertently aided them by stimulating interest in Germanic literature (which he had studied in Germany) among his students at Bowdoin and Harvard College and among American readers in general through his many translations, experimentation with foreign meters in poetry, and use of German sources in such works as *Hyperion*.

L held mixed views of the Transcendentalists. For example, L admired Emerson personally and as a poet and lecturer, and both were longtime members of the Saturday Club.** Emerson struck him as charming, brilliant, and even sublime, and L singled out Emerson's poems "Monadnoc," "Threnody," and "The Humble-bee" "as containing much of the quintessence of poetry." Nevertheless, L found Emerson's ideas obscure, dreamy, and sometimes absurd. Moreover, L knew that many of the Transcendentalists' ideas were unoriginal, and he privately criticized their pretension: "Everybody talks about German literature and German philosophy, as if they knew something of them." There are, to be sure, hints of Transcendentalist ideas in L's work (as expressed, for instance, by Flemming in *Hyperion* and Mr. Churchill in *Kavanagh*), and L occasionally responded with enthusiasm to the German philosophers (going so far as to claim, for instance, that there was more of true Christianity in the lectures of Johann Fichte** than in the sermons of the orthodox who railed against German philosophy). However, L never accepted certain New England Transcendentalist ideas, such as the correspondence** between nature** and the human mind.

The Transcendentalists, in turn, were largely critical of L. Although Emerson occasionally praised L's work, deeming *Kavanagh* "the best sketch we have seen in the direction of the American Novel" and dubbing L's poem "The Birds of Killingworth" "serene, happy, and immortal as Chaucer," L little resembled Emerson's ideal poet. L did not produce the original and prophetic "metre-making argument" that Emerson called for in "The Poet"; rather, his gift lay in the technical virtuosity of his translations and adaptations of foreign literature and folklore. In what is perhaps the classic Transcendentalist critique of L, M. Fuller* declared him not only overrated but also essentially "artificial and imitative" (*New-York Daily Tribune*, 10 December 1845). Fuller judged L an exotic flower transplanted from European soil rather than a truly American poet. Nevertheless, she conceded, "His verse breathes at times much sweetness; and, if not allowed to supersede what is better, may promote a taste for good poetry."

References: The standard edition of L is *The Works of HWL* (1966). A still useful biography, consisting largely of letters and journal entries, is S. Longfellow,* *Life of HWL*, 3 vols. (1891; rpt. 1968). A lucid view of L and the Transcendentalists is Frederick Wagner, "L, Emerson, and Emerson's 'Gossips': [A.B.] Alcott,* [W. Ellery] Channing,* and [H.] Thoreau,*" *Papers Presented at the Longfellow Commemorative Conference, April 1–3, 1982* (1982), 93–109. For the relation between L's and the Transcendentalists' aesthetic theories, see Marjorie J. Elder, *Nathaniel Hawthorne:* Transcendental Symbolist* (1969), 15–41. For a comparative look at L's, Emerson's, and Thoreau's poetics, see Bernard Duffey, *Poetry in America: Expression and Its Values in the Times of Bryant,* Whitman,* and Pound* (1978), 3–57.

Terry J. Martin

LONGFELLOW, SAMUEL (1819–1892), biographer and youngest brother of H. W. Longfellow,* was a Unitarian** preacher who adapted the Transcendentalist philosophy to his sermons and hymns. While attending Harvard Divinity School** in 1842, he heard of a convention being organized by R. W. Emerson* and B. Alcott* and laughed at the " 'phase' of the spirit of the age," adding, "I expect to see funnier things yet." But, like classmates S. Johnson* and T. W. Higginson,* he was to come under the influence of the movement while at the Divinity School, eventually embracing its spiritual idealism** as his own.

Known for his focus on children in his congregation and a kindly, optimistic disposition, L spent many years in conjunction with Johnson working on a new book of hymns for Unitarians. As a minister, he retained the phraseology of Christianity but considered himself a "Theist" (he admitted no mediation between himself and the Divine Spirit) and was poetical rather than mystical—an "intuitionalist."

References: L's hymns have been collected in *A Book of Hymns for Public and Private Devotion* (1846), *Hymns of the Spirit* (1864), *Hymns and Verses* (1894), and "The Anonymous Hymns of SL," ed. Henry Wilder Foote, *HTR* (1917): 362–68. L and Higginson jointly compiled *Thalatta: A Book for the Sea-Side* (1853). His writings are collected in *Memoir and Letters*, ed. Joseph May (1894). His best-known work is his biography of his famous brother, *Life of Henry Wadsworth Longfellow* (1891). For his relationship with his brother, see *Letters of Henry Wadsworth Longfellow*, 6 vols., ed. Andrew Hilen (1967–82).

David Hicks

LORING, ELLIS GRAY (1803–1858), was a successful Boston lawyer and abolitionist** who joined with W. L. Garrison* and ten others to found the New England Anti-Slavery Society on 1 January 1832. A strong believer in human rights, L successfully argued before the Massachusetts Supreme Court, in the celebrated Med Case (1836), that any slave brought by a master into the state of Massachusetts was automatically free. The case established an important legal precedent. Two years later, when A. Kneeland* achieved the questionable distinction of being the last person to be imprisoned for the crime of blasphemy in Massachusetts, L joined with Dr. W. E. Channing* and promulgated the *Petition on Behalf of Abner Kneeland* (1838), which has been seen by many as a seminal document in defense of free speech. Among the signatures that L garnered in support of his position was that of R. W. Emerson,* who at the time was in the middle of the firestorm created by his own heretical Divinity School Address.

L's home in Boston was a center for intellectual, as well as abolitionist, activity. Maria Chapman, Caroline and Deborah Weston, Edmund Quincy, L. M. Child,* W. Phillips,* and Emerson himself were frequent guests. L, like Emerson, also had a strong interest in the then-little-known Scottish writer T. Carlyle.* He had encouraged Emerson to invite Carlyle to America in 1835 and joined with him and others in editing Carlyle's *Critical and Miscellaneous Essays* (4 vols., 1838), which did much to introduce the writer to an American audience.

Emerson's friendship with L dated back to their Boston Latin Grammar School days and, later, Harvard. L's strong commitment to the abolition movement undoubtedly had a direct influence on Emerson's eventual involvement in that reform, as indicated in the (largely unpublished) correspondence between the two. It was L who provided much of the material and detailed advice used by Emerson in preparing his "Emancipation in the British West Indies Address" (1844 [*W*, 11:97–147]), one of his most important and comprehensive antislavery presentations.

References: Surprisingly, little has been written about L. For his relationship with Emerson, see Gougeon (1990); and Len Gougeon, "1838: EGL and a Journal for the Times," *SAR* 1990: 33–47. See also Eleanor Tilton, "Emerson's Lecture Schedule—1837–1838—Revised," *HLB* 21 (October 1973): 382–99). L is mentioned several times in various biographies of Garrison and in Walter Merrill and Louis Ruchames, eds., *The Letters of William Lloyd Garrison,* 6 vols. (1971–81).

Len Gougeon

LOWELL, JAMES RUSSELL (1819–1891), poet, editor, and leading Brahmin intellectual, began his professional writing career imbued with a spirit of reform, evident in his early poems and in his writings for *The Pioneer* (1843) and the *National Anti-Slavery Standard* (1846–50). Although L's cautious nature prevented him from joining with W. L. Garrison* and the more fanatical abolitionists,** his passion for humanitarian reform and his vocal support for the worldwide revolutions of the 1840s provided grounds for an intellectual affinity between himself and the Transcendentalists. However, the increasingly urbane L could never abide the mystical elements in R. W. Emerson's* philosophy nor the eccentricities of the lesser members of the Transcendental group. His natural tendencies toward moderation and sociability discouraged close affiliation with the worshipers of ''self-reliance'' and engendered a deep distrust of any form of political, social, and literary extremism.

Since Emerson was only a philosophical and not a practicing extremist, allowing L to embrace the man without embracing the philosophy, a warm personal friendship developed between them. Emerson's contributions were always welcome while L edited the *Atlantic Monthly*** (1857–61) and the *North American Review*** (1863–72). In fact, Emerson may be viewed as one of L's intellectual mentors, especially in light of the significance each man placed upon the centrality of the creative imagination and the belief in a ''universal mind'' behind the particulars of individual expression. In acknowledgment of an intellectual debt he said he could never repay, L dedicated *Among My Books. Second Series* (1875) to Emerson with ''a love . . . which more than thirty years have deepened.'' Emerson was living proof that a democracy could indeed ''produce a gentleman.''

Personal and philosophical differences doomed the chances for a friendship between L and H. D. Thoreau.* The break between them became permanent when Thoreau accused L of cowardice in censoring a mildly irreligious statement from his essay ''Chesuncook'' in the *Atl.* L took his revenge on Thoreau's posthumous reputation in his famous *NAR* essay ''Thoreau'' (101 [October 1865]: 597–608), a systematic attack on Thoreau as man and writer, labeling him a recluse who embraced nature** because he could not abide mankind, a humorless cynic who had given up on America and its society, and most of all an arrogant egotist inordinately prideful of his own originality.

For L the contagion of egotism undermined any literary merit that might be argued for other members of the Transcendental school: B. Alcott* was a dreamer, Whitman* was crude and contrived, and Fuller,* fiercely lampooned in *A Fable for Critics* (1848), was a creature motivated only by spite. As the century progressed, the ardent reformer of the 1840s became the urbane conservative of the Gilded Age. From his powerful position as cultural arbiter, L helped raise Emerson to a position of international honor as an embodiment of the New England devotion to mind and spirit. But his peevish misjudgments of Emerson's associates, especially Thoreau, provided powerful ammunition for the continued critical assault on Thoreau by other detractors that helped postpone his full acceptance as an American classic writer for at least another generation.

References: The standard biography of L is Martin Duberman, *JRL* (1966); for L's younger years (to the late 1850s), see Leon Howard, *Victorian Knight-Errant* (1952); and for a valiant attempt to organize L's aesthetic theories, Norman Foerster's Introduction to the American Writers Series *JRL* (1947) is still interesting.

Daniel A. Wells

LYELL, CHARLES (1797–1875), a British geologist, helped establish geology as the era's most exciting and accessible science. L's emphasis on the immensity of time, the eternal balance of natural forces, and the continuity between present realities and the mysteries of earth's past appealed to both R. W. Emerson* and H. Thoreau.*

In *Principles of Geology* (3 vols., 1830–33), L argued with passion and skill that ''the former changes of the earth's surface'' could be explained ''by reference to causes now in operation.'' His monumental work marshaled scientific evidence for this key principle of ''uniformitarianism'' and argued strenuously against the mounting evidence for the progressive development of life. L showed how geological evidence, properly interpreted, proved the earth's history was immensely long, cyclical, and static.

The immense antiquity of earth was already widely accepted among geologists, but L impressed the concept on a general audience. Emerson, who first read L around 1836 and visited him in London in 1848, responded imaginatively to Lyellian deep time in ''Nature'' (1844): ''All changes pass without violence, by reason of the two cardinal conditions of boundless space and boundless time. Geology has initiated us into the secularity of nature.''** Thoreau, who read L in 1840, also responded to the image of time layered into the soil under our feet in *A Week*: ''I thrust this stick many aeons deep into its surface, and with my heel make a deeper furrow than the elements have ploughed here for a thousand years. . . . The newest is but the oldest made visible to our senses.''

Deep time explained how the minute changes visible from day to day could accumulate into the massive changes recorded in geological strata, showing the continuity of present and past; for L, the present is our index to eternity, and the history of the earth proves that while nature is in constant flux, nothing ever really changes. As Thoreau put it, ''[G]o where we will we discover infinite change in particulars only—not in generals.'' Or, in the social universe: ''As in geology, so in social institutions, we may discover the causes of all past change in the present invariable order of society'' (Journal and *Week*). In ''Self-Reliance,'' Emerson echoed L's belief in the stable balance of creative and destructive forces: ''Society never advances. It recedes as fast on one side as it gains on the other. . . . For every thing that is given, something is taken.''

Emerson more often expresses a progressive view of life, and though L's vision of a cyclic, steady-state earth defended humanity against the threat posed by developmental theories, in the 1850s L himself admitted a version of evolution. More lasting was his principle of uniform and gradual change, which used science to subdue revolution. Thoreau radicalized this principle: Revolution was generated by the accumulation of small and individual changes. As he observed in his journal,** not only do ''little strokes fall great oaks,'' but ''such, too, is the rise of the oak; little strokes of a different kind and often repeated raise great oaks.''

References: The first edition of *Principles of Geology* has been reprinted (1990–92); see the excellent introduction by Martin S. Rudwick (1: vii–lviii). Also helpful is the discussion of L in Stephen Jay Gould, *Time's Arrow, Time's Cycle* (1987), 99–179. Although a great deal of work has been done on L, little examines L's ideas in the context of American Transcendentalism. For an exception see William Rossi, ''Poetry and Progress: Thoreau, L, and the Geological Principles of *A Week*,'' *AL* 66 (June 1994): 275–300.

Laura Dassow Walls

M

MANN, HORACE (1796–1859), was president of the Massachusetts State Senate and secretary of Massachusetts' first board of education. M's belief in human perfectibility made him friends among Transcendentalists: E. Peabody,* W. E. Channing,* and T. Parker* all encouraged M in his reform interests, which included temperance,** prisons, treatment of the insane, education for the blind and deaf, and the common school system. However, M's conservative insistence on reforming the individual through morally authoritative institutions sharply distinguished his ideas from the Transcendentalist belief in the autonomy of the individual.

M met E. and Mary Peabody while living with them in a boardinghouse in 1832. The sisters encouraged him to run for the state legislature, a position he had abandoned because of personal debts and the death of his first wife. Elizabeth introduced M to Channing, and together they helped him reconstruct a religious faith shattered by Charlotte Mann's death. Channing reassured M of God's love and promise of eternal life and of man's perfectibility. Elizabeth and M shared a close personal relationship, carrying on lengthy discussions about the possibility of reaching moral perfectibility without external pressure. Elizabeth lost M's romantic affections, however, to her sister Mary, who married him in 1843. The Hawthornes* lived with the Manns while Nathaniel completed *The Blithedale Romance,* in which the character Hollingsworth, as a prison reformer, bears striking similarities to M.

R. W. Emerson* took enough interest in M's education reform** ideas to attend his convention in Concord** and even invited M to stay at the Old Manse.** But Emerson was disappointed with M's ideas and wrote in his journal,** "Law has touched the business of education with the point of its pen and instantly it has frozen stiff." A. B. Alcott* expressed interest in M's push for better teacher education, offering to lecture at a normal school, but M rebuffed him. While Alcott and Emerson believed in the innate ability of students to understand moral principles, M believed that only a streamlined and centrally controlled common school system could instill correct moral principles in students. Furthermore, he thought textbooks, teachers, and classrooms should teach general moral principles without religious or political sectarianism, a claim O. Brownson* ridiculed as naive and antiintellectual: "If they exclude whatever is sectarian, they must exclude all that relates to religion." Parker did his best to defend M against accusations of irreligion, as did E. Peabody, who used her personal friendship with Brownson to persuade him to soften his tone.

References: Selections from M's reports to the Massachusetts Board of Education are in *The Republic and the School: HM on the Education of Free Men*, ed. Lawrence A. Cremin (1957). The best biography is *HM*, by Jonathan Messerli (1972). For a detailed examination of M as secretary of the board of education, and an argument that his push for nonsectarian education did not intend separation of church and state, see *HM and Religion in the Massachusetts Public Schools,* by Raymond B. Carver (1969). Michael B. Katz argues that M and other education reformers wanted schools to discipline and homogenize an increasingly large and heterodox working class in *The Irony of Early School Reform* (1969). Arthur Bestor, "HM, Elizabeth Peabody, and Orestes A. Brownson," *Proceedings of the Middle States Association of History and Social Science Teachers* (1941): 47–53, details the clash between M and Brownson over nonsectarian education.

D'Ann Pletcher-George

MARSH, JAMES (1794–1842), was a Congregationalist minister, professor of philosophy at Hampden-Sydney College and Seminary in Virginia and the University of Vermont, and president of the University of Vermont (1826–33). His 1829 edition of S. T. Coleridge's* *Aids to Reflection* introduced Americans to the chief English exponent of the German philosophical thought that ultimately provided the underpinning of Transcendentalism (he later edited *The Statesman's Manual* [1832] and *The Friend* [1833]. *Aids to Reflection* is one of the works that instigated the 1836 formation of the Transcendental Club** in Boston; however, M, never a Transcendentalist, abhorred the opinions he inadvertently fostered. His "Preliminary Essay" to *Aids to Reflection* guided the Transcendentalists' (and other American readers') understanding of Coleridge. M calls particular attention to the distinction between Understanding and Reason, perhaps the key epistemological concept of the Romantic age. But his hope for Coleridge's work was that it would return spirituality to American Congregationalism, not open a path away from orthodoxy.

M believed that Lockean** and Scottish metaphysical philosophies that excluded the possibility of spiritual power and agency were logically incompatible with an essentially spiritual religion. Although he recognized that the principles in *Aids to Reflection* were inconsistent with received theological thought, he discovered in Coleridge the reconciliation of religion and philosophy that reason demanded. Rational knowledge of the central and absolute ground of all being could only be attained through reflection on the mysterious grounds of one's own being.

Understanding, the faculty called reason in the 18th century, is possessed by humans in greater degree, but no difference in form, than by animals. It allows for abstraction, generalization, forethought, and adapting means to ends but does not offer rational grounds for human feelings of free will or moral responsibility.

Reason, as M, and through him the Transcendentalists, interpreted Coleridge, instinctively seeks after (and presumably may find) unity and consistency in the Divine Mind. The real requirements of Reason, and consequently true knowledge of one's self, could be learned through profound reflection. Truths arrived at through reflection could be attributed to Reason and the Divine Mind and, although arrived at individually, would be shared by others who followed the same process. Each man could draw truths from his own depths only for himself, even though the same truths could be discerned by others.

References: Joseph Torrey, *The Remains of the Rev. JM, D.D.* (1843); Peter C. Carafiol, *Transcendent Reason: JM and the Forms of Romantic Thought* (1982), and introduction to *Selected Works*, 3 vols. (1976); John J. Duffy, *Coleridge's American Disciples: The Selected Correspondence of JM* (1973); Ronald Vale Wells, *Three Christian Transcendentalists: JM, Caleb Sprague Henry,* Frederic Henry Hedge** (1943; rptd. & expanded 1972); Douglas McCreary Greenwood, "JM," in Myerson (1984), 343–47.

Leigh Kirkland

MARTINEAU, HARRIET (1802–1876), was a British political economist, journalist, and abolitionist.** From 1834 through 1836, she traveled throughout the United States from New England to New Orleans, meeting a number of well-known Unitarians**, Transcendentalists, and political figures. She stayed with Dr. W. E. Channing* and R. W. Emerson* and met M. Fuller* and B. Alcott,* among many prominent Transcendentalists. M later wrote two books based upon her experiences and the observations she drew: *Society in America* (1837) and *Retrospect of Western Travel* (1838). Her goal in *Society in America* was to examine how well American society measured up to the ideals expressed in the Declaration of Independence; as a result she tends to concentrate her discussion on institutional practices. The great flaw that she found was slavery, and her interest in this issue permeates all of her writings on America. And while she praised American democracy, she believed that women in America were intellectually stifled. *Retrospect of Western Travel* explores her personal experiences and the relationships she established during this trip. Both books had mixed receptions in the United States, but *Society in America* evoked particularly hostile reactions, due both to her gender and to her outspoken praise for the abolition movement.

Although M later rejected Christianity and converted to Necessarianism, she was raised in a prominent Unitarian family and thus had letters of introduction to many Unitarians in the United States. She publicly criticized a number of American Unitarians, however, for distancing themselves from the slavery debate, claiming in *Society in America*, "I can come to no other conclusion than that the most guilty class of the community in regard to the slavery question at present is, not the slave-holding, nor even the mercantile, but the clerical: the most guilty, because . . . they profess to spend their lives in the study of moral relations, and have pledged themselves to declare the whole counsel of God.'' M praised other Unitarians, like her friend Channing, for taking a public stand in favor of abolition.

Despite Emerson's lack of active involvement with the abolition movement, M frequently praised his moral and intellectual independence, traits that she believed others in New England lacked. She saw Emerson deliver ''The American Scholar'' at Cambridge in 1837 and wrote of it: ''His address breathes a truly philosophical reverence for Humanity, and exhibits an elevated conception of what are the right aims and the reasonable discipline of the mind of a scholar and thinker.'' Most important, she noted, was the spirit of ''moral independence which breathe[s] through the whole.'' Emerson was not entirely pleased with her praise, however; he wrote of M to T. Carlyle:* ''Meaning to do me a signal kindness (& a kindness quite out of all measure of justice) she does me a great annoyance—to take away from me my privacy & thrust me before my time, (if ever there be a time) into the arena of the gladiators to be stared at.'' Despite his annoyance with her, M and Emerson enjoyed a cordial relationship. She stayed briefly with the Emersons in Concord** in 1836, and Emerson visited her in 1848 during his trip to England. Although they maintained only an intermittent personal correspondence, they exchanged their works regularly. M also met Fuller during her time in America, and she took credit for drawing Fuller to Emerson's attention.

Although M liked Fuller, she judged her harshly because she could not understand how a woman of Fuller's intellect could fail to be interested in abolition. She explains that during the 1830s and early 1840s, Fuller ''was living and moving in an ideal world, talking in private and discoursing in public about the most fanciful and shallow conceits which the transcendentalists of Boston took for philosophy, [and] she looked down upon persons who acted instead of talking finely. . . . While Margaret Fuller and her adult pupils sat 'gorgeously dressed,' talking about Mars and Venus, Plato** and Göethe,* and fancying themselves the elect of the earth in intellect and refinement, the liberties of the republic were running out as fast as they could go'' (*Autobiography*, 2:71). As J. F. Clarke* points out in his 1877 review essay in the *North American Review*,** M delivers harsh criticism of a person whom she considered a friend. Clarke justifiably concludes that M's reformist zeal made her hostile toward anyone who did not share her beliefs (438). M amended her judgment of Fuller in later years and claimed in both her *Autobiography* and a letter to Emerson that Fuller's experiences during the Italian revolution taught her much-needed compassion.

M's more distant relationship with Alcott brought about mixed results. While she strongly criticized the Temple School,** she did later pass on the *Record of a School* and *Conversations with Children on the Gospels* to J. P. Greaves,* who founded the Alcott House school in England.

References: Several works by M include sections on the Transcendentalists. Most useful are *Society in America*, 3 vols. (1837; abridged rpt. 1968), and *Retrospect of Western Travel*, 3 vols. (1838). *HM's Autobiography, with Memorials by Maria Weston Chapman*, 3 vols. (1877), is another good source for her personal relationships with the Transcendentalists. Clarke's review of her *Autobiography* provides a useful contemporary perspective: *NAR* 124 (1877): 435–50. Also important is John McAleer, *Ralph Waldo Emerson: Days of Encounter* (1984), 217–21. Three biographies focus on M's work in reform movements: Vera Wheatley, *The Life and Work of HM* (1957); R. K. Webb, *HM: A Radical Victorian* (1960); and Valerie Kossew Pichanick, *HM: The Woman and Her Work, 1802–1876* (1980). See also *HM: Selected Letters* (1990).

Karen A. Weyler

MARTINEAU, JAMES (1805–1900), the younger brother of H. Martineau,* was a Unitarian** minister and a prominent British theologian. After serving as a minister in Dublin and Liverpool, he was elected to the post of professor of mental and moral philosophy at Manchester New College in 1841. When the college relocated to London in 1857, M moved as well and took on the additional responsibility of serving as a pastor at the Little Portland Street Chapel.

M's departure from traditional Unitarian views as reflected in his sermons and published writings was well known in New England. Denying the infallibility of the Bible and sharing the Transcendentalists' view that Unitarianism was cold and lifeless, M was an early and enthusiastic reader of *The Dial.* ** His first book, *The Rationale of Religious Inquiry* (1836), was originally a series of six lectures designed to investigate the origins of belief and to establish the human conscience as the guide for correct behavior. G. Ripley* wrote lengthy reviews of M's works in 2 of the 13 articles he wrote for *The Christian Examiner*** between 1830 and 1837. While generally applauding M's *Rationale*, Ripley objected to what he perceived as a lack of full analysis and rigor in M's program of reform for English theology (*ChEx* 21 [1836]: 225–54).

M was visited by both M. Fuller* and R. W. Emerson* on their separate trips to England. Fuller heard M speak in Liverpool in 1846 and observed in one of her New York *Tribune* dispatches that "Mr. M looks like the over-intellectual, the partially developed man, and his speech confirms this impression. He is sometimes conservative, sometimes reformer, not in the sense of eclecticism, but because his powers and views do find a true harmony. On the conservative side he is scholarly acute,—on the other, pathetic, pictorial, generous." In 1847, Emerson met M in Liverpool, drank tea with him, and heard him preach. Although M liked Emerson personally, he was more interested in the works of Dr. W. E. Channing,* with whom he enjoyed a cordial relationship through correspondence.

In addition to the *Rationale*, M published a variety of works of interest to the Transcendentalists during his life, including *The Scheme of Vicarious Redemption Inconsistent with Itself* (1839), *Scope of Mental and Moral Philosophy* (1840), and *The Restoration of Belief* (1852).

REFERENCES: The two biographical studies of M are J. Estlin Carpenter, *JM: Theologian and Teacher: A Study of His Life and Thought* (1906); and A. W. Jackson, *JM: A Biography and Study* (1901). For a contemporaneous account of the relationship of M to Emerson, see William R. Alger, ''Emerson, Spencer, and M,'' *ChEx* 84 (May 1868): 257–87. Fuller's assessment is in *'These Sad but Glorious Days': Dispatches from Europe, 1846–1850 by Margaret Fuller*, ed. Larry J. Reynolds and Susan Belasco Smith (1991), 85–86. See also references in Myerson (1984).

Susan Belasco Smith

MAY, SAMUEL JOSEPH (1797–1871), was a Unitarian** minister, reform advocate, and member of the Transcendental Club.** Though concerned with such causes as temperance,** penal reform, woman's rights,** education reform,** and the plight of Native Americans, he is best remembered as a nonresistant** abolitionist.** Active in the cause of abolition, M, as R. W. Emerson* put it in his journal,** ''goes everywhere & sees the leaders of society everywhere.'' His circle of colleagues and acquaintances included B. Alcott* (his brother-in-law), W. E. Channing,* L. M. Child,* Emerson, W. L. Garrison,* the Grimké sisters, Lucretia Mott, and T. Parker.*

Already active in the cause of abolition and peace, M met Garrison at an 1830 meeting in Boston, telling Garrison, ''I am sure you are called to a great work, and I mean to help you.'' M was an active speaker for reform, asking for but not always receiving permission to speak against slavery from the pulpits of his Unitarian brethren. Though Channing and W. Furness* were dismayed by M's antislavery stand, Emerson allowed him to preach from his Second Church pulpit on 29 May 1831. In that sermon, M pointed to the hypocrisy of American pride in ''our free institutions'' while ''we have been holding *two millions* of our fellow men in the most abject servitude.'' Channing finally overcame his reluctance to align himself with the antislavery movement after a private conversation with M. Acknowledging to M, ''I have been silent too long,'' Channing in the next year published his book on *Slavery*. M took an even more active stand when, after passage of the Fugitive Slave Law, he and others at the October 1851 Syracuse convention effected the rescue of a fugitive slave, Jerry. Thereafter, 1 October was celebrated as Jerry Rescue Day. Though convinced of the need for nonresistance, M did not hesitate to criticize the Unitarian community for refusing ''to speak as a body . . . for the down-trodden.'' Nor was his stand always easy; he was forced to resign from the pastorate of two churches, at Brooklyn, Connecticut, and South Scituate, Massachusetts, and was mobbed five times during his antislavery tour through Vermont in 1835. Nonetheless, he had a reputation for gentleness; Parker noted that mild M had a voice ''made to pronounce the Beatitudes.''

M's concern for equality and humanitarian efforts extended to others. He pondered the example of Lucretia Mott and the propriety of women speaking in public, resolving whatever hesitations he had and inviting the abolitionist Angelina Grimké to speak from his pulpit. He championed the cause of Prudence

Crandall, a schoolteacher who attempted to bring an African-American child into her classroom. He promoted popular education and the improvement of the common schools and served as principal of the Normal School at Lexington, Massachusetts, at the request of H. Mann.* And when Alcott fell on hard financial times, he was "spared house rent by the kindness of Mr. May." So much did M do for others that Alcott dubbed him "God's chore boy."

References: *Some Recollections of Our Antislavery Conflict* (1869) provides a look at the major events and personages as well as M's own involvement in the antislavery movement. See Douglas C. Stange, *Patterns of Antislavery Among American Unitarians, 1831–1860* (1977); *The Journals of Bronson Alcott*, ed. Odell Shepard (1938); W. H. Channing, *Memoir of William Ellery Channing* (1848; 10th ed., 1874); Emerson's *JMN*; and J. Weiss,* *The Life and Correspondence of Theodore Parker* (1864). Also see the biography by Donald Yacovone, *SJM and the Dilemmas of the Liberal Persuasion, 1797–1871* (1991).

Susan L. Roberson

MELVILLE, HERMAN (1819–1891), best known to his contemporaries as the sailor-author of *Typee* (1846) and to 20th-century readers and students as the creator of *Moby-Dick* (1851), was never a part of the New England Transcendentalist movement. But he was notably responsive, both affirmatively and negatively, to Transcendentalist thinking and writing—especially when he heard R. W. Emerson* lecture in 1849 and subsequently read his essays.

Like many of the New England Transcendentalists, M had Unitarian** affiliations: Both his father, Allan, and his wife, Elizabeth, daughter of Chief Justice of Massachusetts Lemuel Shaw,* were Boston Unitarians; by contrast, M's mother, Maria, daughter of the Albany Gansevoorts, was a member of the Calvinist Dutch Reformed Church. Herman and Elizabeth were married in 1847 by a Unitarian clergyman, and in their later years, they attended All Souls Unitarian Church in New York City. But Herman, who knew the Bible intimately, could never free himself from thoughts of the stern Deity of Calvinism (see Puritanism**) and of the Old Testament. After leaving the sea in 1844, he had sought some basis for his personal faith and philosophy in the omnivorous private reading that served to compensate for his limited formal education. While writing *Mardi* (1849) he turned to "Plato** and Proclus** and Verulam," as Emerson, too, had done, and by the time of *Moby-Dick*, like the Transcendentalists as Emerson once described them, he had "fallen upon Coleridge* and Wordsworth* and Goethe,* then on Carlyle,* with pleasure and sympathy."

M professed to know little of Emerson's writing until hearing him lecture, as he declared at the time, but from unsympathetic friends, he had heard of him "as full of transcendentalisms, myths & oracular gibberish." The lecture, however, was a revelation for him—both of Emerson and of his own potential as an author and as what he called a "thought-diver." "Say what they will," he told a correspondent, Emerson is "a great man." Still, he withheld full allegiance, either to Emerson and Transcendentalism or to any idealistic** philosopher from Plato onward. With contemporaries such as N. Hawthorne* and Poe* he could accept and employ the basically Platonic notion of what Emerson called ''correspondence''** between nature** and spirit, for M was an inveterate analogist and symbolist, but for him, nature was indifferent to man or at best neutral toward his strivings. Sometimes, with Ahab in *Moby-Dick*, he thought that ''there's naught beyond'' nature; sometimes, as in the chapter on ''The Whiteness of the Whale,'' he could write that while ''this visible world seems formed in love, the invisible spheres were formed in fright.'' The Transcendentalists, he thought, were insufficiently aware of evil and suffering, and Emerson in particular exhibited both coldness and self-conceit. Yet for all that, M shared Emerson's belief in both a democracy of men and a self-reliant aristocracy of superior individuals.

In 1850 M wrote of Emerson as second only to Hawthorne among contemporary American writers; he also knew Thoreau's* *A Week on the Concord and Merrimack Rivers*, and he probably read *Walden* as well in 1854. But though both *Moby-Dick* and *Pierre* (1852) reflect his absorption of Emerson's thinking and writing, even while they were in progress he was becoming increasingly disenchanted with all forms of transcendental thought, both ancient and modern. He had also been reading authors of another persuasion, from the skeptical Montaigne** to the rationalist Pierre Bayle and the contemporary anti-Transcendentalist Andrews Norton,* and they, too, left their marks on his own work. In *Pierre* he scathingly satirized and dismissed ''Muggletonian Scots and Yankees'' (read Carlyle and Emerson) along with ''their Greek or German Neoplatonical** originals,'' and his Mark Winsome in *The Confidence-Man* (1857) is an unmistakable caricature of Emerson himself. ''He can neither believe, nor be comfortable in his unbelief,'' Hawthorne wrote of M in 1856, ''and he is too honest and courageous not to try to do one or the other.'' During later years he was again reading Emerson and indicating points of both agreement and disagreement while drawing on Emerson's poetry as one of the models for his own unconventional verse. Though he once again affirmed his old reservations, he also praised both the essays and their author as ''noble.''

References: The Northwestern-Newberry Edition of *The Writings of HM* (1968–) is replacing both *The Works of HM* (1922–24) and the incomplete Hendricks House Edition (1947–). Two complementary works have long served as standard biographies: Jay Leyda, *The M Log: A Documentary Life of HM 1819–1891* (1951, 1969), and Leon Howard, *HM: A Biography* (1951); Hershel Parker is revising and expanding the *Log* and writing a new biography based upon it. Discussion of M and Transcendentalism through the early 1980s is reviewed and evaluated by Brian Higgins in the chapter on M in Myerson (1984).

Merton M. Sealts, Jr.

MUIR, JOHN (1838–1914), is, with H. D. Thoreau,* one of America's most admired and influential naturalists. Botanist, mountaineer, glaciologist, ecologist, and conservationist, M was instrumental in creating new national parks from

1890 on, and in 1892, he became the first president of the Sierra Club, which he had helped to found. Heavily influenced by the writings of R. W. Emerson* and Thoreau, M is identified as a Transcendentalist by most of his biographers and admirers who perceive and celebrate apparent correspondences between him and his predecessors of Concord.**

Whereas Emerson's apprehension of Nature** originated with consciousness, however, M's originated with Nature itself. M found Nature in its grandeur ''drenched'' with spirit, but unlike Emerson, he was no Idealist** who insisted on the *primary* power of thought and will—a fundamental difference. The discrepancy between their views appears in M's early modification of Emerson's phrase in *Nature* from ''I am part or parcel of God'' to ''[I] become part and parcel of Nature,'' a distinction often overlooked by those who write of M's Transcendentalism. Although both emphasized the unity, order, and harmony that underlie Nature if observed from the right perspective, M's response required total immersion in the natural world, but Emerson's did not.

In May 1871, Emerson visited M in Yosemite and early the next year urged him to leave his wilderness solitude, proposing that he come east to teach, write, and live among notable people. M, of course, refused, disappointed over Emerson's tepid response to the glorious Sierra. Nevertheless, he continued to carry and mark his copy of Emerson's essays during his treks and climbs in the western wilds, and Emerson listed M in his journal** along with Carlyle,* Thoreau, and several others, among those he called ''My men.''

Born in Dunbar, Scotland, M immigrated at age 11 with his family to a farm in Wisconsin where he grew to maturity under the control of his strict Calvinist father. Like Thoreau, he was mechanically adept and inventive. After attending the University of Wisconsin, M nearly lost his right eye in an accident, and when the eye healed, he decided never again to risk losing sight of the natural world that he craved.

M's reputation as a naturalist evolved chiefly from his writings on Yosemite and his beloved High Sierra. Enchanted by its natural glory, he became a mountaineer and glaciologist. His pantheistic** views appear in *The Mountains of California* (1894), but they do not connote transcendence there on the order of Emerson, Thoreau, and their contemporaries in Concord.

Elsewhere, however, his view seems closer to Emerson's when he writes that the physical senses are inferior to ''those of the mind,'' that the ''spiritual eye sees not only rivers of water but of air,'' and that the ''whole world is in motion to the center.'' Yet even here, M describes not the role of philosophical idealism but of imagination as central to his appreciation for Nature; Emerson, to be sure, would not disagree, but for him, M's awakened understanding does not go nearly far enough.

All in all, M's emphasis on wildness and scientific observation makes him closer akin to Thoreau the naturalist than to Emerson the idealist in whom the divinely inspired Self, not Nature, constitutes the crucial core of his philosophy. As Thoreau's life at Walden**—and his writing of it—led at least as much to a study of self as of the woods and pond, so did exploration of the Sierra serve a comparable purpose for M. With utter devotion, M indexed in pencil each volume of Thoreau's *Works* and maintained a written dialogue with his ''spiritual and literary mentor'' in the margins, occasionally disputing, but usually not. Even with Thoreau, however, M's priorities differed, though the two men shared a profound and compelling affinity for the wild through which each gained access to the higher laws of his own unique quest.

References: The standard edition of M's *Works* is the Sierra Edition, 10 vols., ed. William F. Badé (1915–24); the last two volumes comprise the *Life and Letters*, also by Badé. A valuable selection from the writings, ed. Edwin Way Teale, is *The Wilderness World of JM* (1954); especially relevant are Teale's introduction and a series of extracts entitled ''The Philosophy of JM'' at the end of the volume. The best biocritical overview is Frederick Turner, *Rediscovering America: JM in His Time and Ours* (1985); a helpful compact account is Herbert F. Smith, *JM* (1965). An engaging personalized tracing of M's ''spiritual journey'' is Michael P. Cohen, *The Pathless Way: JM and American Wilderness* (1985). ''JM: Wilderness Sage,'' chap. 6 in Max Oelschlaeger, *The Idea of Wilderness from Prehistory to Ecology* (1991), 172–204, offers a particularly astute analysis of M's putative Transcendentalism. Other relevant essays are by John P. O'Grady, ''JM's Parables of Desire,'' in *Pilgrims to the Wild* (1993), 47–85; Sherman Paul, ''M's Self-Authorizings,'' in *For Love of the World: Essays on Nature Writers* (1992), 221–64; and Jim dale Vickery, ''JM: Footloose in Regions of Light,'' in *Wilderness Visionaries* (1986), 46–104.

For Emerson's visit to M, see the account of a contemporary who accompanied him to Yosemite, James Bradley Thayer, *A Western Journey with Mr. Emerson* (1884), 88–109. M recalls and assesses that visit in *Our National Parks* (1901), 131–36, 235. And see Richard F. Fleck, ''JM's Homage to Henry David Thoreau,'' in a special issue of *Pacific Historian* devoted to M, 29 (summer–fall 1985): 55–64.

Sanford E. Marovitz

MURAT, NAPOLEON ACHILLE (1801–1847), author and nephew to Napoleon Bonaparte, emigrated from France to America in 1823 to escape political persecution and established a plantation in the frontier town of Tallahassee, Florida. There M met young R. W. Emerson,* who had ventured south in 1827 to soothe a respiratory ailment. In March of that year, M and Emerson sailed together from St. Augustine to Charleston, a trip that impacted significantly the intellectual development of both men.

When their paths crossed, M and Emerson came from polar opposites of opinion, especially on religious questions. M the confident atheist confronted Emerson the unwavering believer. Their ideological differences only enhanced their discussions, and in the end, they caused each other to reexamine deeply held orthodoxies. Due to stormy weather, their one-day trip was extended to over a week, causing Emerson to exclaim that he ''blessed my stars for my fine companion and we talked incessantly.'' The conversations expanded Emerson's intellectual horizons on matters of religion. ''My faith,'' Emerson wrote in his journal,** ''in these points is strong and I trust, as I live, indestructible. Meantime, I love and honour this intrepid doubter.'' In a letter to his brother William,* Emerson concluded that M was ''a philosopher, a scholar, a man of the world . . . & an ardent lover of truth.''

In return, Emerson introduced M to Unitarianism,** a faith without the dogma of traditional religion that M dismissed as fanatical. So appealing was this church that M asked Emerson to establish a Unitarian church in Tallahassee. After their brief encounter, M went on to publish three well-received books composed of observations on the American people. However, M is remembered most importantly for his correspondence with Emerson, especially their eight-day trip, which was not only an ocean voyage but an intellectual voyage as well.

References: A. J. Hanna, *A Prince in Their Midst: The Adventurous Life of AM on the American Frontier* (1946), is the only full-scale biography of M. References to M also appear in Mrs. Henry L. Richmond, ''Ralph Waldo Emerson in Florida,'' *Florida Historical Quarterly* 18 (October 1939): 75–83, and Alan J. Downes, ''The Legendary Visit of Emerson to Tallahassee,'' *Florida Historical Quarterly* 34 (April 1956): 334–38. M himself published three books of his observations of America, including *America and the Americans* (1849).

Jonathan Wells

N

NEWCOMB, CHARLES KING (1820–1894), was one of R. W. Emerson's* discoveries who failed to deliver on early promises of genius. His only published work, "The Two Dolons," typified for many contemporaneous critics the ridiculous pretension and vagaries of Transcendental mysticism.

N's father, a distinguished navy lieutenant, died in a shipwreck in 1825, leaving six children to be raised by their mother, Rhoda, a Providence, Rhode Island, bluestocking. Though Charles, the eldest, never broke completely free of his mother's influence, neither did he give himself fully to the literary life she planned for him. Graduated from Brown in 1837, his plans to enter an Episcopal seminary gave way to his attraction to the ritual and symbolism of Catholicism, though his informal association with the Church of Rome never extended to embracing its doctrines.

On 20 May 1841, N joined G. Ripley's* Brook Farm** at West Roxbury, where he boarded until December 1845, though never becoming an official member of the Brook Farm Association. N came to Brook Farm a protégé of M. Fuller* and acquaintance of Emerson, and he spent much of his time there writing. Little is known of his literary efforts, as "The Two Dolons" is his only work that made it into print. A sequel was intended but never materialized. There are indications that N also completed an "Essay on Saints and Poets" and a story, "Edith," the latter of which Emerson refers to in a letter; however, neither has been located, and both may well have been parts of the no-longer extant " 'Book-Journal' " that Emerson refers to in his journal** of June 1842.

"Dolon," which appeared in the July 1842 *Dial*** as "The First Dolon" of "Two Dolons" from "Symphony of Dolon," came only after great urging from Emerson, who had read from the original drafts and believed it contained "native gold": "There are sentences in Dolon worth the printing [of] the Dial." Despite Emerson's own corrections of the proofs, the story was still considered hopelessly obscure, even to its most sympathctic readers; as W. H. Channing* put it, “ ‘Dolon’ is full to crowding with truth and beauty, but . . . has no key-note for earthly instruments” (O. B. Frothingham,* *Memoir of William Henry Channing* [1886], 184).

N’s fellow Brook Farmers remembered him as a retiring eccentric. Georgiana Bruce Kirby, in *Years of Experience* (1887), recalls “a young man with large, devout eyes” and a “want of firmness in his gait.” His room was filled with relics, both natural and Catholic: Engravings of Ignatius Loyola and Jesus surrounded a portrait of German-born ballerina Fanny Elssler. Never married, N formed attachments to Fuller, Elizabeth Hoar,* and C. Sturgis [Tappan].*

After leaving Brook Farm, N spent 20 years in Providence, until the death of his mother in 1865; he then moved to Philadelphia, where he composed over 1,000 erotic poems contained in his journals. N spent the last two decades of his life in Europe, dying in Paris in 1894.

References: The most complete biography is Judith Kennedy Johnson’s introduction to her edition of *The Journals of CKN* (1946). The best sketch of N’s interactions with the Transcendentalists is *NET*Dial, 180–85; also useful is Cooke* (1902), 143–47. N’s later years are examined in Richard Lee Francis, “CKN: Transcendental Hamlet,” *ESQ* 49 (March 1976): 46–52. His place among Emerson’s discoveries is discussed in William M. Moss, “ ‘So Many Promising Youths’: Emerson’s Disappointing Discoveries of New England Poet-Seers,” *NEQ* 49 (March 1976): 46–64. A bibliography of N by Joel Myerson appears in Myerson (1984), 214–15.

Alan D. Brasher

NIETZSCHE, FRIEDRICH (1844–1900), was a German philologist and philosopher whose qualified admiration for R. W. Emerson* represents an important reaction to—and an appropriation of—American Transcendentalism. He first read Emerson while a young adult and would return to him at various times later in his career. N heavily annotated his copies of Emerson’s essays, transcribed selections into his own notebook, and chose a passage from “History”—an essay that had inspired his “On the Use and Disadvantage of History for Life” (1873)—as an epigraph for the first edition of *The Gay Science* (1882).

N especially admired Emerson’s determination to transcend the limitations of history, to “unsettle all things” and rediscover the primitive sources of religion, ethics, and language. Emerson’s refusal to worship traditional notions of “goodness” corresponds strongly with the “transvaluation of all values” that N attempted in *Beyond Good and Evil* (1886) and *Toward a Genealogy of Morals* (1887), and he reveled in Emerson’s boast that no facts were sacred and none profane. In a variety of ways, Emerson’s essays prefigure N’s effort to liberate the forces of Dionysus—change, energy, passion, the will—from the repressive forces of Apollo—stability, order, form, control. N’s recognition of these mutual goals lay behind his claim that he never felt so much at home in someone else’s book as when he read Emerson.

While N considered Emerson to be “the author who has been richest in ideas in this century,” he also believed that Emerson’s “glorious, great nature” needed the guidance of a ''*strict* discipline.'' He found Emerson to be too fond of life, too ready to soften his commitment to the liberated will of the strong man with appeals to the ''divine breath'' that ''blows eternally . . . in the direction of the Right and Necessary.'' N was content to place his faith in the self-protected Over-Man; Emerson's reliance on the guidance of the Over-Soul was an unfortunate capitulation to weakness. In disciplining Emerson, then, N sought to take Transcendentalism the final mile by stripping away the rhetoric of safety and reassurance and setting free the individual will. This, in turn, makes up part of the legacy that N passed on to the wide variety of later thinkers for whom he was such an important influence, from Jack London to Martin Heidegger.

References: Discussion of N and Emerson may be found in Walter Kaufmann's ''Introduction'' in N, *The Gay Science* (1974), 7–13; Hermann Hummel, ''N and Emerson,'' *NEQ* 19 (March 1946): 63–84; Stanley Cavell, ''Aversive Thinking,'' in *Conditions Handsome and Unhandsome* (1990); Stanley Hubbard, *N und Emerson* (1958); and Eduard Baumgarten, ''Mitteilungen und Bemerkungen über den Einfluss Emersons auf N,'' *Jahrbuch für Amerikastudien*, ed. Walter Fischer (1956), 1: 93–152.

Charles Mitchell

NORTON, ANDREWS (1786–1853), biblical scholar and professor at Harvard Divinity School,** influenced a generation of young men associated with Transcendentalism in New England. Called ''Pope Andrews'' by T. Parker* for his sometimes reactionary responses to the ''new views,'' N is best known for his part in the Transcendental Controversy of the late 1830s. In fact, his response was less a tirade against Transcendentalism than it was a principled opposition to the forces of social and educational disruption that the Transcendentalists seemed, for N, to represent.

A Unitarian** liberal early in his career, N was named Dexter Professor at Harvard in 1819. He retired from teaching in 1830 to work on his magnum opus, *Evidences of the Genuineness of the Gospels* (3 vols., 1837–44). N's concern for intellectual responsibility undergirded his role in the Transcendental Controversy. Incensed over what he considered inappropriate speculations by G. Ripley* and O. Brownson,* he complained in a letter to the *Boston Daily Advertiser* (5 November 1836) that Ripley's questioning of biblical miracles** should appear in a Christian publication. Two years later, following R. W. Emerson's* Divinity School Address, he turned once again to the *Advertiser* to castigate the ''new school in literature and religion'' for its ''extraordinary assumption, united with great ignorance, and incapacity for reasoning'' (27 August 1838). His *Discourse on the Latest Form of Infidelity* (1839), in many ways N's manifesto, maintained that ''the divine authority'' of Christ ''was attested, in the only mode in which it could be, by miraculous displays of his powers'' (5), a direct response to the Transcendentalists' questioning of the need for historical miracles to validate Christianity. For the next year, he and Ripley traded pamphlets arguing the more arcane points of German biblical (Higher) criticism.** N withdrew from the controversy in 1840, increasingly alone in his articulation of the conservative response to Transcendentalism. Too easily vilified as the archenemy of the Transcendental group, N found his thinking—as well as his reputation—eclipsed by the ''newness'' of Emerson and Ripley.

References: Aside from an appreciative memorial by William Newell, *ChEx*** 55 (November 1853): 425–52, only two substantive studies of N exist. Lilian Handlin surveys his early years in ''Babylon est delenda—the Young AN,'' in *American Unitarianism, 1805–1865*, ed. Conrad Edick Wright (1989), 53–85. Robert D. Habich analyzes the contexts and tenor of N's remarks on the Transcendentalists in ''Emerson's Reluctant Foe: AN and the Transcendental Controversy,'' *NEQ* 65 (June 1992): 208–37.

Robert D. Habich

NORTON, CHARLES ELIOT (1827–1908), art historian, reformer, and man of letters, was the son of R. W. Emerson's* opponent A. Norton.* N broke with his father's Unitarianism** and worked to disseminate Emerson's ideas, especially those of ''The American Scholar.'' After Emerson's death N collected and edited Emerson's correspondence with T. Carlyle* (1884); he was also an early reviewer of Whitman's* *Leaves of Grass*, finding in it ''an epic directness . . . which belongs to no other adept of the transcendental school.'' N upheld Emerson's faith in the imagination as the source of thought and spirituality, yet after the Civil War, he publicly argued that Emerson's optimism about human progress made him an unfit guide for the more disillusioned Gilded Age.

In N's writings and lectures on culture (his art-history courses at Harvard from 1874 to 1897 were the first in an American university), he located Emerson's ''sincerity'' and ''habitual loftiness of view'' not in the present but in the art, religion, and morality of the Middle Ages and the Florentine Renaissance. He was a disciple (and literary executor) of Ruskin* and a supporter of the Arts and Crafts movement. Yet his opposition to his materialistic era included the 1879–84 campaign to save Niagara Falls from development—the first practical consequence of the Transcendentalist reverence for nature.** Despite his reactionary posture and his pessimism about American democracy, N made himself the custodian of much of the Transcendentalists' spiritual as well as literary heritage.

References: Kermit Vanderbilt, *CEN: Apostle of Culture in a Democracy* (1959), is thorough if not deeply analytical and describes N's relations with Transcendentalism in detail. More provocative is T. J. Jackson Lears, *No Place of Grace: Antimodernism and the Transformation of American Culture, 1880–1920* (1981). Lears's neo-Marxist and psychological studies of conservative figures in 19th-century American culture relate N's public career to Emersonian ideals.

M. David Samson

O

OEGGER, GUILLAUME (circa 1790s–1850s), a Catholic priest from the Lorraine region in France near the border with Germany, became a follower of Swedenborg's** New Church around 1826 and wrote works that particularly inspired Transcendentalism's early belief in a "language of nature"** that corresponds** to spiritual things.

In 1829, O wrote *Le Vrai Messie*, or *The True Messiah*, which was translated into English by E. P. Peabody* in 1835 (not published until 1842). R. W. Emerson* encountered this work in Peabody's manuscript and copied large portions of it into his journals.** Near the end of his "Language" chapter in *Nature*, he summarizes the core of O's influence in New England: " 'Material objects,' said a French philosopher, 'are necessarily kinds of *scoriae* of the substantial thoughts of the Creator, which must always preserve an exact relation to their first origin; in other words, visible nature must have a spiritual and moral side.' " Although O himself believed in the possibility of linking the natural and spiritual worlds through direct illuminations, Emerson and other Transcendentalists stressed O's claim that spiritual meanings lie within the linguistic signs for natural things. For Emerson, such a doctrine of correspondences between natural objects and spirit shows that "the world shall be to us an open book, and every form significant of its hidden life and final cause."

O also offered the concept that human language, before the fall of Adam and Eve, was a natural language in which words initially corresponded to the object they designated. This language was lost and replaced by a corrupted language of convention, in which the word's root meaning has vanished beneath a babble of inaccurate usages. O allowed readers like Emerson to regard the reawakening of the world less as a new creation than as a return to the creation's origins. O provided a quasi-empirical description of language and objects that drew Transcendentalist idealism** surprisingly close to espousing the absolute dependence of individual consciousness on God.

References: A brief biography and excerpt of Peabody's translation of *The True Messiah* appears in Kenneth W. Cameron, *Young Emerson's Transcendentalist Vision* (1971), 295–302. O's other major works include *Manuel de religion et de morale* (Paris, 1829), *Essai d'un dictionnaire de la langue de la nature* (Paris, 1831), *Rapports inattendus établis entre le monde matériel et le monde spirituel* (Paris, 1834), and *Nouvelles questions philosophiques* (Paris, 1835). Karl-Erik Sjodén considers O in the context of French Swedenborgianism in *Swedenborg en France* (Stockholm, 1985), esp. 77–79 and 136–38. See Philip F. Gura, ''Elizabeth Palmer Peabody and the Philosophy of Language,'' *ESQ* 23 (3d Q 1977): 154–63. On Emerson's use of O, see Gura, *The Wisdom of Words* (1981), and John T. Irwin, *American Hieroglyphics* (1980).

Christopher Newfield

OKEN, LORENZ (1779–1855), one of R. W. Emerson's* ''poets in science,'' was a German biologist and philosopher who extended Schelling's* *Naturphilosophie* into natural science, particularly comparative anatomy and embryology. He also spread his left-liberal politics through his scientific journal *Isis* (1817–47) and in 1822 founded the Society of German Scientists and Physicians, the model for both the British and the American Associations for the Advancement of Science. Emerson alludes to O several times in the 1840s, including in ''The Poet,'' and in 1849, both Emerson and B. Alcott* read *Elements of Physiophilosophy* (1809; London, 1847), which orders all natural knowledge in 3,562 oracular paragraphs. O's philosophy also appears in J. B. Stallo's work, from which Emerson transcribed in his journal** some typical O utterances: '' 'Animals are but foetal forms of man.' '' '' 'The limbs are emancipated ribs.' ''

O's writings gave scientific corroboration to some favorite Transcendentalist ideas. For O, all creation began with the primal number zero, ''nothing,'' the infinite, God, out of which originated manyness, numbers, the finite—God realizing himself in matter. The material universe formed through a ''descending creation,'' as the elements of spirit divided, interacted, and subdivided. At the moment of earth's completion the dividing elements began to reunite and differentiate into living bodies, developing in an ''ascending creation'' through successive additions, from mucus or ''infusoria,'' to the lower organisms, to the higher, to man himself—''the summit, the crown of nature's** development'' (*Elements*, 2), by whom God beholds himself.

O's two key ideas both appealed to Emerson. First, since every developing organism parallels and contains the adult stages of all preceding organisms, man comprehends all organisms within himself—he is ''the whole world in miniature'' (*Elements*, 12), a microcosm.** Conversely, all animals are but ''foetal'' or ''irregular'' men; as Emerson wrote in ''Nature,'' ''The animal is the novice and probationer of a more advanced order.'' Second, since development proceeds by repetition of parts, the basic animal body is but a series of vertebrae, elaborated into various appendages—most famously, the skull consists of four vertebrae fused into a composite bone, making the head, as Emerson put it, ''only a new man on the shoulders of the old'' and showing the wonders of the ''iterations or rhymes of nature'' (*Elements*, 408; *JMN*, 11:153–54; see also ''Swedenborg,''** in *Representative Men*). After reading O, Alcott, in one of his ''illuminations,'' saw the universe as ''one vast spinal column.'' Though his direct influence is limited, O provided the Transcendentalists with confirmation and illustration of nature's progressive and self-similar unity.

References: Alfred Tulk's translation of O's *Elements of Physiophilosophy* (1847) remains standard; see also J. B. Stallo's chapter on O in *General Principles of the Philosophy of Nature* (1848). For O and the Transcendentalists, see René Wellek, *Confrontations* (1965), 160–67, 201–12. A useful discussion of O's science appears in Stephen Jay Gould, *Ontogeny and Phylogeny* (1977), 39–45.

Laura Dassow Walls

OSGOOD, SAMUEL (1812–1880), was a Unitarian** minister who edited *The Western Messenger*** and belonged to the Transcendental Club** and Town and Country Club.** O's religious and philosophical thought are well documented in *WM* as he single-handedly brought out four numbers of it and collaborated on one more while living in Louisville, Kentucky (1836–37). He wrote at least 65 articles and is assumed the author of 12 more; he also contributed seven translations. Most of his work appeared in the second and third volumes, but several articles appeared subsequently.

O called his ideological approach, which combined several philosophies, ''eclecticism.'' However, his work ultimately defends standard Unitarian thought. Though he was against the Calvinists and Trinitarians, he was offended by radical Transcendentalists such as T. Parker* (whom O accuses of ''[spiritualizing] the Gospel faith so as to attach comparatively little significance to the Gospel facts'' [''Parker's Discourse,'' *Monthly Miscellany* 7 (August 1842): 149]).

Noteworthy is O's review of *Nature*, the first discussion of R. W. Emerson* printed in *WM* (3 [January 1837]: 385–93). The review has been frequently excerpted but is best read in its entirety. O calls *Nature* ''remarkable'' and praises Emerson for being ''not such a dreamer on the beauties of the universe, as to forget its material uses.'' O praises most sections of the essay, except for ''Idealism,''** which he claims will tempt many ''to shut the book in disgust.'' However, O misunderstands Emerson as thinking that the material world is only ideal. O concludes by praising Emerson as a visionary in contrast to sensualists and materialistic men of ambition.

O was not so pleased with the Divinity School Address, maintaining that Emerson ''ought not to be suffered to preach in any Christian Church.'' His reaction to Transcendentalism was quite mixed, as shown by his reference in a letter to J. F. Clarke* to ''one sided transcendentalists like R. W. E.'' who were unable to ''get out of the *me*.'' O praises G. Ripley's* *Of Discourses on the Philosophy of Religion* yet voices a similar objection to Ripley as against Emerson and Parker. Acknowledging that Ripley's work may have been too short to explain his ideas fully, O notes, ''Only thc spiritual side [of Christianity] is shown [in the book]; the connection between the spiritual and material is not shown'' (*WM* 3:577).

To his credit, O always tries to show the positive points of authors he reviews. Even in ''Parker's Discourse,'' his severe review of Parker's *A Discourse of Matters Pertaining to Religion*, he writes, ''Pained as we are by the dogmatical tone and captious spirit that so often appear, we are thoroughly convinced that no such motive as the love of notoriety, but a determination to express his own honest opinions, mainly dictated the work'' (146).

O served as pastor of the Church of the Messiah in New York City from 1849 to 1869, when he resigned to travel for a year in Europe. When he returned, he became a minister in the Protestant Episcopal Church. O's many books include a translation of De Wette's* *Human Life; or, Practical Ethics* for Ripley's *Specimens of Foreign Standard Literature*** series. He edited the *Christian Inquirer* from 1850 to 1854.

References: See Hutchison (1959); Judith Kent Green, ''A Tentative Transcendentalist in the Ohio Valley: SO and the *WM*,'' *SAR* 1984: 79–92; Charles E. Blackburn, ''Some New Light on the *WM*,'' *AL* 26 (November 1954): 320–36; Robert D. Habich, *Transcendentalism and the* WM (1985); and Habich, ''An Annotated List of Contributions to the *WM*,'' *SAR* 1984: 93–179. Insight into O's thoughts on Transcendentalism and other concerns can be found in his ''Shelley and Pollok'' (*WM* 3 [February 1837]: 474–78), which Habich and Green attribute to O despite the signature initials ''D. L.'' Also of note are O's ''The Real and Ideal in New England,'' *NAR*** 84 (April 1857): 535–59; ''Transcendentalism in New England,'' *IntR* 3 (November 1876): 742–63; and autobiographical *Mile Stones in Our Life-Journey* (1860).

April Selley

OWEN, ROBERT (1771–1858), was a philanthropist who envisioned a perfect society in an industrial world and devoted much of his time, energy, and resources to establishing utopian communities to implement his ideas. A precocious child of an English postal worker, O was said to have ''consumed a book a day'' as a young student. At age 14 he moved to Manchester, where he later entered the textile manufacturing business. He gained the reputation of ''a compassionate taskmaster'' in addition to being a shrewd businessman.

O met and married Caroline Dale, the daughter of the proprietor of a large cotton mill in New Lanark, Scotland. At age 26, he and his partners purchased Dale's mill and set about to build a community to improve the living conditions of his employees. He constructed houses with sanitary facilities for 2,000 families, recreational facilities, and a company store that assured reasonable prices and quality goods. He forbade gin palaces, illicit sex, and child labor. He encouraged parents to send their children between the ages of five and ten to his free school; there was to be no corporal punishment and no lessons to last more than 45 minutes. O dissolved partnership with the owners of the New Lanark mills when they disagreed with his costly benevolent philosophy. He formed a stock company, sold shares, and bought the firm outright. The profits O reaped from his manufacturing business enabled him to experiment in fulfilling his utopian vision of a perfect society.

Heredity played no role whatever in the makeup of the human character, according to O. In his *New Views of Society or Essays on the Formation of Character* (1813), he attempted to shift moral responsibility from the individual to society. He believed that social institutions left a large class of people to be educated in vice rather than virtue; if a person were to be good, the environment must be altered.

In his *New Views of Society* and *Book of the New Moral World* (1845), O developed his socialist views of absolute equity. Since Europe was steeped in hundreds of years of tradition, O thought the American frontier the ideal place for his social experiment. In 1824, he purchased the Rappite Community on the Wabash River in southern Indiana and established New Harmony. Nearly 900 people from all over Europe and America accepted his invitation to inhabit the village, including Thomas Say, Charles Lesueur, Marie Fretageot, William McClure, J. Warren,* and Frances Wright. O delivered his ''Declaration of Mental Independence'' at New Harmony on 4 July 1826, the fiftieth anniversary of the American nation. He claimed that the order of present society had been built on exploitation of the poor by the ''monstrous evils'' of private property, irrational religion, and priestly marriages based on property.

O regarded New Harmony not as perfect but as a ''half-way house'' on the road to a just and equitable society. He believed that through education and experimentation the environment would be conducive to social improvement. But his hopes were soon dashed by what his son called ''a collection of radicals, enthusiastic devotees to principles, honest latitudinarians and lazy theorists with a sprinkling of unprincipled sharpers thrown in'' (Robert Dale Owen, *Threading My Way* [1874]). O's New Harmony experiment lasted a little more than three years. The Owenite movement, however, continued in the formation of other communities in Indiana, Ohio, New York, and Europe, with no more success than the parent community. The Yellow Springs Community in Green County, Ohio, involved about 100 families who purchased 720 acres on which Antioch College was later located. The community there was abandoned the same year it began, in 1825.

Undaunted, O returned to England, where in 1844 he constructed Harmony Hall in Hampshire and continued his philanthropic work. In his later years, he became a firm believer in Spiritualism** and claimed to catch a glimpse of immortality. He reported that he communicated with the deceased Duke of Kent, Thomas Jefferson, Benjamin Franklin, and Shelley. Still he firmly denied a belief in God to the very end. Although O's experiments in utopian communalism were short-lived, he cannot be regarded as a failure, since he was a harbinger of what governments and industries must do in an industrial age to alleviate the inequities of an unchecked materialistic society. O's influence on Transcendentalist utopias, however, was slight compared to that of Fourier* on Brook Farm** or J. H. Noyes on Fruitlands.** B. Alcott* followed education reform** at New Harmony with great interest. But the Owenite movement had generally failed by the time the Transcendentalists were at their height.

References: O's autobiography, *The Life of RO* (1857), includes selections of his writing and correspondence. An account of his utopian vision is found in *A New Society and Other Writings by RO* (1927). George D. H. Cole, *The Forerunners, 1789–1850*, vol. 1 of *A History of Socialist Thought* (1962), is an outstanding summary of Owenite philosophy. Arthur Bestor, *Backwoods Utopias . . . 1663–1829* (1950), has long been standard. A concise, informative biography is Margaret Cole, *RO of New Lanark* (1953). Arthur John Booth, *RO, The Founder of Socialism in England* (1869), is older and quite biased but still useful.

Raymond L. Muncy

P

PALFREY, JOHN GORHAM (1796–1881), was a Unitarian** clergyman, editor, politician, and historian whose best-known connection with the Transcendentalist movement was as the man who (as professor of Sacred Literature and dean of the theological faculty from 1831 to 1839) ''allowed'' R. W. Emerson* to deliver his famed Divinity School Address in 1838. While it was actually the graduates themselves who chose Emerson as their speaker, P was held responsible by some even though he himself felt that ''what was not folly in the address was impiety.''

Andrew Preston Peabody recalls P as a professor who ''invited discussion, welcomed the expression of non-agreement, and even asked his students to prepare in writing, and read to the class their reasons for differing with him.'' Yet, as editor of *The Christian Examiner*** (1824–26) and the *North American Review*** (1835–42), P adhered strictly to the view (in contrast with the philosophy of his fellow Unitarian editor, J. Walker*) that the contents of a magazine must reflect the editor's views. Thus, P was averse to publishing the writings of more radical Unitarians like Emerson, G. Ripley,* and F. H. Hedge,* and his exclusion of them from the pages of the *NAR* contributed to the feeling among Transcendentalists that a journal of their own was needed. P's staunch abolitionist** position in the late 1840s and 1850s brought about a rapprochement with Transcendentalists such as Emerson, whose own increasing concern over the issue led him to support P in the latter's successful bid for a congressional seat in 1847. The final decades of P's life were spent in writing his massive, five-volume *History of New England*.

REFERENCES: Peabody's account of P in *Harvard Reminiscences* (1888), 107–15, is the most personal sketch of P's life. Frank Gatell's *JGP and the New England Conscience* (1963) is the definitive study of P's life and writings. References to P's ideas on moral philosophy** can be found in Howe (1970), and discussions of his impact on Unitarian history can be found in G. W. Cooke,* *Unitarianism in America* (1902); and in Robinson (1985). On P's career as editor of *ChEx*, see Alfred G. Litton, " 'Speaking the Truth in Love': A History of the *Christian Examiner* and Its Relation to New England Transcendentalism" (Diss., Univ. of South Carolina, 1993).

Alfred G. Litton

PALMER, EDWARD (?–?), an obscure figure, is remembered largely for his occasional visits with R. W. Emerson* and for his crusade to abolish money. A native of Belfast, Maine, P was not tied directly to the Transcendental movement, but his preachments against currency demonstrate the wide range of antebellum reform.

In 1840 P published *A Letter to Those Who Think*, an 18-page pamphlet that set forth his basic philosophy. He stressed that the "benevolent and fraternal" should form the basis for business, believing that requiring payment in exchange for goods and services was a "faith-destroying and soul-perverting practice."

In his daily existence, P ran little risk of destroying his faith or perverting his soul. He traveled about New England and exchanged his message on the evils of money for his sustenance. Apparently he managed not only to eke out his livelihood but to gain limited fame. Emerson was sufficiently impressed with P's notions that he considered him a reformer of the same magnitude as S. Graham* and W. L. Garrison.*

P was never attached formally to any of the established Transcendental circles or communities. His ideas, though, reflect well the philosophies of such utopian enterprises as Brook Farm,** Fruitlands,** and New Harmony, all of which sought to establish noncompetitive environments based on universal love and goodness. The primary difference between those visionaries who organized experimental communities and P is that the latter fulfilled his dream.

References: If studies of Transcendentalism mention P, they do so only in passing. Anne C. Rose in *Transcendentalism as a Social Movement, 1830–1850* (1981) offers the most detailed account of him, quoting from his pamphlet and connecting him to such others as J. Warren* who sought to reform the money system. Although he does not mention P, Joseph Dorfman, *The Economic Mind in American Civilization, 1606–1865* (1946), gives insights into the economic climate of P's day. *A Letter to Those Who Think* appears in Goldsmiths'-Kress *Library of Economic Literature* and in the Research Publication microfilm series (1980).

E. Kate Stewart

PALMER, JOSEPH (1791–1875), exemplified in various ways the stereotypical Transcendentalist. This true eccentric did not allow society's conventions to dictate his daily existence. He caught quickly the vision of both B. Alcott* and C. Lane* for the edenic Fruitlands** and stayed with the experiment from its birth to its demise. P's professional life revealed nothing of the man's free-spirit tendencies. A No Town farmer, he later opened a butchery in nearby Fitchburg. But P's insistence upon wearing a beard quickly set him apart from the clean-shaven citizenry of the central Massachusetts community. Despite being called "Old Jew Palmer," being refused the sacraments of the church on one occasion, and being constantly rebuked openly, P kept his whiskers.

Public opinion against his facial hair was such that at one point four men accosted him, wrestled him to the ground, and attempted to give P a shave. Resisting this barbershop quartet, P fought back. Authorities promptly arrested him and charged him with "unprovoked assault." The bearded rebel was jailed for over a year and remained in jail after his sentence was served because he felt cheated at having to pay for his board. He left only after being forcibly removed to the street in a chair. Shortly thereafter he joined Fruitlands. P's son, a Fitchburg dentist, remarked: "Father was a reformer; was early in the field as an anti-slavery man and as a total abstinence advocate." These qualities suggest a person well suited for the plain living and high thinking at Fruitlands.

When Fruitlands failed, P bought the property and there cultivated another unique community. As a trustee of that property, R. W. Emerson* visited P from time to time and, as Sears reports, found "a motley collection of reformers and a host of tramps." Emerson remarked in his journal** for 1848 that "the old beggar [P] went barefoot, & busied himself very much with his toes, as they sat together in the house." Buried in the Old North Leominster cemetery, P rests under a headstone that notes that he was "Persecuted for Wearing the Beard."

References: Clara Endicott Sears gives the most thorough account of P's life in *Bronson Alcott's Fruitlands* (1915). This most unusual of Transcendentalists is mentioned in Donald N. Koster, *Transcendentalism in America* (1975), and Anne C. Rose, *Transcendentalism as a Social Movement, 1830–1850* (1981). P appears as Moses White in L. M. Alcott's* "Transcendental Wild Oats."

E. Kate Stewart

PARKER, THEODORE (1810–1860), became the leading Transcendentalist minister within Unitarianism** after R. W. Emerson* and G. Ripley* abandoned their pulpits. His powerful and controversial South Boston Sermon (1841) rivaled Emerson's Divinity School Address as a manifesto of Transcendentalism. Although P's rationalistic instincts made him distrust the mystical tendencies of Emerson and the Concord** circle, he was a key member of the Transcendental Club,** a regular contributor to *The Dial*,** and a lifelong friend of many Transcendentalists. For nearly 20 years until his death, he remained the nominal leader of the Unitarian reform wing, promoting his own brand of Transcendental Christianity as well as antislavery and other social reforms.

In the early 1830s, when a young teacher in Watertown, P was introduced to liberal religious perspectives by C. Francis,* the local Unitarian minister. While a student at the Harvard Divinity School** in the mid-1830s, P rapidly moved beyond the "supernatural rationalism" of Unitarianism toward his eclectic blend of Christianity, Transcendentalism, and rationalism. After being ordained at West Roxbury, he continued his scholarly researches through wide reading, especially of the liberal and radical biblical critics of Germany. Around the time he graduated from the Divinity School in 1836, P began attending meetings of the newly formed Transcendental Club. As a young minister in West Roxbury, P echoed Transcendentalist ideas in his sermons and in numerous anonymous contributions to periodicals. In 1840, he entered the heated debate between his friend Ripley and the conservative Unitarian leader A. Norton* over the meaning of the biblical miracles** with a lengthy public letter written under the pseudonym "Levi Blodgett" (1840).

P soon openly proclaimed his Transcendentalism in an 1841 ordination sermon, "The Transient and Permanent in Christianity." Known also as the South Boston Sermon for the place of its delivery, this address established P as a leading Transcendentalist radical. P argued that true Christianity had nothing to do with the primitive superstitions and transient false doctrines that had grown up over the ages around the Bible and Jesus but instead meant worshipping "as Jesus did, with no mediator." To P, Jesus was simply a man who had extraordinary but wholly natural religious insights. The essence of Christianity, P argued, was entirely contained in the intuitive spirituality and pure morality that Jesus had modeled.

Many of P's ideas in the South Boston Sermon were familiar Unitarian sentiments. W. E. Channing* and others had already humanized Jesus, deified human consciousness, and proclaimed the Bible to be an imperfect revelation of truth. But like Emerson, though from a rationalistic perspective, P pushed Unitarian ideas to their extremes and expressed them in extreme language. For Unitarians who still held what P referred to scathingly as "an idolatrous regard" for the text of Scripture and the figure of Jesus, P's iconoclastic handling of biblical stories and the figure of Jesus was shocking. Moreover, P seemed to be accusing many Unitarian ministers of teaching a supernatural Christianity in which they no longer believed as well as insisting on conformity to a creed that they professed not to have. A storm of criticism soon arose. The Unitarian *Christian Register, Christian Examiner,*** and *Monthly Miscellany* all issued strong statements in condemnation. Friends began to shy away, and P's pulpit exchanges, a sign of ministerial fellowship, became more and more infrequent. The main Unitarian ministerial organization of Boston debated expelling him but were prevented from doing so by members who insisted on P's right to express himself freely.

The next year, when invited by a group of laymen to lecture on religion in Boston, P seized the opportunity to explain his position more fully. The lectures, published in 1842 in an augmented and annotated form as *A Discourse of Matters Pertaining to Religion*, set out to demonstrate empirically that what P called "Absolute Religion" (later "Theism") was the true religion toward which the religious consciousness of humanity had been groping throughout human history. In these lectures, P argued that all religions originated from an intuitive "sense of dependence" on God (a phrase P borrowed from the liberal German theologian F. Schleiermacher*). However, the limited understanding of each age resulted in misinterpretations and perversions of that original intuition of the divine. By finally escaping all temporary and local interpretations, ''Absolute Religion'' represented pure eternal truth—which to P was simply the recognition of a morally perfect deity and of the highest moral standards of human behavior.

Although P often claimed that further progress in religious consciousness was inevitable, he never admitted that his ''Theism'' might also be a limited, imperfect conception that was historically conditioned. Unlike Emerson, P inconsistently continued to believe in traditional Christian ideas such as a personal deity and an afterlife, two ideas that P claimed were also intuitively verifiable.

A new phase of P's career marked by increasing involvement in reform movements, particularly antislavery, began after a trip to Europe in 1843–44. Friends soon created the Twenty-Eighth Congregational Society of Boston expressly for him, providing a forum that made his battle with conservative Unitarians increasingly irrelevant. For the next 15 years, at Sunday services in the rented Melodeon theater and later the Boston Music Hall, P held forth to thousands. Published sermons, essays, and books, as well as regular lecture tours, made P's controversial views of religion known to tens of thousands more.

From the mid-1840s on, P increasingly became a leading critic of urban industrial society, producing sermons, lectures, and essays on woman's rights,** labor reform, the poor, and many other topics. At the center of his social philosophy was a loosely Jeffersonian conception of an ''industrial democracy'' organized to develop the potential of each individual. Power was to be distributed throughout an educated populace rather than concentrated in the hands of a capitalist aristocracy.

By the late 1840s, P's circle of friends included many of the major social activists of the day. He founded *The Massachusetts Quarterly Review*** (1847–50) to be a clearinghouse for social reform thought. Following the adoption of the new Fugitive Slave Law in 1850, P's time was increasingly absorbed by the antislavery crusade. As chairman of the executive committee of the Boston Vigilance Committee in the 1850s, P led the defense of Boston's fugitive slaves.

In perennially fragile health, P died of tuberculosis in 1860 in Florence without producing the great scholarly work on the history of religion that he had once dreamed of writing. His radical-seeming ''Theism'' turned out to be little more than a guidepost soon passed by the younger Transcendentalist ministers. Nevertheless, his thoroughgoing application of Higher Criticism** to the Bible helped release Unitarianism from traditional theology and clear the way for more radical developments. For the rising generation of ministers that included T. W. Higginson,* S. Johnson,* S. Longfellow,* and D. A. Wasson,* and for many persons dissatisfied with the traditional church or the materialism and inequalities of 19th-century American society, P stood as a model of religious progressivism and social activism.

References: The two main collections of P's writings are Frances Power Cobbe, ed., *The Collected Works of TP*, 14 vols. (1863–71), and T. W. Higginson et al., eds., *Centenary Edition*, 15 vols. (1907–12). The most indispensable biography is still the first, J. Weiss,* *The Life and Correspondence of TP*, 2 vols. (1864), which includes extensive selections of letters and journal passages. Weiss needs to be supplemented by three other biographies based on original research: O. B. Frothingham,* *TP: A Biography* (1874); John White Chadwick, *TP: Preacher and Reformer* (1901); and Henry Steele Commager, *TP* (1936). The best brief modern account of P's place in the Transcendentalist-Unitarian controversy is Hutchison (1959), 98–136, 178–87. See also Conrad Wright, ed., *Three Prophets of Religious Liberalism: Channing, Emerson, P* (1961), 32–46; and Perry Miller's challenging interpretation, "TP: Apostasy within Liberalism," *HTR* 54 (October 1961): 275–95, rpt. in his *Nature's Nation* (1967), 134–49. For P's Transcendentalism, see H. Shelton Smith, "Was TP a Transcendentalist?" *NEQ* 23 (September 1950): 351–64; and Alexander Kern, "The Rise of Transcendentalism, 1815–1860," in *Transitions in American Literary History*, ed. Harry Hayden Clark (1954), 245–314. P's response to Higher Criticism is discussed in Jerry Wayne Brown, *The Rise of Biblical Criticism in America, 1800–1870: The New England Scholars* (1969), 140–70; Richardson (1978), 34–48; and Richard Grusin, "Interpretation and Intuition in TP," *BuR* 28.1 (1983): 21–41. On P's connection to *The Dial*, see *NET*Dial, 185–92. Robert C. Albrecht, *TP* (1971), gives much needed attention to P's later career and writings. Joel Myerson's *TP: A Descriptive Bibliography* (1981) lists all separate publications of P's work. For a bibliography of studies of P, see Gary L. Collison, "TP," in Myerson (1984), 216–32.

Gary L. Collison

PEABODY, ELIZABETH PALMER (1804–1894), educator, reformer, publisher, was involved in many of the most characteristic activities of New England Transcendentalism, including Temple School** and *The Dial*,** and continued to work in postwar reforms that had their roots in "The Newness" of the 1830s to 1850s.

P was born in 1804 in Billerica, Massachusetts, daughter of Elizabeth Palmer, an educator and author, and Dr. Nathaniel Peabody, a physician and dentist. Rigorously taught by both parents, P opened her first private school in 1820 in Lancaster, Massachusetts. In the 1820s and early 1830s she conducted private schools in Maine and eastern Massachusetts. A sustained encounter with W. E. Channing* helped P modify the doctrinaire Unitarianism** she had learned from her mother and opened her to the affective side of religion. In the early 1830s P conducted seminars for adult women on historical subjects, for which she wrote textbooks and study guides. In 1834 B. Alcott* was encouraged to open a private school in Boston, and P, drawn to his philosophy of education, helped him recruit and organize Temple School. Acting as part-time teacher and assistant, P also observed and recorded the classroom activities in *Record of a School* (1835). At first in sympathy with Alcott's belief that education** involved drawing out what already existed in each child, P grew increasingly dissatisfied with Alcott's insistence on introspection and alarmed by the frank discussion of physiology in his *Conversations with Children on the Gospels*. She left Temple in August 1836 and returned to Salem, where she met J. Very* and N. Hawthorne,* encouraging the latter to publish his short stories and introducing him to her sister Sophia,* whom he married in 1842.

In 1840 P opened a bookshop and lending library on West Street in Boston, which soon became the hub of Transcendentalist and reform activity. M. Fuller* conducted several of her Conversations** in the bookshop's parlor, and G. and Sophia Ripley* planned the Brook Farm** experiment there. By now fully engaged in the Transcendentalist movement, friend to R. W. Emerson* and Fuller, member of the Transcendental Club,** P became publisher of *The Dial* from 1841 to 1843. At decade's end, P attempted to found her own journal. *Aesthetic Papers*** only appeared for one number, in May 1849.

With her sisters now married (Mary married H. Mann* in 1843) and two of her three brothers dead, P took her father to Theodore Weld's community at Eagleswood, near Perth Amboy, New Jersey, where she taught in the school from 1854 to 1860. At the end of the decade, P began to hear of the German innovation of kindergartening. In 1860 she opened the first English-speaking kindergarten in America, on Pinckney Street, in Boston.

In 1867–68 P traveled to Europe, meeting the disciples of German educator and theorist Friedrich Froebel, whose concept of the kindergarten as guided play seemed to her a systematic application of the Transcendentalist ideas of education that she and others had practiced three decades earlier. Upon her return, P proselytized for Froebel's kindergarten, editing and writing many of the articles for *The Kindergarten Messenger* and campaigning for the adoption of the Froebellian kindergarten by public school systems.

P participated in the last act of New England Transcendentalism, Alcott's Concord School of Philosophy,** speaking at the 1882 session on ''Childhood'' and at the 1883 session on ''Paradise Lost.'' In the last decade of her life, she kept up a steady, if somewhat less vigorous, pace of reformist activities, including continued advocacy of the kindergarten and of the ill-treated Piute Native Americans. P also turned to reminiscence, publishing her long-awaited memoir of Channing in 1880 and writing several long letters on her first encounters with Very and Hawthorne. In these last years, she became a legendary figure, called by some ''the Grandmother of Boston,'' ridiculed by others as a relic of the naive days of ''high thinking and plain living'' that had marked the antebellum reform era. Although he denied it, H. James's* good-hearted but ineffectual and irrelevant Miss Birdseye in *The Bostonians* appears modeled after Peabody. She is buried in Concord's** Sleepy Hollow Cemetery.**

P appears in virtually every study of Transcendentalism, yet she is overshadowed by such figures as Channing, Alcott, Emerson, and Fuller. Acting as the ''Boswell'' of the movement, as T. Parker* said, P has been treated as one of the supporting cast. However, she deserves her own assessment and analysis. She was a person of enormous intellectual gifts, notably in the areas of language, history, philosophy, and theology. Emerson testified to her accomplishments: ''a wonderful literary head, with extraordinary rapidity of association, and a methodising faculty which enabled her to weave surprising theories very fast, & very finely, from slight materials. Of another sex, she would have been a first-rate academician; and, as it was, she had the ease & scope & authority of a learned professor or high literary celebrity in her talk.''

From the mid-1830s through the 1840s P was near the center of Transcendentalism as a social movement and, to some extent, shared the intellectual views of her contemporaries. But she insisted on the value of a historical consciousness and stressed the self's social identity. To Fuller, P conformed too much to a kind of Unitarian gentility: ''[T]here is so much in you that is hostile to my wishes, as to character, and especially as to the character of a woman.'' On the other hand, P's concern for propriety should be balanced against her support for ''indecorous'' efforts like Temple School or Brook Farm.

P's self-giving devotion to perhaps too many good causes led to a scattered quality in her life, but she was a deeply generous person, nonetheless, often to her own detriment. Her self-forgetfulness coexisted with a shrewd sense of the exigencies of a market economy, particularly for a single woman, whose survival involved marketing and selling her essays, books, ideas, and her skills as a teacher.

References: The most reliable bibliography of P's extensive publications in journal and book form is in Ruth M. Baylor, *EPP, Kindergarten Pioneer* (1965). None of P's publications is currently in print. A selection of her correspondence with introduction and notes is *The Letters of EPP, American Renaissance Woman*, ed. Bruce Ronda (1984). References to the principal secondary works on P may be found in Margaret Neussendorfer, ''EPP,'' in Myerson (1984), 233–41. Earlier biographical studies of P include Gladys Brooks, *Three Wise Virgins* (1957), and Louise Hall Tharp, *The P Sisters of Salem* (1950).

Bruce A. Ronda

PHILLIPS, WENDELL (1811–1884), was one of the leading lights of the abolition** movement and universally recognized as its greatest orator. Unlike many of his abolitionist cohorts, P was a member of a socially prominent family and was educated, like R. W. Emerson,* at Boston Latin Grammar School and Harvard. After his conversion to abolitionism in 1835, he worked closely with W. L. Garrison.* Like Garrison, P had the ability both to impress and to irritate those major Transcendentalists with whom he came into contact. Emerson's initial opinion of him tended to distinguish between the nobility of the cause that he so ably represented and the personality behind the public figure. Thus, in a retrospective journal** entry in the early 1850s, Emerson states, ''[T]he first discovery I made of P was, that while I admired his eloquence, I had not the faintest wish to meet the man.'' Despite such reservations, however, Emerson found himself irresistibly drawn to P and the cause of abolition. On more than one occasion in the early 1840s, Emerson and H. Thoreau* weathered the ire of their conservative neighbors by arguing adamantly and successfully for P's right to speak on antislavery at the Concord** Lyceum.** Following one such presentation, Thoreau sent off his only known ''letter to the editor'' celebrating the event (*Liberator*, 28 March 1845; *RP*, 58–62). In Thoreau's view, P deserved high praise personally because he possessed that ''freedom and steady wisdom, so rare in the reformer, with which he declared that he was not born to abolish slavery, but to do right.'' After this initial contact Emerson was drawn closer to P, as he was to Garrison and other active abolitionists, as the slavery issue became more hotly debated throughout the 1840s and 1850s. The two frequently visited Concord to speak on slavery, and they found ready listeners in Emerson, Thoreau, and many others. After hearing P speak on one of these occasions, Emerson was led to comment to a friend that he ''had not learned a better lesson in many weeks than last night in a couple of hours'' and that P was ''the best generator of eloquence I have met for many a day.''

Despite his early reservations, Emerson came to develop a working alliance with P, whom his wife Lidian* once described as ''the great man of this earth,'' and Emerson's daughter Ellen* points out that over the years, ''Mr P often came to our house.'' In his later career, following the Civil War, P continued his reforming efforts, focusing primarily on the woman's rights** cause and the labor movement.

References: For P's relationship with Emerson, see Gougeon (1990); and Irving H. Bartlett, ''The Philosopher and the Activist,'' *NEQ* 62 (June 1989): 280–96. Recent biographies are Bartlett, *WP, Brahmin Radical* (1961), and *W and Ann P: The Community of Reform, 1840–1880* (1979); and James Brewer Stewart, *WP: Liberty's Hero* (1986). For responses of the Emerson women, see *The Selected Letters of Lidian Jackson Emerson* (1987), 258, and *The Life of Lidian Jackson Emerson* (1980), 130, both ed. Delores Bird Carpenter.

Len Gougeon

PILLSBURY, PARKER (1809–1898), was an abolitionist** and radical reformer widely known among the Transcendentalists. Raised on a farm in Henniker, New Hampshire, P became a farmer and a blacksmith, but his deep interest in religion led him to be ''marked out'' for the ministry by the elders of the local Congregationalist Church. Following two years of seminary study, in 1839 he was licensed to preach by the Suffolk North Association of Congregational Ministers. After a brief stint as an antislavery agent in Worcester County, P became the minister of the church in Loudon, New Hampshire, ''a little den of proslavery as filthy as can be found this side of the Caverns of the pit,'' as he put it in a letter to a friend in the abolitionist movement. In response to his vigorous attacks on church officials who compromised on the issue of slavery, his license to preach was revoked nine months later. In reply, P—one of the earliest ''come-outers''**—excommunicated the Suffolk Association and, later, his church in Henniker.

Having withdrawn from the church, P devoted the remainder of his long life to abolitionism and other crusades for reform. As an agent of the New Hampshire Anti-Slavery Society, he became a close associate of Stephen S. Foster, best known for interrupting church services by standing to testify against slavery, and N. P. Rogers,* the aggressively anticlerical editor of the *Herald of Freedom*. P's communications from the field frequently appeared in the *Herald*, which he edited after Rogers resigned in 1845. During the 1840s P was also a contributor to *The Liberty Bell*, an antislavery annual; and he published his most famous polemical pamphlet, *The Church as It Is; or, The Forlorn Hope of Slavery* (1847). But P gained his reputation as a fiery antislavery lecturer: ''A terrible denouncer, he, / Old Sinai burns unquenchably / Upon his lips,'' as J. R. Lowell* described him in his ''Letter from Boston'' (1846). Unlike Garrison* and some of the other fierce denouncers of slavery, however, P continued his work on behalf of oppressed groups even after slavery was abolished, pleading the cause of freed blacks in the South, laborers in the North, and women. He was one of the few prominent abolitionists to oppose the Fifteenth Amendment because it did not extend the franchise to women, and during the years 1868 to 1870 he and Elizabeth Cady Stanton edited *The Revolution*, a feminist newspaper published by Susan B. Anthony. Nonetheless, the central chapter in P's life had been the antislavery crusade, a drama he powerfully depicted in a book written in his old age, *Acts of the Anti-Slavery Apostles*, an account of those who, like the apostles of old, ''literally 'went everywhere preaching the word.' ''

P's own ''preaching'' brought him into contact with a number of Transcendentalists, especially with those in Concord.** Following a lecture P delivered there in 1846, shortly after the outbreak of the Mexican War, R. W. Emerson* described him as ''that very gift from New Hampshire which we have long expected, a tough oak stick of a man not to be silenced or insulted or intimidated by a mob, because he is more mob than they; he mobs the mob.'' During his frequent visits to Concord, P stayed with the Thoreaus, and he became a close friend of the family. Despite H. Thoreau's* usual antipathy to activist reformers, he evidently respected P. In fact, in political addresses like ''Resistance to Civil Government,'' ''Slavery In Massachusetts,'' and ''A Plea for Captain John Brown,*'' Thoreau assumed militant positions not far removed from P's. More usually, however, Thoreau sought to remain aloof from the social and political issues that so engaged P. Replying to a letter in which P apparently alluded to the election of Lincoln and the possibility of an attack on Fort Sumter, Thoreau affirmed: ''I do not so much regret the present condition of things in this country (provided I regret it at all) as I do that I ever heard of it.'' Shortly before Thoreau's death a year later, a question P asked him elicited an equally memorable response. ''You seem so near the brink of the dark river, that I almost wonder how the opposite shore may appear to you,'' P asked. ''One world at a time,'' Thoreau answered. Despite P's piety, however, he was anything but an otherworldly Christian; on the contrary, few men or women of his time worked so tirelessly for the reform of this world.

References: P's account of his final meeting with Thoreau is quoted in F. B. Sanborn,* *The Personality of Thoreau* (1901), 68–69. P is also mentioned in passing in letters, journals,** and biographies of his better-known friends and associates, as well as in studies of abolitionism and feminism, notably Ellen Carol DuBois, *Feminism and Suffrage: The Emergence of an Independent Women's Movement in America, 1848–1869* (1978). But the only substantial work devoted exclusively to P is Louis Filler, ''PP: An Anti-Slavery Apostle,'' *NEQ* 19 (1946): 315–37. Fortunately, that article offers an excellent portrait based on unpublished letters, antislavery periodicals like the *Herald of Freedom*, and P's writings, especially *Acts of the Anti-Slavery Apostles* (1883).

Linck C. Johnson

POE, EDGAR ALLAN (1809–1849), as a contributor to 19th-century periodicals, was a critic of New England Transcendentalism. Although his scattered remarks on New England writers are damning, more recent attention to P's *Eureka* and other visionary prose pieces has disclosed affinities with Idealistic* and Transcendental thinking.

In a review of N. Hawthorne,* P admonished the New England author to "mend his pen . . . come out from the Old Manse,** cut Mr. Alcott,* hang (if possible) the editor of 'The Dial' "** (*Essays and Reviews*, 587–88). Criticizing Hawthorne's penchant for allegory, he was impatient with stylistic ambiguities imbibed from the "phalanx and phalanstery" atmosphere of Transcendentalism. The "phalanx" to which Hawthorne belonged, moreover, reflected Hawthorne's questionable participation in the social experiment at Brook Farm.**

In drawing from this review important principles of short fiction, literary historians have questioned the accuracy of remarks on Hawthorne, more caustic than those in his 1842 review of *Twice-Told Tales*. By November 1847, the date of the second review in *Godey's Lady's Book*, Hawthorne had left the Old Manse, the experiment at Brook Farm was at the point of collapse, *The Dial* was extinct, and R. W. Emerson* had embarked on a tour of England. Hyperbolic or irate, P's remarks on Hawthorne have been taken to reflect his hostile attitude toward Transcendentalism and its central figures.

In his satires "How to Write a *Blackwood* Article" and "Never Bet the Devil Your Head" P used reductio ad absurdum in referring to Transcendentalism. In assaulting Transcendentalism on stylistic grounds, he questioned the "Carlylisms," "Euphuisms," "Merry Andrewisms," and "metaphor run mad" of this school of writing. Transcendental style, he argued, often amounted to "obscurity for obscurity's sake" or "mysticism for mysticism's sake." Emerson, Carlyle,* and the poet W. E. Channing* were scorned for their inability to distinguish obscurity of expression from expression of obscurity.

He attacked stylistic excesses, but his irreverence extended to the social philosophy of the Transcendentalists. Fashioning himself a member of the Virginia gentry, a social class to which he could only aspire, he objected to Transcendentalist views on abolition* and reform. Hardly discriminating among individual social thinkers, he adopted a hostile stance out of regional bias. He referred to Boston as the "Frogpond" or as headquarters of "the Humanity *clique*" and lumped together writers from this city with Transcendentalists and socialists.

His tumultuous feelings toward Boston, the city of his birth, did not prevent him from seizing economic opportunity when it presented itself. In 1845, using the offices of J. R. Lowell* and hoping to establish a foothold in enemy territory, he spoke before the Boston Lyceum.** Prefacing his recitation with an attack on didacticism, a sin he associated with New England moralism, he read his poem ''Al Aaraaf.'' When he was attacked in the local press, his concealed hostility resurfaced, and he claimed to have chosen the abstruse ''Al Aaraaf'' for an audience of vague thinkers, that is, Transcendentalists. The lyceum fiasco intensified his regional animus, and he crafted ''The Facts in the Case of M. Valdemar,'' a hoax on mesmerism.** Like phrenology,** feminism, and Fourierism,* mesmerism was a fad he associated with the party of Progress in Boston.

His antipathy to the New England establishment notwithstanding, P's attitude toward Transcendentalism does not lend itself to easy generalization. Mindful of the European roots of the movement, he punned on Kant's** name, though his early tales point to a realm beyond the senses akin to the German philosopher's supersensible sublime. Deploring Coleridge's* ''metaphysicianism'' on one hand, he alternatively called Coleridge ''a towering intellect.'' Even his comments on some New England Transcendentalists have a double thrust. He questioned M. Fuller's* feminist proclivities but acknowledged that she had a superior prose style (*Essays and Reviews*, 1176). He could not abide Emersonian mysticism but selectively praised his individual lyrics. Of minor figures associated with the movement, he praised C. P. Cranch* and the elder Channing.*

In a letter to Thomas Holley Chivers, P disclaimed general disdain for the Transcendentalists, reserving criticism only for ''pretenders'' and ''sophists.'' He seemed intent to distinguish an obscure brand of mysticism, to which cultists had fastened, from a deeper philosophic stance. More ''profound'' and ''ennobling'' aspects of Transcendentalism may inform the studies of the heroine in ''Morella,'' who investigates both Fichte** and Schelling.* P does not specify what stores of intuitive knowledge are reflected in ''the many mysteries of . . . transcendentalism'' probed by Ligeia in the tale bearing her name.

Confirmation of a positive kind of Transcendentalism is found in several of P's essays, especially those reflecting his interest in ''supernal beauty.'' His fascination with ideal forms of beauty, latent in reviews from the early 1840s, received full expression in ''The Poetic Principle'' (1850). Other texts that suggest a path to the quasi-Transcendentalism of *Eureka*, in which poetic intuition and scientific logic coalesce into a vision of cosmic unity, include ''The Colloquy of Monos and Una,'' ''Mesmeric Revelation,'' and his 1844 letter to Lowell.

Whether one emphasizes P's satiric thrusts at Transcendentalism or his blend of Transcendental idealism and traditional religious imagery, the reader needs to be attentive to the charged context of his individual comments on figures and texts associated with the movement. To the extent that a heroic and unitary version of Transcendentalism has been challenged by social historians, P's comments on the movement remain pertinent.

References: Ottavio M. Casale has treated P's attitudes in ''P on Transcendentalism,'' *ESQ* 14 (1968): 85–97. An advocate for P's ''psychal transcendentalism'' is E. W. Carlson, ''P's Vision of Man,'' in *Papers on Poe*, ed. Richard Veler (1972). Critical disagreement on the subject is summarized in essays in *Poe and His Times*, ed. B. F. Fisher (1990).

Kent P. Ljungquist

POLIS, JOSEPH "JOE" (1807?–1884?), a Penobscot, was one of H. Thoreau's* representative men. The two met on the Massachusetts man's last trip to Maine in 1857, when P served as Thoreau's guide and the two struck up a friendship. In 1862, in his funeral oration for his old neighbor, R. W. Emerson* claimed that the three great influences on the last years of Thoreau's life were J. Brown,* W. Whitman,* and the aboriginal Maine woodsman. Thoreau himself had said that P "was one of the aristocracy, and was particularly steady and trustworthy."

Though Thoreau liked to think that his Maine guide was "a wild man, indeed," P was a thoroughly postcontact Native American. Comfortable with English, a devout Protestant, tribal representative to the state of Maine, traveler to the nation's capital and other distant cities, he once paid a visit to D. Webster.* (His niece, Clara Neptune, also brushed with notoriety: On the vaudeville stage, she played opposite John Wilkes Booth.) When he was not leading tours, P made a living crafting baskets and canoes and selling local curios. By the time Thoreau met him, he had amassed enough wealth to buy a substantial home in Old Town, Maine. One tale has him a sharpshooter at the battle of Chancellorsville, though the source that hands on this story expresses doubt.

P's woodcraft and native lore fascinated the Concord** naturalist: With tongue only partly in cheek, he portrayed P listening to snakes whistle, and hailing busy muskrats. An important figure in Old Town chronicles, P was remembered as a shaman. Thoreau was impressed by his guide's knowledge of herbal cures and by his warning that Native American knowledge was inaccessible to the white man. That oracular air, a fund of non-Western knowledge, and a playful wit were irresistible to Thoreau, whose remarks on P betray many of the qualities he admired in his Maine guide.

REFERENCES: Scholarship on P is scant. But see Robert F. Sayre, *Thoreau and the American Indians* (1977), esp. 172–87; Philip F. Gura, "Thoreau's Maine Woods Indians: More Representative Men," *AL* 49 (November 1977): 366–84; and the folklore collections of Fannie Hardy Eckstorm. Marion Whitney Smith refers to P in two pamphlets, *Thoreau's West Branch Guides* (1971) and *Abenaki Shamanism* (1963), both collected at the Bangor Historical Society. The Penobscot Indian Nation in Old Town holds scattered primary materials related to the P family.

Barbara Ryan

POWERS, HIRAM (1805–1873), expatriate American sculptor whose studio and home in Florence, Italy, served Anglo-American intellectuals and artists from the 1840s to the 1870s as congenial sites to meet, indulge in progressive experiments in art, and discuss new intellectual movements, is significant to Transcendentalism for his extended friendships with Americans M. Fuller,* H.

Greenough,* N. and S. Hawthorne,* and W. W. Story,* among others, and his facilitating the exchange of ideas between them and his many English friends, including Robert and Elizabeth Barrett Browning, Charles Dickens, and Thomas and Frances Trollope.

Descended from early settlers of Concord, Massachusetts,** P was born in Woodstock, Vermont. Repairing and sculpting wax figures in Cincinnati's Dorfeuille Western Museum, he discovered his gift for detail work, which encouraged him to pursue a career in bust portraiture and sculpture. From 1834 to 1836, he lived in Washington, D.C., where his reputation grew as he produced busts of Andrew Jackson, John C. Calhoun, D. Webster,* and John Marshall. Seeking a more lively (and inexpensive) environment to continue his craft, P left America in 1837 and settled permanently in Florence. There, awed but also inspired by Italy's prominence in art history and encouraged by his early friendship with Greenough, P began his career in sculpture in earnest, and he flourished. The *Greek Slave* (1843) established him as a serious classical artist and is regarded today as one of the greatest achievements in marble executed in the 19th century. Other important pieces include *Eve Before the Fall* (in two versions: 1843 and 1850); *Il Penseroso* (1856), executed according to details from Milton;** *California* (1858), an idealized female nude that art historians believe rivals the *Greek Slave*; and *The Last of the Tribe* (1872), a rare depiction of an Indian maiden. Powers's statues of Thomas Jefferson and Benjamin Franklin decorate the U.S. Capitol.

Though P's reputation has suffered in comparisons between his work and that of Americans Greenough (championed by R. W. Emerson*), Story, and Thomas Crawford, a new biography and catalog of his works along with several comparative studies of American sculpture affirm his position as, possibly, the most accomplished sculptor of his generation. P's importance to Transcendentalism remains his facility at advancing Anglo-American literary and intellectual relations during the mid-19th century. For that, he was a favorite of Fuller, who was captivated by the person and his art. In an ironic premonition of her untimely demise, she wrote to Emerson shortly before leaving Italy for America and, after commenting on the loss of P's first *Eve Before the Fall* at sea, confessed the event created a ''dark feeling'' in her. While estimates of P's service to Anglo-American relations are evident in the personal writings of most who met him, Hawthorne's in his *French and Italian Notebooks* may stand for all. Observing that impressions of P filled his notebooks at the expense of others he met during his travels, Hawthorne stated: ''I had no idea of filling so many pages . . . [with] Mr. Powers; but the man and his talk are fresh, original, and full of bone and muscle, and I enjoy him very much.''

References: Contemporary reports of P abound in the personal writings of the Brownings, the Trollopes, and Hawthorne. The most recent biography and catalog is Richard P. Wunder, *HP: Vermont Sculptor, 1805–1873*, 2 vols. (1991). Comparative studies include Sylvia E. Crane, *White Silence: Greenough, P, and Crawford, American Sculptors in Nineteenth-Century Italy* (1972), Albert TenEyck Gardner, *Yankee Stonecutters: The*

First American School of Sculpture, 1800–1850 (1945), and Margaret Farrand Thorp, *The Literary Sculptors* (1965).

Ronald A. Bosco

PRATT, MINOT (1805–1878), one of the original members of the Brook Farm** community, highlights the connection between Transcendentalism and Unitarianism.** Born in Concord,** he demonstrated as a youth the love of outdoor life and practical skills that would make him a valuable member of the Brook Farm experiment. Before he joined the community, he served as a printer for eight years, working as foreman in the office of the *Christian Register*, a journal devoted to Unitarianism. He arrived just in time to sign the Articles of Association in September 1841 because he was tying up loose ends at the *Register*. P and his wife, Maria, bought five shares in the community for $2,500. He served as one of the directors of agriculture at the farm and, along with C. Dana,* was one of G. Ripley's* most trusted advisers. Although he had listed his occupation as "printer," his commitment and devotion to agriculture** contributed to the survival of the farm and might have saved it from financial ruin if others had shared his practical management skills.

The Ps were one of the original "family groups" at the farm; the last of P's three children was born there. According to accounts of the farm, he and his wife managed the "Hive" where most domestic duties were executed. P, with Ripley and Dana, signed the introductory statement in 1844 that announced the conversion of the Brook Farm Association to a phalanx. Appointed a trustee of the farm a year earlier, he served in that office until leaving in 1845. He wrote Ripley expressing regret at his family's departure and wished the enterprise success. However, he believed that his small children would be a disadvantage to the community. Others also expressed regret. G. W. Curtis* wrote to J. S. Dwight* on the day of the P family's departure: "All Brook Farm in the golden age seemed to be strapped to the rear of their wagon as baggage, for Mrs. P was the first lady I saw at Brook Farm, where ladyhood blossomed so fairly." After P retired to a farm in Concord, he published "Flora of Concord," the fruit of his botanical studies.

References: On P's contribution to Brook Farm and the Transcendentalist movement, see John Thomas Codman, *Brook Farm: Historic and Personal Memoirs* (1894); Lindsay Swift, *Brook Farm* (1900); Marianne Dwight, *Letters from Brook Farm: 1844–1847* (1928); and Henry W. Sams, *Autobiography of Brook Farm* (1958).

Julie M. Norko

R

RAY, ISAAC (1807–1881), was a New England psychiatrist active in reforming the treatment of the insane and in developing the field of forensic psychiatry. He published in both professional and popular journals, including the *American Journal of Insanity, The Christian Examiner,*** and the *North American Review.*** Born in Beverly, Massachusetts, R was educated at Phillips Andover Academy and received medical training in Beverly, in Boston, and at Bowdoin College. He was one of 13 psychiatrists who in 1844 founded the Association of Medical Superintendents of American Institutions of the Insane, now the American Psychiatric Association.

R's interest in the developing science of psychiatry led him to study phrenology.** In the 1834 *ChEx,* his essay on "Moral Aspects of Phrenology" praised G. Combe's* *A System of Phrenology* and suggested that phrenology and Christianity were compatible and complementary. R admitted that phrenologists had not fully explained the workings of the mind but accepted their sense that mental and spiritual attributes were dependent upon physical conditions. He suggested that moral behavior required not a triumph of mind and will over animal instincts, but rather a balance of moral, intellectual, and animal "powers," and urged clergymen to provide congregants with physiological knowledge that would help them achieve this balance. In 1835, R translated portions of Franz Joseph Gall's work on the functions of the brain. Though R's enthusiasm for phrenology waned, even later in life he valued its contribution to developing thought on the mind and its functions and continued to believe in a connection between mental health and physical conditions. In 1850, he exhorted teachers at the Rhode Island Institute of Instruction to learn the physiology of the brain that they were trying to teach. In 1851 he considered "Epidemic Monomania" for *ChEx.* Though he identified monomania's social roots, including "Millerism,** Mesmerism,** Antimasonry, gold-hunting, [and] Abolitionism,"** he was interested as well in physical symptoms of the illness and in the mechanisms by which these symptoms were produced. In 1858, R reviewed Thomas Buckle's *History of Civilization in England* for *NAR*, challenging Buckle's "theory of the supremacy of the intellectual powers in promoting civilization" and arguing that "the improvement of the bodily organism [is] among the most potent agencies for advancing the moral and intellectual condition of the race" (405, 394–95).

R's primary professional concerns, however, were the treatment of insanity in the court system and the reform of mental health care. He published numerous articles on forensic psychiatry, as well as the pioneering *Treatise on the Medical Jurisprudence of Insanity* (1838), written with the advice and assistance of C. Sumner.* In 1840, he was named the superintendent of Maine Insane Hospital and, before assuming his position, traveled abroad to observe the treatment of the mentally ill in other countries. Interested in improving treatment of the insane in the United States, he published "Observations on the Principal Hospitals for the Insane in Great Britain, France, and Germany" (*American Journal of Insanity* [April 1846]), which influenced the construction of the McLean Asylum in Massachusetts, as well as *Ideal Characters of the Officers of a Hospital for the Insane* (1873). Seeking to influence public opinion on this subject, R did not confine his essays to professional journals. In 1854, he published "American Hospitals for the Insane" in *NAR*, advocating compassion and care in the design of mental hospitals (82).

Other important writings include *Mental Hygiene* (1863), *Contributions to Mental Pathology* (1873), and a collection of essays discussing mental illness in historic figures and literary texts. R's address to the Rhode Island Institute of Instruction was published in 1851 as *Education in Its Relation to the Physical Health of the Brain*. After retiring from hospital administration, R continued his written and clinical work, maintained a lucrative consultation practice, and often testified in court as an expert witness.

References: Biographical information is in the *DAB*; Winfred Overholser's introduction to the reprint of *A Treatise on the Medical Jurisprudence of Insanity* (1962); A. W. Stearns, "Psychiatrist and Pioneer in Forensic Psychiatry," *American Journal of Psychiatry* 101.5 (March 1945): 573–84; and *Pioneers in Criminology*, ed. Hermann Mannheim (1960). R's personal collection of papers and books is housed at the IR Library of Butler Hospital, Providence, Rhode Island. On R's view of phrenology, see Benjamin Pasamanick, "An Obscure Item in the Bibliography of IR," *American Journal of Psychiatry* 111.3 (September 1954): 164–71.

Lisa M. Gordis

REDPATH, JAMES (1833–1891), journalist, abolitionist,** reformer, and lecture promoter, was involved with the Transcendentalists, especially through his interest in J. Brown.* R attended the Concord** memorial services for Brown, 2 December 1859, and incorporated those presentations in his best-selling volume *Echoes of Harper's Ferry* (1860). In addition to organizing the service, H. Thoreau,* B. Alcott,* and R. W. Emerson* made a few comments and read selections of verse and prose. R's volume also included ''A Plea for Captain John Brown'' by Thoreau; two speeches by Emerson, one given at Tremont Temple in Boston and one at Salem, to defend Brown and to raise support for his family; a sermon entitled ''Causes and Consequences of the Affair at Harper's Ferry'' by J. F. Clarke;* and a sermon, ''Bunker Hill and Harper's Ferry both Failures,'' by W. Furness.* R also interviewed Thoreau for his biography *The Public Life of Captain John Brown* (1860), which was dedicated to Thoreau, Emerson, and W. Phillips* as ''Defenders of the Faithful, who, when the mob shouted, 'Madman!' said, 'Saint!' '' R's publications helped elevate Brown to the status of martyr for the abolitionist cause.

R, then a correspondent for the New York *Tribune*, first met Brown in Kansas. This association and his travels in the South led R to become an ardent abolitionist who advocated violence and published numerous articles and books attacking slavery. Later he became a promoter for the emigration of African Americans to Haiti and, as joint commissioner representing Haiti in the United States, helped attain recognition of Haitian independence. After the Civil War, R helped reform the state school system in South Carolina and establish an orphan asylum for African American children.

As the organizer of the Boston (later Redpath) Lyceum** Bureau in 1868, R booked lecture tours for Emerson as well as such notables as H. Greeley,* Phillips, and J. W. Howe.* Eventually, he added Mark Twain and other humorists to his list of clients. Later R became interested in Ireland and published a volume of letters on Irish reform. In 1886–87, he edited the *North American Review*.**

REFERENCES: In addition to the volumes on Brown, R's works include *The Roving Editor; or, Talks with Slaves in the Southern States* (1859), *Hand-book to Kansas Territory* (1859), *A Guide to Hayti* (1860), and *Talks About Ireland* (1881). The only biography is Charles F. Horner, *The Life of JR and the Development of the Modern Lyceum* (1926). See also John R. McKivigan, ''JR, John Brown, and Abolitionist Advocacy of Slave Insurrection,'' *Civil War History* 37 (December 1991): 293–313.

Larry R. Long

REED, SAMPSON (1800–1880), was a prominent American disciple and promoter of Swedenborg,** who functioned as an ''early oracle'' to some Transcendentalists, in R. W. Emerson's* phrase. Born in what is now West Bridgewater, Massachusetts, the son of a minister and congressional representative (1795–1801), R attended Harvard College (Class of 1818), where, at age 14, he encountered Swedenborg through a 19-year-old student, Thomas Worcester. An acquaintance of Emerson's at Harvard, he was Emerson's initial point of exposure to Swedenborg's ideas. He particularly impressed Emerson with his early writings ''Oration on Genius'' (1821) and *Observations on the Growth of the Mind* (1826). He became a druggist and eventually the proprietor of Reed, Cutler & Co., a large wholesale drug business, and in 1827 cofounded the

Swedenborgian *New Jerusalem Magazine*,** for which he wrote numerous articles over a period of 50 years.

R's early writing was one source of many of Transcendentalism's most important themes: Nature** exists for the soul to use; a newly awakened age was beginning to fathom the ''godlike form of man''; all elements of the creation are connected to all others in a uniformly lawful divine order; each mind has its own form that is essentially complete at birth; and ''merely physical force'' yields before ''the powers of the mind.'' His *Observations* also offered the doctrine of correspondences** between the realms of nature and spirit: Parts of Emerson's *Nature* (1836) and his other early works are indebted to R's view that the individual mind could find, in the ''relations which exist between created things,'' ''the actively creative will of God.''

R's thought was implicit in a conflict within Transcendentalism between a belief in the innate self-positing genius of the higher mind and the view that ''true genius is reception'' of the divine influx. R lent weight to the latter position. Emerson's later journal** references to R and his essay on Swedenborg suggest that R was more influential through his belief in the divinity of thought and the mental uses of nature than in his views about the literal reality of the ''other world'' and additional Swedenborgian notions. But in folding human agency into the godhead, R may have been more consistent than the more flexible (if not self-contradictory brand of) Transcendentalism that asserted self-positing and divine order equally. Adamant that Swedenborg was a vehicle of the revealed Word of God, R distanced himself from the Transcendentalism of his own day, which he regarded as a perversion of his master's vision. Transcendentalism, R declared in the preface to the 1838 edition of *Observations on the Growth of the Mind*, is the ''product of man's own brain; . . . Transcendentalism is the parasite of sensualism; and when it shall have done its work, it will be found to be itself a worm, and the offspring of a worm.''

References: A useful list of R's decades of contributions to *NJM* can be found in Kenneth Walter Cameron, *Young Emerson's Transcendental Vision* (1971), 285–87. For a defense of R against Emerson's dismissals, see Clarence Paul Hotson, ''SR, a Teacher of Emerson,'' *NEQ* 2 (April 1929): 249–77. Excerpts from R's two most influential early works appear in Miller (1950), 49–59. The Swedenborg Foundation has published *SR: Primary Source Material for Emerson Studies* (1992), which includes the 1838 preface.

Christopher Newfield

RICKETSON, DANIEL (1813–1898), is connected to Transcendentalism by his friendships with some of its central figures, most notably with H. D. Thoreau.* R purchased *Walden* (1854) the day after its publication and immediately dashed off a letter to its author, whom he had never met. He characterized *Walden* as ''a prose poem'' and identified himself as ''a kindred spirit,'' which in part he was, having built in the mid-1840s ''the Shanty,'' a small building for his personal use located some distance from his home, Brooklawn, in New Bedford, Massachusetts. Thoreau first visited R on 25 December 1854. Fond of sketching,

R drew a picture of Thoreau as he appeared at their first meeting. The two men were friends for the remaining eight years of Thoreau's life and wrote one another frequently (although R sent nearly twice as many letters as Thoreau did). R came to Concord** eight times; Thoreau visited his friend in New Bedford on six occasions. Thoreau's journal** entry for 10 April 1857 includes an extended description of R's eccentrically furnished Shanty, where the two spent many hours.

The friendship between R and Thoreau seemed unlikely. A Quaker,** R benefited from inherited wealth and spent much of his life nursing hypochondriacal sicknesses and composing poems of fitful quality. R repeatedly entreated his friend to visit Brooklawn. Thoreau just as regularly declined the invitations. In 1860, their correspondence lapsed for the better part of the year, prompting R to write Thoreau and inquire if he should ''infer from your silence that you decline any farther correspondence and intercourse with me?'' Thoreau responded several weeks later, pointing out that he had ''never promised to correspond with you, and so, when I do, I do more than I promised.'' The correspondence and the friendship resumed.

The nature of the relationship between the two men continues to intrigue scholars. Henry Seidel Canby argues that Thoreau had three categories of friends. He groups R with those Thoreau ''could at any moment have gone back to Walden** and forgotten.'' Yet as Don Mortland and Richard Lebeaux suggest, the friendship may have benefited both men. Mortland speculates that Thoreau found attractive R's lack of presumption; R was well aware of his own character flaws and frequently discussed them with Thoreau. Lebeaux postulates that R ''furnished [Thoreau] with confirmation of his own generativity,'' that as Thoreau's physical strength waned, he found comfort in men like R who acted as his ''disciples.'' Regardless of the periodic ruptures in their friendship, it was to New Bedford to see his friend R that Thoreau made his last trip. R was too overcome by grief to attend his friend's funeral.

R also knew the other important men in Concord's Transcendental circle. He heard R. W. Emerson* lecture in New Bedford in 1854 and found both the content and the presentation wanting, characterizing the experience as ''almost . . . an imposition upon an intelligent audience.'' He liked the Emerson lecture he heard in 1856 better, and their mutual regard for Thoreau led the two men to a friendship. R was a frequent guest in Emerson's home during his visits to Concord. Yet R found Emerson's funeral address for Thoreau inadequate. He wrote to Henry's sister Sophia: ''to strangers the article would fail in some important particulars to convey an idea of [Thoreau's] noblest and highest qualities.'' The poet E. Channing* frequently visited R during his sojourn with the *New Bedford Mercury*, a position R likely helped him attain. In 1857, R observed that he had ''rarely if ever found a more companionable friend'' than Channing, but shortly thereafter the eccentric Channing seems to have abandoned the friendship, deeply offending R in the process. R's relationship with A. B. Alcott* was perhaps the most stable of those he had in the Concord circle.

The two men visited one another during the 1850s and 1860s, and they corresponded periodically throughout their lifetimes. R published several poems about his Concord friends in *The Autumn Sheaf* (1869).

References: Following their father's death, Anna and Walton Ricketson edited two volumes of memorabilia: *DR and His Friends* (containing portions of R's correspondence and his journals) and *DR, Autobiographic and Miscellaneous* (1910). Several useful studies discuss R: Canby, *Thoreau* (1939); Harding (1965); Thomas Blanding, ''DR's Sketch Book,'' *SAR* 1977: 327–28; Earl J. Dias, ''DR and Henry Thoreau,'' *NEQ* 26 (1952): 388–96; Walter Harding, ''DR's Copy of *Walden*,'' *HLB* 15 (October 1967): 401–11; Blanding, ''Beans, Baked and Half-Baked,'' *CS* 17 (December 1984): 46; Lebeaux, *Thoreau's Seasons* (1984); and Mortland, ''Thoreau's Friend R: What Manner of Man?'' *CS* 18 (December 1985): 1–19. See *Corr.* The R family papers (1795–1958) are housed in the Old Dartmouth Historical Society Whaling Museum Library, New Bedford, Massachusetts.

Kathryn B. McKee

RIPLEY, EZRA (1751–1841), Congregational minister and stepgrandfather of R. W. Emerson,* served as pastor, political mediator, historian, and arbiter of taste in Concord, Massachusetts,** for the half century between the American Revolution and the Mexican War. His precise relation to Transcendentalism, as with his precise relation to the rise of Unitarianism** along with other forms of liberal theology and thought in New England, is a matter of continued debate, with little common ground between three distinct positions, no one of which is finally dominant.

The first and possibly most durable reading of R's character and legacy was advanced upon his death by Emerson in a series of biographical sketches eventually collected into the essay ''ER, D.D.'' Emerson identified R with the ideas and practices of New England's old-style, conservative Congregationalism, ''which expired about the same time with him''; in an unusual mix of compliment and censure, Emerson conceded that the remnants of Puritan** ''faith made what was strong and what was weak in Dr. R,'' for he was ''a perfectly sincere man, punctual, severe, but just and charitable, and if he made his forms a strait-jacket to others, he wore the same himself all his years.''

A second and almost as durable estimate of R has been advanced in the annals of Unitarian church history, where reports by, among others, B. Frost,* R's colleague and, later, successor in the First Parish, emphasize his humanitarianism and portray him as one of the ''prophets'' of New England Unitarianism. Rejecting Emerson's allegation of R's inherent formalism, this view stresses that R had challenged both Trinitarian and Calvinistic doctrines by the time he assumed his position in Concord in the 1770s and, seemingly, had rejected them completely by the time a Trinitarian congregation split from the Concord church in 1826, thus preparing the way for Unitarianism in the First Parish.

A third reading of R's character and legacy, decidedly more personal and anecdotal than the first two, is preserved in moments of romantic revisionism discernible in N. Hawthorne's* prose and American notebooks and in collections of the lore and witticisms of post-Revolutionary Concord. Hawthorne, who rented the First Parish parsonage—the "Old Manse"**—for several years after R's death, did not remember R as a prescient Unitarian or as one whose "grim" portrait had been added to those of other Concord ministers; instead, in the preface to *Mosses from an Old Manse,* he portrayed R as the Manse's gentle ghost, whose presence provided relief from the unnerving rustles of his contentious and sulfuric First Parish predecessors, Daniel Bliss (1715–1764) and William Emerson (1743–1776), and as the planter of an orchard on the Manse grounds, that "has a relation to mankind, and readily connects itself with matters of the heart." In a comparable vein, local histories have repeatedly reprised popular versions of R's relation to the people of Concord such as "Concord felt very close to God when R prayed," and each has credited R's prayers with improving a harvest or forestalling an inconvenient thunderstorm. These same histories compliment R as the quintessential New England Yankee, citing, for example, his shrewdness in tying his ministerial stipend to variations in the grain and meat commodity markets, or they transform him into something of a local-style Ben Franklin in their various depictions of R as a young Harvard man from Woodstock, Connecticut, the fifth of 19 children born into a farming family, wintering in Concord in 1775–76 during the British occupation of Cambridge, returning two years later as minister of the town's sole congregation, marrying two years after that his predecessor's widow (and herself the daughter of a former Concord preacher), siring his own line in the place of the Bliss and Emerson families, and appropriating all the Concord lands and property once belonging to them so that he and his might enjoy the fruits of earlier labor.

For almost a century and a half, each of these portraits has vied for position as the definitive estimate of R's character and religious temperament. Yet even when they are read collectively, the portrait that emerges is skewed and incomplete. Between the mixed political motives and the romantic fancy of 19th century writers who chose to remember him, ER—the *essential* ER—has likely ceased to exist. Thus, no one of the portraits cited above should be accepted as a fair, full, or satisfactory account of his character and merit, and certainly, none comes even close to reporting the details of his remarkably long and interesting life or to deciding the means by which, besides longevity, he exerted such a hold on Concord for so long. Although significant local and personal materials relating to R and some 2,500 of his manuscript sermons are preserved in libraries in Concord and at Harvard University, few have come forward to begin the biographical or critical studies that R deserves and that are needed to decide, finally, the nature of both his character and his legacy. Until that work is undertaken and completed, readings of R's relation to Unitarianism and, in consequence, to Transcendentalism remain subject to dispute.

References: For late-in-life self-appraisals of his legacy, see ER, *Half Century Discourse* (1829), and "Memoir," *The Unitarian Advocate, and Religious Miscellany* 3 (1831): 128–32, 163–70, 208–14. For the collection of R's extant manuscript sermons—

complete for the years 1783 to 1837—see all materials cataloged under b MS 64, 490 in the ''ER Collection,'' Andover-Harvard Theological Library, Harvard Divinity School.** Among the most interesting items relating to R in the Concord Free Public Library are records of the Concord First Parish dating from 1739 to 1857 and the detailed ''Records of deaths,'' which R began in 1778 and Frost kept from 1838 to 1856. Reports of R are scattered throughout Emerson's *JMN* and Hawthorne's American notebooks; for Emerson's biographical essay, see ''ER, D.D.'' (first published in *Atl*** in 1883) in *W*, 10:379–95. On R's life and position in Unitarian Church history, see particularly *American Unitarian Biography: Memoirs of Individuals Who Have Been Distinguished . . . in the Cause of Liberal Christianity*, ed. William Ware (1850–51), 1:130ff; William B. Sprague, *Annals of the American Pulpit; or Commemorative Notices of Distinguished Clergymen* (1857–[69]), 8:117ff; and *Heralds,* 1:160–74. For a recent overview of Concord's First Parish and modest appraisals of R's place in its history, see *The Meeting House on the Green*, ed. John Whittemore Teele (1985). Popular histories of Concord include Townsend Scudder, *Concord: American Town* (1947). For recent critical revaluations, see Ronald A. Bosco, '' '[M]ercy to Pardon & Grace to Help': ER's Ordination Diary, 1778–1836,'' *SPAS* 2 (1992): 153–92; and Robert A. Gross, *The Minutemen and Their World* (1976), and ''Much Instruction from Little Reading: Books and Libraries in Thoreau's Concord,'' *PAAS* 97 (April 1987): 129–88.

Ronald A. Bosco

RIPLEY, GEORGE (1802–1880), Unitarian** minister and editor, is best known as founder and director of the utopian community Brook Farm.** On 8 September 1836, he met with three ''like-minded seekers''—R. W. Emerson,* F. H. Hedge,* and George Putnam—at Willard's Hotel in Cambridge for the first meeting of what was to become the Transcendental Club.** From the outset, R's endeavors mirrored the divergent concerns of the Transcendentalists.

Upon graduating from Harvard Divinity School,** R was ordained at Boston's Purchase Street Church in 1826. His essays on such writers as J. Martineau,* Constant,* Schleiermacher,* and Cousin* appeared primarily in *The Christian Examiner*** from 1830 to 1837. He engaged A. Norton* in several printed skirmishes that served in many instances to solidify the Transcendentalist position relative to that of more conventional Unitarians. The first bout, fought over R's liberal interpretation of the gospel miracles,** occurred in 1836 largely in the pages of the *Christian Register*. Two years later, Norton's attack on the Transcendentalists' affinity for German philosophy in his *Discourse on the Latest Form of Infidelity* was the catalyst for yet another series of printed arguments.

In 1838, R began publishing his *Specimens of Foreign Standard Literature*** (1838–42), a 14-volume series of translations of German and French literature to which he added his own translations of Cousin, Jouffroy,* and Constant (2 vols., 1838). In 1839 he served as business manager of *The Dial*,** the fledgling Transcendentalist journal, while M. Fuller* agreed to serve as editor. His growing involvement in the liberal issues and causes surrounding Transcendentalism created a rift between R and his Purchase Street congregation, and he resigned his pulpit in March 1841. Almost immediately R adjourned to Brook Farm, where he served as director until the dissolution of the community around the end of 1847.

Strapped with the debts incurred by the failure of Brook Farm, R moved to New York, where he struggled through a series of low-paying freelance journalistic jobs. In 1849 he became "literary assistant" for H. Greeley's* *Tribune*, a position previously held by Fuller. In 1862, with completion of his 16-volume *Cyclopedia*—edited with his friend C. Dana*—R finally recovered from his financial losses. He could not, however, forget the lesson of Brook Farm and his subsequent years of poverty. For the rest of his life, he steadfastly refused to become closely involved in theological, philosophical, or social reform.

References: There are three full-length biographies: O. B. Frothingham,* *GR* (1882), which includes excerpts from R's letters; Charles Crowe, *GR: Transcendentalist and Utopian Socialist* (1967); and Henry L. Golemba, *GR* (1977). See Mathew David Fisher, "A Selected Annotated Edition of the Letters of GR, 1828–1841" (Diss., Ball State Univ., 1992). On R's significant dissemination of German and French literature to the Transcendentalists, see Pochmann (1957). The Brook Farm years are documented in Lindsay Swift, *Brook Farm, Its Members, Scholars, and Visitors* (1900); J. T. Codman, *Brook Farm, Historic and Personal Memoirs* (1894); and Henry W. Sams, *Autobiography of Brook Farm* (1958), a collection of primary materials. A bibliographical essay by Crowe is in Myerson (1984), 242–49. Most of R's manuscripts are in the Boston Public Library, the Houghton Library, Harvard University, and the Massachusetts Historical Society.

Mathew David Fisher

RIPLEY, SAMUEL (1783–1847), Unitarian** minister in Waltham, Massachusetts, and R. W. Emerson's* half-uncle, was host and friend of Transcendentalists. He was the son of the Rev. Ezra Ripley* of Concord** and Phebe Bliss, widow of William Emerson, grandfather of Ralph Waldo. Graduating from Harvard in 1804, he spent two years as tutor in Virginia and Washington, D.C., where he acquired a taste for politics. With some reluctance he followed the family footsteps into the ministry. From 1809 to 1846 he served in Waltham and, after retiring to Concord, continued to serve the Lincoln congregation until his death.

To supplement his salary in Waltham, he started a school for boys. In 1818, he married Sarah Alden Bradford [Ripley],* a skilled teacher and classical scholar. Together they created one of the most respected preparatory schools in New England. R. W. Emerson and his brothers took turns as tutors at the school during their college years, and their Uncle R continued to provide moral as well as financial support, opening his pulpit for Waldo's first sermon in 1826 and covering expenses for his health-restoring trip south soon thereafter.

R was a Unitarian Christian notable for his generosity of spirit and lack of intellectual pretensions. Declaring their theological flights beyond his scope, he was nonetheless supportive of the Transcendentalists. Although he was alarmed at parts of the Divinity School Address and urged that it not be published, his pulpit was always open to Emerson. C. Francis,* minister in neighboring Watertown, was a beloved colleague. T. Parker* was invited to preach in Waltham at the height of his ostracism by other Unitarian ministers. G. Ripley* found an advocate in his cousin Samuel during the controversy with A. Norton.* When the quiet brilliance of Sarah Alden Ripley drew the Transcendentalist luminaries to Waltham, they could be confident of the parson's warm welcome.

References: A memoir by his son, Christopher Gore Ripley, appears in the *PMHS* 2 (April 1848): 392–94. His son-in-law, James Bradley Thayer, wrote a brief biography, *Rev. SR of Waltham* (1897), which was included in *Memoirs of Members of the Social Circle in Concord*, Third Series (1840–95) (1907), 1–24.

Joan W. Goodwin

RIPLEY, SARAH ALDEN BRADFORD (1793–1867), one of the most respected scholars of her time and place, was a valued member of R. W. Emerson's* extended family, a close friend of C. Francis* and F. H. Hedge,* and an occasional member of the "Transcendental Club."** A descendant of Plymouth Colony founders, S was the daughter of sea captain Gamaliel Bradford of Duxbury and Elizabeth Hickling of Boston. She spent her early years in Boston and Duxbury, lived in Charlestown for five years before her marriage in 1818, and occupied the Waltham parsonage until 1846, when she retired to the Old Manse** in Concord.**

As a child, she was encouraged in her love of learning by liberal and supportive parents and studied Latin and Greek along with modern languages. While her brothers attended Harvard, S independently continued her own education in the classics as well as English, French, and Italian literature and history, mathematics, and science.

The Bradfords were members of William Emerson's congregation at First Church in Boston and friends of the Emerson family. After the minister's death in 1811, his sister, Mary Moody Emerson,* became young S's self-appointed mentor in things spiritual. S was challenged to defend her intellectual pursuits from Miss Emerson's charge that they constituted a detriment to piety. Partly in response to theological questions raised in this relationship, S plunged into New Testament criticism and was among the first in New England to read Johann Jakob Griesbach and Johann Gottfried Eichhorn,** learning German along the way. After moving to Charlestown in 1813, the Bradfords became active in the liberal congregation formed in opposition to the orthodoxy of Jedidiah Morse.

In 1818, S married Mary Moody Emerson's half brother, Samuel Ripley,* minister and schoolmaster in Waltham, and became the mainstay of the Ripley school, where boys were prepared for Harvard and rusticated students were returned to the college the better for her teaching. She also supervised the education of her younger sisters and brother, G. P. Bradford,* raised her own family of seven, and made the Waltham parsonage a favorite gathering place for the ministers and intellectuals associated with Transcendentalism.

S attended the Transcendentalist meeting at Emerson's house on 1 September

1837 and was invited in May 1840, when Emerson was again host. She was enthusiastic about Emerson's lectures and writings, but she would probably not have identified herself as a Transcendentalist, despite her sympathy and close acquaintance with members of the group. During her thirties, her youthful faith gave way to skepticism. She found no scientific evidence for belief in an afterlife, maintaining that the limitations of the human intellect left most tenets of religion in the realm of fancy. Though she read Kant** as well as Goethe* and others of the Romantic school and eagerly discussed German literature with Hedge and Francis, she did not see human reason as synonymous with deity. Her disciplined mind would not allow her to profess what she found lacking in evidence or rationality.

Still, Transcendentalism had its effect on the development of her faith. Gradually she was able to resolve her earlier skepticism. Life, nature,** science, philosophy, and religion came together in her understanding. She moved away from theological controversy and the institutional church to a simple faith nourished by her lifelong love of nature.

S's influence on Emerson is apparent in the number of references to her in his journals** and letters. All of the Transcendentalists knew and admired her and spent rewarding hours in her presence.

REFERENCES: SAR was chosen to represent Massachusetts in the centennial volume *Worthy Women of Our First Century*, ed. Mrs. O. J. Wister and Agnes Irwin (1877). Elizabeth Hoar* wrote the chapter "Mrs. SR," 113–227. Gamaliel Bradford included a chapter on his great aunt, "SAR," in *Portraits of American Women* (1919), 34–64. More recent studies include Frances W. Knickerbocker, "New England Seeker: SBR," *NEQ* 30 (March 1957): 3–22; Patricia Ann Carlson, "SAR—Emerson's *Other* Aunt," *ATQ* no. 40 (fall 1978): 309–21; and Joan Goodwin, "Self-Culture and Skepticism: The Unitarian** Odyssey of SABR," *PUUHS* 22, pt. 1 (1990–91): 35–50, and "SAR, Another Concord Botanist," *CS*, New Series 1 (fall 1993): 77–86. For a manuscript collection, see the SABR Papers at The Schlesinger Library, Radcliffe College.

Joan W. Goodwin

RIPLEY, SOPHIA WILLARD DANA (1803–1861), wife of G. Ripley* and cofounder of Brook Farm,** is best known for her unflagging efforts to promote the utopian community from its conception in 1840 to its collapse in 1847. S was born into the prominent Dana family; her grandfather Joseph Willard was a Harvard president. Her father, however, abandoned her family when she was a young girl, and along with her mother and one of her sisters, she opened a school in Cambridge where she was the "principal instructress."

In 1827 she married G. Ripley, minister to Boston's Purchase Street Church. When her husband and several other liberal Unitarians** formed the Transcendental Club,** the first official meeting was held at the Ripleys', and S attended many of the subsequent meetings. In the early 1840s she was a regular participant at M. Fuller's* "Conversations."** She contributed three articles to *The Dial*:** "Woman" (January 1841) and "Painting and Sculpture" and "Letter" (from a socialist community she and her husband were visiting [July 1841]).

After she and her husband formed the ''Brook Farm Institute of Agriculture and Education,'' it was largely S's diligence and her example that maintained the utopian community for the six years of its existence. O. B. Frothingham,* in his biography of G. Ripley, refers to S's efforts: ''His devoted wife toiled and served at his side unmurmuringly. For ten hours at a time she has been known to labor in the muslin room . . . she was yet so attentive to her classes that in two years she missed only two recitations.'' In fact, the community's school, where S taught history and modern languages, was one of Brook Farm's few consistently profitable enterprises.

S grew disillusioned with the utopian venture when Brook Farm became a Fourierist* phalanx. This discontent with Fourierism, coupled with the encouragement of the recently converted O. Brownson,* caused S's latent interest in Catholicism to blossom. In 1846 she embraced Catholicism—though privately, out of respect for her husband's new faith in Fourierism. When the community finally foundered in September 1847, she and her husband moved to New York, where she took a job teaching while George began his career as literary editor of the *Herald Tribune*. SR completed her conversion to Catholicism in 1847 and died in New York in 1861. Her funeral was held in Boston, in a Catholic church that had once been the same Purchase Street Church where she and George began their lives together.

REFERENCES: The best biographical sources for SR are the standard studies of her husband. All the relevant histories of Brook Farm contain information about her. Henry W. Sams, *Autobiography of Brook Farm* (1958), includes parts of three letters she wrote from Brook Farm. Most of her letters are in the Massachusetts Historical Society.

Mathew David Fisher

ROBBINS, SAMUEL D. (1812–1884), was an enthusiastic, if peripheral, Transcendentalist. He knew major figures, published in Transcendental-leaning magazines—a poem in *The Harbinger*,** a sermon in *The Western Messenger*,** an anonymous article in *The Boston Quarterly Review***—but is rarely mentioned in histories of the period. He was allied briefly with Brook Farm** but never lived there.

According to Clarence Gohdes, R wrote ''Thoughts on Unity, Progress, and Government,'' published anonymously in Brownson's* *BoQR* (1 [April 1838]); Gohdes and John McAleer identify this article as an influence on R. W. Emerson's* Divinity School Address. R writes, ''Individual minds are the best interpreters of the Divinity. The original thinkers, the single-eyed, the holy-hearted, are the purest conductors of infinite truth, the Christs of God'' (192). This individualist strain leads to a mystical, antischolastic conclusion: ''[T]he mysteries in which truth has been shrouded by the initiated, theology by the priest, nature** by the professor, have frightened young and credulous minds from researching the more profound religion of Humanity, the more glorious science of the soul'' (198). Emerson knew R; he briefly but positively reviewed R's sermon ''The Worship of the Soul'' in *The Dial*** 1 (402–4).

R would also have known Emerson from attending Transcendental Club** meetings. B. Alcott** knew R and listed him under the heading "Living Men" in his journal.** (Others Alcott described as "living life to its full potential" were Emerson, T. Parker,* G. Ripley,* and W. E. Channing.* Later R's name was struck.)

W. H. Channing,* R's friend and Divinity School colleague, published a R selection parallel with one by Joseph Priestley in his *WM* (1841). Channing asks readers to "determine for themselves which contains the most truth," adding that "we far prefer the cloudy raptures of the mystic to the dry clearness of the philosopher" (432). Priestley warns against "indulging the vain and delusive imagination of an immediate and supernatural communion with God" (457); R conversely proclaims, "Man is the seed of God; he blossoms here to ripen in the skies. The Infinite is in us" (432). R cites Moses and Christ to demonstrate that "we never truly commune with God till we realize his actual presence pervading all our thoughts" (461).

REFERENCES: For more on Emerson's debt to R, see Gohdes, "Some Remarks on Emerson's *Divinity School Address*," *AL* 1 (March 1929): 27–31 and McAleer, *Ralph Waldo Emerson: Days of Encounter* (1984). On R and the *WM*, see Robert D. Habich, *Transcendentalism and the* Western Messenger (1985).

Stephen N. Orton

ROGERS, NATHANIEL PEABODY (1794–1846), was an abolitionist** and radical reformer whose writings deeply impressed R. W. Emerson* and H. Thoreau.* A descendant of John Rogers, one of the Maryite martyrs and the hero of Foxe's *Acts and Monuments*, R himself became one of the central figures in P. Pillsbury's* *Acts of the Anti-Slavery Apostles* (1883), "a man, the like of whom the world has seldom seen—may not soon see again." R was raised in Plymouth, New Hampshire, and educated at Dartmouth College, where he graduated with honors in 1816. After studying with two distinguished lawyers, R returned to Plymouth and began his own successful practice around 1820. A major turning point in his life came in 1835, when R met W. L. Garrison,* editor of the *Liberator*, and became a contributor to a newly established abolitionist newspaper, the *Herald of Freedom*. Three years later R abandoned his law practice and moved to Concord, New Hampshire, where he became the editor of the newspaper, in the pages of which he mounted a sustained attack on slavery, racism, the military, and other social and political institutions.

Although its circulation was small, the *Herald* gained the attention of a number of Transcendentalists, especially Thoreau, with whom R briefly conducted a kind of correspondence in print. In the April 1844 issue of *The Dial*,** Thoreau published "Herald of Freedom," a laudatory review of R's writings in that "spirited journal." Surprised and gratified "to see the little outcast sheet getting at all the eye of so respectable a periodical" as *The Dial*, R reprinted the review in the 10 May 1844 issue of the *Herald*, concluding his introductory note with the hope that Thoreau would "let Anti-slavery have the benefit of his beautiful pen.'' Four months later Thoreau sent a copy of Emerson's First of August Address, ''Emancipation in the British West Indies,'' to R, who in the 27 September 1844 issue of the *Herald* graciously remarked, ''It adds not a little to its value coming from [Thoreau's] hand.'' Characteristically, however, R did not allow his respect for the sender to blunt his sharply critical review of the address. Pouncing on Emerson's suggestion that the government should purchase the freedom of the slaves, a conciliatory idea that violated the radical abolitionists' policy of immediate, uncompensated abolition, R replied: ''I go for the doctrine that no man can be a slave or ever was. . . . I would suggest to the gifted author of the Address, that a tour of anti-slavery field service would be most healthful to his own powers of writing and speech.''

Despite, or perhaps because of, that rebuke, Emerson also admired R. Although the *Herald of Freedom* was the official organ of the New Hampshire Anti-Slavery Society, R came to view all organizations as coercive, since any corporate action infringed upon the freedom of individuals. In 1844 he therefore began to agitate for the dissolution of the antislavery societies, a campaign that locked him in a bitter dispute with his old friend Garrison, the president of the parent organization, the American Anti-Slavery Society. Emerson privately asserted that R was right, ''against any or all statements,'' adding: ''Is it that we wish once more to know what a society decides, a majority, the reason of fools, the fortress of the weak; or do we want a pamphlet because a genius writes it?'' Nonetheless, in 1845 the board of the New Hampshire Society wrested control of the *Herald* from R, who briefly edited a competing antislavery newspaper before he died in October 1846. A few months later, Emerson observed in his journal,** ''N. P. R spoke more truly than he knew, perchance, when he recommended an Abolition-Campaign to me. I doubt not, a course of mobs would do me much good.''

Thoreau, too, still found R's words compelling. After reading a collection of R's newspaper writings published in June 1847, Thoreau revised ''Herald of Freedom'' for inclusion in the ''Thursday'' chapter of *A Week on the Concord and Merrimack Rivers*. Following the final paragraph in *The Dial* version, where he had praised R's expressions of ''genuine indignation and humanity,'' Thoreau in the 1847 version of ''Herald of Freedom'' continued, ''But since our voyage R has died, and now there is no one in New England to express the indignation or contempt which may still be felt at any cant or inhumanity.'' Although he finally omitted the revised version of ''Herald of Freedom'' from *A Week*, R's writings may have inspired Thoreau to offer his own radical critique of American institutions in a lecture delivered in 1848 and published in 1849 as ''Resistance to Civil Government.'' Indeed, that famous lecture—now widely known as ''Civil Disobedience''**—was itself a kind of oblique tribute to R and other radical social critics of the 1840s, whose views profoundly influenced Thoreau and, through him, such influential figures as Mahatma Gandhi and Martin Luther King, Jr.

References: A reliable account of R's life is Robert Adams, "NPR: 1794–1846," *NEQ* 20 (1947): 365–76. R is also at least briefly discussed in biographies of prominent abolitionists like Garrison and W. Phillips,* as well as in more general studies of radical abolitionism. The only collection of R's writings is *A Collection from the Newspaper Writings of NPR* (1847; rpt. 1849). Thoreau's interest in R is documented by Wendell Glick, "Thoreau and the 'Herald of Freedom,' " *NEQ* 22 (1949): 193–204. An edited text of Thoreau's "Herald of Freedom," first published in *The Dial* 4 (1844): 507–12, is included in the Princeton edition of *RP*. As Linck C. Johnson has argued, however, the text in *RP* incorporates revisions and additions Thoreau made in 1847, when he revised "Herald of Freedom" for inclusion in *A Week*: see " 'Native to New England': Thoreau, 'Herald of Freedom,' and *A Week*," *SB* 36 (1983): 213–20.

Linck C. Johnson

ROWSE, SAMUEL WORCESTER (1822–1901), lithographer and painter, is best remembered for his crayon portraits of H. D. Thoreau* and R. W. Emerson.* Born in Bath, Maine, he was trained in Augusta as an engraver and moved to Boston to learn lithography. He remained in Boston from 1852 to 1880 and kept a studio on Tremont Street.

In summer 1854 R boarded at the Thoreaus' in Concord,** and Henry records taking him on nature** walks. Acquaintances variously recalled how at the breakfast (or dinner) table R glimpsed a particular expression on Henry's face and rushed off to sketch in solitude. Emerson liked the portrait, and Sophia Thoreau declared, "His friends all consider it an excellent likeness." Not *all*, for Henry's Aunt Maria, H. G. O. Blake,* and F. B. Sanborn* found fault with it, and B. Alcott,* granting it "the best we have," thought it "made too much of a gentleman out of its subject." When the Alcotts bought the Thoreaus' Main Street house in 1877, they presented the portrait to the Concord Free Public Library, as Sophia had requested.

In spring 1858 C. E. Norton* commissioned R to draw Emerson, who in his journal** paraphrases R on portraiture: "R said that a portrait should be made by a few continuous strokes giving the great lines, but if made by labor & by many corrections, though it became at last accurate, it would give an artist no pleasure,—would look muddy." R's first try at his Emerson portrait suffered such a fate. Emerson writes on 19 July that the portrait has been left "imperfect" for six weeks. E. W. Emerson* remembered that by trying "to improve the mouth a little" R ruined the first version and started over. Lidian* liked the first sketch well enough to have it photographed, and Waldo's letters record sending copies to his brother William* and to another admirer. Norton liked the second sketch and proudly hung the finished portrait at Shady Hill; today these hang in the Emerson house in Concord.

A. H. Clough* declared the photo sent by Norton "the best portrait I know of anyone I know." The artist William J. Stillman considered it "the most masterly" rendering of character he had "ever seen," "represent[ing Emerson] in his most characteristic mood, the subtile intelligence mingling with the kindly humor in his face, thoughtful, cordial, philosophic." Sanborn preferred the original sketch for capturing "the lofty air of cheerful courage and hospitality, so native to Emerson, yet so hard for his photographers and painters to reproduce." Edward thought the portrait "a good likeness, but tightly drawn and with a weak mouth." R was widely praised for what his friend Norton called "depth and delicacy of sentiment." But the defect of this virtue in his art is a tendency to soften and idealize his subjects, making them appear younger than their years.

Commercially successful, R also did celebrated portraits of Clough, N. Hawthorne,* H. W. Longfellow,* and J. R. Lowell,* and he was in demand for his crayon portraits of children. He was characterized by E. W. Emerson as "kindly . . . yet sometimes uncomfortably modest and aloof in company." Yet he was sufficiently sociable to be elected to the Saturday Club** in 1864, and R. W. Emerson wrote in his journal, "Wasson* is good company for prince or plowman. R also." In 1872 R visited London, where he met Ruskin.* He enjoyed traveling but insisted that his muse could do without Old World charm, writing from Paris, "The proper study of mankind is man, and I can study him and myself better in America than anywhere else. America is to me the centre and the head of the world—the last incarnation." R relocated to New York in 1880 and died at Morristown, New Jersey.

References: See Frederick W. Coburn's entry in *DAB*; Thoreau's journal in *Wr*; Emerson's *JMN* and *L*; B&M (1985); Mantle Fielding, *Dictionary of American Painters, Sculptors and Engravers*, enlarged ed. (1974); Thomas Blanding and Walter Harding, *A Thoreau Iconography*, Thoreau Society Booklet 30 (1980; rpt. from *SAR* 1980: 1–35); Fritz Oehlschlaeger and George Hendrick, eds., *Toward the Making of Thoreau's Modern Reputation* (1979); E. W. Emerson, *The Early Years of the Saturday Club 1855–1870* (1918), 388–91; [William J. Stillman,] "R's Portrait of Emerson," *Atl* 3 (May 1859): 653–54; F. B. Sanborn, "The Portraits of Emerson," *NEMag* n.s. 15, no. 4 (December 1896): 449–68 (rpt. *ESQ* 59.2 [spring 1970]: 67–86). R crayon sketches of Waldo and Lidian Emerson are reproduced in Kenneth Walter Cameron, "The R Drawings of the Emersons," *ATQ* 13.2 (winter 1972): 49–52.

Wesley T. Mott

ROY, RAMMOHAN (1772–1833), Hindu scholar and social activist whose early commitment to the reformation of Hindu religion and society has earned him the epithet of "father of modern India," exemplified to Western sympathizers, and particularly his Unitarian** admirers in England and America, an ideal of purified monotheism, concern for social justice, and a rational appropriation of scriptural traditions. Known to the Transcendentalists chiefly through his groundbreaking translations and commentaries of selected texts of the Vedas and Upaniṣads, R was especially influential for Unitarians in the early 1820s. Among them was the young R. W. Emerson,* whose views on India and the Orient he helped shape.

Born to a family of wealthy, landholding brahmins in a small town of modern West Bengal, R quickly distinguished himself for his precocious intellect and extraordinary aptitude for languages. Upon completing the standard Bengali education, he was sent to Patna, a traditional center of Islamic power, for training in Persian and Arabic, still the languages for social and political advancement in India. Intensive study of the Qur'ān and Sufi poets under the tutelage of his Muslim instructors nurtured an abiding respect for the Muslim doctrine of *tawhid*, the absolute unity of God, and a growing discomfort with contemporary expressions of Hindu polytheism and image worship. Ostracized from family and friends for his heterodox opinions, R resolved to pursue his study of religions further, for a time in Tibet studying Buddhism, and later in Benares, the traditional seat of Hindu learning on the Ganges, where he immersed himself in Sanskrit and the ancient expressions of the Vedic tradition. Out of his study of the classical texts of these several traditions, R developed a syncretistic theology in which a neo-Vedāntin unity of God served as the foundation for his critique of contemporary Hindu and other religious forms.

In 1803, having in the meantime also acquired a command of English, R secured an appointment with the British East India Company, where he worked in several capacities throughout the following decade. This contact led to a study of Christianity, as well as Western literatures and languages generally, which would eventually culminate in a working knowledge also of Latin, Greek, and Hebrew. In 1814, R retired from civil service to his family estate in Calcutta to pursue his career as a scholar, journalist, and social reformer full-time. Repelled by what he saw as contemporary distortions of the pure classical faith of the Upaniṣads, R launched a campaign calling for reform of Hindu religious life that continued unabated till his death in England at age 61. Among his targets were "idolatry," the still widespread practice of "suttee" (*satī*), which he was instrumental in helping to abolish, and the traditional caste restrictions on access to Vedic study (*adhikāra*). In addition, he became a vigorous proponent of woman's rights** and the extension to India's masses of modern systems of education. Especially significant was his founding in 1828 of the Brāhma Samāj (Society of God), which, under the subsequent leadership of a series of charismatic teachers, became the principal agency in the 19th and early 20th centuries of Hindu religious and cultural reform.

R's first major work, *Tuḥfat al-muwāḥḥidīn* (A Gift to Monotheists), published in Persian and Arabic in 1804, signaled R's advocacy of a natural theology** and, to some extent, his continued indebtedness to Islam. In 1815, he began publishing a series of translations, first into Bengali and then English, of selected texts of the Vedas, Upaniṣads, and the Vedānta school of Indian philosophy, a project that helped to consolidate his reputation as a reformer in India and as an exponent of classical Hindu teachings in the West. R's most influential collection, and the one by which H. Thoreau* was introduced to him in 1850, was his *Translation of Several Principal Books, Passages and Texts of the Veds* (1832).

With the publication of *The Precepts of Jesus* in 1820, R's public life took a new turn. Intended to expound the merits of the New Testament's ethical teachings to fellow Hindus, *Precepts* inadvertently triggered a storm of protest from members of the Baptist Mission at nearby Serampore on the grounds that it dismissed Christian ''doctrines'' and the Bible's ''miraculous relations'' as problematic. In response to the missionaries' attacks, R quickly published ''An Appeal to the Christian Public, in Defense of the Precepts of Jesus,'' the first in a series of three rebuttals that sought to amplify his objections to Christian Trinitarianism. Two years later, the antagonism between the Serampore Mission and R was further exacerbated when one of the missionaries, William Adam, formally abandoned the Trinitarian position and converted to Unitarianism, under the tutelage and at the inspiration of R. Having found R's theology more reasonable than that of his Baptist peers, Adam devoted the next seven years of his life to establishing a Unitarian Mission in India. Though R supported Adam's efforts and for a time even participated in his meetings, in the end, he found the evangelical thrust of the English missionaries unpalatable and left to establish his own community based largely on Hindu traditions.

As early as 1816, periodicals in England and the United States began publishing accounts of R's teachings and his remarkable career. Emerson likely read a few of these in 1821 while preparing his Harvard College Commencement composition on the topic of ''Indian Superstition.'' When news arrived the next year of R's theological skirmishing with the Baptist missionaries in India, and particularly the conversion to Unitarianism of William Adam, the Unitarian press seized upon the story with excitement and covered it in great detail. For several months, beginning in May 1822, the Boston-based *Christian Register* devoted extended treatments to the theological controversy, the writings of R, and the work of William Adam. His journals** indicate that Emerson himself perused these accounts. At the time, R appears to have been significant to Emerson for the same reasons he was significant to other Unitarians—as a noteworthy victory in the contest between liberal and orthodox faiths—but by the next decade, R had so risen in Emerson's overall estimate as to be included in a list of his representative men.

References: The standard account of R's life is Sophie Dobson Collet, *The Life and Letters of Raja RR*, 3d ed., ed. D. K. Biswas and P. C. Ganguli (1962). R's English writings are available in *The English Works of Raja RR*, 6 vols., ed. Kalidas Nag and Debajyoti Burman (1945). A helpful account of early Unitarian interest in India is Spencer Lavan, *Unitarians in India: A Study in Encounter and Response* (1977). For Emerson's interest in R, see Alan D. Hodder, ''Emerson, RR, and the Unitarians,'' *SAR* 1988: 133–48.

Alan D. Hodder

RUSKIN, JOHN (1819–1900), British art critic and social reformer, the 19th century's major English-language writer on art, spread ideas on nature** and culture that complemented Transcendentalism. R shared with American Transcendentalists a strong Protestant religiosity, the vocabulary of Romanticism, and the conviction that minutiae of the natural world were microcosms** of a spiritual whole. However, where the Americans wrote on the individual's direct confrontation with nature and spirit, R tracked consciousness of God's nature in painting, architecture, decorative arts, and secular society at large. R's *Modern Painters* (1843–46, 1856–62) and *The Stones of Venice* (1851–53) explained the arts as impressions or recapitulations of the natural world, remade through the imagination and hand of the artist. Artistic styles were the evidence of a society's ability to live by nature's truths.

R came to the Transcendentalists' attention in the late 1840s, when his writings began to be popular in America. *The Massachusetts Quarterly Review*** praised *Modern Painters'* doctrine of seeking "the common idea" behind the details of nature. H. Thoreau* was a serious, if frequently dissatisfied, reader of R, impressed by the passion behind the writing on nature but uninterested in its treatment of art theory and painting.

For the generation that followed R. W. Emerson's* and Thoreau's, R's relation of nature to high culture and public life was indispensable. William J. Stillman, a young acquaintance and admirer of Emerson, founded the art journal *The Crayon* (1855–61) to argue that American devotion to nature should be expressed through painters' Ruskinian fidelity to the details of nature. (W. C. Bryant* was a more enthusiastic backer of the journal than were the New England writers.) In the 1860s the American branch of R's followers in painting, the Pre-Raphaelite artists around the journal *The New Path* (1863–65), tended to separate R's ideas on art from the general nature worship that had fueled his American popularity. After this point, American Ruskinianism split. Progressive architects like Peter B. Wight developed R's ideas on Gothic architecture into a functionalist theory that exemplified an "Emersonian" honesty of form. The art historian and reformer C. E. Norton,* admirer of Emerson and R's closest American friend, argued that Emerson's spiritual values were best seen in the Arts and Crafts movement launched by R and William Morris. By 1900 the Arts and Crafts celebration of natural materials and the joy of handwork was often backed up with quotations from Emerson, Thoreau, and Whitman.* The most important product of this loose joining of R's and Emerson's ideas is the architecture of Frank Lloyd Wright.

References: J. D. Hunt, *The Wider Sea: A Life of JR* (1982), is a good recent biography. Elizabeth K. Helsinger, *R and the Eye of the Beholder* (1982), is an important recent study. Roger B. Stein, *JR and Aesthetic Thought in America, 1840–1890* (1967), remains the starting point for its topic; it suggests that ties between the Transcendentalists and R were weak. "Ruskinian" art is the subject of Linda S. Ferber and William H. Gerdts, *The New Path: R and the American Pre-Raphaelites* (1985). For the figure who did most to fuse R's and Emerson's thought, see Kermit Vanderbilt, *Charles Eliot Norton: Apostle of Culture in a Democracy* (1959).

M. David Samson

S

SALT, HENRY STEPHENS (1851–1939), English socialist and author, wrote what is widely regarded as the most useful and most sympathetic early biography of Thoreau.* *The Life of Henry David Thoreau* (London, 1890) includes both information about its subject's life and a critical examination of Thoreau's writing. In composing the book, S relied heavily on his personal correspondence with Americans like D. Ricketson,* F. B. Sanborn,* and H. G. O. Blake * because S himself did not know Thoreau nor had he ever visited the United States. Nevertheless, Ricketson wrote to S: "It seems remarkable to me, who knew him so intimately, that you should have been able to make so lifelike a portraiture of him" (*Daniel Ricketson and His Friends*, ed. Anna and Walter Ricketson [1906], 258). In the biography and elsewhere, S maintained that most readers and critics ignored Thoreau's humanitarianism in favor of exploring the idiosyncrasies of his character. He repeatedly praised Thoreau's pacifism, his vegetarianism, and the simplicity of his lifestyle, all priorities that S shared. Yet S was aware of Thoreau's human foibles. In fact, he enumerates them in the closing paragraphs of the *Life*: "his lack of geniality, his rusticity, his occasional littleness of tone and temper." Nevertheless, S counsels, Thoreau's "incidental failings . . . did not mar the essential nobility of his nature. We shall do wisely in taking him just as he is." S defended Thoreau from accusations he considered unjust and ventured "to doubt whether [R. W.] Emerson* had really gauged his friend's mind as fully as he imagined."

Despite favorable reviews when the biography appeared in England, it sold poorly. S revised the volume, and in 1896 Walter Scott released a shorter and less expensive version of it that included several factual emendations. Although the book never sold in impressive numbers, S had evidence that his words and Thoreau's had reached one important reader: In 1929 Mahatma Gandhi wrote to S and indicated that he had read the biography. S began revising Thoreau's *Life* for a third time but did not complete his work before his death.

A socialist, S found Thoreau's attitudes toward established government, wealth, and religion attractive. S's first essay about Thoreau, published in the 14 November 1885 issue of *Justice*, the weekly publication of the Social Democratic Federation, constitutes his most strenuous effort to align Thoreau and socialism. S resists actually designating Thoreau a socialist but proclaims that "Thoreau did a real service to the cause of Socialism by practically demonstrating the truth of Socialist calculations and proving how little labour is sufficient to support mankind." A year later, S published a less propagandistic essay about Thoreau in *Temple Bar*, a periodical with a wider circulation than *Justice*, and admitted that "Thoreau cannot be called a Socialist; he was rather an Individualist of the most uncompromising type" ("Henry D. Thoreau," *Temple Bar* 78 [November 1886]: 373).

His appreciation for Thoreau's individualism eventually prohibited S from assigning him membership in any group, particularly the Transcendentalists. S disliked Transcendentalism for its "vague mysticism," a characteristic he noted in H. Melville's* writing. Thoreau's "sound practical frame of mind" saved him from sharing that weakness. S described *Walden* (1854) in the *Life* as "agriculture** and mysticism combined" and in *Temple Bar* declared that volume "alone . . . sufficient to win [Thoreau] a place among the immortals" (382). "Thoreau's genius will eventually be at least as highly valued as Emerson's," S predicted in the *Life*, for "of all the Concord** group, by far the most inspired, stimulating, and vital personality is Thoreau's." S also published a number of articles about Thoreau and discusses him in two of his five autobiographical works: *Seventy Years Among Savages* (1921) and *Company I Have Kept* (1930). A chapter about Thoreau appears in one of S's three naturalist books, *The Call of the Wildflower* (1922), as well as in his *Literary Sketches* (1888). S edited three posthumous compilations of Thoreau's works: *Anti-Slavery and Reform Papers* (1890); *Selections from Thoreau* (1895); and *Poems of Nature*, edited with Sanborn (1895).

REFERENCES: George Hendrick, *HS: Humanitarian, Reformer and Man of Letters* (1977), is a valuable survey of S's accomplishments, with extensive discussion of S's work on Thoreau and a review of S's other literary studies. In "H S. S, the Late Victorian Socialists, and Thoreau," *NEQ* 50 (1977): 409–22, Hendrick maintains that individual socialists like S and Edward Carpenter, and not British socialist groups, introduced Thoreau to the English public eye. The *Life* of Thoreau has been rpt. in 1968 and in 1993, ed. Hendrick et al.

Kathryn B. McKee

SANBORN, FRANKLIN BENJAMIN (1831–1917), journalist, abolitionist,** social reformer, social scientist, and memorialist of the Transcendental movement, was signally important in perpetuating the ideas and works of R. W. Emerson,* H. Thoreau,* and other Transcendentalists into the 20th century. Born in Hampton Falls, New Hampshire, S became interested enough in Emerson's work to walk to Concord** from Harvard College, where he was a student, for a ten-minute meeting with Emerson in July 1853. That meeting eventually led in late 1854 to S's being offered the position of schoolmaster at the private school in Concord where the children of Emerson and other distinguished citizens of the town were enrolled. S's subsequent move to and life in Concord became the basis of his work as editor and biographer of A. B. Alcott,* Emerson, Thoreau, and other writers and thinkers associated with American Transcendentalism.

S's interests were not exclusively literary, however. Once settled in Concord, he pursued his passion for social reform, most notably the cause of abolition, serving on committees for the colonization and defense of Kansas and even as the secretary of the Massachusetts Free Soil Association, a position that took him on an inspection tour of the West in 1856. Late that year, S met John Brown* and soon became one of the ''secret six'' who helped to plan the raid on the arsenal in Harpers Ferry, Virginia. When Brown's raid failed in October 1859, S's role as a member of Brown's inner circle came under the scrutiny of the U.S. Senate, which dispatched marshals to arrest S and bring him to Washington, D.C., but that attempt was thwarted by Emerson and other Concord citizens, and the Senate warrant for S's arrest was eventually declared illegal by the Massachusetts Supreme Court. S also directed his considerable philanthropic energies into serving on the Massachusetts Board of Charities from 1865, organizing the American Social Science Association, serving as an officer of the National Prison Association and National Conference of Charities, and participating in the founding of the Clarke Institution for the education of the deaf. He used his expertise in these and related areas as a special lecturer on social science at Cornell University from 1884 to 1887.

S's career as a journalist included succeeding his friend M. Conway* as editor of the antislavery weekly *The Commonwealth* (1863–67) and filling a number of roles for *The Springfield Republican*, including that of resident editor from 1884 to 1887. The work S seems to have been best suited for, though, is that of chronicler of Transcendentalism. In 1879 he even had a role in founding, with Alcott, Emerson, and others, the Concord School of Philosophy,** which was devoted to teaching Transcendentalist philosophy to a new generation. But S's greatest service to the memory of the movement was somewhat undercut by the liabilities of the work he produced. His editions of Thoreau, notably *The Familiar Letters of Henry David Thoreau* (1894) and *Walden* (1909), were produced with little regard for editorial accuracy and contain ample evidence of S's willingness to revise Thoreau's lean prose to bring it into line with his own taste. S's biographies and memoirs are similarly flawed. His three biographies of Thoreau—*Henry D. Thoreau* (1882), *The Personality of Thoreau* (1901), and *The Life of Henry D. Thoreau* (1917)—feature grossly inaccurate transcriptions of Thoreau's work and may overstate the closeness of S's relationship to his subject. Problems of inaccuracy also plague his two biographies of Alcott—*A. Bronson Alcott: His Life and Philosophy*, written with W. T. Harris* (1893), and *Bronson Alcott at Alcott House, England, and Fruitlands,*** *New England (1842–1844)* (1908)—and his work on Emerson—*Ralph Waldo Emerson* (1901) and *The Personality of Emerson* (1903)—seems to focus as much on S as his subject. S also edited several works by E. Channing,* wrote a biography of N. Hawthorne,* and would have edited T. Parker's* papers if Parker's widow, perhaps leery of S's reputation, had not refused him access to her husband's work.

It is perhaps too easy to find fault with S the scholar, but his work on such valuable projects as *The Genius and Character of Emerson* (1885), a superb collection of essays that originated at the Concord School of Philosophy, remind us of the value of S's indefatigable efforts to keep Transcendentalist ideas alive and to translate the movement's idealism** into meaningful social action.

References: S's autobiography is *Recollections of Seventy Years*, 2 vols. (1909). Kenneth Walter Cameron has compiled numerous sources for S; see especially "Some Memorabilia of FBS," *ESQ* (3d Q 1959): 23–30, and *Transcendental Youth and Age: Chapters in Biography and Autobiography by FBS* (1981). The best listing of S's published work is John W. Clarkson, "A Bibliography of FBS," *PBSA* 60 (1st Q 1966): 73–85; and the best and most recent discussion of work on S is Robert E. Burkholder, "FBS," in Myerson (1984), 253–59. The best available biography is Benjamin Blakely Hickock, "The Political and Literary Careers of F. B. S" (Diss., Michigan State Univ., 1953).

Robert E. Burkholder

SCHELLING, FRIEDRICH WILHELM JOSEPH VON (1775–1854), German idealist philosopher, the "poet of the transcendental movement," was the most influential of post-Kantian thinkers; because of its organicism, antirationalism, and emphasis on the individual, the value of art, and the problem of freedom, S's transcendental idealism** has been called the "epitome" of German romantic philosophies. Yet his work is the least translated of these thinkers and the least known to the English-speaking world.

S's thought stands between the subjective idealism of Fichte** and the abstract philosophy of Hegel.* All three attempted to overcome the dualism created by Kant's** critiques: the divorce of subject and object implied by his distinction of the realms of pure and practical reason. For R. W. Emerson* in *Nature* (following Coleridge's* borrowing from Kant), the problem of philosophy was "for all that exists conditionally to find a ground unconditioned and absolute." S located the absolute in the union of the real and the ideal: He sought to include the finite (nature,** matter, the object, life, science) within the infinite (consciousness, thought, spirit, the subject, faith) without depriving the finite of its reality. S sought, says Copleston, to show the absolute as "eternal essence or Idea objectifying itself in Nature, returning to itself as subjectivity in the world of representation and then knowing itself, in and through philosophical reflection, as the identity of the real and the ideal, of Nature and spirit." This "positive" approach dealt with experience, in contrast to Hegel's "negative" conceptual philosophy.

This inclusive theme first unfolded in more than 15 books published between 1793 and 1809. Beginning in 1797, S expounded his *naturphilosophie*, defining nature as the expression and manifestation of spirit. His *System of Transcendental Idealism* (1800) develops a philosophy of knowledge, including the subject-object distinction, the roles of the will and imagination, the nature of history, art, and aesthetics. By 1803, he had developed his *identitäts-system*, positing an undifferentiated absolute as the ground of nature and spirit; his *Philosophical Inquiries into the Nature of Human Freedom* was published in 1809.

Although philosophically congruent with American Transcendentalism, none of S's work was known directly by Emerson when he published *Nature* in 1836. Lacking English translations, Americans had to rely on mediaries such as G. de Staël,** V. Cousin,* and especially Coleridge for S's transcendental philosophy. In his notes toward a ''dynamic philosophy'' in the *Biographia Literaria*, Coleridge borrowed from S in defining philosophy's task as the search for the absolute, the ''science of being altogether,'' knowledge as the ''coincidence of an object with a subject,'' the identity of ''realism'' with ''idealism,'' and connecting the objective as ''nature'' and the subjective as ''self or intelligence.'' *Aids to Reflection* and *The Friend* also made secondhand S available to English readers.

Another important mediary was F. H. Hedge,* who had studied in Germany from 1819 to 1822 and was the only member of the Transcendentalist circle who knew German well. In his 1833 review essay ''Coleridge,'' he called Coleridge's leading ideas the core of the ''transcendental philosophy.'' Though Coleridge had not interpreted German metaphysics, Hedge took on the task, which requires rising to a ''transcendental'' point of view—the interior consciousness—that regards objects outside the subject as determined by our cognitions. In his primary concern with the object, S ''endeavours to show that the outward world is of the same essence with the thinking mind, both being different manifestations of the same divine principle.''

After 1841, when S was called to Berlin by the king of Prussia to combat the negative philosophy of Hegel, American knowledge of S changed somewhat. Hailed as the prophet of a new era, S delivered a popular series of lectures on the philosophy of revelation, attempting to harmonize faith and science. Attending these lectures were not only such later well-known Europeans as Kierkegaard, Engels, and Bakunin but several young Americans, recent Harvard graduates, including C. S. Wheeler,* John Francis Heath, and J. E. Cabot.* In correspondence sent to Emerson and published in *The Dial*** in 1843, Wheeler provided the gist of the introductory and concluding lectures in this series. The next year, Cabot returned to Boston a convert to S's thought. In 1845, he loaned Emerson his manuscript translation of the still-unpublished essay on human freedom, and an English translation of *The Philosophy of Art* appeared. In 1848, Cabot's translation of the oration ''On the Relation of the Plastic Arts to Nature'' was printed in Hedge's *The Prose Writers of Germany*, with Hedge's short introduction. Also, in 1848, Johann Bernardt Stallo's *General Principles of the Philosophy of Nature* included a chapter on S. Since then, only two works by S have appeared in English: the essay on freedom in 1936 and *The Ages of the World* in 1942.

REFERENCES: Frederic Copleston's three chapters on S in *A History of Philosophy*, vol. 7, pt. 1 (''Modern Philosophy: Fichte to Hegel''), remain the best introduction; see also Adam Margoshes' entry in *EP*. *The Dial* 3 (July 1842, January & April 1843): 136, 387–92, and 541–43, prints Wheeler's dispatches from Berlin. Hedge's comments are in ''Coleridge's Literary Character,'' *ChEx* 14 (March 1833): 108–29, and *The Prose Writers of Germany* (1848), 509–10. Rene Wellek discusses S briefly in ''Emerson and German Philosophy,'' *NEQ* 16 (March 1943): 41–62. Pochmann (1957) centers on Emerson's knowledge of the post-Kantians, with an interesting look at Emerson's shift from Carlyle* to Coleridge as the better expositor of German metaphysics and at Stallo's contribution. Stanley M. Vogel, in *German Literary Influences on the American Transcendentalists* (1955), stresses the similarity of thought between S and the Concord** ''post-Kantians'' and credits Hedge and especially Coleridge with popularizing S in New England. The question of Coleridge's ''plagiarism'' from S is explored by Thomas McFarland in *Coleridge and the Pantheist** Tradition* (1969).

Nancy Craig Simmons

SCHLEGEL, AUGUST WILHELM VON (1767–1845), was one of the most influential exponents of the ideas of the Romantic movement in Germany and, as such, had an impact, either directly or through such intermediaries as Coleridge,* upon the thinking of the American Transcendentalists. After studying Greek and Latin literature and aesthetics at the University of Göttingen, S was associated briefly with Schiller* at Jena (1796–97), then with his brother Friedrich* edited the *Athenäum*, which became the main voice of the German Romantic movement (1798–1800). Also in Jena he began the monumental task of translating Shakespeare's** plays into German, eventually finishing about half; the complete Schlegel-Tieck translations are landmarks of German literature. In 1801 he went to Berlin, where he gave a well-received series of lectures on literature and art. Between 1804 and 1817 he was Madame de Staël's** adviser on German literature and culture, traveling with her throughout France, Switzerland, Italy, Austria, Sweden, and Germany. Upon her death, he became a professor of literature at the University of Bonn (1818), where, for the rest of his life, he devoted himself to the study of Sanskrit language and literature; he is regarded as the founder of Sanskrit studies in Germany.

The most direct link between S and the American Transcendentalists lies in his belief in the ''organic''** nature of character, national culture, and art. Unlike the classical ideal, which is concerned with immutable forms and concepts, the Romantic vision, said S, sees life as a developing entity. Consequently, artistic expression must arise out of the author's awareness of his own mutable life and thought, and of his roots in his culture. In his lectures on Shakespeare, given in Vienna in 1808, S saw Shakespeare's supremacy as grounded in his ability to show the development and interplay of feelings in and between his characters; their passions and behavior arise out of their individual natures and adapt to changing occasions. It is this ability that is the basis of Shakespeare's well-noted "universality" in character depiction.

R. W. Emerson* owned S's *A Course of Lectures on Dramatic Art and Literature*, translated by John Black (1833); his views on organic growth and on Shakespeare were undoubtedly influenced by his readings in S. M. Fuller* was familiar with S through her readings in German literature during the 1830s.

References: S's collected works were edited by Eduard Böcking in 12 vols. (1846–47; rpt. 1971), and his letters by Josef Körner (1930); biographies (in German) were published by Bernard von Brentano (1943) and by Ruth Schirmer (1986). S's influence on Emerson and other American writers is the subject of Carola Elfriede Wittmann, "Schlegelian Traces in Early Nineteenth Century American Literature" (Diss., Univ. of Washington, 1990). There is no comprehensive edition of his writings in English.

Ralph H. Orth

SCHLEGEL, FRIEDRICH VON (1772–1822), like his older brother, was influential in the German Romantic movement. More restless and less successful than August,* he believed in the necessity of a fusion between Greek "objectivity" and modern "subjectivity," a view set forth in *Über das Studium der griechischen Poesie* (1797). Following a growing separation from August, F, with his wife, Dorothea, the daughter of Moses Mendelssohn, converted to Roman Catholicism in 1808. A growing conservatism led to his support of the Austrian monarchy as the only legitimate heir of the European tradition, and from 1820 to 1823 he was the editor of *Concordia*, the voice of Viennese (Catholic) Romanticism. In the late 1820s he delivered three series of lectures in Vienna on life, history, and language, respectively; R. W. Emerson* owned *The Philosophy of History*, trans. James Burton Robertson (1835), drawn from the second series.

References: Individual volumes of a critical edition of FS's writings, ed. Ernst Behler, have been appearing since 1958; a biography and critical study in English is by Hans Eichner (1970).

Ralph H. Orth

SCHLEIERMACHER, FRIEDRICH (ERNST DANIEL) (1768–1834), was a German theologian and philologist whose works W. Emerson* read and advised his younger brother R. W.* to read. After passing his theological examinations, S assumed pastorates and theological professorships at Landsberg, University of Halle, and Trinity Church in Berlin. Among his most famous writings are *Die Weihnachsfeier* (1805; Christian Celebration) and *Kurze Darstellung des theologischen Studiums* (1811; Brief Outline of the Study of Theology).

Drawn to the works of Plato,** Kant,** and German Romantics like Friedrich von Schlegel,* S believed that God was immanent,** one with all of his creation. For him, religious experiences were immediate and the potential was ever present. God did not have to be reached through the study of a historical time, place, and person. The soul could feel a oneness with God, a sense of communion with the Infinite and Eternal in the present. S emphasized the eternal, mystical moment when man becomes aware of God and his own oneness with creation. Believing that man could find the answers to moral laws within himself, he thought man should contemplate nature** and its ever-present miracles.**

S's ideas by influence or coincidence are the very ones Emerson expresses in *Nature* (the mystical moment in the transparent eye-ball); "Self-Reliance" (children of God whose influence comes from above); and Divinity School Address ("Trust thyself . . . God is here within").

S's thought influenced theology through the early 20th century but came under attack from 1925 to 1955 by the Word of God followers (Karl Barth and Emil Prunner) for emphasizing man rather than God.

References: S's works are available in three parts: *Theologie, Predigen* (sermons), and *Philosophie.* His biography, Martin Redeker's *FS: Leben und Werke* (1968), was translated into English in 1973. Also available is his *Brief Outline of the Study of Theology*, trans. Terrence N. Tice (1970), and *The Christian Faith*, trans. H. R. Machintosh and J. S. Stewart (1963). Richard B. Brandt, *The Philosophy of S: The Development of His Theory of Scientific and Religious Knowledge* (1914), and Richard R. Niebuhr, *S on Christ and Religion: A New Introduction* (1964), are good secondary sources.

Karen L. Kalinevitch

SHAW, FRANCIS GEORGE (1809–1882), was an Associationist, reformer, translator of George Sand, Fourier,* and Zschokke, and a major advocate of Henry George's theory that the major reason for inequality is the possession of land. Cooke* calls S "one of the staunchest friends and supporters of Brook Farm,"** although S never belonged to the community. To the Brook Farm publication *The Harbinger,*** S contributed articles, book reviews, and translations of George Sand's *Consuelo* and *The Countess of Rudolstadt* (the only fiction ever published in that periodical).

S's thoughtful and humane contributions to *The Harbinger* provide evidence why he was much admired in his time. In his article "The Women of the Boston Anti-Slavery Fair," he presents some ideas similar to M. Fuller's* in *The Great Lawsuit*: that American women were in "a state of subjection and slavery" (1.17.268–70); that marriage tended to be degrading to women; and that "the salvation of the race" and "the advancement of humanity" depended upon women (269). In other articles, S criticizes the eviction of Scottish peasants by the lords who "own" the land ("British Mercy" [1.5.78–79]); condemns religious bigotry (review of G. Cheever,* *Wanderings of a Pilgrim Under the Shadow of Mount Blanc* [1.20.316]); expresses a need for compassion toward criminals and the better education** of children to prevent their becoming criminals ("Teaching not Education" [1.5.79] and review of Dorothea Dix, *Remarks on Prisons and Prison Discipline in the United States* [1.22.346–47]); and condemns the physical and moral conditions under which children labor ("Children in Workshops Near Paris" [1.22.351–52]).

S defends a fellow advocate of Fourierism in "The Writings of George Sand"

(4.14.223–24). His reviews of translations from older and contemporary Italian writers show that he, like R. W. Emerson,* was open to inspiration from learned men; however, like Emerson, he believed that any literature read by Americans should be relevant to American experience. Reviewing *Gertrude: A Tale*, he writes, ''It is entirely an English book, in our opinion by no means adapted to this country, and without interest in a general point of view'' (1.14.220).

A few personal references to S appear in *JMN* and *L*. A close friend of S and his wife, Emerson stayed at their home occasionally and spoke at a meeting (20 March 1863) to raise funds for their son Robert Gould Shaw's 54th Negro regiment. Upon Colonel Shaw's death, Emerson sent the Ss a note of condolence and a poem, ''Voluntaries,'' which were published in *Memorial R. G. S.* (1864 [160–64]). S was probably also one of those who demonstrated generosity and concern over the fire at Emerson's house.

S was an overseer of the poor, justice of the peace, member of the school committee of West Roxbury, foreman of the jury of Norfolk County that first proposed the establishment of a state reform school, longtime president of the Freedman's Bureau, and trustee for a number of organizations, including the Seaman's Retreat and the Sailor's Fund.

References: Except for the entry in *National Cyclopedia of American Biography*, vol. 8 (1898), there is little information on S. His morality play *A Piece of Land* is in the appendix of a book dedicated to him, Henry George, *Social Problems* (1883), 361–66. In the play, S notes the proper conjunction of Labor and Capital and the unfairness of the greedy Landowner toward Labor[ers]. S's short articles and reviews are listed in Sterling Delano, The Harbinger *and New England Transcendentalism* (1983), 202–3.

April Selley

SHAW, LEMUEL (1781–1861), chief justice of the Supreme Judicial Court of Massachusetts from 1830 to 1860 and father-in-law to H. Melville,* promoted individualism in American law through his highly influential decisions. Although occasionally criticized by leading Transcendentalists such as R. W. Emerson* and H. Thoreau* for his conservatism, S shared with the Transcendentalists a belief in the virtues of self-reliance and individual free will.

Two key cases in tort law highlight Chief Justice S's commitment to individualism. In *Farwell v. Boston and Worcester Railroad Co.* (1842), he established the Fellow/Servant Rule and the legal doctrine of Assumption of Risk, both of which emphasized free will and personal responsibility by holding the individual accountable for industrial accidents. In *Brown v. Kendall* (1850), S affirmed the principle of contributory negligence in which individual actions remained paramount in determining liability. These two decisions demonstrate S's adherence to the principles of the common law, which, as historian Leonard Levy has suggested, assumed a posture of ''extreme individualism'' in legal controversies. S allowed exceptions for mentally ill defendants because they did not act out of free will. Throughout his judicial career, S, like the Transcendentalists, repeatedly emphasized the importance of recognizing individual responsibility and self-reliance.

References: Only two biographies of S have been published within the last 75 years: Leonard Levy, *The Law of the Commonwealth and Chief Justice S* (1957), and Elijah Adlow, *The Genius of LS* (1962); Levy's contains the most penetrating analysis of S's personal and professional life. Levy and Adlow are also responsible for virtually all of the scholarly essays on S. Among the most useful are Levy, ''LS: America's Greatest Magistrate,'' *Villanova Law Review* 7 (spring 1962):389–406; and Adlow, ''LS and the Common Law,'' *Boston University Law Review* 41 (winter 1961):1–34.

Jonathan Wells

SIMMONS, GEORGE FREDERICK (1814–1855), graduated from Harvard Divinity School** in 1838 and served on the committee of three inviting R. W. Emerson* to give the ''customary address.'' The committee's letter of thanks to Emerson following the lecture noted that not all assented to his views but did not reveal the members' own sentiments.

S went as a Unitarian** evangelist to Mobile, Alabama, but was forced to leave because of his antislavery views. He then settled in Waltham, Massachusetts, with Samuel Ripley* as associate. From 1843 to 1845 he studied at the University of Berlin under Neander, noted Lutheran theologian and disciple of Schleiermacher.* On his return, he married Mary Emerson Ripley, daughter of Samuel and Sarah Alden Ripley,* and subsequently served congregations in Springfield, Massachusetts, and Albany, New York.

Known first as a brilliant speaker, S turned inward to become a scholar and mystic. J. F. Clarke* characterized him as a liberal Christian who moved beyond narrow Unitarianism toward the moderate orthodoxy of Germany. Through his connection with the Ripleys, S was well known to Emerson and others of the Transcendentalist circle.

References: A memoir of S is included in William B. Sprague, *Annals of the American Pulpit* (1865), 8:554–59. Henry Whitney Bellows's obituary of S appeared in the *New York Enquirer*, 15 September 1855. J. F. Clarke wrote an article about S, ''Abolition in Mobile,'' in *WM* 8, no. 4 (August 1840): 184–87.

Joan W. Goodwin

SMITH, ELIZABETH OAKES (1806–1893), born in Portland, Maine, was a poet, novelist, journalist, feminist activist, and lecturer. She was one of the first women on the lyceum** circuit and lectured on ''Women's Rights''** at the Concord** Lyceum on 31 December 1851. She had lectured with W. Phillips,* and in Boston with R. W. Emerson* as early as 1855. She stayed at the Emerson home for several weeks at the end of 1851, spending time with H. Thoreau* and B. Alcott,* whom she knew from the western lecture circuit. Thoreau did not like her, although they might have found more common ground under different circumstances, since in 1849 OS became the first white woman to climb Mount Ktaadn, three years after Thoreau's climb. She knew M. Fuller* and G.

Ripley* in New York, all having written for the New York *Tribune*. In 1858 Alcott sent her some of L. M. Alcott's* stories while OS was editing *Emerson's Magazine and Putnam's Monthly*** with her husband, Seba Smith.

References: See Mary Alice Wyman, *Selections from the Autobiography of EOS* (1924); Wyman, *Two American Pioneers: Seba Smith and EOS* (1927); and *PJ*, 4: 233–34, 235. OS's manuscript papers are in the New York Public Library.

Leigh Kirkland

SPURZHEIM, JOHANN GASPAR (CASPER) (1776–1832), was the German-born associate of Franz Josef Gall, a fellow countryman and founder of phrenology,** a revolutionary science that attempted to map out the structure of the brain in order to explain human behavior. Phrenology had already caused considerable stir in Austria, Germany, France, and Great Britain when S arrived on these shores in August 1832 to lecture on this subject, chiefly in the Boston area. Despite his untimely death three months later, S succeeded in generating widespread enthusiasm about this discipline, thereby preparing the way for the triumphant reception accorded G. Combe* in 1838 through 1840 and popular interest in phrenology under the aegis of the Fowler brothers, Orson Squire and Lorenzo Niles. As taught by S, phrenology appeared to address many of the Transcendentalists' own concerns about the conduct of social and individual life, education,** legislation, the arts, morals, and even metaphysics. R. W. Emerson* was later to attribute to the enthusiasm accorded phrenology a reaction against ''too formal science, religion and social life,'' declaring that it brought instead a refreshing ''sharpness of criticism, an eagerness for reform'' (''Historic Notes of Life and Letters in New England'' [1880]). Phrenology also matched the Transcendentalists' own penchant for amassing empirical data to bolster intuitively derived truths.

Several Transcendentalists knew S firsthand: W. E. Channing* corresponded with and met S, and J. F. Clarke,* as a student at Harvard Divinity School,** attended S's Cambridge lectures; several essays in Clarke's *Self-Culture* (1890) mention S by name and enlist the vocabulary of phrenology to describe the mind's faculties and organization.

Most of the New Englanders, however, knew S either through his works (in the three years following his death, seven of S's titles were published in Boston) or by reputation. In a lengthy review in *The Christian Examiner*** F. H. Hedge* dismissed S's *Phrenology, or the Doctrine of the Mental Phenomena* (1833) as a ''branch of the sensual school,'' of Bacon and Common Sense philosophy** (17 [November 1834]: 249–69), and O. Brownson* accused the doctrines of Combe and S of fatalism that denies men accountability for either vice or virtue (''Pretensions of Phrenology,'' *BoQR* [April 1839]: 205–29). Others were more favorably impressed. In an 1846 review of *Phrenology* W. Whitman* averred that phrenology ''has at last gained a position . . . among the sciences'' (*Brooklyn Daily Eagle*, ''Notices of New Books,'' 16 November), while M. Fuller* (*Boston Daily Advertiser*, 27 November 1834) respectfully referred to S as a ''keen observer . . . [who] warned the people of this country that their great danger lay in the want of reverence.'' S's death affected E. Peabody* profoundly: As late as 1836, in a letter to her sister Mary, she admits to being still ''too violently affected by Dr. S's death just at the moment when I thought I might possibly gain from him the resurrection & life.''

Emerson evidently read S's *Outlines of Phrenology* (1832), having borrowed it from the Boston Library Society on 23 October 1837. Of all the Transcendentalists, he returned most often to the subject of phrenology, his many references to phrenology in his published works, letters, and notebooks wavering between cautious hope that it was a grand theory of nature** and his uneasiness that it might be merely ''innocent entertainment.'' In an 1835 letter to Fuller he disparaged S's materialism: ''I had rather not understand in God's world than understand thro' and thro' in . . . S's''; but in a notebook entry in 1842 he expressed a hope that phrenology might develop a useful system for indicating ''the signs of probity, of sanity.'' His views shifted again in ''New England Reformers'' (1844), where he lumped ''the adepts of homoeopathy, of hydropathy, of mesmerism,** of phrenology'' in the same class with foes of leavened bread, defenders of the insect world, and the like. However, disparaging phrenology was easier than dismissing it outright: In ''Fate'' (1851) he gloomily acknowledges the power of temperament as described by S, conceding that man's fate might very well reside in ''his skull, spine, and pelvis.'' Though he never arrived at a final assessment, his most characteristic response appears in ''Demonology'' (1839), where he concedes the possibility that ''a man's fortune may be read . . . in the outlines of the skull, by craniology,'' but concluded that the man who can decipher the spiritual facts these outlines represent has yet to appear.

Writers were quick to recognize the potential phrenology had for accurately delineating human character. ''Awed'' by S's exposition of the laws of human nature in *Education: Its Elementary Principles* (''Lighting the Light,'' *Brooklyn Daily Eagle*, 10 March 1847), Whitman appears to have incorporated S's division of the prepubertal life of a child from infancy through adolescence in the first two sections of his poem ''There Was a Child Went Forth.'' In his earlier works especially, Whitman drew on the concepts and vocabulary of phrenology; however, distinguishing his specific debts to S, as distinct from other authorities—especially Combe and O. S. Fowler—is impossible. This is true for other writers who employed the language and concepts of a more or less generic phrenology in their fiction—most notably Poe,* Melville,* and Hawthorne*—and then only to disparage satirically its vocabulary and pretensions.

References: For important contemporaneous discussions, see [Park Benjamin], ''The Late Dr. S,'' *NEMag* 4 (January 1833): 40–47; ''Dr. S's Works,'' *Boston Literary Magazine* 5 (January 1833): 434–40; and ''Review of S on *Education*,'' *American Annals of Education* 3 (March 1833): 122–28. An exhaustive treatment of S's brief tour in America is Anthony A. Walsh, ''The American Tour of Dr. S,'' *Journal of the History of Medicine* *and Allied Sciences* 27 (April 1972): 187–205. Articles treating generally phrenology's reception among the Transcendentalists include John B. Wilson, ''Phrenology and the Transcendentalists,'' *AL* 28 (May 1956): 220–25; Stephen S. Conroy, ''Emerson and Phrenology,'' *AQ* 16 (summer 1964): 215–18; and Madeleine B. Stern, ''Emerson and Phrenology,'' *SAR* 1984: 213–28. Harold Aspiz recognizes Spurzheimean doctrines in ''Educating the Kosmos,'' *AQ* 18 (winter 1966): 655–66.

Arthur Wrobel

STETSON, CALEB (1793–1870), a Unitarian** minister, was among the regular members of the original Transcendental Club,** which on at least one occasion met at his home in Medford, Massachusetts. S graduated in 1827 from the Harvard Divinity School,** where his contemporaries included R. W. Emerson,* J. F. Clarke,* G. Ripley,* F. H. Hedge,* and G. Bradford.* His pamphlet ''The Apostle Paul, a Unitarian'' was published by the American Unitarian Association in the 1820s. Not an especially vocal or active member of the club, and not a contributor to *The Dial*,** S was nonetheless on friendly terms with Emerson, H. Thoreau,* Ripley, and M. Fuller.* He was in the audience on 31 August 1837 for Emerson's Phi Beta Kappa oration, ''The American Scholar,'' at Harvard and later (with Fuller) for Hedge's oration ''Conservatism and Reform'' on 26 August 1841.

Writing for *The Christian Examiner*** (37 [September 1844]: 274–76), S published a generally favorable review of Fuller's *Summer on the Lakes*, calling it ''a work of varied interest, rich in fine observation; profound reflection and striking anecdote. It breathes throughout a spirit of perfect benignity and love—generous, humane, and free from prejudices of every kind.'' Commenting on the subjective nature of Fuller's observations of Niagara Falls, the plains of Illinois, and Lake Superior, S observed that Fuller recorded ''what is passing in her own soul'' instead of ''the objective realities which present themselves to the senses.'' Sympathetic to Fuller's ''free expression'' of her reflections about the scenes she visited, S was nonetheless critical of the passages about European art and literature as being ''strained, unnatural, and out of place.'' Anticipating later criticism of Fuller's prose, he found her style difficult, suggesting that there is ''something cold, stately, almost *statuesque*, in her language.''

S was peripherally involved in the abolition** movement in New England. When the antislavery women of Concord** held their meeting at Thoreau's cabin at Walden Pond** on 1 August 1846, S joined Emerson and W. H. Channing* in giving speeches. S also joined in the efforts to find a suitable successor to *The Dial*, a new journal that would continue to challenge the conservatism of most periodicals and advance the ideas of reform. With B. Alcott,* T. Parker,* Thoreau, Channing, C. Sumner,* and others, S met at Emerson's house on 15 April 1847 to discuss plans for a new journal, *The Massachusetts Quarterly Review*.** Generally more conservative than his former Harvard classmates, however, S appears to have drifted away from the Transcendentalist circle after the late 1840s.

References: For brief references to S, see *L*, 3:391–92; *JMN*, 10: 54; Harding (1965); Robert N. Hudspeth, *The Letters of Margaret Fuller* (1983–94), 2: 228; Hutchison (1959); and *NET*Dial.

Susan Belasco Smith

STONE, THOMAS TREADWELL (1801–1895), Unitarian** minister, author, reformer, and lecturer, was as Nicholas P. Gilman stated in a necrology ''a born Platonist** and Transcendentalist'' and was in the New England Transcendental movement ''a ready convert and inspired herald.'' He was a personal friend and ally of most of the major Transcendentalists and was variously connected with them in pulpit exchanges, literary endeavors, and reform activities.

S's background and early training were Calvinistic, but from the beginning, he was sympathetic to Broad Church views. He preached in orthodox Congregational churches in Andover, Maine (1824–30), and in East Machias, Maine (1832–36). At the latter he developed into a superior literary scholar, an eloquent and erudite minister, and an active social reformer who espoused the causes temperance,** pacificism, women's suffrage, and abolitionism.** The last of these became a passion with him. He was a personal friend of the martyred abolitionist editor Elijah Parish Lovejoy. He was associated in the antislavery cause with J. G. Whittier,* W. L. Garrison,* W. Phillips,* Edmund Quincy, T. Parker,* George B. Emerson, and John Quincy Adams. In East Machias he began to embrace the thought of the Boston-area Transcendentalists. S first met R. W. Emerson* at Waterford, Maine, in summer 1832 and shortly thereafter entertained him at Bridgton, Maine. They kept in touch through S's correspondence with Emerson's aunt M. M. Emerson,* and periodically visited in each other's homes. B. Alcott* numbered S with the members of the Transcendental Club** (''Conversations on the Transcendental Club,'' 1), but there is no record of what meetings he attended. He and Emerson quite likely kept their friendship fresh in these meetings. Emerson, M. Fuller,* and F. H. Hedge* enlisted him in 1840 as a contributor to *The Dial*.** Two pieces from his pen eventually appeared in the journal: ''Man and the Ages'' (January 1841), a Transcendental essay, and ''Calvinist's Letter'' (January 1842), a part of a letter written originally to M. M. Emerson in which S assessed the strengths and weaknesses of the Transcendentalists' faith. He found their faith too weak and uncertain (an opinion with which Emerson agreed). He was asked to submit other pieces to *The Dial* but never found time to do so. He did, however, on 14 April 1847 meet in Concord** with Emerson, Parker, Alcott, and several others to discuss establishing a journal to succeed *The Dial*. The result was the founding of the mundane *Massachusetts Quarterly Review*** (1847–50).

S's desire to learn more of Transcendentalism prompted him to convert to Unitarianism and accept a call to become the pastor of the First Church (Unitarian) in Salem in 1846. Here, sometimes to the distress of a few of his parishioners, he exchanged pulpits from time to time with Parker and other controversial Transcendentalist ministers. At his home at 360 Essex Street he often entertained his Transcendentalist friends and notable literati. Alcott conducted his Conversations** there. Emerson, N. Hawthorne,* S. P. Hawthorne,* E. Peabody,* and J. Very* were sometimes his guests. G. Ripley* and C. Dana* discussed the Brook Farm** enterprise in his parlor. His ministry at the First Church came to an abrupt end in 1852, when as a consequence of his uncompromising antislavery views and insistence upon hiring a church pew to a Negro, he was voted out of his pulpit by a majority of one. Unbitter and undaunted he soon settled over the Unitarian Church in Bolton, Massachusetts, where he served until 1860. Here he found more time for reading, writing, and lecturing. Two books published in this period are quite Transcendental in spirit and content: *Sermons* (1854) and *The Rod and the Staff* (1856), a collection of religious, social, and philosophical essays. Both books place S in the liberal wing of the Unitarian Church, but the second especially is an apologetic for a Transcendental faith. In it the thoughts on such matters as the primacy of spirit, immanence,** and intuition are much the same as those held by Emerson. At Bolton he continued to conduct lectures before lyceums** and various societies, notable instances being before the Salem Lyceum in 1854–55 on European history, and the Lowell Institute in Boston in 1858 on British literature. These lectures were not published, but reports and summaries in the newspapers attest to their excellence and their success. He delivered an important address (later published) entitled "The Preacher" before the senior class at the Harvard Divinity School** on 13 July 1856. Somewhat reminiscent of Emerson's famous address of 1838, it was a call for the young divines to draw from within themselves and not become too attached to historical Christianity. His final ministerial charge was over the First Ecclesiastical Society in Brooklyn, Connecticut, from 1863 to 1871, where, with most of the causes he had championed either won or vindicated, he continued to preach in a Transcendental spirit. E. E. Hale* wrote to William B. Weeden on 15 July 1866: "I hear that dear T T. S is preaching for your people today. The wisest, kindest, loveliest of mankind, lives utterly in the seventh heaven now, and is so far unfitted for communion with the earth, but excellent for an occasional lark-song heard from the empyrean above, which makes us wonder why we do not at daybreak go out into the present Heaven every morning."

REFERENCES: The best account of S's life is in *Heralds*, 3: 358–60, much of which originally appeared in Nicholas P. Gilman, "TTS, D.D.," *ChReg*, 28 November 1895, 785. The best accounts of his connections with the major Transcendentalists are Cooke* (1902) and *NET*Dial. The library at Bowdoin College, S's alma mater (Class of 1820), has a large body of miscellaneous holographic manuscripts and printed materials related to S's life and career. The Boston Public Library, Massachusetts Historical Society, and Houghton and Divinity School Libraries at Harvard University hold small but important deposits of letters and documents by and about S. Substantial references to and sometimes letters by and to S appear in the published journals** and letters of most of those in the Transcendental circle. A few are Leonora Cranch Scott, *The Life and Letters of Christopher Pearse Cranch** (1917); *JMN* and *L*; and Nancy Craig Simmons, *The Letters of*

Mary Moody Emerson (1993). For Francis, see *SAR* 1991: 53; for Hale, Edward E. Hale, Jr., *The Life and Letters of Edward Everett Hale* (1917), 2:87.

Guy R. Woodall

STORY, WILLIAM WETMORE (1819–1895), was an expatriate American sculptor whose success also as a poet, essayist, and attorney encouraged his intimates to believe he was an original ''Renaissance man.'' While S found current intellectual movements interesting, he never formally subscribed to any, including Transcendentalism; instead, during brief sojourns in Italy in the 1840s, and as a permanent resident after 1856, he served aesthetic and political ideas by facilitating them among his many American and English friends who gathered at his studio on Rome's Via Sistina. From the 1840s on, S was a key figure in Italy's Anglo-American communities, which over time included M. Fuller,* N. and S. Hawthorne,* Robert and Elizabeth Barrett Browning, H. Greenough,* Harriet Hosmer, J. R. Lowell,* and H. Powers.*

Reared in the elite circles of Cambridge and Boston and a graduate of Harvard and the Harvard Law School, S was always inclined to mix careers. In the 1840s, when he was beginning a successful law practice and serving as a commissioner on the Massachusetts federal courts, he also delivered the Phi Beta Kappa poem at Harvard, wrote several essays and poems for the *Boston Miscellany* and Lowell's *Pioneer*, and published two books on the law and a volume of poems—all between 1844 and 1847. His interests also included music, modeling in clay, and painting, but literature and law vied for his principal attentions until 1847, when he accepted a commission from Mount Auburn Cemetery for a statue of his father, the eminent jurist Joseph Story.

Balancing for a time between a career in art and a new life in Italy or a return to the law and America, S elected the former. Appreciation of his art was slow in coming, but after his earliest marbles, *Cleopatra* and *Lybian Sibyl*, were acclaimed at the International Exhibition in London in 1862, S was never without patrons. Art historians agree that, along with those early pieces, *Medea* (1864), *Salome* (1870), *Jerusalem in Her Desolation* (1873), and *Alcestis* (1874)—ideal representations of literary and religious subjects executed in the classical style—are S's most enduring works. At the same time, his early literary efforts anticipated later achievements such as *The Life and Letters of Joseph Story* (1851); *Roba di Roma* (1862), a collection of essays recreating midcentury Italy for American readers; *The Proportion of the Human Figure* (1866), art criticism and theory; and occasional poems, plays, and ''idyls.''

In the end, S always returned to his sculpture, and it is in that field that his reputation remains measured today. He often feared that as a master of many talents he bore a multiple risk of being remembered for none. Yet in their respective views, Hawthorne, his closest American friend, and H. James,* his biographer, preserve S's luster. S and his ''magnificent'' *Cleopatra* are featured in the preface to *The Marble Faun*, where Hawthorne argues S's claim in public testimony that equals remarks in private such as these from his *French and Italian Notebooks*: "Mr. S is the most variously accomplished and brilliant person—the fullest of social life and fire—whom I have ever met" (4 October 1858). But the ultimate compliment to S's achievement remains that from James, who opened *WWS and His Friends* with this testimony: "[H]e . . . succeeded in living the real life of his mind."

References: S is prominent in the private writings of most authors and artists who frequented Italy's Anglo-American communities from the 1840s to the 1890s; Fuller, Hawthorne, Lowell, and the Brownings provide the most sustained commentary. James, *WWS and His Friends*, 2 vols. (1903), remains the standard biography; Mary E. Phillips, *Reminiscences of WWS, the American Sculptor and Author* (1897), is useful for its full chronology of S's career, otherwise lacking in James. William H. Gerdts, Jr., "WWS," *American Art Journal* 4 (November 1972): 16–33, briefly revisits S's career in sculpture.

Ronald A. Bosco

STOWE, HARRIET BEECHER (1811–1896), daughter of the eminent Congregationalist minister Lyman Beecher, is best remembered for the epic antislavery novel *Uncle Tom's Cabin*, first published in 1851. Raised under the strict rule of her father, who preached the Calvinist doctrines of human depravity and irresistible grace, HB found Transcendentalist teachings incompatible with her own religious orientation.

Enrolling at age 12 in the Hartford Female Seminary, founded by her sister, Catherine, H continued her religious education. In 1832, the entire clan moved to Cincinnati, Ohio, where Lyman Beecher assumed the presidency of the Lane Theological Seminary, and in 1836, H married Calvin Ellis Stowe, a professor of biblical literature at Lane. Although she gave birth to seven children, S found the time to write—publishing domestic sketches and sentimental tales. In 1850, however, passage of the Fugitive Slave Act fueled her desire to write a powerful antislavery tract that preached the need for Christian compassion. An immediate best-seller, *Uncle Tom's Cabin* sold nearly 3 million copies prior to the Civil War. Legend has it that when she met President Lincoln in 1863, he greeted her as "the little lady who made this big war." S insisted throughout her lifetime, however, that God was the author of the novel; she was simply the instrument through which he spoke.

Although never considered part of the tight New England literary circle, S was acquainted with many of its members. With Holmes* and Whittier* she was friendly; Lowell* she held in especial high esteem. While initially critical of Hawthorne's* writing, she came to admire his artistry. R. W. Emerson,* however, epitomized Transcendentalism, and S was disinclined to accept his work. Of her writing, however, Emerson was somewhat more generous, praising *Uncle Tom's Cabin* in his essay "Success" for its ability to speak "to the universal heart."

References: The success of *Uncle Tom's Cabin* tends to eclipse S's other work, which was considerable. In addition to a second antislavery novel, *Dred* (1856), other major works include *The Mayflower; or, Sketches of Scenes and Characters among the De-*

*scendants of the Puritans*** (1843); *The Minister's Wooing* (1859); *The Pearl of Orr's Island: A Story of the Coast of Maine* (1862); *Oldtown Folks* (1869); *Lady Byron Vindicated* (1870); *Palmetto-Leaves* (1873); and *Poganuc People: Their Loves and Lives* (1878). Annie Fields's *Life and Letters of HBS* (1897) is perhaps the best biography by a contemporary of S. Forrest Wilson's Pulitzer Prize–winning *Crusader in Crinoline: The Life of HBS* (1941) remains invaluable. Edward Charles Wagenknecht's *HBS: The Known and the Unknown* (1965) is highly informative and thoroughly rendered. And see Joan D. Hedrick, *HBS: A Life* (1994).

Denise D. Knight

STRAUSS, DAVID FRIEDRICH (1808–1874), German theologian, was only 27 when he wrote *Das Leben Jesu kritisch bearbeitet* (The life of Jesus critically examined), perhaps the most controversial theological work of the 19th century. Although S was to pursue a distinguished career as a theologian, politician, and man of letters, none of his later writings had the impact or influence of this, his first book. It forced the Transcendentalists to reconsider their assumptions about the historical Jesus.

When *Das Leben Jesu* was published, in 1835, two opposed camps of New Testament interpreters dominated the German theological scene. The supernaturalists believed, with most ordinary Christians, that the Gospel narratives were literally true. By contrast, the rationalists, among whose ranks numbered many prominent intellectuals, held that although the Gospels were generally historical, the stories of the miracles** were merely exaggerated or misinterpreted accounts of mundane events. S in his book demolishes both positions; neither, he argues, can explain the Gospels without falling into contradictions and absurdities. Instead, he proposes a disturbingly plausible alternative: The Gospels were made up almost entirely of myths. These had arisen as early Christians sought to make the story of Jesus' life conform to their messianic expectations, which existed quite independently of him. S concluded that almost nothing could be known about the historical Jesus. Christianity, he thought, must be rebuilt on new foundations and in Hegelian* terms as a religion of humanity.

Among the New England Transcendentalists, S probably had the greatest direct influence on T. Parker.* Parker is supposed to have read one of the first copies of *Das Leben Jesu* to reach Boston and wrote the first substantial review the book received in America (*Christian Examiner*** [July 1840]). He even took the title of what became his most famous sermon, *A Discourse of the Transient and Permanent in Christianity* (1841), from an essay S published in 1838, ''Über Vergängliches und Bleibendes im Christenthum'' (later translated as *Soliloquies on the Christian Religion* [1845]). Although Parker rejected S's radically negative conclusions—maintaining that the words and general character of Jesus, at least, could still be known—he admired S for his brilliance and for his bravery in raising fundamental questions about the origins of Christianity. S helped convince Parker that the Gospels were not reliable historical documents and that the Christian miracles were not historical events.

References: The standard English translation of *Life of Jesus* remains that of George Eliot, first published in London in 1846; see the valuable introduction by Peter Hodgson to the Fortress Press edition (1972). A useful account of S's life and work is Horton Harris, *DFS and His Theology* (1973). For S's influence in America, see Pochmann (1957); and Dean Grodzins, ''The Transient and Permanent in Theodore Parker's Christianity,'' *PUUHS* 22:1 (1990–91):1–18.

Dean David Grodzins

SUMNER, CHARLES (1811–1874), senator from Massachusetts (1851–74), began his political career as an opponent of slavery. Having graduated from Harvard College (1830) and Harvard Law School (1834), S eventually became acquainted with many of New England's leading intellectuals and writers including H. W. Longfellow,* Dr. W. E. Channing,* and W. Phillips.* As an early opponent of slavery, S, like R. W. Emerson,* H. Thoreau,* B. Alcott,* and others among the Transcendentalists, opposed the admission of Texas into the Union as a slave state in 1845. In the same year, S followed the example of Emerson in boycotting the New Bedford Lyceum** because of their racist membership policy. S's letter of protest, along with Emerson's, was later published in the *Liberator* (16 January 1846). Earlier in August Emerson had the opportunity to hear directly from this outspoken young man. Invited to deliver the annual Phi Beta Kappa Address at Harvard, S, to the chagrin of some Harvard officials who wished to avoid the topic of slavery entirely, celebrated Dr. Channing's commitment to antislavery principles and urged his audience, using Channing's words, ''to free themselves from all support of slavery.'' Emerson was delighted with the performance and recorded in his journal** the observation, ''At Phi Beta Kappa S's oration was marked with a certain magnificence which I do not know well where to parallel.''

In spring 1851 S was elected to the United States Senate from the Free Soil Party and began what would be a long and distinguished career. Coincidentally, at this same time, in his first foray into the political arena, Emerson was campaigning throughout the Middlesex District delivering his acerbic ''Fugitive Slave Law Address'' (1851 [*W*, 11:177–214]) in an unsuccessful effort to elect J. G. Palfrey* to Congress, also on the Free Soil ticket. S was delighted with Emerson's stump oration, which was widely reported, and wrote to him that ''your judgment of the Fugitive Slave Bill posterity will adopt, even if the men of our day do not.''

Emerson, and several other Transcendentalists, admired S because, in many ways, he seemed to be an unpolitical politician. That is, he placed principle first and never compromised for purposes of political expediency. Indeed, shortly after his election to the Senate, T. Parker* wrote to S and reminded him, ''You told me once that you were in morals, not in politics. Now I hope you will show that you are still in morals, although in politics. I hope you will be the *senator with a conscience*.''

Thoreau's acquaintance with S began in 1850 when he went to Fire Island to look for M. Fuller's* body and found instead S's brother who had also been drowned. The two remained friends for the rest of Thoreau's life. Four years later Henry sent S one of the first copies of *Walden*.

S's opposition to slavery became even more strident throughout the first half of the decade of the 1850s, culminating with his famous ''Crime Against Kansas'' speech in May 1856 in which he attacked in scathing terms the position taken by Senators Butler from South Carolina and Mason from Virginia. The speech included personal invective, and in response, on 22 May, S was attacked and severely beaten on the floor of the Senate by Rep. Preston Brooks of South Carolina, a nephew of Senator Butler. S would not completely recover from his injuries for three years. Transcendentalists, abolitionists,** and others throughout the North were shocked by this act of barbarism. An indignation meeting was held in Concord** on 26 May and Emerson delivered his famous ''Assault upon Mr. S'' speech (*W*, 11:245–52), in which he attacked the slave oligarchy soundly. He asserted, ''I think we must get rid of slavery, or we must get rid of freedom.''

Eventually S recovered from his wounds and resumed his Senate seat from whence he continued to wage his war against slavery and social injustice until his death in 1874. Throughout this period, Emerson remained a strong and vocal supporter of the senator and, joined by J. G. Whittier,* would serve as a pallbearer at his funeral.

References: S's writings appear as *CS, His Complete Works*, with an introduction by George Frisbee Hoar, 20 vols. (1900; rpt. 1969). An interesting early biography by a friend of E. W. Emerson,* and S's onetime secretary, is Moorfield Storey, *CS* (1900). Substantive later biographical studies are David H. Donald, *CS and the Coming of the Civil War* (1960), and *CS and the Rights of Man* (1970). On Emerson's relationship with S, see Gougeon (1990). Also of interest is Bill Ledbetter, ''CS: Political Activist for the New England Transcendentalists,'' *The Historian, a Journal of History* 44 (May 1982): 347–63.

Len Gougeon

T

TAPPAN, CAROLINE STURGIS (1819–1888), minor Transcendentalist poet, was a lifelong friend of both R. W. Emerson* and M. Fuller.* Daughter of wealthy maritime merchant prince William Sturgis and Elizabeth M. Davis, she met Fuller in 1832, following her mother's temporary—and traumatic—departure from home. For the adventurous, impressionable girl, Fuller became a mentor. At first an ardent student, for a period in the late 1830s C was suddenly a hesitant correspondent, for her father saw Fuller as a bad influence. Their friendship revived, only to falter again as Fuller devoted herself to the mentoring of Anna Barker (Ward).* They settled on a regular, if not intimate, friendship up until Fuller's death in 1850; to C, Fuller confided the details of her stay in Italy.

On 22 July 1836, when Fuller came to Concord** to meet Emerson, she brought along C; Emerson had known Captain Sturgis and probably knew C as a little girl; his friendship with her as an adult would last the rest of his life. During the next decade, C, relishing her unsettled life, came often to Concord. She befriended the prominent figures there, enjoying a brief love affair and longtime friendship with E. Channing* and sharing the Old Manse** for a while with the Hawthornes.* CS had some of her poems—including "Bettina," "Light in Shade," and "Windmill"—published in *The Dial*.** Emerson linked her poetry with Channing's as "honest, great, but crude." Her best poems, he later assessed, "are blasphemies, which greatly take me." Of S personally, Emerson was quite fond, eventually calling her "the Ideal Friend." "Of all the persons I know," he wrote in his journal,** "this child, called romantic & insane & exaggerating, is the most real." Like Fuller, S had strong feelings for the paternal Emerson, which infringed upon his concepts of propriety (he encouraged a fraternal relationship); but unlike Fuller, she probably did not fall in love with him. While evidently captivated by her youth and enthusiasm (as he would be later with Barker), Emerson was sure to keep their relationship fraternal: "my Parian sister," he called her.

S eventually discarded her once-ardent Transcendentalism as she married, inherited her father's fortune, had two children, and reensconced herself in upper-crust New England society. The Tappans were close friends of the James* family and played host to prominent New Englanders. They rented their Lenox home to the Hawthornes in the early 1850s, an agreement that ended unhappily.

References: S wrote *The Magician's Show Box, and Other Stories* (1887). George Dimock emphasizes her break with Transcendentalism, as illustrated in her photographs of Europe, in *CST and the Grand Tour: A Collection of 19th Century Photographs* (1982). C. K. Newcomb's* letters to S are at the Houghton Library at Harvard. See also Francis Dedmond, ed., "The Letters of CS and Margaret Fuller," *SAR* 1988: 201–51; on their relationship, Laurie James, *Men, Women, and Margaret Fuller* (1990). For S's relationship with Emerson, see Gay Wilson Allen, *Waldo Emerson* (1981) and *JMN*.

David Hicks

TAYLOR, EDWARD THOMPSON (1793–1871), preacher at the Seamen's Bethel in Boston and model for H. Melville's* Father Mapple in *Moby-Dick*, epitomized intuitive, natural eloquence to his age. His celebrated extemporaneous sermons—marked by nautical imagery and wit—deeply moved common sailors, politicians, and writers alike. Charles Dickens, H. Martineau,* and W. Whitman* wrote of his power, as did R. W. Emerson,* who called him "that living Methodist, the Poet of the Church." Emerson contemplated "Taylor's muse" with wonder: "It is a panorama of images from all nature** & art, whereon the sun & stars shine but go up to it & nothing is there. His instinct unconscious instinct is the nucleus or point of view, & this defies science & eludes it."

Born in Richmond, Virginia, to unknown parents, T went to sea at age seven. Captured by the British during the War of 1812, he began preaching for his fellow prisoners. The Methodist Conference assigned him a circuit along the Massachusetts coast in 1819, and in 1829 he was called to minister to seamen in Boston. In 1833 he moved into the new Bethel he would make an international mecca for almost 40 years.

An evangelical Methodist, "Father" T was no Transcendentalist and thought T. Parker* bound for hell. Impatient with doctrine and impulsively good-hearted, he was otherwise tolerant of other sects, being on especially good terms with Boston Unitarians,** who had helped fund the Bethel and other projects. The rugged "sailor preacher" remained fond of the contrastingly mild Emerson, who as pastor of Second Church had briefly been T's contemporary in the Boston ministry and supported his work; in 1835, two and a half years after resigning his own pulpit, Emerson preached for T in the Bethel (*Sermons*, 4: 236–43). Though T could not fathom Emerson's position on the Lord's Supper,** he was quick to defend his young friend against snide comments by the orthodox, in one anecdote declaring that "Mr. Emerson might think this or that, but he was more like Jesus Christ than any one he had ever known." T lectured before the Transcendental Club** in 1840 and occasionally stayed with the Emersons in

Concord.** Emerson was astonished by the broad appeal of T, who, when he preached in Concord on 22 June 1845, attracted area ministers and farmers as well as H. Thoreau,* H. Mann,* and E. Channing.*

T labored tirelessly on behalf of sailors and their families, but—except for temperance**—he had little interest in the reforms that kindled Transcendentalists' enthusiasm. Though he held forth passionately on the dangers of demon rum, his mercurial nature and hot temper made him unsuited for leadership of any movement. His enduring appeal for the likes of Emerson was his compelling eloquence. "There is beauty in that man," Emerson wrote to M. Fuller,* "& when he is well alive with his own exhortations it flows out from all the corners of his great heart & steeps the whole rough man in its gracious element." Even more than orator-heroes like E. Everett* and D. Webster,* Father T seemed rhetorically and physically suffused with the glory of his vision—nature's own preacher.

References: The most complete biography, richly anecdotal but occasionally unreliable, is Gilbert Haven and Thomas Russell, *Father T, the Sailor Preacher* (1872). Useful but somewhat derivative is Robert Collyer, *Father T* (1906). Good overviews are Allan MacDonald, "A Sailor Among the Transcendentalists," *NEQ* 8 (September 1935): 307–19, and R. E. Watters, "Boston's Salt-Water Preacher," *SAQ* 45 (July 1946): 350–61. Because T did not publish his sermons, eyewitness reports are valuable. A newspaper account and commentary are presented in Sargent Bush, "The Pulpit Artistry of Father T: An 1836 Account," *AL* 50 (March 1978): 106–9. Emerson's friendship with T is surveyed in John McAleer, *Ralph Waldo Emerson: Days of Encounter* (1984), 170–77. T's literary impact is cited in David S. Reynolds, *Beneath the American Renaissance* (1988).

Wesley T. Mott

THERIEN, ALEK (1812–1885), was the French Canadian woodchopper and day laborer whose portrait is drawn by H. Thoreau* in the "Visitors" chapter of *Walden*, although his name does not appear in the text. T, like the Irish workers Thoreau also describes, belonged to a growing but largely invisible immigrant labor class in New England. He lived in a succession of boardinghouses in the Concord** and Lincoln area and, at one time, perhaps inspired by the example of Thoreau himself, lived alone in a shanty of his own construction in the Lincoln woods. He later married, had three children born during the 1860s, and died in Concord. Besides his portrayal in *Walden* and occasional mention in Thoreau's journal,** T is also the source of a well-known anecdote about Thoreau that R. W. Emerson* recorded in his journal in 1862, just before Thoreau's death: "T came to see Thoreau on business, but Thoreau at once perceived that he had been drinking; and advised him to go home & cut his throat, and that speedily. T did not well know what to make of it, but went away, & Thoreau said, he learned that he had been repeating it about town, which he was glad to hear, & hoped that by this time he had begun to understand what it meant."

Despite his foreign ancestry, in *Walden* T is portrayed as thoroughly naturalized and resembles, with his axe and dog and ability to live off the land, the figure of the frontiersman as much as the immigrant laborer. Along with the somewhat similar character of the Irishman John Field in ''Baker Farm,'' T is one of the few significant human presences in *Walden* besides Thoreau himself. As drawn, he is a foil for the narrator, a man thoroughly at home and happy in his life and in nature** but without much evidence of other development: ''But the intellectual and what is called spiritual man in him were slumbering as in an infant.'' Although the narrator blames T's lack of intellectual development in part on his education by Catholic priests in Canada, his character serves to complicate and even potentially to call into question the narrator's own quest for spiritual enlightenment. T not only resists Thoreau's efforts to get him to take a higher view of things, but he also demonstrates that human life in nature flows in many productive channels, not all of them uplifting. Like the sometimes tragic lives of *Walden*'s ''Former Inhabitants,'' T's life is a counterpoint to Thoreau's own and hints at forces that could constrain the narrator's optimistic quest for transcendence. But he appears only briefly in this one chapter, so his character is only sketchily drawn at best. The narrator never solves the puzzle of T's life or encounters him again but instead becomes progressively more absorbed in the possibilities of his own transcendent relation with nature.

REFERENCE: The only detailed consideration of Thoreau's relationship with T is Robert Bradford, ''Thoreau and T,'' *AL* 34 (1963): 499–506.

Robert Sattelmeyer

THOREAU, HENRY DAVID (1817–1862), was one of the defining figures of American Transcendentalism. Born and raised in Concord, Massachusetts,** T was educated at Harvard but received his direction in life from the writings and friendship of R. W. Emerson.* T became a writer and, by his own account, a mystic, a naturalist, and a Transcendentalist. He was also, at various times, a teacher, a pencil-maker, and a land surveyor. He never married; he lived almost his entire life in Concord, most of it at his family's home, with brief sojourns at Walden Pond,** at Emerson's home, and at Emerson's brother's home on Staten Island. Briefest of all was his sojourn in Concord Jail following his arrest for nonpayment of his poll tax, an event that led to his feisty and celebrated essay ''Civil Disobedience''** (first published in 1849 as ''Resistance to Civil Government''). T also wrote against slavery and in favor of J. Brown,* though most of his life was devoted to writing about nature.** From his first book, *A Week on the Concord and Merrimack Rivers* (1849), to his posthumous volumes *The Maine Woods* (1864) and *Cape Cod* (1865), to his 2-million word *Journal* (1906), and his unfinished projects on the dispersion of seeds and the ripening of fruits, T produced a body of writing on nature and our place in nature that remains the standard against which subsequent similar work has been measured.

His greatest book, *Walden; or, Life in the Woods* (1854), is the prose epic not only of Transcendentalism but of *practical* Transcendentalism. It is concerned with ''that economy of living which is synonymous with philosophy.''

In his life and writings, T sought to reattach the philosophy of transcendental idealism** to real life.

Readers doggedly remain dubious of Transcendentalism, both as a word and as an activity because we suspect, rightly enough, that its mere existence implies a rebuke to the ordinary pursuits that constitute and consume our own lives. Even in its own day, Transcendentalism quickly became a byword for nonsense and moonshine. Kant,** Schelling,* and Coleridge* all tried to guard against misunderstanding by making a sharp distinction between the *transcendental method*, which they defined—and approved of—as ''the patient and rigorous analysis of experience itself,'' and *transcendent*, by which they meant—and meant to condemn—''any question or theorem which might pass beyond possible experience.'' T was aware of this problem of terminology, but to his credit, he did not adopt this confusing and hair-splitting distinction. He is as interested in the transcendental method as any, but he also uses the word *transcendent* in its ordinary English sense (according to Samuel Johnson's *Dictionary*) of ''excellent, supremely excellent, passing others'' as when he refers to the ''transcendent beauty of the pickerel'' in chapter 16 of *Walden*. We should be clear about what Transcendentalism did not mean to T. It was not an interest in anything that transcends—in the sense of rejects—experience but rather an interest in a fuller experience than that offered by materialism. T's Transcendentalism embraces, supplements, and completes ordinary experience. The higher life, the higher consciousness includes the lower, although it finds the lower insufficient by itself.

T accepted the label of Transcendentalist, just as he accepted the fact that it set him apart. Reflecting, in 1853, on an inquiry from the secretary of the Association for the Advancement of Science as to what branch of science he was interested in, T noted in his journal** for 5 March, ''The fact is I am a mystic, a transcendentalist and a natural philosopher to boot.''

Walden is T's book-length effort to translate transcendental idealism from an abstract and technical discussion in the work of a few professional philosophers into a generally accessible and even practicable way of life. *Walden* is a manual for the practicing Transcendentalist; it belongs on the shelf with the great enchiridions and devotional handbooks. If William Law hadn't already used the phrase, *Walden* could have been titled *A Serious Call to a Devout and Holy Life in Nature*.

The first chapter of *Walden*, both in its title (''Economy'') and its subject matter (food, shelter, clothing, fuel, wages, and expenses), is a considered reply to the charge that Transcendentalism is oblivious to the hard material facts of life. T shows how we can free ourselves for what he calls the ''finer fruits of life'' by reducing our material wants to workable minimums. He indulges in no cheap talk about transcending material life—indeed, he relishes it—but he is impatient with the contracted horizons of the purely material life and, worst of all, the meandering drift of comfortable lives that see no farther than the next meal. ''I went to the woods,'' he writes in chapter 2, ''because I wished to live deliberately, to front the essential facts of life, and see if I could not learn what it had to teach, and not, when I came to die, discover that I had not lived.''

This appetite for experience is an important aspect of Thoreauvian Transcendentalism. *Walden* undertakes by means of what may be called T's transcendental procedure to establish and clarify a transcendental point of view. For every material fact or observation, T finds a transcendental counterpart. The transcendental vision wishes to see past the surfaces of things. ''I perceive that we inhabitants of New England live this mean life that we do because our vision does not penetrate the surface of things. We think that *is* which *appears* to be.'' T's greatest desire is for that classical transcendental attribute, truth. ''Rather than love, than money, than fame, give me truth,'' he wrote in the last chapter of *Walden*.

What are the classical transcendental attributes? For Plato,** Aristotle, and Plotinus,** the ''transcendentals'' were those conceptions of being that transcended Aristotle's ten categories of being. (The ten kinds of things that Aristotle said can be predicated of an object are substance, quantity, quality, relation, location, duration, position, state, activity, and passivity.) Transcending these material attributes are the attributes of unity, truth, goodness, and beauty. Albertus Magnus, following Avicenna, added *res* (thingness) and *aliquid* (otherness) to the list of transcendentals. Aquinas's list comprised thingness, unity, otherness, truth, and goodness. In the late 18th century Kant redefined transcendentals, considering them no longer as attributes of being but rather as logical conditions preliminary to the comprehension of any object. In his *Critique of Pure Reason*, Kant wrote, ''I apply the term transcendental to all knowledge which is not so much occupied with objects as with the mode of our cognition of those objects.'' For Kant, the transcendentals were elements of the basic structures of consciousness. Far from being the products of experience, they were the built-in aspects of mind that provide us access to what we call experience. Schelling works this out most completely in his *System of Transcendental Idealism* (1800), in which he shows, according to Copleston, ''how the ultimate immanent principle of consciousness produces the objective world as the condition of its attainment of self-consciousness.''

The ideas of Kant and Schelling came first to America via de Staël,** Carlyle,* and Coleridge. Building on all of them, Emerson wrote in ''The Transcendentalist'' (1841) that Transcendentalism ''affirms facts not affected by the illusions of sense, facts which are of the same nature as the faculty which reports them.'' He argued that while the materialist ''took his departure from the natural world,'' the idealist—the Transcendentalist—''takes his departure from his consciousness.'' Emerson's transcendentals or transcendental realities are ''the eternal triangle of truth, beauty and goodness.'' He gives a peculiarly American twist to the subject by insisting that Transcendentalists ''are lovers of nature also, and find an indemnity in the inviolable order of the world for the violated order and grace of man.'' The way back to human wholeness lies through nature. This is so because, as Schelling puts it in a bold formulation, nature is externalized mind, and mind is internalized nature.

T pushes every subject in *Walden* until it yields a transcendental correlative, a truth. In chapter 3, ''Reading,'' he urges us not just to read but to read the best books; then he goes on to urge us to read not books but our own lives. In ''Sounds'' he attends not only to written language but to ''the language which all things and events speak.'' The transcendental method is to interrogate everything until it gives up a higher sense; the transcendental point of view assures him that such a method will in fact work. Business becomes the business of living; from hunting stories he moves to proposing that we become hunters and fishers of men. Instead of going around the world to explore the blank spots on the map, he urges us to explore our own higher latitudes. He planted beans his first year at Walden Pond but found that beans were not enough. ''I will not plant beans and corn with so much industry another summer, but such seeds, if the seed is not lost, as sincerity, truth, simplicity, faith, innocence and the like.''

In chapter 9, ''The Ponds,'' which is for many readers the symbolic and spiritual center of the book, T first describes in minute and affectionate detail the shape and depth of the pond, its banks, its bottom, and the levels, sources, and clarity of its water. T's love of the natural world, in and for itself, has been often imitated but seldom equaled. Perhaps this is because for him the natural world, though never to be relinquished, is never quite enough. What T was really measuring, as he patiently sounded and probed back and forth across the pond, were his own depths. Remarkably, he knew this at the time. ''A lake is the landscape's most beautiful and expressive feature,'' he wrote. ''It is earth's eye; looking into which the beholder measures the depth of his own nature.'' And there is something beyond even that perception. Walden becomes a character in its own book and T says, ''[O]f all the characters I have known, perhaps Walden wears best, and best preserves its purity.'' He sees that while life is marked by change, Walden is the same as it always was; it is ''the same water which my youthful eyes fell on; and all the change is in me.'' Of all T's interlocutors, Walden best recalls him to his own purest self, and then to something altogether beyond that self. Gazing at the pond, he is struck anew. ''Why, here is Walden, the same woodland lake that I discovered so many years ago . . . the same thought is welling up to its surface that was then; it is the same liquid joy and happiness to itself its Maker, ay, and it *may* be to me.'' There is a sober note of caution in that ''*may*,'' but it is clear nevertheless that T recognizes the deepest truth about himself and about life as he looks into the pond. Narcissus saw only his own reflection in the pool. T sees that as well, but beneath it he also sees the maker of both pool and reflection. ''He rounded this water with his hand, and deepened and clarified it in his thought, and in his will bequeathed it to Concord. I see by its face that it is visited by the same reflection; and I can almost say, Walden, is it you?''

T's transcendental method becomes most pronounced and explicit in the last three chapters of *Walden*. For every natural fact, there is a corresponding spiritual or imaginative fact. After carefully sounding the pond (107 feet at the deepest point) he declares, ''[Y]et not an inch of it can be spared by the imagination.'' He found by measurement that Walden is deepest just where the straight line representing its widest point intersects the straight line representing its greatest length. The same rule holds true in ethics, he says. ''Draw lines through the length and breadth of the aggregate of a man's particular daily behaviour and waves of life into his coves and inlets, and where they intersect will be the height and depth of his character.'' T's Transcendentalism is essentially compatible with science, a subject T became more interested in as he grew older. This is because he understood Transcendentalism not as a rejection of material facts but as a search for the natural laws behind and governing visible facts. ''If we knew all the laws of nature, we should need only one fact, or the description of one actual phenomenon, to infer all the particular results at that point.''

In ''The Pond in Winter,'' T notes that even when the pond is frozen, as people say, ''solid,'' the level of the ice on the pond fluctuates continually. ''It is well known,'' says T of surveying, ''that a level cannot be used on ice.'' What this means to T the scientist, and to T the Transcendentalist, is that even in winter the pond is alive. This is an all-important, a determining idea of *Walden*. Everything in nature is alive and continually changing. ''The very globe continually transcends and translates itself,'' T writes in ''Spring.'' Transcendentalism is, in ''Spring,'' the method of nature itself.

As T became ever more interested in science, he fretted that he was subsiding into a mere data-gatherer and losing his power of imaginative correlation. But his interest in science, which is pronounced from his early *A Week on the Concord and Merrimack Rivers* onward, is not finally hostile to Transcendentalism. His late interests in science show him exploring the minute and particular ways in which nature keeps transcending and transforming itself.

T never lost sight of particulars. At the same time, he never lost the transcendental point of view, and he never abandoned the transcendental method. T saw, with a steadiness of vision attained by no other American writer, that the transcendental is revealed to us through the natural and in no other way. He spent his life seeking the truth, and he found—as we *may*—that it lies everywhere around us. Looking at the reflection of the sky in a hole in the ice of Walden Pond in winter, he says, ''Heaven is under our feet.'' This is the highest, the culminating image or symbol of T's transcendental point of view. ''Men esteem truth remote, in the outskirts of the system, beyond the furthest star, before Adam and after the last man. . . . But all these times and places and occasions are now and here. God himself culminates in the present moment.''

References: For T's writings, see the Walden or Manuscript edition (1906), in 20 vols. Many of the titles have been superseded by the ongoing Princeton edition of The Writings of HD.T (1971–). See also *Corr.* For general treatments of T's life and work, see Harding (1965); and R. D. Richardson, Jr., *HT: A Life of the Mind* (1986). Michael

Meyer's bibliographical essay in Myerson (1984), 260–85, is indispensable. A quarterly bibliography is published in *TSB*.

For the literary side of T's Transcendentalism, see Buell (1973). On T's early work, see K. W. Cameron, *Transcendental Apprenticeship* (1976), and Linck Johnson, *T's Complex Weave: The Writing of* A Week on the Concord and Merrimack Rivers (1986). On the German influence, see Pochmann (1957). For Asian influence and analogs, see Arthur Christy, *The Orient in American Transcendentalism* (1932), and Carl Jackson, *The Oriental Religions and American Thought* (1981). For science and T's thought, see Nina Baym, "T's View of Science," *JHI* 26 (April–June 1965): 221–34; R. D. Richardson, "T and Science," in R. Scholnick, *Science and American Literature* (1992); and Lawrence Buell, *The Environmental Imagination* (1994). Excellent new studies are William Rossi, "Poetry and Progress: T, Lyell,* and the Geological Principles of *A Week*," *AL* 66 (June 1994): 275–300; and Laura Dassow Walls, *Seeing New Worlds* (1995). For T's interest in language, see Philip F. Gura, *The Wisdom of Words* (1981). For philosophical matters, see Frederick Charles Copleston, *A History of Philosophy* (1946), and the articles on Transcendentalism in the *New Catholic Encyclopedia* (1967) and the *Encyclopedia of Religion and Ethics*, ed. James Hastings (1908, 1926).

Robert D. Richardson, Jr.

THOREAU, JOHN, JR. (1815–1842), was a schoolteacher and the older brother of H. Thoreau.* John (and their sister Helen) taught school in order that Henry might go to Harvard College, although most in Concord** thought J the more promising of the Thoreau brothers. From 1839 to 1841, J and Henry ran the Concord Academy together, until J's health failed as a result of tuberculosis, and the school closed. They both courted Ellen Sewall and may have both proposed marriage to her in 1841.

In the fall of 1839 they made the river trip that Henry later retold as *A Week on the Concord and Merrimack Rivers* (1849). The book was initially conceived as a memorial to J, and Henry's evident grief over his brother's death shapes the narrative. On 1 January 1842, J cut his finger while stropping a razor, rapidly developed lockjaw (tetanus), and died on 11 January. His younger brother developed sympathetic psychosomatic symptoms after J's death and did not fully recover for several months. The influences of J's life, rather than his death, on Henry's life included the flute and a detailed bird book that Henry and their younger sister Sophia continued.

REFERENCES: See Harding (1965), esp. 134–37; *PJ* vol. 1; Linck C. Johnson, "Historical Introduction" to *A Week on the Concord and Merrimack Rivers*, ed. Carl F. Hovde, William L. Howarth, and Elizabeth Hall Witherell (1980); Max Cosman, "Apropos of JT," *AL* 12 (May 1940): 241–42; and Joel Myerson, "More Apropos of JT," *AL* 45 (March 1973): 104–6.

Leigh Kirkland

TICKNOR, GEORGE (1791–1871), was a Harvard professor of modern languages whose lectures on language and literature inspired many young men, including W. Emerson,* to study in Europe. T was born in Boston, where his father, Elisha, a former teacher, was a successful businessman. After graduating from Dartmouth in 1807, T apprenticed in a law office and was admitted to the bar in 1813 but lost interest. He toured America, met Thomas Jefferson at Monticello, and traveled to Europe. He studied at the University of Göttingen (1815–17), where he found literature more appealing than theology, and assumed a Harvard professorship in 1819. In 1821 he married Anna Eliot, daughter of prosperous Boston merchant Samuel Eliot. T retired and traveled to Europe in 1835; H. W. Longfellow* took his position.

When T returned home in 1838, he wrote *History of Spanish Literature* (3 vols.) with the advice of historian-friend William Hickling Prescott. T traced the origins of the Spanish language and the progress of Spanish literature to the early 19th century. Sales and reception far exceeded expectations. Considered one of the best literary histories ever written, the work went through several revisions, reaching its definitive edition in 1872. To perfect his language skills and to do research, T traveled several times to Europe, where he met A. von Humboldt,* Mme. de Staël,** Goethe,* Scott, Wordsworth,* and Southey.

Although T's attempts to reform the curriculum by grouping related studies met with resistance from colleagues and Harvard president John Thornton Kirkland, following T's retirement, his wife's nephew, President Charles W. Eliot, implemented this system. T helped found the Boston Public Library in 1852, bequeathing his personal volumes to it, and was a member of the board of visitors at the U.S. Military Academy at West Point.

References: See *Life, Letters and Journals of GT* (1876), with an introduction by Ferris Greenslet. T's works include *Syllabus of a Course of Lectures on the History of Criticism of Spanish Literature* (1832), *Outline of the Principal Events in the Life of General Lafayette* (1825), *Remarks on Changes Lately Proposed or Adopted in Harvard University* (1825), *The Remains of Nathaniel Appleton Haven, with a Memoir of His Life* (1827), *Remarks on the Life and Writings of Daniel Webster** (1831), and *A Lecture on the Best Methods of Teaching the Living Languages* (1833).

Karen L. Kalinevitch

TYNDALL, JOHN (1820–1893), born in Carlow, Ireland, was originally educated as a mechanic and worked as a young man for three years as a railway engineer. His reading of R. W. Emerson* and Carlyle,* to whom he dedicated numerous tributes throughout his life, inspired him to become a scientist. He valued Emerson for stimulating him to act independently and to develop his individual potential. While his friends discouraged him from deserting the security of his engineering career, T first accepted a position as a mathematics and surveying teacher at Queenwood College, Hampshire. Discouraged by a lack of opportunity to do any real scientific work there, T sought further instruction in chemistry, physics, and mathematics at the University of Marburg. While T moved to Germany despite a comparative shortage of money, it exposed him to the cutting-edge natural philosophy he so desired. T earned his Ph.D. from Marburg after attending lectures by noteworthy German scientists such as Robert W. Bunsen.

T's first significant scientific work dealt with magnetism in relation to the density of crystals. This work led to his being named professor of natural philosophy at the Royal Institution in London, where he worked closely with Michael Faraday as a colleague and friend. T succeeded Faraday as superintendent of the Royal Institution upon Faraday's death in 1867. The increasingly renowned natural philosopher remained actively involved with the Royal Institution for the rest of his life. In the course of this career, and as a result of his original interest in the dynamics of crystals, T probed the causes and effects of glacial movement in the formation of the Alps. His on-site studies led to his becoming an enthusiastic mountain climber.

Later, T turned from crystalline solids to study the properties of gases, with which he made his most famous discoveries. His studies of air led him to answer the age-old question of why the sky is blue by demonstrating that air without suspended particles did not reflect light waves, a phenomenon later described in theoretical form by Lord Rayleigh. T's work with suspended particles in air led to his decisive settlement of the dispute over spontaneous generation by demonstrating that the bacteria responsible for food rotting is airborne. This experiment led T to work further on sterilization of liquids, which produced valuable information on the properties of bacteria. T extended his work with particles suspended in air in order to develop more efficient fog signals. For this purpose he conducted several experiments with sound waves to determine the role of clouds in producing acoustic echoes.

T's writings extended the results of his experiments in nontechnical language for a popular audience. Thus, his writings were useful in informing laypeople of 19th-century scientific advances. T's view of science as a tool with which man may effectively deal with his environment was responsible for his highly controversial address to the British Association at Belfast in 1874 in which he discussed the relation between science and theology. Here he presented theology as at odds with the aims of science to uncover objectively the nature of the universe. Hailing in the same breath Darwin* and Carlyle, he discussed the aims of art and science as equally important expressions of separate aspects of the human mind. Art, said T, satisfies man's moral and emotional desires, while science satisfies his desire to understand. Theology functions to stifle these desires and should therefore be regarded, according to T, as hostile to the development of the mind.

References: See A. S. Eve and C. H. Creasey's biography, *Life and Work of JT* (1945). T's own reflections on his life may be found in *Fragments of Science*, vols. 1–2 (1896–97), and in *New Fragments* (1897). T's famous Belfast lecture is recorded in full in *Fragments of Science*, 2: 135–201. The resulting controversy is briefly described in Frothingham* (1876), 210–13. T's reverence for Emerson and the Transcendentalist movement is described in *Fragments of Science* and *New Fragments* and is further documented by ''The Contributor's Club'' (Anon.), *Atl* 73 (Feb. 1894): 281; ''A Tribute to Emerson'' (Anon.), *New York Times*, 27 October 1882, 1; and ''T and Emerson'' (Anon.), London *Telegram*, 28 October 1882.

Elisa E. Beshero

V

VERY, JONES (1813–1880), in his determination to speak and write only as the Spirit bade him, established himself as the quintessential Transcendentalist poet, seeming to fulfill for a short time R. W. Emerson's* call in the Divinity School Address for a "new-born bard of the Holy Ghost." The Transcendental community was divided as to whether V was insane or inspired.

Born in Salem, Massachusetts, V graduated (1836) from Harvard College second in his class. For the next two years he was employed as tutor in Greek at the college while studying at the Harvard Divinity School.** In the meantime, he was writing poetry for college publications as well as for the *Knickerbocker*. He was also breaking into the Transcendentalist circle: E. P. Peabody,* having heard him lecture in Salem, drew him to the attention of Emerson, who, impressed with his promise, entertained him at Concord** and included him in several meetings of the Transcendental Club.** V read Emerson's *Nature* and was probably also influenced by his Divinity School Address of 1838. A few months later, V underwent a mystical experience that profoundly affected his writing and his relationships.

This psychological/spiritual crisis and V's evangelical fervor in communicating his new insights to his Greek class, Harvard professors, and the Unitarian** clergy resulted in his dismissal from Harvard and a one-month confinement at the McLean Asylum. At the time of his institutionalization V was writing an essay on Shakespeare** in which Emerson was much interested, and at about the same time, he began writing a new, ecstatic kind of poetry. When he spent several days in Concord with Emerson shortly following his release from the asylum, Emerson found him fascinating. He was delighted to find a person so free of cant and pretension who was willing to confront directly a visiting minister or Emerson himself on matters of religion and personal integrity. Peabody, to whom V had delivered his "revelation," had tried to forewarn Emerson, observing that there was talk associating V with Emerson and with A. Kneeland,* recently imprisoned in Boston for the crime of blasphemy. But Emerson stoutly defended V: ''He is profoundly sane,'' he wrote Peabody, and to M. Fuller* he suggested ''Mono*Sania*'' as the explanation for V's excited state.

When Emerson saw the new poetry that was the result of V's illumination, he was surprised and enthralled, writing to V, ''Do not, I beg you, let a whisper or sigh of the muse go unattended to or unrecorded.'' He proposed helping V publish a volume of his works; V agreed, but difficulties arose when Emerson took editorial license with poems that V insisted should remain unchanged, arguing that they were the utterances of the Spirit. Further, Emerson, who controlled the selection of poems, excluded the most radical of V's poems, those in which he assumed a divine persona. Nevertheless, *Essays and Poems* (1839), edited by Emerson, eventually resulted.

V's ecstatic period lasted no longer than about 18 months beginning in fall 1838, but during that period, he wrote about a third of the nearly 900 poems he produced in his lifetime. The best of these ecstatic poems are characterized by the imagery of mystical experience, by biblical language, and by turns a breathless intensity or a sense of serene passiveness. They were apparently very nearly spontaneous utterances: Surviving manuscripts from this period show little evidence of revision. V's later work tended toward conventional nature,** religious, and occasional poetry that he published in local newspapers and Unitarian periodicals. He became a Unitarian supply preacher and lived out the remainder of his life in Salem.

Besides Emerson, B. Alcott* and J. F. Clarke* were V's chief promoters among the Transcendentalists. Alcott felt a special affinity for V, writing of Emerson and V that ''I get more from these men than from others now extant.'' Yet he was ambivalent about both V's mental health and his poetry, objecting (as did Emerson) to his Hebraic diction. Clarke published a number of V's poems in *The Western Messenger*,** prefacing them with a defense of V's sanity. After V's death, he collaborated with V's sisters to publish a purportedly complete edition of his poems.

Among the other Transcendentalists, Peabody was the first to recognize V's talents, and she and her entire family acted as V's friends during the thick of his crisis. She believed, however, that he was manifestly insane and urged Emerson to distance himself from V. She was especially eager to establish a distinction ''between trusting the Soul & giving up one's mind to these *individual illuminations*.'' Fuller did not share Emerson's wholesale enthusiasm for V's poetry but wrote for *The Boston Quarterly Review*** the first published review of *Essays and Poems*. H. Thoreau* admired V's work but does not seem to have been personally close to him.

With the exception of his impact on Emerson, V's influence on the Transcendentalist circle was intense and brief. And for Emerson, the enduring fascination was with V the man (''our brave saint,'' he called him) rather than the poet. The figure of V continued to echo through Emerson's journals** for decades after they had ceased seeing each other, and he became the model for a remarkable passage in Emerson's essay ''Friendship'': ''I knew a man who under a certain religious frenzy cast off this drapery [hypocrisy], and omitting all compliment and commonplace, spoke to the conscience of every person he encountered, and that with great insight and beauty. . . . To stand in true relations with men in a false age is worth a fit of insanity, is it not?''

References: A modern scholarly edition is *JV: The Complete Poems*, ed. Helen R. Deese (1993). The two biographies of V are William Irving Bartlett, *JV: Emerson's ''Brave Saint''* (1942), and Edwin Gittleman, *JV: The Effective Years, 1833–1840* (1967); the latter covers in detail almost all of V's association with the Transcendentalists. The chapter on V and Whitman* in Buell (1973) includes some of the most provocative criticism to date of V's poems. Articles of significance include Yvor Winters, ''JV and R. W. Emerson: Aspects of New England Mysticism,'' *Maule's Curse* (1938), 125–36; David Robinson, ''JV, the Transcendentalists, and the Unitarian Tradition,'' *HTR* 68 (April 1975): 105–24; and Robinson's indispensable bibliographical essay ''JV,'' in Myerson (1984), 286–94.

Helen R. Deese

W

WALKER, JAMES (1794–1874), was a leading Unitarian** clergyman whose career and writings as a minister, editor, and educator had a profound influence on the Transcendentalist movement and its acceptance within Unitarian circles. A member of the first official class of students graduating from the newly organized Divinity School** at Harvard in 1817, W became minister of the Unitarian Church in Charlestown (1818–39). After resigning this position, W accepted the Alford Professorship of Natural Religion** and Moral Philosophy** at Harvard (1839–53), a post he held until becoming the university's president from 1853 through 1860.

It was in his last decade as a minister in Charlestown that W had his greatest impact on Transcendentalism, for during that period (1831–39), he also served as editor of *The Christian Examiner.*** W dramatically altered the mission of that periodical. Under earlier editors such as H. Ware, Jr.,* and J. G. Palfrey,* *ChEx* had been the leading organ for Unitarianism in its debate with Calvinists. During his editorship, however, W pledged himself to a policy of "free inquiry," publishing the works of mainstream Unitarians as well as works by O. A. Brownson,* F. H. Hedge,* G. Ripley,* and others associated with the nascent Transcendentalist movement. In the case of Ripley's works, W was criticized by Unitarians such as A. Norton* who did not share W's view of the magazine as an open forum. Ripley's review of J. Martineau's* *Rationale of Religious Inquiry*, appearing in *ChEx* in 1836, sparked a major controversy among Unitarians and their radical Transcendentalist "brethren" over the miracles** of the Bible. Norton, Palfrey, and others felt that *ChEx* should present only articles that accurately reflected mainstream, "official" Unitarian views on theological subjects, and they resented W's policy of including such "infidel" pieces.

As editor of *ChEx* W published his most famous (and many say his most Transcendental) work, a lecture on *The Philosophy of Man's Spiritual Nature* *in Regard to the Foundation of Faith* (1834). Younger Transcendentalists eagerly embraced the work because of W's assertion that spiritual experiences are "not a matter of sensation, nor of logic; but of consciousness [i.e., intuition] alone" (*ChEx* 17 [September 1834]: 4). This work and his later lecture (no longer extant) before the Boston Society for the Diffusion of Useful Knowledge in 1838 prompted J. F. Clarke* and others to conclude that W had "gone over" to the New School. Even conservative Unitarians such as Charles Upham thought that W "favored" Transcendentalist views, writing to Norton that "his appointment to Cambridge was hailed as the first step toward bringing the college and Unitarianism to Transcendentalism." At Harvard, however, W was temperamentally moderate and his tenure proved uneventful.

References: Andrew Preston Peabody's sketch of W (*Harvard Graduates Whom I Have Known* [1890], 123–36) is the most detailed biographical treatment. In Howe (1970) and in "The Cambridge Platonists" (*American Unitarianism, 1805–1865*, ed. Conrad Edick Wright [1989], 87–119), D. W. Howe offers scattered but significant analyses of W's moral philosophy. The most detailed examination of W's philosophy is Wilson Smith, in *Professors & Public Ethics* (1956), 149–85. For W's connection with *ChEx*, see Alfred G. Litton, " 'Speaking the Truth in Love': A History of the *Christian Examiner* and Its Relation to New England Transcendentalism" (Diss., Univ. of South Carolina, 1993), and Hutchison (1959), 52–97.

Alfred G. Litton

WALKER, TIMOTHY (1802–1856), was a reform-oriented educator, an author of textbooks, an essayist and orator, a law editor, and a judge. He wrote for such periodicals as *The Christian Examiner*** and the *North American Review*** and gave speeches from Ohio to Boston, especially on issues of law and education. W was a very empirical thinker and naturally bridled at the mystical components of Transcendentalism, as might be expected of a conservative Unitarian** geometry teacher and law professor.

W graduated from Harvard College in 1826 and joined the faculty of G. Bancroft's* progressive Round Hill School in Northampton as a mathematics teacher. During his time at Round Hill he found time to publish two editions of a well-received geometry textbook; C. C. Felton* praises the book's structure and proofs for clarity and simplicity in the *NAR* (30 [1830]). W remained involved with education throughout his life.

In 1830 W moved to Cincinnati and became a lawyer. He helped found Cincinnati Law School in 1833, served as its head, and published another textbook, on law, which also went through several editions. He became a judge in 1843 and the *Western Law Review*'s first editor as well as a frequent contributor. In 1850 he delivered an "Oration on the Reform Spirit of the Day" to the Phi Beta Kappa Society of Harvard.

W tangentially strikes at the American Transcendental movement in an *NAR* (33 [July 1831]) article on "The Signs of the Times," by T. Carlyle.* In this glib attack, W praises the "Mechanism" that Carlyle's essay deplores, defending Locke** and the advances of science and technology. Despite his philosophical conservatism, W believed in education reform,** although his reasons have nothing to do with individualism. In the *NAR* (29 [July 1829]), in an article called ''On Popular Education,'' he supports broad-based education of the lower classes, arguing in favor of the lyceum** system and for the necessity of inexpensive books on basic topics, written with simple approaches. He does not want to do away with the class system; in fact, he reassures the privileged that they will get smarter at the same rate as the poor and so maintain their superiority (252). One motive for education reform is to protect the Republic from ''demagogues'' who might take advantage of an ignorant electorate (258).

References: See the *NAR* 38 (January 1834) for more on W's mechanism. See Miller (1950) for a contemporary view of W and excerpts from his article on Carlyle, 39–43.

Stephen N. Orton

WARD, ANNA HAZARD BARKER (1813–?), is best known for her beauty, her friendship with the Transcendentalists, and her marriage to S. G. Ward.* Often referred to as a Southern belle, in actuality she was born in New York City to Quaker** parents and was raised in New England. She was a descendant of Benjamin Franklin. AB was 21 when the family relocated in New Orleans after a series of financial setbacks.

A's father, Jacob Barker, was noted for his flamboyancy and his love of public attention. Her mother, in contrast, was described as quiet, Quaker-simple, and naturally elegant; from her mother A apparently inherited her own beauty and charm. These qualities most enthralled R. W. Emerson* and the other Transcendentalists. AB was one of M. Fuller's* ''diamonds''—a distinction given to Fuller's bright young friends whom Elizabeth Hoar* described as being displayed by Fuller as diamonds around her neck. However, B shocked her Transcendentalist friends by first refusing the marriage proposal of S. G. Ward and later suddenly changing her mind and hastily marrying him.

References: Although little information is available on ABW, Eleanor M. Tilton, ''The True Romance of AHB and Samuel Gray Ward,'' *SAR* 1987, and David Baldwin, ''The Emerson-Ward Friendship: Ideals and Realities,'' *SAR* 1984, are helpful. ABW's diary of 1845 to 1852 is in the S. G. Ward Collection at the Massachusetts Historical Society. For anecdotal material, see E. T. Emerson,* *The Life of Lidian Jackson Emerson** (1980).

Barbara Downs Wojtusik

WARD, SAMUEL GRAY (1817–1907), was involved in Transcendentalism through his long friendship with R. W. Emerson* and other of its associates. Early in his life, W met E. Channing* when they both attended Round Hill School, an experimental, private school in Northampton, Massachusetts. Later, at Harvard, W was a classmate of J. Very.* Also in Cambridge he met Anna Barker [Ward],* whom he eventually married. In 1835 W became acquainted with M. Fuller,* who became his literary mentor and frequent companion. Through Fuller, W was introduced to Emerson and his circle of budding Transcendentalists including C. S. [Tappan],* who later married William Aspinwall Tappan, and her sister E. S. Hooper.*

After graduating from Harvard in 1836, W spent a year touring the art centers of Europe and refining his knowledge of art. Upon returning to America, he renewed his association with the Transcendentalists. In 1838 W went to work in the mercantile business of his father, Thomas Wren W, in the New Orleans branch. As Anna Barker and her family were living there at the time, it is likely that her renowned beauty and charm influenced the move. W introduced Barker to Emerson and his following in 1839. Thus began several years of round-robin letter writing among the group, and various visits to Concord.**

With the advent of *The Dial*** in 1840, W became a contributor. Four of his poems and a selection of his letters written from his European trip were published in the first issue. However, in October 1840, he was married, and further submissions did not appear in *The Dial* until the third volume. Four more pieces by W, including "Notes on Art and Architecture" and "Translation of Dante,"** were published in the fourth volume. Although W did not continue a literary career, Emerson selected three of W's poems to be published in *Parnassus* (1874), Emerson's collection of his favorite poetry.

After three years spent working in a brokerage firm in Boston, W and family ventured off to Lenox, where he built "Highwood," a house of his own design, and established himself as an Emersonian gentleman-farmer-scholar. He is credited with being the first "cottager," those who constructed lavish summer homes in the Berkshires. Although family obligations and needs caused W to remove to New York City, he continued his Transcendentalist friendships throughout his life.

REFERENCES: Information on the W family can be found in the *W Family Papers*, ed. SGW (1900). W's personal papers are at the Houghton Library, Harvard University. Thomas Wren W's papers are at the Massachusetts Historical Society. See David Baldwin, "The Emerson-W Friendship: Ideals and Realities," *SAR* 1984: 299–324; Carl F. Strauch, "Hatred's Swift Repulsions: Emerson, Margaret Fuller, and Others," *SIR* 7 (winter 1968): 65–103; and Eleanor Tilton, "The True Romance of Anna Hazard Barker and SGW," *SAR* 1987: 53–72. Essential is *NET*Dial. C. E. Norton* edited a selection of *Letters from Ralph Waldo Emerson to a Friend, 1838–1853* (1899). Nancy Craig Simmons discusses W, among others, in "Thoreau as Napoleon; or a Note on Emerson's Big, Little, and Good Endians," *ESP* 4 (spring 1993): 1–4. For W's later life in the Berkshires, see Richard D. Birdsall, *Berkshire County: A Cultural History* (1959).

Barbara Downs Wojtusik

WARE, HENRY, JR. (1794–1843), was R. W. Emerson's* predecessor as minister of the Second Church, Boston, and one of the most influential antebellum Unitarian** ministers. His preaching and ministerial practice exemplified a pietistic element in early Unitarianism that was a formative influence on the Transcendentalists. W was the son of another important Unitarian minister, Henry Ware (1764–1845), whose election as Hollis Professor of Divinity at Harvard in 1805 signalled the beginning of the Unitarian Controversy with the more doctrinally conservative Congregationalists. The younger W's ministry at the Second Church coincided with the period of the Unitarian Controversy, and he was a strong defender of the liberal position and an advocate for the Unitarians' assumption of a separate identity. His 1825 sermon *The Faith Once Delivered to the Saints*, a response to an earlier sermon of the same title by the Calvinist leader Lyman Beecher, is an important formulation of the Unitarian outlook. W argues that the individual "is placed in a state of trial and probation, for the purpose of forming and bringing out his character," and that the powers of "reason and conscience" are the essential tools of this effort. This dual faith in rational judgment and the moral sense, and the conception of religion as a process of character building and self-culture, were hallmarks of antebellum Unitarian theology and essential premises of Transcendentalism as well.

W's ministry at the Second Church, which began in 1817, helped rejuvenate the church and set an example of the engaged ministry that he would later teach at Harvard Divinity School.** He emphasized the nurturing role of the pastor, whom he conceived less as an authority figure than a friend and helper to his congregation. W also helped to reform Unitarian preaching through his advocacy of a more spontaneous form of extemporaneous address, in which the sermon was conceived less as a dry recitation of doctrines than a lively and direct effort to engage the listener.

W's unstinting efforts as a pastor, however, also contributed to the collapse of his health in 1828. Emerson was brought in to assist him as junior pastor during his recovery, but W never returned to his post, accepting an appointment as professor of Pulpit Eloquence and the Pastoral Care at Harvard Divinity School in 1830, where he extended his influence over a generation of ministers. His pietistic approach to religion is best exemplified in *The Formation of the Christian Character* (1831), a devotional manual that advocated the Christian's entire submission to God and delineated specific forms of devotional practice, such as prayer and meditation, as the means of this surrender.

While W's theology and ministerial practice were in many ways conducive to the evolution of Transcendentalism out of Unitarianism, he did not endorse the drift of Emerson and others toward antisupernatural and post-Christian positions. W expressed his opposition to these tendencies in a critique of Emerson's Divinity School Address, entitled *The Personality of the Deity* (1838), in which he argued that the achievement of both religious faith and moral virtue depended on a conception of a personal God, which he felt that Emerson had rejected in his address. W's early death in 1843 was a severe loss to the Unitarian movement and the Harvard faculty, but he had made an important impact on both during his remarkable career.

REFERENCES: For W's theological works, see *The Works of HW, Jr., D.D.*, 4 vols. (1846–47). The chief source of biographical information is John Ware, *Memoir of the Life of HW, Jr.*, 2 vols. (1846). For important information on W's Unitarian context, see Howe (1970). W's contributions to Unitarian theology and ministerial practice, and his relation with Emerson, are discussed in David Robinson, *Apostle of Culture: Emerson as Preacher and Lecturer* (1982); ''Poetry, Personality, and the Divinity School Address,'' *HTR* 82 (1989): 185–99; and ''The Sermons of Ralph Waldo Emerson: An Introductory Historical Essay,'' *Sermons*, 1:1–32. On W's work at Harvard Divinity School, see Gary Collison, '' 'A True Toleration': Harvard Divinity School Students and Unitarianism, 1830–1859,'' in *American Unitarianism, 1805–1861*, ed. Conrad Edick Wright (1989), 209–37.

David M. Robinson

WARREN, JOSIAH (1799–1874), was the founder of philosophical anarchism in America. His theory of society based upon the ''sovereignty of the individual'' appealed to the Transcendentalists' concern with individualism. David S. Reynolds identifies W as a ''Thoreau*-like figure.'' In his essay ''On Liberty,'' J. S. Mill praised W's ideas, which were grounded upon the assumption that exchanges of goods and services should be based entirely on cost to the producer, rather than worth or value to the receiver. As W wrote in *True Civilization*, ''The *value* of bread to a starving man is equal to the value of his life; and if the price of a thing should be what it will bring, then a vender might demand of the passengers of a wrecked vessel, the whole of their future lives in servitude, as the proper price of the bread that saved their lives! . . . If the producers, carriers, and venders of the bread had bestowed one hour's labor upon that given to each passenger, then one hour's labor from each . . . would constitute the just compensation for the bread.''

W, a Boston native, put his theory of ''cost the limit of price'' into practice in 1827 when the first of his ''time'' or ''equity'' stores was established in Cincinnati. He operated the store for two years without loss or gain and then closed it, satisfied that he had proven the efficacy of such an arrangement. By 1855, the Equity movement had spread to Boston, where a short-lived ''House of Equity'' was started in the city's North End.

W's primary works, *Equitable Commerce* (1846), *True Civilization: An Immediate Necessity* (1863), and *True Civilization: A Subject of Vital and Serious Interest to All People* (1869), espouse a theory of strong individualism. His ideas were formed in reaction to his negative experience with communal living. W, who had been a professional musician, inventor of a lard-burning lamp, and founder of a lamp factory, became a follower of R. Owen* and moved to the reformer's commune at New Harmony, Indiana, in 1825. W lived for a year at New Harmony, an antecedent to communistic experiments such as Brook Farm,** and came to reject the principles of communal living and all forms of government.

In 1850, W moved to New York, where he met S. P. Andrews,* who became his protégé and the literary exponent of the philosophy of Equity. Soon after, W established the town of Modern Times, a Long Island community based upon the principle of individual sovereignty that lasted until 1862. W spent his later years near Boston and is buried at Mount Auburn Cemetery in Cambridge.

References: *JW: The First American Anarchist*, by William Bailie (1906; rpt. 1972), provides the fullest biographical portrait. W is also mentioned in G. B. Lockwood, *The New Harmony Movement* (1905). His theories are discussed in S. P. Andrews, *The Science of Society* (1888; rpt. 1970), and *The Basic Outline of Universology* (1872). See Reynolds, *Beneath the American Renaissance* (1988), 98.

Mark J. Madigan

WASSON, DAVID ATWOOD (1823–1887), was a prominent second-generation Transcendentalist minister, essayist, and poet. Though he would preach at the prestigious churches of T. Parker* and T. W. Higginson,* W was never able to sustain a permanent ministry, owing largely to ill health. Yet W was active in numerous intellectual circles, speaking before the ''Concord Club'' and the Free Religious Association,** helping organize the Radical Club,** and contributing significantly to *The Radical*,** the *Atlantic Monthly*,** and the *North American Review*.**

Born in Brooksville, Maine, the son of a farmer and shipbuilder, W displayed the independence of rural New England. Following preparatory education at Phillips Andover Academy, he entered Bowdoin College in 1845. His suspension after his sophomore year is attributed variously to his attending a neighboring church instead of the orthodox college chapel or ''refusing to testify in a case of discipline where he had no certain knowledge.'' In any case, his studies of Greek and Roman literature made him skeptical of American and French democracy. The classical doctrine of democracy seemed to him seldom realized, and he became disillusioned by this discrepancy. Restless, he studied law at Belfast, Maine, for a year, abandoning this pursuit as well.

Still seeking his calling, W attended the Bangor Theological Seminary. He was installed as minister of the Congregational Church and Society of Groveland, Massachusetts, in 1851, a position secured with the local influence of Abbie Smith, whom he married in 1852. Within a year, W was dismissed, his beliefs and sermons critical of Calvinist tenets and noticeably influenced by the ideas of R. W. Emerson* and Parker. W had finally found his niche. He founded an independent religious society in Groveland, before which he continued to preach his liberal doctrine.

In 1855, W temporarily filled the pulpit of Higginson in Worcester, Massachusetts. Higginson returned in 1856, and the two became colleagues. W's literary output increased dramatically. Initially, his writings centered on attempts to define his religious philosophy but gradually expanded into social theory. Most notable were his series of articles for the *Atlantic*, including ''Ease in Work,'' ''Individuality,'' ''Hinderance,'' and ''Originality.'' His talents were noticed by Emerson, who wrote to Senator C. Sumner* on 8 December 1864, recommending W as a possible emissary abroad: ''He is known to me as a man of superior understanding, and of a broad comprehensive genius, an excellent writer, and, as a preacher, the first choice of the 'Fraternity' people after Parker. . . . He is one of those who ought to be gratified, as it is the saving and maturing of a great man.'' W was appointed in 1865 to the ministry of the Twenty-Eighth Congregational Society in Boston to succeed the late Parker.

Unfortunately, this promising ministry came to a rapid end, as W's ill health forced him to resign. Numerous illnesses, including poor eyesight, painful back problems, and a nervous disorder, had plagued him for much of his life. These and his naturally restless spirit and a reputation for sermons too deep and subtle for popular taste combined to hamper his professional stability. In 1873, W took a three-year excursion to Stuttgart, where he wrote on cultural differences between Germany and America. Upon his return, he continued to publish searching social criticism until his death. W's essays were generally considered dry, if original and well ordered; his poetry, however, was much admired by his contemporaries. An important figure in the final decades of Transcendentalism, he deserves attention as a prolific and versatile writer.

REFERENCES: A complete bibliography of W's publications, compiled by Robert C. Albrecht, is included in *Beyond Concord:*** *Selected Writings of DAW*, ed. Charles H. Foster (1965). Foster's book is by far the most complete source of biographical material on W, with a good sampling of his major works. J. Wade Caruthers gives a brief introduction in the *DLB* volume *The American Renaissance in New England*, ed. Joel Myerson. Frank Preston Stearns's *Sketches from Concord to Appledore* (1895) mentions W. See also Abby A. Wasson, ''DAW,'' in *Heralds*, 3:373–76. W's posthumous *Essays: Religious, Social, Political* (1889) includes a ''Memoir'' of W and a bibliography by O. B. Frothingham.*

Nathaniel T. Mott

WEBSTER, DANIEL (1782–1852), was the preeminent American lawyer and statesman of his age, and throughout most of his career, he was revered by many of the Transcendentalists for his godlike powers, unsurpassed oratory, and spirited defense of freedom, especially in such famed speeches as the Plymouth Rock oration (1820), the Bunker Hill oration (1825), and eulogy on Adams and Jefferson (1826). In addition, W gained fame as defender of the Union (as against states' rights), most notably in his reply to Hayne (1829). However, when W backed the Fugitive Slave Law as part of the Compromise of 1850** to keep the South in the Union, the Transcendentalists' subsequent denunciation, in which they were joined by many other prominent New England intellectuals, was so prolonged and intensive that W's reputation has never since recovered.

R. W. Emerson* was, in Irving H. Bartlett's phrase, ''[t]he most famous and eloquent of all the W watchers.'' Indeed, W had embodied Emerson's ideal of manhood: Emerson frequently praised W's great intellect, rhetorical power, majestic form and strength, undaunted courage, and exemplary self-reliance. Emerson was willing, at least until 1850, to excuse W's apparent avarice, gluttony, ambition, and occasional pandering to financial and political interests. However, the passage of the Fugitive Slave Law shocked and angered Emerson out of his customary reticence toward the abolitionist** cause, and he denounced W publicly in ''The Fugitive Slave Law'' (1851) for having ''no moral sentiment,'' declaring, ''All the drops of his blood have eyes that look downward.'' When W died in 1852, Emerson's journal** entry, although more balanced, nevertheless expressed his lingering grief and disappointment: W had been the ''completest man,'' but ''alas! he was the victim of his ambition.''

Almost all of the Transcendentalists shared Emerson's deep sense of loss and of betrayal. For example, in the *Discourse* on W, T. Parker* admitted having loved and honored W, lamenting, ''Never was there such a fall.'' Nevertheless, Parker compared W to Benedict Arnold and blasted W for his hypocrisy, egotism, and ''practical atheism,'' claiming, ''No living man has done so much to debauch the conscience of the nation.'' Parker especially criticized W for scoffing at ''the Higher Law''** and for declaring protection of property to be the chief aim of government. For his part, G. Ripley,* in an article in the *Tribune* in 1852, considered W ''the great high-priest of the practical understanding'' and therefore ''inferior to the poet or philosopher.'' Ripley did not believe that the Compromise of 1850, whereby W was widely supposed to have saved the Union, was anything more than a temporary patchwork. Unlike the others, H. Thoreau* was never a great admirer of W. Throughout the 1840s Thoreau criticized W in his journal for the latter's venality, narrowly political outlook, incompetent farming and management, and lack of economy, evident in the inordinate size and low productivity of Marshfield, W's country estate. Thoreau expressed his harshest criticism in ''Slavery in Massachusetts'' (1854), likening W to a ''dirt-bug,'' worthy only of being trampled upon.

W seems to have paid little attention to the Transcendentalists, whom he suspected of promulgating empty abstractions.

References: For exemplary Transcendentalist analyses of W, see T. Parker's *Discourse* on W (1853; rpt. *Theodore Parker's Review of W* [1970]); *JMN*, esp. 11:344–64 and 13: 111–12; and both versions of Emerson's ''The Fugitive Slave Law'' in *W*, 11:177–244. Bartlett covers W's views and public image in *DW* (1978). John McAleer analyzes Emerson's evolving response toward W in *Ralph Waldo Emerson: Days of Encounter* (1984).

Terry J. Martin

WEISS, JOHN, JR. (1818–1879), a Unitarian** minister, was the foremost biographer of T. Parker* and a prolific contributor to *The Radical*,** *The Christian Examiner*,** and *Atlantic Monthly*.** His published sermons and lectures powerfully addressed topics ranging from slavery (including the rendition of Anthony Burns) to immortality.

The grandson of a German Jew, W was born in Boston and raised in Worcester, where his father was a barber. W was noted for his pointed humor and maintained a liberal and independent stance throughout his life. He graduated from Harvard College in the Class of 1837 with H. D. Thoreau* and entered Harvard Divinity School,** spending a winter studying at Heidelberg University before graduating in 1843. W characterized Thoreau as ''cold and unimpressible'' yet respected his reserve and praised his keen observation and imagination. As both close friend and successor to the Watertown pulpit of C. Francis,* W became an influential member of the Transcendentalist circle. He was a member of the Radical Club,** H. G. O. Blake's* "Worcester Circle," and B. Alcott's* Town and Country Club;** and he helped found the Free Religious Association** in 1867. In one FRA address he declared, "Time was that when the brain was out a man would die, but now they make a Unitarian minister of him." His young friend Minot Savage thought this wit the product of years of denominational strife; but he saw also in W something "whimsical," "a certain boyishness." "With this," Savage went on, "was mingled something prankish, almost elfish. There was a subtle, mystic quality about him which gave him a personal fascination and charm." W challenged his more idealistic** contemporaries with an outlook that, said O. B. Frothingham,* "tread the border-land between religion and science, recognizing the claims of both" and exemplified the balance sought by the Transcendentalist soul.

W admired R. W. Emerson,* as is evident in a 4 February 1852 letter to Emerson expressing interest in retiring from the pulpit and pursuing literature, much as Emerson had done in 1832. His important translations of works of Novalis,** Schiller,** and Goethe* during his ministry in New Bedford were testimony to his literary abilities. His own originality was demonstrated in numerous essays on politics, literature, and theology. With the publication of his major *The Life and Correspondence of Theodore Parker* (2 vols. [1864]), W became centrally identified with Transcendentalism. Although W's other works have not received the acclaim enjoyed by many of his contemporaries, he was described by Frothingham as "purely poetic, imaginative" and was highly regarded in his time. His biography of Parker is sometimes criticized for its personal references and occasional lack of objectivity, yet to this day it remains the authority on Parker's life. His many periodical contributions, including poems, are scattered and nearly forgotten. The importance of W to the Transcendentalist movement, however, cannot be forgotten or overemphasized.

References: No single source fully details W's accomplishments. A biography to have been written by Frothingham was never published owing to objections of the W family. Minot J. Savage wrote a memoir of W in *Heralds*, 3:376–80. Modern sketches include George Harvey Genzmer in the *DAB* and J. Wade Caruthers in the *DLB* volume *The American Renaissance in New England.* Robert E. Burkholder provides a helpful bibliographical essay in Myerson (1984), 295–98. Frothingham (1876) offers a limited but interesting assessment. W's portrait of Thoreau, from *ChEx* (July 1865), is reprinted in Walter Harding, ed., *Henry David Thoreau: A Profile* (1971), 36–43. His major works include *The Life and Correspondence of Theodore Parker*, 2 vols. (1864), *American Religion* (1871), *Wit, Humor, and Shakespeare. Twelve Essays* (1876), and the posthumous *The Immortal Life* (1880).

Nathaniel T. Mott

WHEELER, CHARLES STEARNS (1816–1843), was one of the most promising of the younger Transcendentalists, but his death at the age of 26 brought his brief career to a close. Born in Lincoln, Massachusetts, of an old New

England family, he grew up a few miles from H. Thoreau's* Walden Pond,** and the two boys, friends, attended both the Concord Academy and Harvard (Class of 1837) together. A summer vacation that the two spent in a cabin W had constructed on the shores of Flint's (Sandy) Pond in Lincoln in 1837 is generally believed to have been a source of inspiration for Thoreau's later and more famous residence at Walden.

W was a brilliant student at Harvard, and when in 1838 J. Very,* then a Greek tutor at Harvard, suffered a nervous breakdown, W was immediately hired to replace him, a position he held for four years. He early became acquainted with R. W. Emerson* and the other Transcendentalists, and when Emerson decided to publish for the first time in book form T. Carlyle's* *Sartor Resartus*, W volunteered to take over the tedious tasks of making a printer's copy and seeing it through the press while he was still an undergraduate. In 1838 he edited a two-volume edition of Carlyle's *Miscellanies*, adding a third and a fourth volume in 1839, thus helping introduce Carlyle to the Transcendentalists. In 1840 he edited a volume of *Critical and Miscellaneous Essays* of Thomas Babington Macaulay, then persuaded Tennyson to edit a new volume of poems that W saw through the American press. Perhaps his most notable literary contribution was his edition of *Herodotus*, published in 1842 and immediately accepted as a textbook by Harvard and a number of other American colleges.

In 1842, accompanied by his Harvard friends J. Weiss* and LeBaron Russell, W sailed for Europe, intending to spend two years studying in Germany and visiting Carlyle and Tennyson in England. He spent six months at Heidelberg, one at Göttingen, and two in Leipzig, where he contracted gastric fever and died in July 1843. His body was eventually brought back to this country, and he was interred in Mount Auburn Cemetery, in Cambridge, Massachusetts.

REFERENCES: Shortly before his death W wrote several accounts of intellectual activities in the German universities, and these were published in 1843 in *The Dial*** and in J. R. Lowell's* *Pioneer*. A memorial volume collecting together selections from his writing, proposed shortly after his death, was never carried out. The only study of his life and work is John Olin Eidson, *CSW: Friend of Emerson* (1951).

Walter Harding

WHIPPLE, EDWIN PERCY (1819–1886), was, according to Gerald Gerber, "an important disseminator of romantic organic** critical theory in an ethical New England environment." W's critical theory, according to his article "The Vital and the Mechanical," takes root in his assumption that every thing—literature, religion, politics, science—"either grows or is put together, is a living organism or a contrived machine." Thomas Starr King wrote in "W's *Lectures*" that the critic struggled "to know the essence, laws, and philosophy of [the] genius" of the authors, "and therefore he reads a book not only to discover what the characteristics of the book are . . . but also to determine what *the man is*."

W ardently supported a national literature, and he advocated independence from international literary influence. He elevated the position of critic in this country from one who clashes with the author to one who engages in a shared interpretive spirit with the author. W asserted that criticism should be a science, with interpretive laws appropriate and natural to that science. Arbitrary rules and impressions had to give way to organic criticism.

W was born in Gloucester, Massachusetts, on 8 March 1819. His father died of cholera when W was only 18 months old. An avid reader, W graduated from Salem High School, then worked with various banking establishments. While working as the chief clerk at a banking and brokerage firm in Boston, he co-founded ''The Attic Nights Club,'' a venue that allowed him practice as a speaker, writer, and critic. During this time, he wrote reviews for various newspapers, mostly anonymously, including a review of Poe* and of the first volume of R. W. Emerson's* essays. W claimed to have coined the appellation ''a Greek-Yankee—a cross between Plato** and Jonathan Slick'' about Emerson in an unknown ''penny paper'' review of the essays.

W's criticism was voluminous. He contributed articles to many periodicals, including *Graham's Magazine, Literary World*, and *American Review. Essays and Reviews* is a two-volume compilation of his journalistic critiques, and his six-volume *Works* includes *Literature and Life, Essays and Reviews, Character and Characteristic Men, Success and Its Conditions*, and *The Literature of the Age of Elizabeth.* He also wrote four other books, including a two-volume work on Charles Dickens.

Writers as diverse as R. Griswold,* Emerson, Poe, N. Hawthorne,* and Whittier* had high praise for W, and his influence in New England was pervasive. He was awarded honorary degrees from Harvard University in 1848 and from University of Vermont in 1851. However, not everyone considered W a great critic. Often he was charged with being too generous in his assessment of the author to be honestly critical of the work. W's most significant influence was upon Hawthorne. His reviews of Hawthorne's works were generally positive, although they did blame any faults in the tales on the author's ''dark passions.'' Perhaps because of W's remarks on *The Scarlet Letter*, Hawthorne attempted to better balance gloom and humor in his next novel, *The House of the Seven Gables*. Hawthorne asked W to look over the manuscript of *The Blithedale Romance* for inconsistencies, and he asked the critic to help him find a title. W probably helped Hawthorne with the conclusion of the novel as well. He also reviewed *The Marble Faun*, once again noting Hawthorne's genius and ascribing problems in the novel to the author's melancholic personality.

References: See W's *Works*, 6 vols. (1885–87). His important writings include *Essays and Reviews*, 2 vols. (1848–49); ''Nathaniel Hawthorne,'' *Atl*** 5 (May 1860): 614–22; rev. of *The Blithedale Romance, GrMag* 41 (September 1852): 333–34; rev. of *The House of the Seven Gables, GrMag* 38 (June 1851): 467–68; rev. of *The Scarlet Letter, GrMag* 36 (May 1850): 345–46; and ''The Vital and the Mechanical,'' *GrMag* 37 (July 1850): 1–6. On W, see Richard H. Fogle, ''Organic Form in American Criticism, 1840–1870,'' in Floyd Stovall, ed., *The Development of American Literary Criticism* (1955), 75–111;

Gerald E. Gerber, ''EPW,'' *DLB*, vol. 64, ed. John Rathbun and Monica Grecu (1987); Thomas Starr King, ''W's Lectures,'' *UQ* 7 (January 1850): 77–90; and John Paul Pritchard, *Criticism in America* (1956).

David J. Sorrells

WHITMAN, WALT (1819–1892), is the greatest American poet who was influenced by R. W. Emerson* and therefore by Transcendentalism. His personal philosophy, however, as expressed in his poetry and as it evolved over the decades, differed in many respects from those of Emerson and H. Thoreau.*

W acknowledged Emerson's importance to his development. ''I was simmering, simmering simmering,'' he is said to have remarked in 1860; ''Emerson brought me to a boil.'' What he most likely meant by this was that a youth of temperamental but uninspired nonconformity arrived at a mature and confident creativity when W heard and read Emerson's message of self-reliance. It encouraged originality and individualism within a vision of a benign Over-Soul—something different from the self-indulgence and aggressive self-aggrandizement that American democracy seemed to be encouraging. Moreover, Emerson called for a ''scholar'' who would see the value in common things (''The American Scholar'') and for a poet who would radically depart from the conventions, subjects, and values of the past (''The Poet''). Beginning in the late 1840s W managed by conscious effort to become such a poet. When, in 1855, he published the first edition of *Leaves of Grass*, it was no doubt to Emerson that he sent a copy with most confidence.

His confidence was not misplaced. Emerson wrote back in a famous letter greeting the unknown poet ''at the beginning of a great career'' and describing the book as ''the most extraordinary piece of wit & wisdom that America has yet contributed.'' W used the letter as an endorsement for his second edition (1856). Emerson visited W the next year, and a few years later (1860), they discussed a third edition (to be published in Boston) while they walked under the elms of Boston Common. The phenomenon of W was eagerly registered by all the major Transcendentalists. Thoreau and B. Alcott* went all the way to Brooklyn to visit him in 1856; Thoreau wanted to know whether W knew Oriental** philosophy (W, perhaps not completely candidly, said no, and asked to be told about it). After these initial acts of mutual self-recognition, W's personal contact with the New England Transcendentalists waned. *Leaves of Grass,* however, that ever-evolving book of his person and his life, might be read as an ongoing discussion with Emerson and Thoreau, a book of both affirmations and dissents from Transcendentalism.

Leaves of Grass represents above all the creation of what Emerson called for—an ''original relation to the universe'':

> You shall no longer take things at second or third hand, nor look through the eyes of the dead, nor feed on the spectres in books,
> You shall not look through my eyes either, nor take things from me.
> You shall listen to all sides and filter them from your self. (''Song of Myself'')

Leaves celebrates the individual as the center of being and value, with the result that a powerfully autobiographical book can be seen as representative: "what I assume you shall assume, / For every atom belonging to me as good belongs to you." It regards the place and destiny of mankind and indeed the entire universe optimistically: "I believe the soggy clods shall become lovers and lamps." And both at the level of the individual line and in the best poems as wholes, it rests upon a belief in an organic** relation between form and expression, upon an Emersonian trust in the relation between the symbolism of nature** and the symbolic nature of language. W says in the 1855 preface to *Leaves of Grass*: "The rhyme and uniformity of perfect poems show the free growth of metrical laws and bud from them as unerringly and loosely as lilacs or roses on a bush, and take shapes as compact as the shapes of chestnuts and oranges and melons and pears, and shed the perfume impalpable to form. . . . All beauty comes from beautiful blood and a beautiful brain." W's life and poetry were the most powerful practical demonstration of much that Emerson and Thoreau advocated.

For all that, W was conscious of the extent to which his sense of life, of what was real and what mattered, departed from Emerson's. To begin with, there was the fundamental question of the importance of the material world, therefore of the body, and therefore of sex. Although there are moments when W sounds as though he grants the merely apparitional character of the material world that is predominant in Emerson, his most vigorously stated utterances are at pains to deny this. "Crossing Brooklyn Ferry" concludes with a grand affirmation of the permanence of the material world and its necessity to the very existence of a soul, a mind, a perceiver, an individual or collective human identity. Again and again "Song of Myself" declares the unity of the body with the soul. Its spiritual ecstasies are physically realized, and not merely metaphorically so. W's delight in the body—even in "the scent of these armpits"—is literal, and when natural metaphors are used, they serve precisely to purify one's sense of the body. Thus, he addresses his genitals as one of the "particular" things of "my body" that "I worship": "Root of washed sweet-flag, timorous pond-snipe, nest of guarded duplicate eggs, it shall be you." This is very far from Thoreau's purifying cold morning baths in Walden Pond.** Indeed, much of W's program is to remove the vestigial squeamishness about the body, especially the body's sexuality, from the otherwise successful Transcendental revolt against both Puritanical** shame and Unitarian** intellectuality. When Emerson attempted to persuade him to drop the "Children of Adam" poems from *Leaves of Grass* (evidently not recognizing that the *Calamus* poems were even more unconventional in their presentation of sexual desire and experience), W firmly insisted that he would "adhere to my own theory, and exemplify it." That theory, as exemplified in "Children of Adam," where he is "singing the phallus, / Singing the song of procreation," is explicit: "all were lacking if sex were lacking . . . / Sex contains all." The result is an erotic landscape quite alien to Transcendental perception.

W positions himself in opposition to Transcendentalism also in that his persona is both gregarious and city-loving. It delights in crowds and recognizes no class distinctions. Recalling Emerson's chilling remark that "We descend to meet," we see how differently W feels in not only assuming equality everywhere but actively seeking to "merge." The fact that this very desire may be born of the alienation and loneliness of a "solitary singer" only makes it more authentic and intense as a value. It is also part of a conscious democratic politics (shared only equivocally by Emerson and Thoreau) that finds its life in the city. On their preference for woods and ponds, the Transcendentalists were not equivocal. When W turned to nature at all, he found it primarily as simplified into a few symbols, mainly two: the mighty ocean-mother and the blade of grass. And even the first surged in tidal swells between parts of his beloved city, while the grass grew everywhere, and nowhere more significantly than out of the graves of densely populated cemeteries. There are few passages on nature in *Leaves of Grass* as sensuously realized as the descriptions of the city: "the blab of the pave. . . . the tires of carts and sluff of bootsoles and talk of the promenaders." W risks entirely losing himself in this effort to weave the song of his "self" out of "such as these." But it is a way to find and realize the self very different from the aloof withdrawals of the Transcendentalists.

Finally, even before his direct witnessing of tragic suffering and loss in the Civil War, W confronted the facts of physical pain, disease, and death more intensely than one finds them realized or even acknowledged in Emerson. Many of his poems—from occasional lines in his earliest to entire lyrics in his last years—do try to give comforting notions of death and the afterlife, rather vaguely and with no clear ontological basis. But here, too, W at his poetically most authentic (that is, when speaking in imagery rather than in banal phrases) did not "transcend." One of the battle scenes in "Song of Myself" shows

> Formless stacks of bodies and bodies by themselves. . . . dabs of flesh upon the masts and spars [. . .]
> The hiss of the surgeon's knife and the gnawing teeth of his saw,
> The wheeze, the cluck, the swash of falling blood. . . . the short wild scream, the long dull tapering groan,
> These so. . . . these irretrievable.

These irretrievable. No theory of "compensation"** here. It is true that after the horrors of the war, registered in the "Drum-Tap" poems, and after the death of Lincoln, W could search for, and find, "retrievements out of the night." But these are, simply, the fact of love, the beauty of grief, and the attraction of death. Transcendentalists knew nothing of these topics, or at least nothing that they wished to express, even to themselves in their journals,** in words that persuade.

W probably would not have become a poet without the invigorating spirit that Transcendentalism breathed into the American air after 1836; but he would not have been himself—or true to Emerson's and Thoreau's own idea of the individual—if he had not first selectively and tentatively affirmed what they affirmed, then consciously gone his own way to create his own vision.

REFERENCES: The 22 volumes of *The Collected Writings of WW* (1965–) include the well-annotated *Comprehensive Reader's Edition of Leaves of Grass*; the Library of America edition, *WW: Complete Poetry and Collected Prose* (1982), is also excellent. The best biographies are Gay Wilson Allen, *The Solitary Singer* (1955; rev. 1985), and Justin Kaplan, *WW: A Life* (1980). Both of these extensively treat W's connections with Transcendentalism, particularly with Emerson. The classic study of the relationship is Matthiessen (1941). Recent studies that treat W and Transcendentalism include Jerome Loving, *Emerson, W and the American Muse* (1984), and M. Wynn Thomas, *The Lunar Light of W's Poetry* (1987). Still useful is Gay Wilson Allen's *New WW Handbook* (1986).

William L. Vance

WHITTIER, JOHN GREENLEAF (1807–1892), Quaker** militant but not a Transcendentalist, was in the decades preceding the Civil War among the most influential writers in the abolitionist** movement. He was a distant though cordial friend of R. W. Emerson,* never met but learned to admire H. D. Thoreau,* and in W. Whitman's* later ill health gave a small contribution toward Whitman's medical expenses. In short, the Transcendentalists had a greater impact on W than W had on them.

W wrote to Emerson in September 1844, asking him to speak at an abolitionist meeting, but Emerson, according to John B. Pickard, "kept himself somewhat aloof from the practical aspects of reform movements like abolition and temperance,** believing that inner reform must come before any external social reform could be realized." Emerson had long spoken against slavery but, in an address in August 1844, gave much more open support to abolition. W respected Emerson, but, according to Pickard, "the two men were never close." Emerson had four of W's collections of poems in his personal library but did not make notes on any of them.

Just after Thoreau's *Walden* appeared, W wrote to a friend in August 1854, "It is capital reading but very wicked and heathenish. The practical moral of it seems to be that if a man is willing to sink himself into a woodchuck, he can live as cheaply as that quadruped; but after all, for me I prefer walking on two legs." "W did not hold this view permanently," says Pickard, "for in later years he spoke of that 'wise, wonderful Thoreau,' of his 'rare genius,' and in 1886 that he 'loved' both Thoreau and Emerson."

W had only a small and indirect effect on Whitman, writing "confidential" on an 1885 letter to a friend: "I have been pained by some portions of WW's writings, which for his own sake, and that of his readers, I wish could be omitted." Whitman had been the object of much hostile criticism for his sexual themes.

Though Emerson did not derive his philosophy of life, so much like the Quakers', from W—the roots lie elsewhere, and deeper—a compelling case can and has been made for Quakerism as one of Emerson's major intellectual influences. Frederick B. Tolles quotes, most tellingly, Emerson's answer to a kinsman, the Reverend David Greene Haskins, when asked to define his religious position; Emerson answered ''with greater deliberateness, and longer pauses between his words than usual, 'I am more of a Quaker than anything else. I believe in the ''still, small voice,'' and that voice is Christ within us.' ''

References: See Tolles, ''Emerson and Quakerism'' (1938), rpt. in *On Emerson: The Best from ''American Literature*,'' ed. Edwin H. Cady and Louis J. Budd (1988), 19–42. W grew closer to Emerson on the issue of institutional versus individual reform, but they differed over the Inner Light/Inner Voice—see Harry Hayden Clark, ''The Growth of W's Mind—Three Phases,'' in Jayne K. Kribbs, *Critical Essays on JGW* (1980), 192–206. Clark also points to W's and Thoreau's shared skepticism of mere technological progress. Pickard, in ''The Basis of W's Critical Creed'' in the same volume, says, ''Following Emerson's organic** view of art, W believed that goodness, truth, and beauty were one and that the material was only a reflection of the Divine archetype'' (66); this is Emerson's view of the ''correspondence''** between the material and spiritual worlds. See ''W and Whitman'' in Lewis E. Weeks, Jr., *Memorabilia of JGW* (1968), 65–75. Pickard edited *The Letters of JGW*, 3 vols. (1975).

Reid Huntley

WILLIS, NATHANIEL PARKER (1806–1867), was the most popular writer out of New England in his time, being well known both in the United States and abroad. He was poet, editor of magazines and newspapers, traveler, foreign correspondent, playwright, dandy, bon vivant, and close observer of European and American ''high society.'' His relationship to the American Transcendentalist movement was collateral and ambivalent but of signal importance. Although W loved to mix with titled aristocrats of distinguished birth, he was republican and democratic in his personal sentiments. He believed in the ''natural nobility'' of human beings and upheld the importance of education and self-cultivation, especially in respect to the arts and to letters. In his fiction, he even upheld the concept of the ''noble savage'' by using the American Indian or the Near Eastern gypsy by way of illustration. In his work, he also promoted the scenic beauties of nature,** took liberal and secular attitudes toward Christianity, and in the action of his fiction stressed the importance of self-reliance.

Besides primitivism, W added orientalism** to his menu, including the Near East (from Jerusalem to Constantinople) and the Far East (China). However, unlike the Transcendentalists, he was not interested in discovering the ''Over-Soul'' in the Hindu scriptures; he preferred Sardinian gypsies of neoclassical mold (à la John Gibson, English sculptor who tried to revive the classical practice of ''polychromy'') and ancient Chinese scholar-poets (T'ao Ch'ien, c. 375–426, author of the prose-poem ''Peach-Blossom Spring''; and Li Po, c. 700–762, great lyric poet notable for his wine bibbing). Also unlike the Transcendentalists, he exploited sentimental infatuation between the opposite sexes under the fantasy of ''romantic love,'' having been infected by Rousseau's** *Julie, or the New Héloise* and Goethe's* *The Sorrows of Young Werther*. He favored

Della-Cruscan style in his poetry and aristocratic ''silver-fork'' style in his fiction, sometimes mixed with some ''low life.'' W was a facile rather than a ''good'' writer. His poetry reads smoothly and is metrically almost faultless, but it is too ornamental, riddled with romantic clichés and lacking in punch and profundity. In fiction, he continually goes beyond credibility and is lacking in dramatic sense. He invariably allows description to slow down the action to snail speed. His one novel, *Paul Fane* (1857), is mostly sensibility and talk. However, it does anticipate the international novel of H. James.* His play *Tortesa the Usurer* (1839) was praised by Poe.* But ''his prose at its best,'' as Professor William P. Trent put it, ''is that of the talented gossip and reporter.''

W was born in Portland, Maine. In 1812 his orthodox Calvinist family moved to Boston, where his father, a journalist, founded and edited a religious newspaper. W graduated from Yale in 1827 and returned to Boston. Yale's orthodox Calvinism, however, had failed to curb his fondness for gaiety, fashionable clothes, and theater attendance. He was a smooth versifier, a lover of luxury, a sentimental worshiper of pretty women, and a clever social climber. O.W. Holmes* later described young W as ''something between a remembrance of Count D'Orsay and an anticipation of Oscar Wilde.'' In 1829 W founded the *American Monthly Magazine*, which he edited for two years. Feeling restricted in staid Boston, he removed to the more exciting pastures of New York City. There he obtained the position of coeditor with George P. Morris of the *New York Mirror*. In 1833 he was made its foreign correspondent and immediately left for Le Havre, France. Thus, W began a glamorous and highly successful journalistic career. Except for a short break, he remained an associate of Morris until the latter's death in 1864. After the *New York Mirror* ceased publication in 1842, they started the *Weekly Mirror* and the *Evening Mirror* in 1844, hiring Poe as a staff member. In 1846 they started the *National Press*, which name soon changed to *Home Journal*. W died at his country estate, ''Idlewild,'' on the Hudson near West Point, New York. Although much overrated as a litterateur in his own day, he was a talented journalist who left some pieces worth reading still. A minor writer, to be sure, he did represent the popular taste at a time when R. W. Emerson,* N. Hawthorne,* and Poe were struggling for serious recognition.

References: W's letters to the *Mirror* were published in *Pencillings by the Way* (1835). His short stories appeared in *Inklings of Adventure* (1836). His poems were published in *Melanie and Other Poems* (1835); *Poems of Passion* (1843); and *The Lady Jane and Other Poems* (1835). Other successful books were *Loiterings of Travel* (1839) and *Outdoors at Idlewild* (1854). The sole biography is Henry E. Beers, *NPW* (1885). See Barrett Wendell, *A Literary History of America* (1900), 222–30; William P. Trent, *A History of American Literature, 1607–1865* (1905), 452–56; Robert E. Spiller, *The American in England* (1926); Fred Lewis Pattee, *The Development of the American Short Story* (1923); Arthur H. Quinn, *A History of the American Drama from the Beginning to the Civil War* (1943); and Cortland P. Auser, *NP.W* (1969). Among several articles discussing W's influence on Poe, see Kenneth L. Daughrity, ''Poe's 'Quiz on W,' '' *AL* 5

(1933): 55–62; and Richard P. Benton, ''The Works of N.P.W as a Catalyst of Poe's Criticism,'' *AL* 39 (1967): 315–24.

Richard P. Benton

WOODBERRY, GEORGE EDWARD (1855–1930), was an American poet, teacher, and literary scholar whose career spanned the crucial years in the development of modern American literary criticism. New England born and bred, W imbibed a genteel refinement of Transcendentalism at Harvard in the 1870s, most notably at the feet of J. R. Lowell.* While he eagerly embraced the idealism** and individualism of R. W. Emerson* and others, he deeply regretted the Transcendentalists' failure to acknowledge the importance of history and tradition. At the same time, he was contemptuous of the gritty realism of his day for its rejection of the ''higher aims'' of literature. In his own work, then, he sought to create a critical aesthetic that rooted Transcendental idealism in classical traditions of order and eternal truth.

W's ambivalence toward the literature of Transcendentalism is representative of the view of many of the critics of his generation. With them, he saw the New England writers as constituting the high point of 19th-century American literature but doubted their relevance for future generations: The mysticism and innocent optimism that sustained the likes of A. B. Alcott* were of little practical value to men of the 20th century. W makes this point most succinctly in *Ralph Waldo Emerson* (1907), where, after attesting to the emotional power of Emerson's work, he concludes, ''[N]o modern mind can abide in his ideas.'' An influential critic in his day, and a much admired teacher at Columbia University (1891–1904), W's reflections on Emerson and his circle became part of an increasingly condescending assessment of Transcendentalism shared by critics as diverse as Paul Elmer More, H. L. Mencken, and V. F. Calverton.

References: W's major works include *Nathaniel Hawthorne** (1902), *America in Literature* (1903), and *Ralph Waldo Emerson* (1907). For his biography, see Michael Burduck, ''GEW,'' in *DLB*, 71: 297–305. See also John Paul Pritchard, *Criticism in America* (1956), 156–62, and Charles Glicksburg, *American Literary Criticism: 1900–1950* (1952), 91–108.

Charles Mitchell

WORDSWORTH, WILLIAM (1770–1850), the English poet, was, along with his collaborator S. T. Coleridge,* the initiator of Romanticism in English. W first scandalized the British critical establishment, then later became a poetic icon by rebelling against neoclassical formalism to emphasize a poetics utilizing the everyday language and experience of the common people and stressing the need for imagination and emotional identification. W was especially known for introducing the detailed, original observation of ordinary natural landscapes;** for his optimistic, morally elevated tone; and for his emphasis on the primacy of even the most socially despised individual.

R. W. Emerson* was born in the same year that W and Coleridge's pioneering work, *Literary Ballads,* was published in America, 1803, and W's *The Excursion* first introduced Emerson to the literary potential of the common man, as well as to such favorite themes as compensation** and self-reliance. Further, W intimated the existence of an individual moral standard by which decisions could be made in contradistinction to social custom. Perhaps most important, W displayed the symbolic use of nature,** which would become Emerson's most notable theme.

Another of W's major influences upon Emerson, and through him upon the whole of American Romanticism, resulted from his reading of W's famous prefatory works. W's conception of the role of the poet as an individual of greater insight and humanitarianism, who served as a moral exemplar, or representative man, was as important as his theory of poetical creation, in which the poet reproduced experiences of emotional significance that were later ''recollected in tranquillity.'' Foremost, although rarest, among these experiences was the epiphany. As described by W in *The Prelude* and Emerson in *Nature,* this is a mystical or ecstatic experience, an eternal moment in which the soul unites with nature and thereby with God, the ''World Soul,'' in W's terms, which Emerson rechristened the ''Over-Soul.'' The essential qualities of poetry, then, are truth, nature, and moral insight, and all of these ideals were passed on to and through Emerson.

H. Thoreau* had known W's works since his college years, and, like Emerson, he owned copies of the four-volume *Poetical Works* and later *The Prelude.* Thoreau's journal** quotes or refers to W repeatedly, praising his ''simple pathos,'' ''feminine gentleness,'' ''heroism,'' and ''unquestionable and persevering genius.'' W in the journals thus served Thoreau as an exemplar for the ''brave and hopeful human life'' Thoreau himself wished to create, although he felt that W's praise of natural beauty was too ''cold.'' Thoreau also adopted W's theory of poetic creation, calling it the technique of ''relaxed attention,'' and reflects W's use of the Poet as a representative of ideal humanity in his deliberately constructed narrative persona in *Walden* and other works. Moreover, Thoreau inherited W's conviction that the true Poet would necessarily operate outside of—and thus against—the social context of convention and conformity, creating Thoreau's literary position as the quintessential Romantic individualist and outsider.

Thoreau repeats W's recognition of the need for an attitude of reverence toward nature even while respecting its darker and more destructive aspects, and for a use of nature as teacher and physician as well as muse. Both Emerson and Thoreau adapt W's usage of localized natural phenomena in their depiction of Concord's** woods and wildlife. Thoreau, like Emerson, reflects W's ideal of nature not only as a symbol but as a manifestation of spirit and thus as a path to that ultimate goal of life and literature, truth.

Both Emerson and Thoreau diverge from the Wordsworthian ethos, however, in that they stress the need for solitude where W relied upon companionship, especially that of his beloved sister Dorothy. Similarly, while the Americans respect W's emphasis on childhood memory as a source of innocence, spontaneity, and wonder, they stress the possibility of experiencing eternity in the present moment, transcending W's insistence upon the supremacy of the recollected past.

Whitman* was certainly aware of W, having read several of his poems and, more important for Whitman, W's famous preface to *Lyrical Ballads,* in which he had set forth both his poetic theory and his view of the ideal Poet. Whitman even kept a collection of clippings from magazine articles referring to W. Although Whitman only rarely refers to W in his correspondence and other writings, the massive influence of W's preface can be seen particularly in Whitman's own prefaces to works from *Leaves of Grass* onward, which echo W's very phrasing, as well as his emphasis upon the need for a philosophical poetry rooted in spontaneous emotion. Like W, too, Whitman relates the destructive as well as creative aspects of nature and of human life. Further, Whitman shares W's concern for "intimations of immortality," although Whitman's is a less Christianized eternity that includes possibilities such as reincarnation and evolution. And Whitman comes closer to W than even Emerson or Thoreau in his insistent advocacy of the common, working-class man and woman.

Whitman's ideal projected poetic persona was derived directly from W's preface. Both see the life of the poet as an almost mystic calling and hold the imagination to be truly sacred. Through the inspired use of the imagination, the poet in solitude creates the divine chant that was, as Whitman states in his preface to *Leaves of Grass,* the only "means of morally influencing the world." Due to this elevated conception of poetry, Whitman follows W's use of the epiphany, although Whitman's mystical experiences involve not only the assimilated presence of a spiritualized nature but also a sexual component. To a far greater extent than any other Romantic poet, for Whitman, as for W, the ultimate goal of poetry is not only truth but also love. Yet for Whitman this is not so much the personal love of W for his sister but the "kelson" or binding force of the universe, love as a universal principle even more than a personal experience.

Though mentioned by critics only in passing, Dickinson's* debt to W was indeed immense, while her awareness of his work paralleled the critics' awareness of his influence—subliminal, respected without being consciously recognized, accepted without scrutiny as part of the intellectual background. An initial estimate of the concepts Dickinson drew from W, possibly through Emerson as intermediary, must recognize the use of indigenous, common, natural phenomena. Like the Transcendentalists, Dickinson breaks from the neoclassical verse traditions of nightingales and orchids in formal gardens to observe robins and buttercups on her own walkway. As with all the Transcendentalists, Dickinson finds nature a healing, teaching, and inspiring influence but remains aware of the dark side of nature and echoes the visionary experience of W, in which humanity and nature become one, thus representing an apotheosis of the natural symbolism whose development W had initiated. As with W, her poetry deals with such central themes as immortality, the Romantic image of the child and the importance of early spiritual influences, and the assertion of independence and individualism, possibly colored by Emersonian self-reliance. Dickinson agrees in general with W's estimate of the role and the importance of the Poet; indeed, like Whitman, in her letters she shares his hope that such verse could duplicate not only the consoling but even the healing effect of natural surroundings.

Even Dickinson's poetic process follows W's prescription in his preface for a "spontaneous overflow of powerful feelings" experienced in seclusion. Dickinson's use of nonsyntactical phrases connected by dashes creates a new poetic form that enables her to capture the elements of surprise and even ecstasy, which Emerson, following W, had defined as the provenance of poetry.

Thus, the Transcendentalists, while finding in W a source for their most resonant ideals, expressed them in a more radical manner, both thematically and technically. This uniquely American version of W's poetic values would form the intellectual background for generations of American writers.

References: Recent criticism includes John Michael, "Emerson's Chagrin: Benediction and Exhortation in 'Nature' and 'Tintern Abbey,' " *MLN* 101 (December 1986): 1067–85; David Bromwich, "From W to Emerson," in *Romantic Revolutions: Criticism and Theory,* ed. Kenneth R. Johnston et al. (1990), 202–18; Karen Kalinevitch, " 'Apparelled in Celestial Light/Bathed in So Pure a Light': Verbal Echoes in W's and Thoreau's Works," *TJQ* 12 (April 1980): 27–30; Lorrie Smith, " 'Walking' from England to America: Re-viewing Thoreau's Romanticism," *NEQ* 58 (1985): 221–41; Gary Simon, "Craft, Theory, and the Artist's Milieu," *WWR* 22 (1976): 58–66; Erma Ermmighausen Kelly, "Whitman and W: Childhood Experience and the Future Poet," *WWR* 23 (1977): 59–68; Benjamin Lease, *Anglo-American Encounters* (1981); and Robert Weisbuch, *Atlantic Double-Cross: American Literature and British Influence in the Age of Emerson* (1986).

Armida Gilbert

Bibliographical Essay

Contrary to a persistent stereotype, most Transcendentalists were not preoccupied with detached meditation on nature or spirit. The central concern of New England Transcendentalists was character, or what Ralph Waldo Emerson called the moral sublime. Their interest in self-culture drew them not simply to private forms of autobiography such as the journal but also to biography. All of the Transcendentalists read classical and contemporary lives, and several practiced the art of biography, on the lyceum platform and in essays and books. Emerson's *Representative Men* (1850) is only the best-known example of this Transcendentalist impulse.

Fortunately for modern students, the Transcendentalists also wrote lives of each other, and a second and third generation memorialized the movement in histories and biographies that are still of great value. Some of these works, however important for their information or as historical documents themselves, are notoriously unreliable because of either their compilers' biases (e.g., *Memoirs of Margaret Fuller Ossoli*, ed. Emerson, W. H. Channing, and J. F. Clarke [1852]) or their author's self-promotional motives and methodological flaws (e.g., F. B. Sanborn's biographies and editions of Emerson, Thoreau, and Alcott). Of the major "first-generation" Transcendentalists, Emerson and Henry D. Thoreau, and to lesser extents Margaret Fuller, Theodore Parker, and A. Bronson Alcott, were best served by early memoirists; each has also been the subject of excellent 20th-century biographies, with Emerson, Thoreau, and Fuller receiving the most consistent and substantial biographical and critical treatment in the last 50 years. The most significant contemporaneous and modern biographies are cited in the individual entries in this volume and assessed in detail in *The Transcendentalists: A Review of Research and Criticism*, ed. Joel Myerson (New York: Modern Language Association of America, 1984).

Scores of figures central to the emergence and growth of Transcendentalism have received spotty attention, however, and this *Dictionary* is the first comprehensive reference work to include "major" and "minor" American figures, international counterparts, critics of the movement, and great artists who, not necessarily Transcendentalists themselves, creatively grappled with the tenets of Transcendentalism.

Several biographical sources—some hard to come by today—remain indispensable to scholars of Transcendentalism. Octavius Brooks Frothingham's *Transcendentalism in New England: A History* (New York: G. P. Putnam's Sons, 1876; rpt. Univ. of Pennsylvania Press, 1972) offers valuable commentary on many less-known figures and traces philosophical roots of the movement. Because so many Transcendentalists were Unitarian ministers, an especially useful work has been *Heralds of a Liberal Faith*, 3 vols., ed. Samuel A. Eliot (Boston: American Unitarian Assn., 1910). This must be supplemented by David M. Robinson's thorough *The Unitarians and the Universalists* (Westport, Conn.: Greenwood Press, 1985).

Contributors to the Transcendentalist journal *The Dial* have been especially well covered in George Willis Cooke's *An Historical and Biographical Introduction to Accompany* The Dial, 2 vols. (Cleveland: Rowfant Club, 1902), still valuable but superseded by Joel Myerson, *The New England Transcendentalists and the* Dial*: A History of the Magazine and Its Contributors* (Rutherford, N.J.: Fairleigh Dickinson Univ. Press, 1980). Important studies of other periodicals are Sterling F. Delano, The Harbinger *and New England Transcendentalism: A Portrait of Associationism in America* (Rutherford, N.J.: Fairleigh Dickinson Univ. Press, 1983), and Robert D. Habich, *Transcendentalism and the* Western Messenger*: A History of the Magazine and Its Contributors, 1835–1841* (Rutherford, N.J.: Fairleigh Dickinson Univ. Press, 1985). Though anecdotal and dated, the following are still important for the study of participants in Transcendentalist reform ventures: John Thomas Codman, *Brook Farm: Historic and Personal Memoirs* (Boston: Arena, 1894), Lindsay Swift, *Brook Farm: Its Members, Scholars, and Visitors* (New York: Macmillan, 1900), and Clara Endicott Sears, *Bronson Alcott's Fruitlands* (Boston: Houghton Mifflin, 1915).

Entries on many of the Transcendentalists are found in the standard *Dictionary of American Biography*, 20 vols., ed. Dumas Malone (New York: Scribners, 1928–37); this monumental work is in process of being superseded by the *American National Biography* (Oxford Univ. Press). The best one-volume biographical source, with in-depth coverage of several figures, is Joel Myerson's *The American Renaissance in New England* (Detroit: Gale, 1978), in the *Dictionary of Literary Biography* series.

Besides consulting entries in this volume for the best full-length biographies and other sources, check for new biographical and other studies in *American Literary Scholarship: An Annual* (Durham: Duke Univ. Press); published since 1965, *ALS* has bibliographical chapters on "Emerson, Thoreau, Fuller, and Transcendentalism" (Fuller added to the chapter title in 1992) and on "Whitman and Dickinson." The *MLA International Bibliography* (New York: Modern Language Assn. of America) is also published annually. *Emerson Society Papers* (published by The Ralph Waldo Emerson Society) has an annual Emerson bibliography, and *Thoreau Society Bulletin* (published by The Thoreau Society), a quarterly Thoreau bibliography.

Index

Italicized numbers indicate a main entry

About the Editor and Contributors

Richard P. Benton is Associate Professor Emeritus of English and comparative literature, Trinity College, Hartford, Connecticut.

Elisa E. Beshero is a graduate student in English at Pennsylvania State University, University Park.

Ronald A. Bosco is Distinguished Service Professor of American Literature at the University at Albany, State University of New York, and an editor of the Emerson Papers at the Houghton Library, Harvard University.

Alan D. Brasher is Visiting Assistant Professor of English at the University of South Carolina.

Robert E. Burkholder is Associate Professor of English at the Pennsylvania State University, University Park, and past president of the Ralph Waldo Emerson Society.

Larry A. Carlson, Professor and Director of the Graduate Program in English, teaches courses in American literature and American studies at the College of Charleston.

Phyllis Cole is Associate Professor of English and women's studies at Penn State University, Delaware County Campus.

Gary L. Collison, Associate Professor of English at Penn State, York, teaches courses in American literature and culture.

Helen R. Deese is Professor of English at Tennessee Technological University and Caroline Healey Dall editor for the Massachusetts Historical Society.

Jane Donahue Eberwein is Professor of English at Oakland University and a founding board member of the Emily Dickinson International Society.

Lesli J. Favor is a doctoral candidate at the University of North Texas, where she teaches literature and writing.

Mathew David Fisher is Assistant Professor of English at Ball State University and Director of the College of Architecture and Planning's Writing in the Design Curriculum program.

Armida Gilbert is Assistant Professor at Kent State University.

Joan W. Goodwin is an independent scholar who received her bachelor's degree from Barnard College and an honorary Doctorate of Humane Letters from Starr King School for the Ministry.

Lisa M. Gordis is Assistant Professor of English at Barnard College, where she teaches courses in American literature.

Len Gougeon is Professor of American literature at the University of Scranton.

Ezra Greenspan is Associate Professor of English at the University of South Carolina.

Dean David Grodzins is a Postdoctoral Fellow in history at Harvard University and editor of the *Proceedings of the Unitarian-Universalist Historical Society.*

Robert D. Habich is Professor of English and Director of Graduate Programs at Ball State University.

Eric L. Haralson is Assistant Professor of English at the State University of New York at Stony Brook.

Walter Harding, who died in 1996, was Distinguished University Professor Emeritus, State University of New York at Geneseo, was the secretary of the Thoreau Society from 1941 to 1991.

Richard D. Hathaway is Professor of English, State University of New York, the College at New Paltz.

Kathleen M. Healey is a doctoral candidate in English at Pennsylvania State University.

David Hicks is Associate Professor and Assistant Chair of literature and communications at Pace University, Pleasantville, New York.

Alan D. Hodder is a member of the faculty of the School of Humanities and Arts at Hampshire College.

Reid Huntley is Associate Professor of English at Ohio University.

Linck C. Johnson is Professor of English at Colgate University, where he teaches American literature.

Karen L. Kalinevitch is Professor of English at St. Louis Community College.

Leigh Kirkland is Editorial and Production Manager for the scholarly edition of Thoreau's journal in THE WRITINGS OF HENRY D. THOREAU, in progress at Georgia State University.

Denise D. Knight is Associate Professor of English at the State University of New York College at Cortland, where she specializes in 19th-century American literature.

Alfred G. Litton is Assistant Professor of English at Texas Woman's University.

Kent P. Ljungquist is Professor of English at Worcester Polytechnic Institute and edits the *Poe Studies Association Newsletter.*

Larry R. Long is Professor and Director of Honors at Harding University.

David P. McKay, Professor Emeritus in music at Worcester Polytechnic Institute, is a musicologist who has specialized in the music of early America.

Kathryn B. McKee is a doctoral student in American literature to 1900 and southern literature at the University of North Carolina at Chapel Hill.

Mark J. Madigan teaches in the English Department at the University of Vermont.

Robert Durwood Madison is Associate Professor of English at the U.S. Naval Academy in Annapolis, Maryland.

Jo Ann Manfra is Professor of history at Worcester Polytechnic Institute.

Sanford E. Marovitz is Professor of English at Kent State University.

Terry J. Martin is Associate Professor of English at Baldwin-Wallace College.

James W. Mathews recently retired after 32 years as Chair of Humanities and English at West Georgia College, Carrollton.

Laura Jehn Menides, Associate Professor of English at Worcester Polytechnic Institute, teaches American literature, especially poetry and fiction.

Charles Mitchell is Assistant Professor of American studies at Elmira College, Elmira, New York.

Joseph J. Moldenhauer is Mody C. Boatright Regents Professor at the University of Texas at Austin.

Nathaniel T. Mott, a graduate of Gettysburg College, is a freelance writer and served as an intern in newspapers and serials at the American Antiquarian Society.

Wesley T. Mott is Professor of English at Worcester Polytechnic Institute, secretary of the Ralph Waldo Emerson Society, which he organized in 1989, and managing editor of *Emerson Society Papers*.

Raymond L. Muncy, who died in January 1994, was Distinguished Professor and former Chair of the Department of History and Social Science at Harding University.

Joel Myerson is Carolina Research Professor of American literature at the University of South Carolina and editor of the annual *Studies in the American Renaissance*.

Layne Neeper is Assistant Professor of English at Morehead State University, where he teaches courses in 19th- and 20th-century American literature.

Christopher Newfield is Assistant Professor of English at the University of California at Santa Barbara.

Julie M. Norko is a doctoral student at the University of North Carolina at Chapel Hill, where she is working on a dissertation on the Transcendentalists.

Ralph H. Orth is Corse Professor of English language and literature at the University of Vermont.

Stephen N. Orton is a doctoral student specializing in American literature at the University of North Carolina at Chapel Hill.

Barbara L. Packer is Associate Professor of English at the University of California at Los Angeles and is author of *Emerson's Fall* (1982).

Joe Pellegrino is a doctoral candidate at the University of North Carolina at Chapel Hill, where his recent work concerns the connections between philosophy and literature.

D'Ann Pletcher-George, a doctoral candidate in American literature and composition and rhetoric at the University of North Carolina at Chapel Hill, also teaches writing at Towson State University.

Moumin Manzoor Quazi is a doctoral candidate in English literature at the University of North Texas.

Robert D. Richardson, Jr., is an independent scholar living in Middletown, Connecticut, and author of *Henry David Thoreau: A Life of the Mind* (1986) and *Emerson: The Mind on Fire* (1995).

Susan L. Roberson is Instructor of English at Auburn University.

David M. Robinson is Distinguished Professor of American literature at Oregon State University.

Bruce A. Ronda is Associate Professor of English and Director of the American Studies Program at Colorado State University.

Barbara Ryan is a junior member of the Michigan Society of Fellows and Assistant Professor in the University of Michigan's Program in American Culture.

Susan M. Ryan is a doctoral student in American literature at the University of North Carolina at Chapel Hill, where her research interests include 19th-century reform movements and Transcendentalism.

John P. Samonds is a doctoral student at the University of North Carolina at Chapel Hill, specializing in American literature and 20th-century American and British literature.

M. David Samson is Assistant Professor of art history in the Department of Humanities and Arts, Worcester Polytechnic Institute.

Robert Sattelmeyer is Professor of English at Georgia State University and General Editor for the *Journal* in THE WRITINGS OF HENRY D. THOREAU.

Heidi M. Schultz is a doctoral candidate and Director of the Writing Center at the University of North Carolina at Chapel Hill.

Merton M. Sealts, Jr., is Henry A. Pochmann Professor of English, Emeritus, at the University of Wisconsin at Madison.

April Selley is Associate Professor of English at the College of Saint Rose in Albany, New York.

Daniel Shealy is Associate Professor of English and Associate Dean of the Graduate School at the University of North Carolina at Charlotte.

Frank Shuffelton is Professor of English at the University of Rochester and commutes between early American literature and the Transcendentalists.

Nancy Craig Simmons is Associate Professor of Humanities and English at Virginia Tech.

Susan Belasco Smith is Associate Professor of English at the University of Tulsa.

David J. Sorrells is instructor of English at Lamar University–Port Arthur, in Port Arthur, Texas.

Madeleine B. Stern, partner, Leona Rostenberg & Madeleine Stern—Rare Books, has written numerous books on 19th-century feminism, publishing history, and biography.

E. Kate Stewart is Associate Professor of English at the University of Arkansas at Monticello.

Maggie Stier, formerly curator at Fruitlands Museums, is a freelance writer, museum consultant, and educator living in Norwich, Vermont.

Patricia Dunlavy Valenti is Associate Professor in the Department of Communicative Arts at Pembroke State University.

Gustaaf Van Cromphout is Professor of English at Northern Illinois University, where his main research interest is New England Transcendentalism, especially Emerson and Fuller.

William L. Vance is Professor of English at Boston University and has published articles on Whitman and on American novelists from Cooper to Hemingway. He is the author of *America's Rome* (2 vols., 1989).

Laura Dassow Walls is Assistant Professor of English at Lafayette College, and author of *Seeing New Worlds: Thoreau and Nineteenth-Century Natural Science* (1995).

Daniel A. Wells is Professor of American literature at the University of South Florida in St. Petersburg.

Jonathan Wells is a graduate student in history at the University of Michigan, specializing in 19th-century American political and intellectual history.

Karen A. Weyler is a doctoral candidate in the English Department at the University of North Carolina at Chapel Hill, specializing in early American fiction.

Sarah Ann Wider is Associate Professor of English at Colgate University, where her most recent work focuses on women's self-representation within Unitarian culture.

Doni M. Wilson is a doctoral candidate in American literature and a Teaching Fellow at the University of North Carolina at Chapel Hill.

Peter Lamborn Wilson has taught at the Jack Kerouac School of Disembodied Poetics since 1987, is editor of *Semiotext(e)/Autonomedia*, and broadcasts fortnightly on WBAI radio in New York.

Barbara Downs Wojtusik is an English teacher in the Bristol, Connecticut, Public Schools.

Guy R. Woodall is Professor of English, Emeritus, at Tennessee Technological University, where he retired at the end of 1991 after teaching more than 40 years.

Arthur Wrobel is Associate Professor of English at the University of Kentucky and has been editor of *ANQ: A Quarterly Journal of Short Articles, Notes, and Reviews* since 1982.

ISBN 0-313-28836-4
90000>
EAN
9 780313 288364
HARDCOVER BAR CODE